THE HARVARD CLASSICS
EDITED BY CHARLES W ELIOT LL D

JOHN STUART MILL

AUTOBIOGRAPHY
ESSAY ON LIBERTY

THOMAS CARLYLE

CHARACTERISTICS
INAUGURAL ADDRESS
ESSAY ON SCOTT

WITH INTRODUCTIONS AND NOTES

VOLUME 25

P F COLLIER & SON
NEW YORK

Designed, Printed, and Bound at
The Collier Press, New York

CONTENTS

By John Stuart Mill

AUTOBIOGRAPHY JOHN STUART MILL

PAGE

Chapter I 7
Chapter II 30
Chapter III 45
Chapter IV 60
Chapter V 88
Chapter VI 120
Chapter VII 143

ON LIBERTY

Chapter I 203
Chapter II 218
Chapter III 260
Chapter IV 281
Chapter V 302

By Thomas Carlyle

CHARACTERISTICS 333

INAUGURAL ADDRESS AT EDINBURGH 375

SIR WALTER SCOTT 409

INTRODUCTORY NOTE

John Stuart Mill *was born in London, May 20, 1806. He was the eldest of the nine children of James Mill, the chief disciple of Bentham and one of the most important leaders in the Utilitarian movement in England. J. S. Mill as a child was almost incredibly precocious. He began Greek at three, and by the time he was eight had read such authors as Herodotus and Plato in the original, besides such English historians as Gibbon and Hume. At twelve he was studying logic "seriously"; at thirteen he went through a complete course in political economy which his father gave him in conversation during their walks, and the summaries he made of these talks were the basis of James Mill's treatise on this subject. These and other intellectual feats will be found related in the "Autobiography," not in a spirit of boastfulness, but in support of more profitable educational methods.*

So far young Mill had been educated entirely by his father; but when he was fourteen he was sent to France for a year, where he mastered the language, learned much of French society and politics, and continued his studies in mathematics, economics, and science. In 1823 he entered the India House as a clerk in the examiner's office, of which his father was the head; rose rapidly, and finally succeeded to his father's position as chief examiner.

His official labors left him considerable leisure, which he employed with the industry that had been habitual with him almost from infancy. He wrote for the papers, helped his father on the "Westminster Review," and, before he was twenty, edited Bentham's "Treatise on Evidence." His first original work of importance was his "Essays upon Unsettled Questions of Political Economy," written when he was about twenty-four, but not published till 1844.

In religion, Mill had been brought up an agnostic, and, in philosophy, a utilitarian of the school of Bentham; but after a nervous illness in 1836, he began to be dissatisfied with the high and dry intellectualism of his father's circle. He "learnt that happiness was to be found not in directly pursuing it, but in the pursuit of other ends; and learnt, also, the importance of a

3

steady cultivation of the feelings." He had already a wide ac-
quaintance among the most active minds in London, and some
of these, like F. D. Maurice and John Sterling, aided in the proc-
ess of humanising Mill's philosophy. He became a disciple of
Wordsworth's and a friend of Carlyle's; and a second visit to
France still further helped to broaden his views and sympathies,
more especially through the influence of the St. Simonian school
and Comte. Important also among the friendships which af-
fected his development was that with Mrs. Taylor, an invalid
lady of whose intellectual powers Mill had the most exalted
opinion, and whom he ultimately married.

In 1835, the "London Review," later combined with the "West-
minster Review," and for a time owned by Mill, was started as
the organ of the "philosophical radicals"; and till he gave it up
in 1840 he wrote much in it on political and literary topics, and
sought to make it an influence in practical politics. But the
party it represented fell for the time into obscurity, and Mill
resumed his logical studies, which culminated in 1843 in the pub-
lication of his "Logic." This work, which met with great and
immediate success, established Mill as the leader of the empiri-
cal school of thought in England, and it holds its position still
as a standard work on the subject.

His interest now passed for the time to economics, and within
five years he issued his "Principles of Political Economy," a
treatise which stands on the political side, as his "Logic" does
on the philosophical, as the representative statement of the prin-
ciples of the school of philosophical radicalism. Much in its
teaching is still regarded by economists as valuable, and the book
ranks as perhaps the most important systematic treatise on the
subject since "The Wealth of Nations."

In 1858 the East India Company was dissolved, the administra-
tion of India being taken over by the English Government,
and Mill retired on a pension. The same year his wife died, just
after completing with her husband the revision of his famous
"Essay on Liberty." In this book, along with his "Representa-
tive Government" (1860) and his "Utilitarianism" (1861) one
may find an exceedingly compact presentation of his views on
the most important questions of social and political philosophy.
His function with regard to the Utilitarian doctrines in which
he had been trained by his father was that of broadening and

elevating the conception of "the greatest happiness of the greatest number" as the true end of human conduct, by the recognition of difference of quality among pleasures, and by the addition of a new sanction for altruism in a "feeling of unity with his fellow creatures" which makes it a "natural want" of a person of "properly cultivated moral nature" that his aims and theirs should harmonize. With the rise of the evolutionist school on the one hand and the spread of the doctrines of Kant and his successors on the other, the influence of Mill's philosophy has declined.

Mill's philosophical activity culminated in his searching "Examination of Sir William Hamilton's Philosophy," originally published in 1865, and reissued later with replies to critics. In this work he reviewed thoroughly all the main points of difference between the empirical and the intuitional schools; and though, with the shifting of issues in the progress of philosophic thought, the controversy has now died down, the criticism remains an interesting and lively example of Mill's acuteness and skill as a controversialist.

So far Mill's part in politics had been confined to the writing of pamphlets and articles, but in 1865 he was elected to Parliament as member for Westminster. In spite of a weak voice and a nervous manner, he impressed the House by his fluency and exactness in speech, and by his honesty and independence of judgment. He favored the extension of the franchise, and the reform of the Irish land laws; and he argued in favor of a number of projects which long after his time were carried into effect. When Parliament dissolved in 1868, he was not re-elected.

He now returned to literature, writing frequently in the "Fortnightly Review," then edited by his friend John Morley; and in 1869 he issued his "Subjection of Women," in the production of which both his wife and his step-daughter had had a share. During his Parliamentary career he had urged the granting of the voting power to the other sex, and this work is still a standard plea for the rights of women. His health now began to give way, and he died on May 8, 1873.

Although the dominant impression conveyed by the record of Mill's life in his candid and interesting "Autobiography" is one of intellectuality, he was a man of high sensibility and of a tender and affectionate nature. The purity of his motives, the vigor of his thinking, and the energy and independence with which he strove for the realization of his ideals, had their effect not merely on the large circle with whom he came into personal contact, but in the stimulating and elevating of the general intellectual and moral life of his time.

It is as the story of such a man's life, told by himself when it was about six years from its close, that his "Autobiography" is here printed. The "Essay on Liberty" has an interest of a different kind. It belongs to that splendid series of pleas for intellectual freedom, which, beginning with Milton's "Areopagitica," or speech for the Liberty of Unlicensed Printing, and coming down through Locke's "Letters concerning Toleration" to the utterances of Mill himself and his friend and fellow liberal Morley, form the literary expression of the gradual realization of the passion for individual freedom which is one of the glories of the English-speaking peoples.

AUTOBIOGRAPHY
JOHN STUART MILL

CHAPTER I

CHILDHOOD AND EARLY EDUCATION

IT seems proper that I should prefix to the following
biographical sketch, some mention of the reasons which
have made me think it desirable that I should leave
behind me such a memorial of so uneventful a life as mine.
I do not for a moment imagine that any part of what I have
to relate, can be interesting to the public as a narrative, or
as being connected with myself. But I have thought that
in an age in which education, and its improvement, are the
subject of more, if not of profounder study than at any
former period of English history, it may be useful that there
should be some record of an education which was unusual
and remarkable, and which, whatever else it may have done,
has proved how much more than is commonly supposed may
be taught, and well taught, in those early years which, in the
common modes of what is called instruction, are little better
than wasted. It has also seemed to me that in an age of transition in opinions, there may be somewhat both of interest
and of benefit in noting the successive phases of any mind
which was always pressing forward, equally ready to learn
and to unlearn either from its own thoughts or from those
of others. But a motive which weighs more with me than
either of these, is a desire to make acknowledgment of the
debts which my intellectual and moral development owes to
other persons; some of them of recognised eminence, others
less known than they deserve to be, and the one to whom
most of all is due, one whom the world had no opportunity
of knowing. The reader whom these things do not interest,

7

has only himself to blame if he reads farther, and I do not
desire any other indulgence from him than that of bearing
in mind, that for him these pages were not written.

I was born in London, on the 20th of May, 1806, and
was the eldest son of James Mill, the author of the History
of British India. My father, the son of a petty tradesman
and (I believe) small farmer, at Northwater Bridge, in the
county of Angus, was, when a boy, recommended by his
abilities to the notice of Sir John Stuart, of Fettercairn, one
of the Barons of the Exchequer in Scotland, and was, in
consequence, sent to the University of Edinburgh, at the
expense of a fund established by Lady Jane Stuart (the
wife of Sir John Stuart) and some other ladies for educating young men for the Scottish Church. He there went
through the usual course of study, and was licensed as a
Preacher, but never followed the profession; having satisfied himself that he could not believe the doctrines of that
or any other Church. For a few years he was a private
tutor in various families in Scotland, among others that of
the Marquis of Tweeddale, but ended by taking up his
residence in London, and devoting himself to authorship.
Nor had he any other means of support until 1819, when he
obtained an appointment in the India House.

In this period of my father's life there are two things
which it is impossible not to be struck with: one of them
unfortunately a very common circumstance, the other a
most uncommon one. The first is, that in his position, with
no resource but the precarious one of writing in periodicals,
he married and had a large family; conduct than which
nothing could be more opposed, both as a matter of good
sense and of duty, to the opinions which, at least at a later
period of life, he strenuously upheld. The other circumstance, is the extraordinary energy which was required to
lead the life he led, with the disadvantages under which he
laboured from the first, and with those which he brought
upon himself by his marriage. It would have been no small
thing, had he done no more than to support himself and his
family during so many years by writing, without ever being
in debt, or in any pecuniary difficulty; holding, as he did,
opinions, both in politics and in religion, which were more

odious to all persons of influence, and to the common run of prosperous Englishmen in that generation, than either before or since; and being not only a man whom nothing would have induced to write against his convictions, but one who invariably threw into everything he wrote, as much of his convictions as he thought the circumstances would in any way permit: being, it must also be said, one who never did anything negligently; never undertook any task, literary or other, on which he did not conscientiously bestow all the labour necessary for performing it adequately. But he, with these burdens on him, planned, commenced, and completed, the History of India; and this in the course of about ten years, a shorter time than has been occupied (even by writers who had no other employment) in the production of almost any other historical work of equal bulk, and of anything approaching to the same amount of reading and research. And to this is to be added, that during the whole period, a considerable part of almost every day was employed in the instruction of his children in the case of one of whom, myself, he exerted an amount of labour, care, and perseverance rarely, if ever, employed for a similar purpose, in endeavouring to give, according to his own conception, the highest order of intellectual education.

A man who, in his own practice, so vigorously acted up to the principle of losing no time, was likely to adhere to the same rule in the instruction of his pupil. I have no remembrance of the time when I began to learn Greek, I have been told that it was when I was three years old. My earliest recollection on the subject, is that of committing to memory what my father termed vocables, being lists of common Greek words, with their signification in English, which he wrote out for me on cards. Of grammar, until some years later, I learnt no more than the inflexions of the nouns and verbs, but after a course of vocables, proceeded at once to translation; and I faintly remember going through Æsop's Fables, the first Greek book which I read. The Anabasis, which I remember better, was the second. I learnt no Latin until my eighth year. At that time I had read, under my father's tuition, a number of Greek prose authors, among whom I remember the whole of Herodotus, and of

Xenophon's Cyropædia and Memorials of Socrates; some of the lives of the philosophers by Diogenes Laertius; part of Lucian, and Isocrates ad Demonicum and Ad Nicoclem. I also read, in 1813, the first six dialogues (in the common arrangement) of Plato, from the Euthyphron to the Theoctetus inclusive: which last dialogue, I venture to think, would have been better omitted, as it was totally impossible I should understand it. But my father, in all his teaching, demanded of me not only the utmost that I could do, but much that I could by no possibility have done. What he was himself willing to undergo for the sake of my instruction, may be judged from the fact, that I went through the whole process of preparing my Greek lessons in the same room and at the same table at which he was writing: and as in those days Greek and English lexicons were not, and I could make no more use of a Greek and Latin lexicon than could be made without having yet begun to learn Latin, I was forced to have recourse to him for the meaning of every word which I did not know. This incessant interruption, he, one of the most impatient of men, submitted to, and wrote under that interruption several volumes of his History and all else that he had to write during those years.

The only thing besides Greek, that I learnt as a lesson in this part of my childhod, was arithmetic: this also my father taught me: it was the task of the evenings, and I well remember its disagreeableness. But the lessons were only a part of the daily instruction I received. Much of it consisted in the books I read by myself, and my father's discourses to me, chiefly during our walks. From 1810 to the end of 1813 we were living in Newington Green, then an almost rustic neighbourhood. My father's health required considerable and constant exercise, and he walked habitually before breakfast, generally in the green lanes towards Hornsey. In these walks I always accompanied him, and with my earliest recollections of green fields and wild flowers, is mingled that of the account I gave him daily of what I had read the day before. To the best of my remembrance, this was a voluntary rather than a prescribed exercise. I made notes on slips of paper while reading, and from these in the morning walks, I told the story to him; for the books

were chiefly histories, of which I read in this manner a
great number: Robertson's histories, Hume, Gibbon; but
my greatest delight, then and for long afterwards, was Watson's Philip the Second and Third. The heroic defence of
the Knights of Malta against the Turks, and of the revolted
Provinces of the Netherlands against Spain, excited in me an
intense and lasting interest. Next to Watson, my favourite
historical reading was Hooke's History of Rome. Of Greece
I had seen at that time no regular history, except school
abridgments and the last two or three volumes of a translation of Rollin's Ancient History, beginning with Philip
of Macedon. But I read with great delight Langhorne's
translation of Plutarch. In English history, beyond the
time at which Hume leaves off, I remember reading Bur-
net's History of his Own Time, though I cared little for anything in it except the wars and battles; and the historical
part of the "Annual Register," from the beginning to about
1788, where the volumes my father borrowed for me from
Mr. Bentham left off. I felt a lively interest in Frederic of
Prussia during his difficulties, and in Paoli, the Corsican
patriot; but when I came to the American war, I took my
part, like a child as I was (until set right by my father), on
the wrong side, because it was called the English side. In
these frequent talks about the books I read, he used, as opportunity offered, to give me explanations and ideas respecting civilization, government, morality, mental cultivation,
which he required me afterwards to restate to him in my
own words. He also made me read, and give him a verbal
account of, many books which would not have interested
me sufficiently to induce me to read them of myself: among
others, Millar's Historical View of the English Government, a book of great merit for its time, and which he
highly valued; Mosheim's Ecclesiastical History, McCrie's
Life of John Knox, and even Sewell and Rutty's Histories
of the Quakers. He was fond of putting into my hands books
which exhibited men of energy and resource in unusual
circumstances, struggling against difficulties and overcoming
them; of such works I remember Beaver's African Memo-
randa, and Collins's Account of the First Settlement of New
South Wales. Two books which I never wearied of read-

ing were Anson's Voyages, so delightful to most young
persons, and a collection (Hawkesworth's, I believe) of
Voyages Round the World, in four volumes, beginning with
Drake and ending with Cook and Bougainville. Of children's books, any more than of playthings, I had scarcely
any, except an occasional gift from a relation or acquaintance: among those I had, Robinson Crusoe was pre-eminent,
and continued to delight me through all my boyhood. It
was no part, however, of my father's system to exclude
books of amusement, though he allowed them very sparingly.
Of such books he possessed at that time next to none, but
he borrowed several for me; those which I remember are
the Arabian Nights, Cazotte's Arabian Tales, Don Quixote,
Miss Edgeworth's Popular Tales, and a book of some reputation in its day, Brooke's Fool of Quality.

In my eighth year I commenced learning Latin, in conjunction with a younger sister, to whom I taught it as I
went on, and who afterwards repeated the lessons to my
father: and from this time, other sisters and brothers being successively added as pupils, a considerable part of my
day's work consisted of this preparatory teaching. It was
a part which I greatly disliked; the more so, as I was held
responsible for the lessons of my pupils, in almost as full a
sense as for my own: I, however, derived from this discipline the great advantage, of learning more thoroughly
and retaining more lastingly the things which I was set
to teach: perhaps too, the practice it afforded in explaining
difficulties to others, may even at that age have been useful.
In other respects, the experience of my boyhood is not
favourable to the plan of teaching children by means of one
another. The teaching, I am sure, is very inefficient as
teaching, and I well know that the relation between teacher
and taught is not a good moral discipline to either. I
went in this manner through the Latin grammar, and a considerable part of Cornelius Nepos and Cæsar's Commentaries,
but afterwards added to the superintendence of these lessons,
much longer ones of my own.

In the same year in which I began Latin, I made my
first commencement in the Greek poets with the Iliad. After
I had made some progress in this way, my father put Pope's

translation into my hands. It was the first English verse I had cared to read, and it became one of the books in which for many years I most delighted: I think I must have read it from twenty to thirty times through. I should not have thought it worth while to mention a taste apparently so natural to boyhood, if I had not, as I think, observed that the keen enjoyment of this brilliant specimen of narrative and versification is not so universal with boys, as I should have expected both *à priori* and from my individual experience. Soon after this time I commenced Euclid, and somewhat later, Algebra, still under my father's tuition.

From my eighth to my twelfth year, the Latin books which I remember reading were, the Bucolics of Virgil, and the first six books of the Æneid; all Horace, except the Epodes; the Fables of Phædrus; the first five books of Livy (to which from my love of the subject I voluntarily added, in my hours of leisure, the remainder of the first decade); all Sallust; a considerable part of Ovid's Metamorphoses; some plays of Terence; two or three books of Lucretius; several of the Orations of Cicero, and of his writings on oratory; also his letters to Atticus, my father taking the trouble to translate to me from the French the historical explanations in Mingault's notes. In Greek I read the Iliad and Odyssey through; one or two plays of Sophocles, Euripides, and Aristophanes, though by these I profited little; all Thucydides; the Hellenics of Xenophon; a great part of Demosthenes, Æschines, and Lysias; Theocritus; Anacreon; part of the Anthology; a little of Dionysius; several books of Polybius; and lastly Aristotle's Rhetoric, which, as the first expressly scientific treatise on any moral or psychological subject which I had read, and containing many of the best observations of the ancients on human nature and life, my father made me study with peculiar care, and throw the matter of it into synoptic tables. During the same years I learnt elementary geometry and algebra thoroughly, the differential calculus, and other portions of the higher mathematics far from thoroughly: for my father, not having kept up this part of his early acquired knowledge, could not spare time to qualify himself for removing my difficulties, and left me to deal with them, with little other aid than that of books; while I was continually incurring his displeasure by my inability to solve difficult problems for which he did not see that I had not the necessary previous knowledge.

As to my private reading, I can only speak of what I remember. History continued to be my strongest predilection, and most of all ancient history. Mitford's Greece I read continually; my father had put me on my guard against the Tory prejudices of this writer, and his perversions of facts for the whitewashing of despots, and blackening of popular institutions. These points he discoursed on, exemplifying them from the Greek orators and historians, with such effect that in reading Mitford my sympathies were always on the contrary side to those of the author, and I could, to some extent, have argued the point against him: yet this did not diminish the ever new pleasure with which I read the book. Roman history, both in my old favourite, Hooke, and in Ferguson, continued to delight me. A book which, in spite of what is called the dryness of its style, I took great pleasure in, was the Ancient Universal History, through the incessant reading of which, I had my head full of historical details concerning the obscurest ancient people, while about modern history, except detached passages, such as the Dutch War of Independence, I knew and cared comparatively little. A voluntary exercise, to which throughout my boyhood I was much addicted, was what I called writing histories. I successively composed a Roman History, picked out of Hooke; an Abridgment of the Ancient Universal History; a History of Holland, from my favourite Watson and from an anonymous compilation; and in my eleventh and twelfth year I occupied myself with writing what I flattered myself was something serious. This was no less than a History of the Roman Government, compiled (with the assistance of Hooke) from Livy and Dionysius: of which I wrote as much as would have made an octavo volume, extending to the epoch of the Licinian Laws. It was, in fact, an account of the struggles between the patricians and plebeians, which now engrossed all the interest in my mind which I had previously felt in the mere wars and conquests of the Romans. I discussed all the constitutional points as they arose: though quite ignorant of Niebuhr's researches, I, by such lights as my father had given me, vindicated the Agrarian Laws on the evidence of Livy, and upheld, to the best of my ability, the Roman Democratic party. A few years later, in my contempt of my childish efforts, I destroyed all these papers, not then anticipating that I could ever feel any curiosity about my first attempts at writing and reasoning. My father encouraged me in this useful amusement, though, as I think judiciously, he never asked to see what I wrote; so that I did not feel that in writing it I was accountable to any one, nor had the chilling sensation of being under a critical eye.

But though these exercises in history were never a compulsory lesson, there was another kind of composition which was so, namely, writing verses, and it was one of the most disagreeable of my tasks. Greek and Latin verses I did not write, nor learnt the prosody of those languages. My father, thinking this not worth the time it required, contented himself with making me read aloud to him, and correcting false quantities. I never composed at all in Greek, even in prose, and but little in Latin. Not that my father could be indifferent to the value of this practice, in giving a thorough knowledge of these languages, but because there really was not time for it. The verses I was required to write were English. When I first read Pope's Homer, I ambitiously attempted to compose something of the same kind, and achieved as much as one book of a continuation of the Iliad. There, probably, the spontaneous promptings of my poetical ambition would have stopped; but the exercise, begun from choice, was continued by command. Conformably to my father's usual practice of explaining to me, as far as possible, the reasons for what he required me to do, he gave me, for this, as I well remember, two reasons highly characteristic of him: one was, that some things could be expressed better and more forcibly in verse than in prose: this, he said, was a real advantage. The other was, that people in general attached more value to verse than it deserved, and the power of writing it, was, on this account, worth acquiring. He generally left me to choose my own subjects, which, as far as I remember, were mostly addresses to some mythological personage or allegorical abstraction; but he made me translate into English verse many of Horace's shorter poems: I also remember his giving me Thomson's "Winter" to read, and afterwards making me attempt (without book) to write something myself on the same subject. The verses I wrote were, of course, the merest rubbish, nor did I ever attain any facility of versification, but the practice may have been useful in making it easier for me, at a later period, to acquire readiness of expression.[1] I had read, up to this time, very little English poetry. Shakspeare my father had put into my hands, chiefly for the sake of the historical plays, from which, however, I went on to the others. My father never was a great admirer of Shakspeare, the English idolatry of whom he used to attack with some severity. He cared little for any English poetry except Milton (for whom he had the highest admiration), Goldsmith, Burns, and Gray's Bard, which he preferred to his Elegy: perhaps I may add Cowper and Beattie. He had some value for Spenser, and I remember his reading to me (unlike his usual practice of making me read to him), the first book of the Faerie Queene; but I took little pleasure in it. The poetry of the present century he saw scarcely any merit in, and I hardly became acquainted with any of it till I was grown up to manhood, except the metrical romances of Walter Scott, which I read at his recommendation and was intensely delighted with; as I always was with animated narrative. Dryden's Poems were among my father's books, and many of these he made me read, but I never cared for any of them except Alexander's Feast, which, as well as many of the songs in Walter Scott, I used to sing internally, to music of my own: to some of the latter, indeed, I went so far as to compose airs, which I still remember. Cowper's short poems I read with some pleasure, but never got far into the longer ones; and nothing in the two volumes interested me like the prose account of his three hares. In my thirteenth year I met

[1] In a subsequent stage of boyhood, when these exercises had ceased to be compulsory, like most youthful writers I wrote tragedies; under the inspiration not so much of Shakspeare as of Joanna Baillie, whose "Constantine Paleologus" in particular appeared to me one of the most glorious of human compositions. I still think it one of the best dramas of the last two centuries.

with Campbell's poems, among which Lochiel, Hohenlinden, The Exile of Erin, and some others, gave me sensations I had never before experienced from poetry. Here, too, I made nothing of the longer poems, except the striking opening of Gertrude of Wyoming, which long kept its place in my feelings as the perfection of pathos.

During this part of my childhood, one of my greatest amusements was experimental science; in the theoretical, however, not the practical sense of the word; not trying experiments—a kind of discipline which I have often regretted not having had—nor even seeing, but merely reading about them. I never remember being so wrapt up in any book, as I was in Joyce's Scientific Dialogues; and I was rather recalcitrant to my father's criticisms of the bad reasoning respecting the first principles of physics, which abounds in the early part of that work. I devoured treatises on Chemistry, especially that of my father's early friend and schoolfellow, Dr. Thomson, for years before I attended a lecture or saw an experiment.

From about the age of twelve, I entered into another and more advanced stage in my course of instruction; in which the main object was no longer the aids and appliances of thought, but the thoughts themselves. This commenced with Logic, in which I began at once with the Organon, and read it to the Analytics inclusive, but profited little by the Posterior Analytics, which belong to a branch of speculation I was not yet ripe for. Contemporaneously with the Oragnon, my father made me read the whole or parts of several of the Latin treatises on the scholastic logic; giving each day to him, in our walks, a minute account of what I had read, and answering his numerous and searching questions. After this, I went in a similar manner, through the " Computatio sive Logica " of Hobbes, a work of a much higher order of thought than the books of the school logicians, and which he estimated very highly; in my own opinion beyond its merits, great as these are. It was his invariable practice, whatever studies he exacted from me, to make me as far as possible understand and feel the utility of them: and this he deemed peculiarly fitting in the case of the syllogistic logic, the usefulness of which had been impugned by so

many writers of authority. I well remember how, and in
what particular walk, in the neighbourhood of Bagshot
Heath (where we were on a visit to his old friend Mr.
Wallace, then one of the Mathematical Professors at Sand-
hurst) he first attempted by questions to make me think
on the subject, and frame some conception of what constituted the utility of the syllogistic logic, and when I had
failed in this, to make me understand it by explanations.
The explanations did not make the matter at all clear to
me at the time; but they were not therefore useless; they
remained as a nucleus for my observations and reflections
to crystallize upon; the import of his general remarks being interpreted to me, by the particular instances which
came under my notice afterwards. My own consciousness
and experience ultimately led me to appreciate quite as
highly as he did, the value of an early practical familiarity
with the school logic. I know of nothing, in my education,
to which I think myself more indebted for whatever capacity
of thinking I have attained. The first intellectual operation
in which I arrived at any proficiency, was dissecting a bad
argument, and finding in what part the fallacy lay: and
though whatever capacity of this sort I attained, was due to
the fact that it was an intellectual exercise in which I was
most perseveringly drilled by my father, yet it is also true that
the school logic, and the mental habits acquired in studying
it, were among the principal instruments of this drilling. I
am persuaded that nothing, in modern education, tends so
much, when properly used, to form exact thinkers, who attach a precise meaning to words and propositions, and are
not imposed on by vague, loose, or ambiguous terms. The
boasted influence of mathematical studies is nothing to it;
for in mathematical processes, none of the real difficulties of
correct ratiocination occur. It is also a study peculiarly
adapted to an early stage in the education of philosophical
students, since it does not presuppose the slow process of
acquiring, by experience and reflection, valuable thoughts of
their own. They may become capable of disentangling the
intricacies of confused and self-contradictory thought, before their own thinking faculties are much advanced; a
power which, for want of some such discipline, many other-

wise able men altogether lack; and when they have to answer opponents, only endeavour, by such arguments as they can command, to support the opposite conclusion, scarcely even attempting to confute the reasonings of their antagonists; and, therefore, at the utmost, leaving the question, as far as it depends on argument, a balanced one.

During this time, the Latin and Greek books which I continued to read with my father were chiefly such as were worth studying, not for the language merely, but also for the thoughts. This included much of the orators, and especially Demosthenes, some of whose principal orations I read several times over, and wrote out, by way of exercise, a full analysis of them. My father's comments on these orations when I read them to him were very instructive to me. He not only drew my attention to the insight they afforded into Athenian institutions, and the principles of legislation and government which they often illustrated, but pointed out the skill and art of the orator—how everything important to his purpose was said at the exact moment when he had brought the minds of his audience into the state most fitted to receive it; how he made steal into their minds, gradually and by insinuation, thoughts which, if expressed in a more direct manner, would have roused their opposition. Most of these reflections were beyond my capacity of full comprehension at the time; but they left seed behind, which germinated in due season. At this time I also read the whole of Tacitus, Juvenal, and Quintilian. The latter, owing to his obscure style and to the scholastic details of which many parts of his treatise are made up, is little read, and seldom sufficiently appreciated. His book is a kind of encyclopædia of the thoughts of the ancients on the whole field of education and culture; and I have retained through life many valuable ideas which I can distinctly trace to my reading of him, even at that early age. It was at this period that I read, for the first time, some of the most important dialogues of Plato, in particular the Gorgias, the Protagoras, and the Republic. There is no author to whom my father thought himself more indebted for his own mental culture, than Plato, or whom he more frequently recommended to young students. I can bear similar testimony in regard to myself. The Socratic method, of which the Platonic dialogues are the chief example, is unsurpassed as a discipline for correcting the errors, and clearing up the confusions incident to the *intellectus sibi permissus,* the understanding which has made up all its bundles of associations under the guidance of popular phraseology. The close, searching *elenchus* by which the man of vague generalities is constrained either to express his meaning to himself in definite terms, or to confess that he does not know what he is talking about; the perpetual testing of all general statements by particular instances; the siege in form which is laid to the meaning of large abstract terms, by fixing upon some still larger class-name which includes that and more, and dividing down to the thing sought—marking out its limits and definition by a series of accurately drawn distinctions between it and each of the cognate objects which are successively parted off from it—all this, as an education for precise thinking, is inestimable, and all this, even at that age, took such hold of me that it became part of my own mind. I have felt ever since that the title of Platonist belongs by far better right to those who have been nourished in, and have endeavoured to practise Plato's mode of investigation, than to those who are distinguished only by the adoption of certain dogmatical conclusions, drawn mostly from the least intelligible of his works, and which the character of his mind and writings makes it uncertain whether he himself regarded as anything more than poetic fancies, or philosophic conjectures.

In going through Plato and Demosthenes, since I could now read these authors, as far as the language was concerned, with perfect ease, I was not required to construe them sentence by sentence, but to read them aloud to my father, answering questions when asked: but the particular attention which he paid to elocution (in which his own excellence was remarkable) made this reading aloud to him a most painful task. Of all things which he required me to do, there was none which I did so constantly ill, or in which he so perpetually lost his temper with me. He had thought much on the principles of the art of reading, especially the most neglected part of it, the inflections of the voice, or *modulation* as writers on elocution call it (in contrast with *articulation* on the one side and *expression* on the other), and had reduced it to rules, grounded on the logical analysis of a sentence. These rules he strongly impressed upon me, and took me severely to task for every violation of them: but I even then remarked (though I did not venture to make the remark to him) that though he reproached me when I read a sentence ill, and *told* me how I ought to have read it, he never, by reading it himself, *showed* me how it ought to be read. A defect running through his otherwise admirable modes of instruction, as it did through all his modes of thought, was that of trusting too much to the intelligibleness of the abstract, when not embodied in the concrete. It was at a much later period of my youth, when practising elocution by myself, or with companions of my own age, that I for the first time understood the object of his rules, and saw the psychological grounds of them. At that time I and others followed out the subject into its ramifications and could have composed a very useful treatise, grounded on my father's principles. He himself left those principles and rules unwritten. I regret that when my mind was full of the subject, from systematic practice, I did not put them, and our improvements of them, into a formal shape.

A book which contributed largely to my education, in the best sense of the term, was my father's History of India. It was published in the beginning of 1818. During the year previous, while it was passing through the press, I used to read the proof sheets to him; or rather, I read the manuscript to him while he corrected the proofs. The number of new ideas which I received from this remarkable book, and the impulse and stimulus as well as guidance given to my thoughts by its criticisms and disquisitions on society and civilization in the Hindoo part, on institutions and the acts of governments in the English part, made my early familiarity with it eminently useful to my subsequent progress. And though I can perceive deficiencies in it now as compared with a perfect standard, I still think it, if not the most, one of the most instructive histories ever written, and one of the books from which most benefit may be derived by a mind in the course of making up its opinions.

The Preface, among the most characteristic of my father's writings, as well as the richest in materials of thought, gives a picture which may be entirely depended on, of the sentiments and expectations with which he wrote the History. Saturated as the book is with the opinions and modes of judgment of a democratic radicalism then regarded as extreme; and treating with a severity, at that time most unusual, the English Constitution, the English law, and all parties and classes who possessed any considerable influence in the country; he may have expected reputation, but certainly not advancement in life, from its publication; nor could he have supposed that it would raise up anything but enemies for him in powerful quarters: least of all could he have expected favour from the East India Company, to whose commercial privileges he was unqualifiedly hostile, and on the acts of whose government he had made so many severe comments: though, in various parts of his book, he bore a testimony in their favour, which he felt to be their just due, namely, that no Government had on the whole given so much proof, to the extent of its lights, of good intention towards its subjects; and that if the acts of any other Government had the light of publicity as completely let in upon them, they would, in all probability, still less bear scrutiny.

On learning, however, in the spring of 1819, about a year after the publication of the History, that the East India Directors desired to strengthen the part of their home establishment which was employed in carrying on the correspondence with India, my father declared himself a candidate for that employment, and, to the credit of the Directors, successfully. He was appointed one of the Assistants of the Examiner of India Correspondence; officers whose duty it was to prepare drafts of despatches to India, for consideration by the Directors, in the principal departments of administration. In this office, and in that of Examiner, which he subsequently attained, the influence which his talents, his reputation, and his decision of character gave him, with superiors who really desired the good

government of India, enabled him to a great extent to throw
into his drafts of despatches, and to carry through the ordeal
of the Court of Directors and Board of Control, without
having their force much weakened, his real opinions on
Indian subjects. In his History he had set forth, for the first
time, many of the true principles of Indian administration:
and his despatches, following his History, did more than
had ever been done before to promote the improvement of
India, and teach Indian officials to understand their business.
If a selection of them were published, they would, I am
convinced, place his character as a practical statesman fully
on a level with his eminence as a speculative writer.

This new employment of his time caused no relaxation
in his attention to my education. It was in this same year,
1819, that he took me through a complete course of political
economy. His loved and intimate friend, Ricardo, had
shortly before published the book which formed so great an
epoch in political economy; a book which never would have
been published or written, but for the entreaty and strong
encouragement of my father; for Ricardo, the most modest
of men, though firmly convinced of the truth of his doctrines,
deemed himself so little capable of doing them justice in
exposition and expression, that he shrank from the idea
of publicity. The same friendly encouragement induced
Ricardo, a year or two later, to become a member of the
House of Commons; where during the few remaining years
of his life, unhappily cut short in the full vigour of his intellect, he rendered so much service to his and my father's
opinions both on political economy and on other subjects.

Though Ricardo's great work was already in print, no
didactic treatise embodying its doctrines, in a manner fit for
learners, had yet appeared. My father, therefore, commenced instructing me in the science by a sort of lectures,
which he delivered to me in our walks. He expounded
each day a portion of the subject, and I gave him next day a
written account of it, which he made me rewrite over and
over again until it was clear, precise, and tolerably complete.
In this manner I went through the whole extent of the
science; and the written outline of it which resulted from
my daily *compte rendu,* served him afterwards as notes from

which to write his Elements of Political Economy. After this I read Ricardo, giving an account daily of what I read, and discussing, in the best manner I could, the collateral points which offered themselves in our progress.

On Money, as the most intricate part of the subject, he made me read in the same manner Ricardo's admirable pamphlets, written during what was called the Bullion controversy; to these succeeded Adam Smith; and in this reading it was one of my father's main objects to make me apply to Smith's more superficial view of political economy, the superior lights of Ricardo, and detect what was fallacious in Smith's arguments, or erroneous in any of his conclusions. Such a mode of instruction was excellently calculated to form a thinker; but it required to be worked by a thinker, as close and vigorous as my father. The path was a thorny one, even to him, and I am sure it was so to me, notwithstanding the strong interest I took in the subject. He was often, and much beyond reason, provoked by my failures in cases where success could not have been expected; but in the main his method was right, and it succeeded. I do not believe that any scientific teaching ever was more thorough, or better fitted for training the faculties, than the mode in which logic and political economy were taught to me by my father. Striving, even in an exaggerated degree, to call forth the activity of my faculties, by making me find out everything for myself, he gave his explanations not before, but after, I had felt the full force of the difficulties; and not only gave me an accurate knowledge of these two great subjects, as far as they were then understood, but made me a thinker on both. I thought for myself almost from the first, and occasionally thought differently from him, though for a long time only on minor points, and making his opinion the ultimate standard. At a later period I even occasionally convinced him, and altered his opinion on some points of detail: which I state to his honour, not my own. It at once exemplifies his perfect candour, and the real worth of his method of teaching.

At this point concluded what can properly be called my lessons: when I was about fourteen I left England for more than a year; and after my return, though my studies went on under my father's general direction, he was no longer my schoolmaster. I shall therefore pause here, and turn back to matters of a more general nature connected with the part of my life and education included in the preceding reminiscences.

In the course of instruction which I have partially re-traced, the point most superficially apparent is the great effort to give, during the years of childhood, an amount of knowledge in what are considered the higher branches of education, which is seldom acquired (if acquired at all) until the age of manhood. The result of the experiment shows the ease with which this may be done, and places in a strong light the wretched waste of so many precious years as are spent in acquiring the modicum of Latin and Greek commonly taught to schoolboys; a waste which has led so many educational reformers to entertain the ill-judged pro-posal of discarding these languages altogether from general education. If I had been by nature extremely quick of apprehension, or had possessed a very accurate and retentive memory, or were of a remarkably active and energetic char-acter, the trial would not be conclusive; but in all these natural gifts I am rather below than above par; what I could do, could assuredly be done by any boy or girl of average capacity and healthy physical constitution: and if I have accomplished anything, I owe it, among other for-tunate circumstances, to the fact that through the early training bestowed on me by my father, I started, I may fairly say, with an advantage of a quarter of a century over my contemporaries.

There was one cardinal point in this training, of which I have already given some indication, and which, more than anything else, was the cause of whatever good it effected. Most boys or youths who have had much knowledge drilled into them, have their mental capacities not strengthened, but overlaid by it. They are crammed with mere facts, and with the opinions or phrases of other people, and these are accepted as a substitute for the power to form opinions of their own: and thus the sons of eminent fathers, who have spared no pains in their education, so often grow up mere parroters of what they have learnt, incapable of using their

minds except in the furrows traced for them. Mine, however, was not an education of cram. My father never permitted anything which I learnt to degenerate into a mere
exercise of memory. He strove to make the understanding
not only go along with every step of the teaching, but, if
possible, precede it. Anything which could be found out by
thinking I never was told, until I had exhausted my efforts
to find it out for myself. As far as I can trust my remembrance, I acquitted myself very lamely in this department;
my recollection of such matters is almost wholly of failures,
hardly ever of success. It is true the failures were often
in things in which success in so early a stage of my progress,
was almost impossible. I remember at some time in my
thirteenth year, on my happening to use the word idea,
he asked me what an idea was; and expressed some displeasure at my ineffectual efforts to define the word: I recollect also his indignation at my using the common expression
that something was true in theory but required correction
in practice; and how, after making me vainly strive to define
the word theory, he explained its meaning, and showed the
fallacy of the vulgar form of speech which I had used;
leaving me fully persuaded that in being unable to give
a correct definition of Theory, and in speaking of it as
something which might be at variance with practice, I had
shown unparalleled ignorance. In this he seems, and perhaps was, very unreasonable; but I think, only in being
angry at my failure. A pupil from whom nothing is ever
demanded which he cannot do, never does all he can.

One of the evils most liable to attend on any sort of
early proficiency, and which often fatally blights its promise, my father most anxiously guarded against. This was
self-conceit. He kept me, with extreme vigilance, out of the
way of hearing myself praised, or of being led to make self-
flattering comparisons between myself and others. From
his own intercourse with me I could derive none but a very
humble opinion of myself; and the standard of comparison
he always held up to me, was not what other people did,
but what a man could and ought to do. He completely succeeded in preserving me from the sort of influences he so
much dreaded. I was not at all aware that my attainments

were anything unusual at my age. If I accidentally had my attention drawn to the fact that some other boy knew less than myself—which happened less often than might be imagined—I concluded, not that I knew much, but that he, for some reason or other, knew little, or that his knowledge was of a different kind from mine. My state of mind was not humility, but neither was it arrogance. I never thought of saying to myself, I am, or I can do, so and so. I neither estimated myself highly nor lowly: I did not estimate myself at all. If I thought anything about myself, it was that I was rather backward in my studies, since I aways found myself so, in comparison with what my father expected from me. I assert this with confidence, though it was not the impression of various persons who saw me in my childhood. They, as I have since found, thought me greatly and disagreeably self-conceited; probably because I was disputatious, and did not scruple to give direct contradictions to things which I heard said. I suppose I acquired this bad habit from having been encouraged in an unusual degree to talk on matters beyond my age, and with grown persons, while I never had inculcated on me the usual respect for them. My father did not correct this ill-breeding and impertinence, probably from not being aware of it, for I was always too much in awe of him to be otherwise than extremely subdued and quiet in his presence. Yet with all this I had no notion of any superiority in myself; and well was it for me that I had not. I remember the very place in Hyde Park where, in my fourteenth year, on the eve of leaving my father's house for a long absence, he told me that I should find, as I got acquainted with new people, that I had been taught many things which youths of my age did not commonly know; and that many persons would be disposed to talk to me of this, and to compliment me upon it. What other things he said on this topic I remember very perfectly; but he wound up by saying, that whatever I knew more than others, could not be ascribed to any merit in me, but to the very unusual advantage which had fallen to my lot, of having a father who was able to teach me, and willing to give the necessary trouble and time; that it was no matter of praise to me, if I knew more than those who had not had a similar advantage, but the deepest disgrace to me if I did not. I have a distinct remembrance, that the suggestion thus for the first time made to me, that I knew more than other youths who were considered well educated, was to me a piece of information, to which, as to all other things which my father told me, I gave implicit credence, but which did not at all impress me as a personal matter. I felt no disposition to glorify myself upon the circumstance that there were other persons who did not know what I knew; nor had I ever flattered myself that my acquirements, whatever they might be, were any merit of mine: but, now when my attention was called to the subject, I felt that what my father had said respecting my peculiar advantages was exactly the truth and common sense of the matter, and it fixed my opinion and feeling from that time forward.

It is evident that this, among many other of the purposes of my father's scheme of education, could not have been accomplished if he had not carefully kept me from having any great amount of intercourse with other boys. He was earnestly bent upon my escaping not only the corrupting influence which boys exercise over boys, but the contagion of vulgar modes of thought and feeling; and for this he was willing that I should pay the price of inferiority in the accomplishments which schoolboys in all countries chiefly cultivate. The deficiencies in my education were principally in the things which boys learn from being turned out to shift for themselves, and from being brought together in large numbers. From temperance and much walking, I grew up healthy and hardy, though not muscular; but I could do no feats of skill or physical strength, and knew none of the ordinary bodily exercises. It was not that play, or time for it, was refused me. Though no holidays were allowed, lest the habit of work should be broken, and a taste for idleness acquired, I had ample leisure in every day to amuse myself; but as I had no boy companions, and the animal need of physical activity was satisfied by walking, my amusements, which were mostly solitary, were in general, of a quiet, if not a bookish turn, and gave little stimulus to any other kind even of mental activity than that which was already called forth by my studies: I consequently remained long, and in a less degree have always remained, inexpert in anything requiring manual dexterity; my mind, as well as my hands, did its work very lamely when it was applied, or ought to have been applied to the practical details which, as they are the chief interest of life to the majority of men, are also the things in which whatever mental capacity they have, chiefly shows itself. I was constantly meriting reproof by inattention, inobservance, and general slackness of mind in matters of daily life. My father was the extreme opposite in these particulars: his senses and mental faculties were always on the alert; he carried decision and energy of character in his whole manner and into every action of life: and this, as much as his talents, contributed to the strong impression which he always made upon those with whom he came into personal contact. But the children of energetic parents, frequently grow up unenergetic, because they lean on their parents, and the parents are energetic for them. The education which my father gave me, was in itself much more fitted for training me to *know* than to *do*. Not that he was unaware of my deficiencies; both as a boy and as a youth I was incessantly smarting under his severe admonitions on the subject. There was anything but insensibility or tolerance on his part towards such shortcomings: but, while he saved me from the demoralizing effects of school life, he made no effort to provide me with any sufficient substitute for its practicalizing influences. Whatever qualities he himself, probably, had acquired without difficulty or special training, he seems to have supposed that I ought to acquire as easily. He had not, I think, bestowed the same amount of thought and attention on this, as on most other branches of education, and here, as well as in some other points of my tuition, he seems to have expected effects without causes.

CHAPTER II

IN my education, as in that of everyone, the moral influences, which are so much more important than all
others, are also the most complicated, and the most
difficult to specify with any approach to completeness.
Without attempting the hopeless task of detailing the circumstances by which, in this respect, my early character
may have been shaped, I shall confine myself to a few leading points, which form an indispensable part of any true
account of my education.

I was brought up from the first without any religious
belief, in the ordinary acceptation of the term. My father,
educated in the creed of Scotch Presbyterianism, had by his
own studies and reflections been early led to reject not only
the belief in Revelation, but the foundations of what is
commonly called Natural Religion. I have heard him say,
that the turning point of his mind on the subject was reading
Butler's Analogy. That work, of which he always continued to speak with respect, kept him, as he said, for some
considerable time, a believer in the divine authority of
Christianity; by proving to him, that whatever are the
difficulties in believing that the Old and New Testaments
proceed from, or record the acts of a perfectly wise and
good being, the same and still greater difficulties stand in
the way of the belief, that a being of such a character can
have been the Maker of the universe. He considered Butler's argument as conclusive against the only opponents for
whom it was intended. Those who admit an omnipotent as
well as perfectly just and benevolent maker and ruler of
such a world as this, can say little against Christianity but
what can, with at least equal force, be retorted against them-

selves. Finding, therefore, no halting place in Deism, he remained in a state of perplexity, until, doubtless after many struggles, he yielded to the conviction, that, concerning the origin of things nothing whatever can be known. This is the only correct statement of his opinion; for dogmatic atheism he looked upon as absurd; as most of those, whom the world has considered Atheists, have always done. These particulars are important, because they show that my father's rejection of all that is called religious belief, was not, as many might suppose, primarily a matter of logic and evidence: the grounds of it were moral, still more than intellectual. He found it impossible to believe that a world so full of evil was the work of an Author combining infinite power with perfect goodness and righteousness. His intellect spurned the subtleties by which men attempt to blind themselves to this open contradiction. The Sabæan, or Manichæan, theory of a Good and an Evil Principle, struggling against each other for the government of the universe, he would not have equally condemned; and I have heard him express surprise, that no one revived it in our time. He would have regarded it as a mere hypothesis; but he would have ascribed it to no depraving influence. As it was, his aversion to religion, in the sense usually attached to the term, was of the same kind with that of Lucretius: he regarded it with the feelings due not to a mere mental delusion, but to a great moral evil. He looked upon it as the greatest enemy of morality, first, by setting up fictitious excellences, —belief in creeds, devotional feelings, and ceremonies, not connected with the good of human-kind,—and causing these to be accepted as substitutes for genuine virtues: but above all, by radically vitiating the standard of morals; making it consist in doing the will of a being, on whom it lavishes indeed all the phrases of adulation, but whom in sober truth it depicts as eminently hateful. I have a hundred times heard him say, that all ages and nations have represented their gods as wicked, in a constantly increasing progression, that mankind have gone on adding trait after trait till they reached the most perfect conception of wickedness which the human mind can devise, and have called this God, and prostrated themselves before it. This *ne plus ultra* of wickedness he considered to be embodied in what is commonly presented to mankind as the creed of Christianity. Think (he used to say) of a being who would make a Hell—who would create the human race with the infallible foreknowledge, and therefore with the intention, that the great majority of them were to be consigned to horrible and everlasting torment. The time, I believe, is drawing near when this dreadful conception of an object of worship will be no longer identified with Christianity; and when all persons, with any sense of moral good and evil, will look upon it with the same indignation with which my father regarded it. My father was as well aware as any one that Christians do not, in general, undergo the demoralizing consequences which seem inherent in such a creed, in the manner or to the extent which might have been expected from it. The same slovenliness of thought, and subjection of the reason to fears, wishes, and affections, which enable them to accept a theory involving a contradiction in terms, prevents them from perceiving the logical consequences of the theory. Such is the facility with which mankind believe at one and the same time things inconsistent with one another, and so few are those who draw from what they receive as truths, any consequences but those recommended to them by their feelings, that multitudes have held the undoubting belief in an Omnipotent Author of Hell, and have nevertheless identified that being with the best conception they were able to form of perfect goodness. Their worship was not paid to the demon which such a Being as they imagined would really be, but to their own ideal of excellence. The evil is, that such a belief keeps the ideal wretchedly low; and opposes the most obstinate resistance to all thought which has a tendency to raise it higher. Believers shrink from every train of ideas which would lead the mind to a clear conception and an elevated standard of excellence, because they feel (even when they do not distinctly see) that such a standard would conflict with many of the dispensations of nature, and with much of what they are accustomed to consider as the Christian creed. And thus morality continues a matter of blind tradition, with no consistent principle, nor even any consistent feeling, to guide it.

HC

It would have been wholly inconsistent with my father's
ideas of duty, to allow me to acquire impressions contrary
to his convictions and feelings respecting religion: and he
impressed upon me from the first, that the manner in which
the world came into existence was a subject on which nothing was known: that the question, "Who made me?" cannot
be answered, because we have no experience or authentic
information from which to answer it; and that any answer
only throws the difficulty a step further back, since the
question immediately presents itself, "Who made God?"
He, at the same time, took care that I should be acquainted
with what had been thought by mankind on these impenetra-
ble problems. I have mentioned at how early an age he
made me a reader of ecclesiastical history; and he taught
me to take the strongest interest in the Reformation, as the
great and decisive contest against priestly tyranny for liberty of thought.

I am thus one of the very few examples, in this country,
of one who has, not thrown off religious belief, but never
had it: I grew up in a negative state with regard to it. I
looked upon the modern exactly as I did upon the ancient
religion, as something which in no way concerned me. It
did not seem to me more strange that English people should
believe what I did not, than that the men I read of in
Herodotus should have done so. History had made the
variety of opinions among mankind a fact familiar to me,
and this was but a prolongation of that fact. This point in
my early education had, however, incidentally one bad consequence deserving notice. In giving me an opinion contrary to that of the world, my father thought it necessary
to give it as one which could not prudently be avowed to the
world. This lesson of keeping my thoughts to myself, at
that early age, was attended with some moral disadvantages;
though my limited intercourse with strangers, especially
such as were likely to speak to me on religion, prevented me
from being placed in the alternative of avowal or hypocrisy.
I remember two occasions in my boyhood, on which I felt
myself in this alternative, and in both cases I avowed my
disbelief and defended it. My opponents were boys, considerably older than myself: one of them I certainly stag-

gered at the time, but the subject was never renewed
between us: the other who was surprised and somewhat
shocked, did his best to convince me for some time,
without effect.

The great advance in liberty of discussion, which is
one of the most important differences between the present
time and that of my childhood, has greatly altered the
moralities of this question; and I think that few men of my
father's intellect and public spirit, holding with such intensity of moral conviction as he did, unpopular opinions
on religion, or on any other of the great subjects of thought,
would now either practise or inculcate the withholding of
them from the world, unless in the cases, becoming fewer
every day, in which frankness on these subjects would either
risk the loss of means of subsistence, or would amount to
exclusion from some sphere of usefulness peculiarly suitable
to the capacities of the individual. On religion in particular
the time appears to me to have come, when it is the duty of
all who being qualified in point of knowledge, have on mature consideration satisfied themselves that the current
opinions are not only false but hurtful, to make their dissent
known; at least, if they are among those whose station or
reputation gives their opinion a chance of being attended
to. Such an avowal would put an end, at once and for ever,
to the vulgar prejudice, that what is called, very improperly,
unbelief, is connected with any bad qualities either of mind
or heart. The world would be astonished if it knew how
great a proportion of its brightest ornaments—of those most
distinguished even in popular estimation for wisdom and
virtue—are complete sceptics in religion; many of them
refraining from avowal, less from personal considerations,
than from a conscientious, though now in my opinion a most
mistaken apprehension, lest by speaking out what would
tend to weaken existing beliefs, and by consequence (as
they suppose) existing restraints, they should do harm instead of good.

Of unbelievers (so called) as well as of believers, there
are many species, including almost every variety of moral
type. But the best among them, as no one who has had
opportunities of really knowing them will hesitate to affirm,

are more genuinely religious, in the best sense of the word religion, than those who exclusively arrogate to themselves the title. The liberality of the age, or in other words the weakening of the obstinate prejudice which makes men unable to see what is before their eyes because it is contrary to their expectations, has caused it to be very commonly admitted that a Deist may be truly religious: but if religion stands for any graces of character and not for mere dogma, the assertion may equally be made of many whose belief is far short of Deism. Though they may think the proof incomplete that the universe is a work of design, and though they assuredly disbelieve that it can have an Author and Governor who is *absolute* in power as well as perfect in goodness, they have that which constitutes the principal worth of all religions whatever, an ideal conception of a Perfect Being, to which they habitually refer as the guide of their conscience; and this ideal of Good is usually far nearer to perfection than the objective Deity of those, who think themselves obliged to find absolute goodness in the author of a world so crowded with suffering and so deformed by injustice as ours.

My father's moral convictions, wholly dissevered from religion, were very much of the character of those of the Greek philosophers; and were delivered with the force and decision which characterized all that came from him. Even at the very early age at which I read with him the Memorabilia of Xenophon, I imbibed from that work and from his comments a deep respect for the character of Socrates; who stood in my mind as a model of ideal excellence: and I well remember how my father at that time impressed upon me the lesson of the " Choice of Hercules." At a somewhat later period the lofty moral standard exhibited in the writings of Plato operated upon me with great force. My father's moral inculcations were at all times mainly those of the " Socratici viri;" justice, temperance (to which he gave a very extended application), veracity, perseverance, readiness to encounter pain and especially labour; regard for the public good; estimation of persons according to their merits, and of things according to their intrinsic usefulness; a life of exertion in contradiction to one of self-indulgent ease and sloth. These and other moralities he conveyed in brief sentences, uttered as occasion arose, of grave exhortation, or stern reprobation and contempt.

But though direct moral teaching does much, indirect does more; and the effect my father produced on my character, did not depend solely on what he said or did with that direct object, but also, and still more, on what manner of man he was.

In his views of life he partook of the character of the Stoic, the Epicurean, and the Cynic, not in the modern but the ancient sense of the word. In his personal qualities the Stoic predominated. His standard of morals was Epicurean, inasmuch as it was utilitarian, taking as the exclusive test of right and wrong, the tendency of actions to produce pleasure or pain. But he had (and this was the Cynic element) scarcely any belief in pleasure; at least in his later years, of which alone, on this point, I can speak confidently. He was not insensible to pleasures; but he deemed very few of them worth the price which, at least in the present state of society, must be paid for them. The greater number of miscarriages in life, he considered to be attributable to the over-valuing of pleasures. Accordingly, temperance, in the large sense intended by the Greek philosophers—stopping short at the point of moderation in all indulgences—was with him, as with them, almost the central point of educational precept. His inculcations of this virtue fill a large place in my childish remembrances. He thought human life a poor thing at best, after the freshness of youth and of unsatisfied curiosity had gone by. This was a topic on which he did not often speak, especially, it may be supposed, in the presence of young persons: but when he did, it was with an air of settled and profound conviction. He would sometimes say, that if life were made what it might be, by good government and good education, it would be worth having: but he never spoke with anything like enthusiasm even of that possibility. He never varied in rating intellectual enjoyments above all others, even in value as pleasures, independently of their ulterior benefits. The pleasures of the benevolent affections he placed high in the scale; and used to say, that he had never known a happy old man, except those who were able to live over again in the pleasures of the young. For passionate emotions of all sorts, and for everything which has been said or written in exaltation of them, he professed the greatest contempt. He regarded them as a form of madness. " The intense " was with him a bye-word of scornful disapprobation. He regarded as an aberration of the moral standard of modern times, compared with that of the ancients, the great stress laid upon feeling. Feelings, as such, he considered to be no proper subjects of praise or blame. Right and wrong, good and bad, he regarded as qualities solely of conduct—of acts and omissions; there being no feeling which may not lead, and does not frequently lead, either to good or to bad actions: conscience itself, the very desire to act right, often leading people to act wrong. Consistently carrying out the doctrine, that the object of praise and blame should be the discouragement of wrong conduct and the encouragement of right, he refused to let his praise or blame be influenced by the motive of the agent. He blamed as severely what he thought a bad action, when the motive was a feeling of duty, as if the agents had been consciously evil doers. He would not have accepted as a plea in mitigation for inquisitors, that they sincerely believed burning heretics to be an obligation of conscience. But though he did not allow honesty of purpose to soften his disapprobation of actions, it had its full effect on his estimation of characters. No one prized conscientiousness and rectitude of intention more highly, or was more incapable of valuing any person in whom he did not feel assurance of it. But he disliked people quite as much for any other deficiency, provided he thought it equally likely to make them act ill. He disliked, for instance, a fanatic in any bad cause, as much or more than one who adopted the same cause from self-interest, because he thought him even more likely to be practically mischievous. And thus, his aversion to many intellectual errors, or what he regarded as such, partook, in a certain sense, of the character of a moral feeling. All this is merely saying that he, in a degree once common, but now very unusual, threw his feelings into his opinions; which truly it is difficult to understand how any one who possesses much of both, can fail to do. None but

those who do not care about opinions, will confound this
with intolerance. Those, who having opinions which they
hold to be immensely important, and their contraries to be
prodigiously hurtful, have any deep regard for the general
good, will necessarily dislike, as a class and in the abstract,
those who think wrong what they think right, and right
what they think wrong: though they need not therefore be,
nor was my father, insensible to good qualities in an opponent, nor governed in their estimation of individuals by
one general presumption, instead of by the whole of their
character. I grant that an earnest person, being no more
infallible than other men, is liable to dislike people on account
of opinions which do not merit dislike; but if he neither himself does them any ill office, nor connives at its being done by
others, he is not intolerant: and the forbearance which flows
from a conscientious sense of the importance to mankind of
the equal freedom of all opinions, is the only tolerance
which is commendable, or, to the highest moral order of
minds, possible.

It will be admitted, that a man of the opinions, and the
character, above described, was likely to leave a strong moral
impression on any mind principally formed by him, and that
his moral teaching was not likely to err on the side of
laxity or indulgence. The element which was chiefly deficient in his moral relation to his children was that of
tenderness. I do not believe that this deficiency lay in his
own nature. I believe him to have had much more feeling
than he habitually showed, and much greater capacities of
feeling than were ever developed. He resembled most
Englishmen in being ashamed of the signs of feeling, and by
the absence of demonstration, starving the feelings themselves. If we consider further that he was in the trying
position of sole teacher, and add to this that his temper
was constitutionally irritable, it is impossible not to feel
true pity for a father who did, and strove to do, so much
for his children, who would have so valued their affection,
yet who must have been constantly feeling that fear of him
was drying it up at its source. This was no longer the
case later in life, and with his younger children. They
loved him tenderly: and if I cannot say so much of myself,

I was always loyally devoted to him. As regards my own education, I hesitate to pronounce whether I was more a loser or gainer by his severity. It was not such as to prevent me from having a happy childhood. And I do not believe that boys can be induced to apply themselves with vigour, and what is so much more difficult, perseverance, to dry and irksome studies, by the sole force of persuasion and soft words. Much must be done, and much must be learnt, by children, for which rigid discipline, and known liability to punishment, are indispensable as means. It is, no doubt, a very laudable effort, in modern teaching, to render as much as possible of what the young are required to learn, easy and interesting to them. But when this principle is pushed to the length of not requiring them to learn anything *but* what has been made easy and interesting, one of the chief objects of education is sacrificed. I rejoice in the decline of the old brutal and tyrannical system of teaching, which, however, did succeed in enforcing habits of application; but the new, as it seems to me, is training up a race of men who will be incapable of doing anything which is disagreeable to them. I do not, then, believe that fear, as an element in education, can be dispensed with; but I am sure that it ought not to be the main element; and when it predominates so much as to preclude love and confidence on the part of the child to those who should be the unreservedly trusted advisers of after years, and perhaps to seal up the fountains of frank and spontaneous communicativeness in the child's nature, it is an evil for which a large abatement must be made from the benefits, moral and intellectual, which may flow from any other part of the education.

During this first period of my life, the habitual frequenters of my father's house were limited to a very few persons, most of them little known to the world, but whom personal worth, and more or less of congeniality with at least his political opinions (not so frequently to be met with then as since) inclined him to cultivate; and his conversations with them I listened to with interest and instruction. My being an habitual inmate of my father's study made me acquainted with the dearest of his friends, David Ricardo, who by his benevolent countenance, and kindliness of manner, was very attractive to young persons, and who after I became a student of political economy, invited me to his house and to walk with him in order to converse on the subject. I was a more frequent visitor (from about 1817 or 1818) to Mr. Hume, who, born in the same part of Scotland as my father, and having been, I rather think, a younger schoolfellow or college companion of his, had on returning from India renewed their youthful acquaintance, and who coming like many others greatly under the influence of my father's intellect and energy of character, was induced partly by that influence to go into Parliament, and there adopt the line of conduct which has given him an honourable place in the history of his country. Of Mr. Bentham I saw much more, owing to the close intimacy which existed between him and my father. I do not know how soon after my father's first arrival in England they became acquainted. But my father was the earliest Englishman of any great mark, who thoroughly understood, and in the main adopted, Bentham's general views of ethics, government and law: and this was a natural foundation for sympathy between them, and made them familiar companions in a period of Bentham's life during which he admitted much fewer visitors than was the case subsequently. At this time Mr. Bentham passed some part of every year at Barrow Green House, in a beautiful part of the Surrey Hills, a few miles from Godstone, and there I each summer accompanied my father in a long visit. In 1813 Mr. Bentham, my father, and I made an excursion, which included Oxford, Bath and Bristol, Exeter, Plymouth, and Portsmouth. In this journey I saw many things which were instructive to me, and acquired my first taste for natural scenery, in the elementary form of fondness for a "view." In the succeeding winter we moved into a house very near Mr. Bentham's, which my father rented from him, in Queen Square, Westminster. From 1814 to 1817 Mr. Bentham lived during half of each year at Ford Abbey, in Somersetshire (or rather in a part of Devonshire surrounded by Somersetshire), which intervals I had the advantage of passing at that place. This sojourn was, I think, an important circumstance in my education. Nothing contributes more to nourish elevation of sentiments in a people than the large and free character of their habitations. The middle age architecture, the baronial hall, and the spacious and lofty rooms, of this fine old place, so unlike the mean and cramped externals of English middle class life, gave the sentiment of a larger and freer existence, and were to me a sort of poetic cultivation, aided also by the character of the grounds in which the Abbey stood; which were *riant* and secluded, umbrageous, and full of the sound of falling waters.

I owed another of the fortunate circumstances in my education, a year's residence in France, to Mr. Bentham's brother, General Sir Samuel Bentham. I had seen Sir Samuel Bentham and his family at their house near Gosport in the course of the tour already mentioned (he being then Superintendent of the Dockyard at Portsmouth), and during a stay of a few days which they made at Ford Abbey shortly after the peace, before going to live on the Continent.

In 1820 they invited me for a six months' visit to them in the south of France, which their kindness ultimately prolonged to nearly a twelvemonth. Sir Samuel Bentham, though of a character of mind different from that of his illustrious brother, was a man of very considerable attainments and general powers, with a decided genius for mechanical art. His wife, a daughter of the celebrated chemist, Dr. Fordyce, was a woman of strong will and decided character, much general knowledge, and great practical good sense of the Edgeworth kind: she was the ruling spirit of the household, as she deserved, and was well qualified, to be. Their family consisted of one son (the eminent botanist) and three daughters, the youngest about two years my senior. I am indebted to them for much and various instruction, and for an almost parental interest in my welfare. When I first joined them, in May 1820, they occupied the Château of Pomignan (still belonging to a descendant of Voltaire's enemy) on the heights overlooking the plain of the Garonne between Montauban and Toulouse. I accompanied them in an excursion to the Pyrenees, including a stay of some duration at Bagnères de Bigorre, a journey to Pau, Bayonne, and

Bagnères de Luchon, and an ascent of the Pic du Midi de Bigorre.

This first introduction to the highest order of mountain scenery made the deepest impression on me, and gave a colour to my tastes through life. In October we proceeded by the beautiful mountain route of Castres and St. Pons, from Toulouse to Montpellier, in which last neighbourhood Sir Samuel had just bought the estate of Restinclière, near the foot of the singular mountain of St. Loup. During this residence in France, I acquired a familiar knowledge of the French language, and acquaintance with the ordinary French literature; I took lessons in various bodily exercises, in none of which however I made any proficiency; and at Montpellier I attended the excellent winter courses of lectures at the Faculté des Sciences, those of M. Anglada on chemistry, of M. Provençal on zoology, and of a very accomplished representative of the eighteenth century metaphysics, M. Gergonne, on logic, under the name of Philosophy of the Sciences. I also went through a course of the higher mathematics under the private tuition of M. Lenthéric, a professor at the Lycée of Montpellier. But the greatest, perhaps, of the many advantages which I owed to this episode in my education, was that of having breathed for a whole year, the free and genial atmosphere of Continental life. This advantage was not the less real though I could not then estimate, nor even consciously feel it. Having so little experience of English life, and the few people I knew being mostly such as had public objects, of a large and personally disinterested kind, at heart, I was ignorant of the low moral tone of what, in England, is called society; the habit of, not indeed professing, but taking for granted in every mode of implication, that conduct is of course always directed towards low and petty objects; the absence of high feelings which manifests itself by sneering depreciation of all demonstrations of them, and by general abstinence (except among a few of the stricter religionists) from professing any high principles of action at all, except in those preordained cases in which such profession is put on as part of the costume and formalities of the occasion. I could not then know or estimate the difference between this manner of existence, and that of a people like the French, whose faults, if equally real, are at all events different; among whom sentiments, which by comparison at least may be called elevated, are the current coin of human intercourse, both in books and in private life; and though often evaporating in profession, are yet kept alive in the nation at large by constant exercise, and stimulated by sympathy, so as to form a living and active part of the existence of great numbers of persons, and to be recognised and understood by all. Neither could I then appreciate the general culture of the understanding, which results from the habitual exercise of the feelings, and is thus carried down into the most uneducated classes of several countries on the Continent, in a degree not equalled in England among the so-called educated, except where an unusual tenderness of conscience leads to a habitual exercise of the intellect on questions of right and wrong. I did not know the way in which, among the ordinary English, the absence of interest in things of an unselfish kind, except occasionally in a special thing here and there, and the habit of not speaking to others, nor much even to themselves, about the things in which they do feel interest, causes both their feelings and their intellectual faculties to remain undeveloped or to develop themselves only in some single and very limited direction; reducing them, considered as spiritual beings, to a kind of negative existence. All these things I did not perceive till long afterwards; but I even then felt, though without stating it clearly to myself, the contrast between the frank sociability and amiability of French personal intercourse, and the English mode of existence in which everybody acts as if everybody else (with few, or no exceptions) was either an enemy or a bore. In France, it is true, the bad as well as the good points, both of individual and of national character, come more to the surface, and break out more fearlessly in ordinary intercourse, than in England; but the general habit of the people is to show, as well as to expect, friendly feeling in every one towards every other, wherever there is not some positive cause for the opposite. In England it is only of the best bred people, in the upper or upper middle ranks, that anything like this can be said.

In my way through Paris, both going and returning, I passed some time in the house of M. Say, the eminent political economist, who was a friend and correspondent of my father, having become acquainted with him on a visit to England a year or two after the peace. He was a man of the later period of the French Revolution, a fine specimen of the best kind of French Republican, one of those who had never bent the knee to Bonaparte though courted by him to do so; a truly upright, brave, and enlightened man. He lived a quiet and studious life, made happy by warm affections, public and private. He was acquainted with many of the chiefs of the Liberal party, and I saw various noteworthy persons while staying at his house; among whom I have pleasure in the recollection of having once seen Saint-Simon, not yet the founder either of a philosophy or a religion, and considered only as a clever *original*. The chief fruit which I carried away from the society I saw, was a strong and permanent interest in Continental Liberalism, of which I ever afterwards kept myself *au courant,* as much as of English politics: a thing not at all usual in those days with Englishmen, and which had a very salutary influence on my development, keeping me free from the error always prevalent in England, and from which even my father with all his superiority to prejudice was not exempt, of judging universal questions by a merely English standard. After passing a few weeks at Caen with an old friend of my father's, I returned to England in July, 1821; and my education resumed its ordinary course.

CHAPTER III

LAST STAGE OF EDUCATION, AND FIRST OF SELF-EDUCATION

FOR the first year or two after my visit to France, I continued my old studies, with the addition of some new ones. When I returned, my father was just finishing for the press his Elements of Political Economy, and he made me perform an exercise on the manuscript, which Mr. Bentham practised on all his own writings, making what he called "marginal contents;" a short abstract of every paragraph, to enable the writer more easily to judge of, and improve, the order of the ideas, and the general character of the exposition. Soon after, my father put into my hands Condillac's Traité des Sensations, and the logical and metaphysical volumes of his Cours d'Etudes; the first (notwithstanding the superficial resemblance between Condillac's psychological system and my father's) quite as much for a warning as for an example. I am not sure whether it was in this winter or the next that I first read a history of the French Revolution. I learnt with astonishment, that the principles of democracy, then apparently in so insignificant and hopeless a minority everywhere in Europe, had borne all before them in France thirty years earlier, and had been the creed of the nation. As may be supposed from this, I had previously a very vague idea of that great commotion. I knew only that the French had thrown off the absolute monarchy of Louis XIV. and XV., had put the King and Queen to death, guillotined many persons, one of whom was Lavoisier, and had ultimately fallen under the despotism of Bonaparte. From this time, as was natural, the subject took an immense hold of my feelings. It allied itself with all my juvenile aspirations to the character of a democratic champion. What had happened so lately, seemed as if it might easily happen again: and the most transcendent

45

glory I was capable of conceiving, was that of figuring, successful or unsuccessful, as a Girondist in an English Convention.

During the winter of 1821-2, Mr. John Austin, with whom at the time of my visit to France my father had but lately become acquainted, kindly allowed me to read Roman law with him. My father, notwithstanding his abhorrence of the chaos of barbarism called English Law, had turned his thoughts towards the bar as on the whole less ineligible for me than any other profession: and these readings with Mr. Austin, who had made Bentham's best ideas his own, and added much to them from other sources and from his own mind, were not only a valuable introduction to legal studies, but an important portion of general education. With Mr. Austin I read Heineccius on the Institutes, his Roman Antiquities, and part of his exposition of the Pandects; to which was added a considerable portion of Blackstone. It was at the commencement of these studies that my father, as a needful accompaniment to them, put into my hands Bentham's principal speculations, as interpreted to the Continent, and indeed to all the world, by Dumont, in the Traité de Législation. The reading of this book was an epoch in my life; one of the turning points in my mental history.

My previous education had been, in a certain sense, already a course of Benthamism. The Benthamic standard of "the greatest happiness" was that which I had always been taught to apply; I was even familiar with an abstract discussion of it, forming an episode in an unpublished dialogue on Government, written by my father on the Platonic model. Yet in the first pages of Bentham it burst upon me with all the force of novelty. What thus impressed me was the chapter in which Bentham passed judgment on the common modes of reasoning in morals and legislation, deduced from phrases like "law of nature," "right reason," "the moral sense," "natural rectitude," and the like, and characterized them as dogmatism in disguise, imposing its sentiments upon others under cover of sounding expressions which convey no reason for the sentiment, but set up the sentiment as its own reason. It had not struck me before, that Bentham's principle put an end to all this. The feeling rushed upon me, that all previous moralists were superseded, and that here indeed was the commencement of a new era in thought. This impression was strengthened by the manner in which Bentham put into scientific form the application of the happiness principle to the morality of actions, by analysing the various classes and orders of their consequences. But what struck me at that time most of all, was the Classification of Offences, which is much more clear, compact, and imposing in Dumont's *rédaction* than in the original work of Bentham from which it was taken. Logic and the dialectics of Plato, which had formed so large a part of my previous training, had given me a strong relish for accurate classification. This taste had been strengthened and enlightened by the study of botany, on the principles of what is called the Natural Method, which I had taken up with great zeal, though only as an amusement, during my stay in France; and when I found scientific classification applied to the great and complex subject of Punishable Acts, under the guidance of the ethical principle of Pleasurable and Painful Consequences, followed out in the method of detail introduced into these subjects by Bentham, I felt taken up to an eminence from which I could survey a vast mental domain, and see stretching out into the distance intellectual results beyond all computation. As I proceeded further, there seemed to be added to this intellectual clearness, the most inspiring prospects of practical improvement in human affairs. To Bentham's general view of the construction of a body of law I was not altogether a stranger, having read with attention that admirable compendium, my father's article on Jurisprudence : but I had read it with little profit, and scarcely any interest, no doubt from its extremely general and abstract character, and also because it concerned the form more than the substance of the *corpus juris,* the logic rather than the ethics of law. But Bentham's subject was Legislation, of which Jurisprudence is only the formal part: and at every page he seemed to open a clearer and broader conception of what human opinions and institutions ought to be, how they might be made what they ought to be, and how far removed from it they are now. When I laid down the last volume of the Traité, I had become a different being. The "principle of utility" understood as Bentham understood it, and applied in the manner in which he applied it through these three volumes, fell exactly into its place as the keystone which held together the detached and fragmentary component parts of my knowledge and beliefs. It gave unity to my conceptions of things. I now had opinions; a creed, a doctrine, a philosophy; in one among the best senses of the word, a religion; the inculcation and diffusion of which could be made the principal outward purpose of a life. And I had a grand conception laid before me of changes to be effected in the condition of mankind through that doctrine. The Traité de Législation wound up with what was to me a most impressive picture of human life as it would be made by such opinions and such laws as were recommended in the treatise. The anticipations of practicable improvement were studiously moderate, deprecating and discountenancing as reveries of vague enthusiasm many things which will one day seem so natural to human beings, that injustice will probably be done to those who once thought them chimerical. But, in my state of mind, this appearance of superiority to illusion added to the effect which Bentham's doctrines produced on me, by heightening the impression of mental power, and the vista of improvement which he did open was sufficiently large and brilliant to light up my life, as well as to give a definite shape to my aspirations.

After this I read, from time to time, the most important of the other works of Bentham which had then seen the light, either as written by himself or as edited by Dumont. This was my private reading: while, under my father's direction, my studies were carried into the higher branches of analytic psychology. I now read Locke's Essay, and wrote out an account of it, consisting of a complete abstract of every chapter, with such remarks as occurred to me: which was read by, or (I think) to, my father, and discussed throughout. I performed the same process with Helvetius de l'Esprit, which I read of my own choice. This preparation of abstracts, subject to my father's censorship, was of great service to me, by compelling precision in conceiving and expressing psychological doctrines, whether accepted as truths or only regarded as the opinion of others. After Helvetius, my father made me study what he deemed the really master-production in the philosophy of mind, Hartley's Observations on Man. This book, though it did not, like the Traité de Législation, give a new colour to my existence, made a very similar impression on me in regard to its immediate subject. Hartley's explanation, incomplete as in many points it is, of the more complex mental phenomena by the law of association, commended itself to me at once as a real analysis, and made me feel by contrast the insufficiency of the merely verbal generalizations of Condillac, and even of the instructive gropings and feelings about for psychological explanations, of Locke. It was at this very time that my father commenced writing his Analysis of the Mind, which carried Hartley's mode of explaining the mental phenomena to so much greater length and depth. He could only command the concentration of thought necessary for this work, during the complete leisure of his holiday of a month or six weeks annually: and he commenced it in the summer of 1822, in the first holiday he passed at Dorking; in which neighbourhood, from that time to the end of his life, with the exception of two years, he lived, as far as his official duties permitted, for six months of every year. He worked at the Analysis during several successive vacations, up to the year 1829 when it was published, and allowed me to read the manuscript, portion by portion, as it advanced. The other principal English writers on mental philosophy I read as I felt inclined, particularly Berkeley, Hume's Essays, Reid, Dugald Stewart and Brown on Cause and Effect. Brown's Lectures I did not read until two or three years later, nor at that time had my father himself read them.

Among the works read in the course of this year, which contributed materially to my development, I ought to mention a book (written on the foundation of some of Bentham's manuscripts and published under the pseudonyme of Philip Beauchamp) entitled "Analysis of the Influence of Natural Religion on the Temporal Happiness of Mankind." This was an examination not of the truth, but of the usefulness of religious belief, in the most general sense, apart from the peculiarities of any special Revelation; which, of all the parts of the discussion concerning religion, is the most important in this age, in which real belief in any religious doctrine is feeble and precarious, but the opinion of its necessity for moral and social purposes almost universal; and when those who reject revelation, very generally take refuge in an optimistic Deism, a worship of the order of Nature, and the supposed course of Providence, at least as full of contradictions, and perverting to the moral sentiments, as any of the forms of Chistianity, if only it is as completely realized. Yet, very little, with any claim to a philosophical character, has been written by sceptics against the usefulness of this form of belief. The volume bearing the name of Philip Beauchamp had this for its special object. Having been shown to my father in manuscript, it was put into my hands by him, and I made a marginal analysis of it as I had done of the Elements of Political Economy. Next to the Traité de Législation, it was one of the books which by the searching character of its analysis produced the greatest effect upon me. On reading it lately after an interval of many years, I find it to have some of the defects as well as the merits of the Benthamic modes of thought, and to contain, as I now think, many weak arguments, but with a great over-balance of sound ones, and much good material for a more completely philosophic and conclusive treatment of the subject.

I have now, I believe, mentioned all the books which had any considerable effect on my early mental development. From this point I began to carry on my intellectual cultivation by writing still more than by reading. In the summer of 1822 I wrote my first argumentative essay. I remember very little about it, except that it was an attack on what I regarded as the aristocratic prejudice, that the rich were, or were likely to be, superior in moral qualities to the poor. My performance was entirely argumentative, without any of the declamation which the subject would admit of, and might be expected to suggest to a young writer. In that department however I was, and remained, very inapt. Dry argument was the only thing I could manage, or willingly attempted; though passively I was very susceptible to the effect of all composition, whether in the form of poetry or oratory, which appealed to the feelings on any basis of reason. My father, who knew nothing of this essay until it was finished, was well satisfied, and as I learnt from others, even pleased with it; but, perhaps from a desire to promote the exercise of other mental faculties than the purely logical, he advised me to make my next exercise in composition one of the oratorical kind: on which suggestion, availing myself of my familiarity with Greek history and ideas and with the Athenian orators, I wrote two speeches, one an accusation, the other a defence of Pericles, on a supposed impeachment for not marching out to fight the Lacedæmonians on their invasion of Attica. After this I continued to write papers on subjects often very much beyond my capacity, but with great benefit both from the exercise itself, and from the discussions which it led to with my father.

I had now also begun to converse, on general subjects, with the instructed men with whom I came in contact: and the opportunities of such contact naturally became more numerous. The two friends of my father from whom I derived most, and with whom I most associated, were Mr. Grote and Mr. John Austin. The acquaintance of both with my father was recent, but had ripened rapidly into intimacy. Mr. Grote was introduced to my father by Mr. Ricardo, I think in 1819, (being then about twenty-five years old,) and sought assiduously his society and conversation. Already a highly instructed man, he was yet, by the side of my father, a tyro in the great subjects of human opinion; but he rapidly seized on my father's best ideas; and in the department of political opinion he made himself known as early as 1820, by a pamphlet in defence of Radical Reform, in reply to a celebrated article by Sir James Mackintosh, then lately published in the Edinburgh Review. Mr. Grote's father, the banker, was, I believe, a thorough Tory, and his mother intensely Evangelical; so that for his liberal opinions he was in no way indebted to home influences. But, unlike most persons who have the prospect of being rich by inheritance, he had, though actively engaged in the business of banking, devoted a great portion of time to philosophic studies; and his intimacy with my father did much to decide the character of the next stage in his mental progress. Him I often visited, and my conversations with him on political, moral, and philosophical subjects gave me, in addition to much valuable instruction, all the pleasure and benefit of sympathetic communion with a man of the high intellectual and moral eminence which his life and writings have since manifested to the world.

Mr. Austin, who was four or five years older than Mr. Grote, was the eldest son of a retired miller in Suffolk, who had made money by contracts during the war, and who must have been a man of remarkable qualities, as I infer from the fact that all his sons were of more than common ability and all eminently gentlemen. The one with whom we are now concerned, and whose writings on jurisprudence have made him celebrated, was for some time in the army, and served in Sicily under Lord William Bentinck. After the peace he sold his commission and studied for the bar, to which he had been called for some time before my father knew him. He was not, like Mr. Grote, to any extent, a pupil of my father, but he had attained, by reading and thought, a considerable number of the same opinions, modified by his own very decided individuality of character. He was a man of great intellectual powers which in conversation appeared at their very best; from the vigour and richness of expression with which, under the excitement of discussion, he was accustomed to maintain some view or other of most general subjects; and from an appearance of not only strong, but deliberate and collected will; mixed with a certain bitterness, partly derived from temperament, and partly from the general cast of his feelings and reflections. The dissatisfaction with life and the world, felt more or less in the present state of society and intellect by every discerning and highly conscientious mind, gave in his case a rather melancholy tinge to the character, very natural to those whose passive moral susceptibilities are more than proportioned to their active energies. For it must be said, that the strength of will of which his manner seemed to give such strong assurance, expended itself principally in manner. With great zeal for human improvement, a strong sense of duty, and capacities and acquirements the extent of which is proved by the writings he has left, he hardly ever completed any intellectual task of magnitude. He had so high a standard of what ought to be done, so exaggerated a sense of deficiencies in his own performances, and was so unable to content himself with the amount of elaboration sufficient for the occasion and the purpose that he not only spoilt much of his work for ordinary use by overlabouring it, but spent so much time and exertion in superfluous study and thought, that when his task ought to have been completed, he had generally worked himself into an illness, without having half finished what he undertook. From this mental infirmity (of which he is not the sole example among the accomplished and able men whom I have known), combined with liability to frequent attacks of disabling though not dangerous ill-health, he accomplished, through life, little in comparison with what he seemed capable of; but what he did produce is held in the very highest estimation by the most competent judges; and, like Coleridge, he might plead as a set-off that he had been to many persons, through his conversation, a source not only of much instruction but of great elevation of character. On me his influence was most salutary. It was moral in the best sense. He took a sincere and kind interest in me, far beyond what could have been expected towards a mere youth from a man of his age, standing, and what seemed austerity of character. There was in his conversation and demeanour a tone of highmindedness which did not show itself so much, if the quality existed as much, in any of the other persons with whom at that time I associated. My intercourse with him was the more beneficial, owing to his being of a different mental type from all other intellectual men whom I frequented, and he from the first set himself decidedly against the prejudices and narrownesses which are almost sure to be found in a young man formed by a particular mode of thought or a particular social circle.

His younger brother, Charles Austin, of whom at this time and for the next year or two I saw much, had also a great effect on me, though of a very different description. He was but a few years older than myself, and had then just left the University, where he had shone with great *éclat* as a man of intellect and a brilliant orator and converser. The effect he produced on his Cambridge contemporaries deserves to be accounted an historical event; for to it may in part be traced the tendency towards Liberalism in general, and the Benthamic and politico-economic form of it in particular, which showed itself in a portion of the more active-minded young men of the higher classes from this time to 1830. The Union Debating Society, at that time at the height of its reputation, was an arena where what were then thought extreme opinions, in politics and philosophy, were weekly asserted, face to face with their opposites, before audiences consisting of the *élite* of the Cambridge youth: and though many persons afterwards of more or less note, (of whom Lord Macaulay is the most celebrated), gained their first oratorical laurels in those debates, the really influential mind among these intellectual gladiators was Charles Austin. He continued, after leaving the University, to be, by his conversation and personal ascendancy, a leader among the same class of young men who had been his associates there: and he attached me among others to his car. Through him I became acquainted with Macaulay, Hyde and Charles Villiers, Strutt (now Lord Belper), Romilly (now Lord Romilly and Master of the Rolls), and various others who subsequently figured in literature or politics, and among whom I heard discussions on many topics, as yet to a certain degree new to me. The influence of Charles Austin over me differed from that of the persons I have hitherto mentioned, in being not the influence of a man over a boy, but that of an elder contemporary. It was through him that I first felt myself, not a pupil under teachers, but a man among men. He was the first person of intellect whom I met on a ground of equality, though as yet much his inferior on that common ground. He was a man who never failed to impress greatly those with whom he came in contact, even when their opinions were the very reverse of his. The impression he gave was that of boundless strength, together with talents which, combined with such apparent force of will and character, seemed capable of dominating the world. Those who knew him, whether friendly to him or not, always anticipated that he would play a conspicuous part in public life. It is seldom that men produce so great an immediate effect by speech, unless they, in some degree, lay themselves out for it; and he did this in no ordinary degree. He loved to strike, and even to startle. He knew that decision is the greatest element of effect, and he uttered his opinions with all the decision he could throw into them, never so well pleased as when he astonished any one by their audacity. Very unlike his brother, who made war against the narrower interpretations and applications of the principles they both professed, he, on the contrary, presented the Benthamic doctrines in the most startling form of which they were susceptible, exaggerating everything in them which tended to consequences offensive to any one's preconceived feelings. All which, he defended with such verve and vivacity, and carried off by a manner so agreeable as well as forcible, that he always either came off victor, or divided the honours of the field. It is my belief that much of the notion popularly entertained of the tenets and sentiments of what are called Benthamites or Utilitarians had its origin in paradoxes thrown out by Charles Austin. It must be said, however, that his example was followed, *haud passibus æquis,* by younger proselytes, and that to *outrer* whatever was by anybody considered offensive in the doctrines and maxims of Benthamism, became at one time the badge of a small coterie of youths. All of these who had anything in them, myself among others, quickly outgrew this boyish vanity; and those who had not, became tired of differing from other people, and gave up both the good and the bad part of the heterodox opinions they had for some time professed.

It was in the winter of 1822-3 that I formed the plan of a little society, to be composed of young men agreeing in fundamental principles—acknowledging Utility as their standard in ethics and politics, and a certain number of the principal corollaries drawn from it in the philosophy I had accepted—and meeting once a fortnight to read essays and discuss questions conformably to the premises thus agreed on. The fact would hardly be worth mentioning, but for the circumstance, that the name I gave to the society I had planned was the Utilitarian Society. It was the first time that any one had taken the title of Utilitarian; and the term made its way into the language from this humble source. I did not invent the word, but found it in one of Galt's novels, the "Annals of the Parish," in which the Scotch clergyman, of whom the book is a supposed autobiography, is represented as warning his parishioners not to leave the Gospel and become utilitarians. With a boy's fondness for a name and a banner I seized on the word, and for some years called myself and others by it as a sectarian appellation; and it came to be occasionally used by some others holding the opinions which it was intended to designate. As those opinions attracted more notice, the term was repeated by strangers and opponents, and got into rather common use just about the time when those who had originally assumed it, laid down that along with other sectarian characteristics. The Society so called consisted at first of no more than three members, one of whom, being Mr. Bentham's amanuensis, obtained for us permission to hold our meetings in his house. The number never, I think, reached ten, and the society was broken up in 1826. It had thus an existence of about three years and a half. The chief effect of it as regards myself, over and above the benefit of practice in oral discussion, was that of bringing me in contact with several young men at that time less advanced than myself, among whom, as they professed the same opinions, I was for some time a sort of leader, and had considerable influence on their mental progress. Any young man of education who fell in my way, and whose opinions were not incompatible with those of the Society, I endeavoured to press into its service; and some others I probably should never have known, had they not joined it. Those of the members who became my intimate companions—no one of whom was in any sense of the word a disciple, but all of them independent thinkers on their own basis—were William Eyton Tooke, son of the eminent political economist, a young man of singular worth both moral and intellectual, lost to the world by an early death; his friend William Ellis, an original thinker in the field of political economy, now honourably known by his apostolic exertions for the improvement of education; George Graham, afterwards official assignee of the Bankruptcy Court, a thinker of originality and power on almost all abstract subjects; and (from the time when he came first to England to study for the bar in 1824 or 1825) a man who has made considerably more noise in the world than any of these, John Arthur Roebuck.

In May, 1823, my professional occupation and status for the next thirty-five years of my life, were decided by my father's obtaining for me an appointment from the East India Company, in the office of the Examiner of India Correspondence, immediately under himself. I was appointed in the usual manner, at the bottom of the list of clerks, to rise, at least in the first instance, by seniority; but with the understanding that I should be employed from the beginning in preparing drafts of despatches, and be thus trained up as a successor to those who then filled the higher departments of the office. My drafts of course required, for some time, much revision from my immediate superiors, but I soon became well acquainted with the business, and by my father's instructions and the general growth of my own powers, I was in a few years qualified to be, and practically was, the chief conductor of the correspondence with India in one of the leading departments, that of the Native States. This continued to be my official duty until I was appointed Examiner, only two years before the time when the abolition of the East India Company as a political body determined my retirement. I do not know any one of the occupations by which a subsistence can now be gained, more suitable than such as this to any one who, not being in independent circumstances, desires to devote a part of the twenty-four hours to private intellectual pursuits. Writing for the press, cannot be recommended as a permanent resource to any one qualified to accomplish anything in the higher departments of literature or thought: not only on account of the uncertainty of this means of livelihood, especially if the writer has a conscience, and will not consent to serve any opinions except his own; but also because the writings by which one can live, are not the writings which themselves live, and are never those in which the writer does his best. Books destined to form future thinkers take too much time to write, and when written come, in general, too slowly into notice and repute, to be relied on for subsistence. Those who have to

support themselves by their pen must depend on literary
drudgery, or at best on writings addressed to the multitude;
and can employ in the pursuits of their own choice, only such
time as they can spare from those of necessity; which is
generally less than the leisure allowed by office occupations,
while the effect on the mind is far more enervating and
fatiguing. For my own part I have, through life, found office
duties an actual rest from the other mental occupations
which I have carried on simultaneously with them. They
were sufficiently intellectual not to be a distasteful drudgery,
without being such as to cause any strain upon the mental
powers of a person used to abstract thought, or to the labour
of careful literary composition. The drawbacks, for every
mode of life has its drawbacks. were not, however, unfelt
by me. I cared little for the loss of the chances of riches
and honours held out by some of the professions, particularly the bar, which had been, as I have already said, the
profession thought of for me. But I was not indifferent to
exclusion from Parliament, and public life: and I felt very
sensibly the more immediate unpleasantness of confinement
to London; the holiday allowed by India-House practice not
exceeding a month in the year, while my taste was strong
for a country life, and my sojourn in France had left behind
it an ardent desire of travelling. But though these tastes
could not be freely indulged, they were at no time entirely
sacrificed. I passed most Sundays, throughout the year, in
the country, taking long rural walks on that day even when
residing in London. The month's holiday was, for a few
years, passed at my father's house in the country: afterwards a part or the whole was spent in tours, chiefly pedes-
trian, with some one or more of the young men who were
my chosen companions; and, at a later period, in longer
journeys or excursions, alone or with other friends. France,
Belgium, and Rhenish Germany were within easy reach of
the annual holiday: and two longer absences, one of three,
the other of six months, under medical advice, added Switzer-
land, the Tyrol, and Italy to my list. Fortunately, also, both
these journeys occurred rather early, so as to give the benefit
and charm of the remembrance to a large portion of life.

I am disposed to agree with what has been surmised by

others, that the opportunity which my official position gave me of learning by personal observation the necessary conditions of the practical conduct of public affairs, has been of considerable value to me as a theoretical reformer of the opinions and institutions of my time. Not, indeed, that public business transacted on paper, to take effect on the other side of the globe, was of itself calculated to give much practical knowledge of life. But the occupation accustomed me to see and hear the difficulties of every course, and the means of obviating them, stated and discussed deliberately with a view to execution; it gave me opportunities of perceiving when public measures, and other political facts, did not produce the effects which had been expected of them, and from what causes; above all, it was valuable to me by making me, in this portion of my activity, merely one wheel in a machine, the whole of which had to work together. As a speculative writer, I should have had no one to consult but myself, and should have encountered in my speculations none of the obstacles which would have started up whenever they came to be applied to practice. But as a Secretary conducting political correspondence, I could not issue an order or express an opinion, without satisfying various persons very unlike myself, that the thing was fit to be done. I was thus in a good position for finding out by practice the mode of putting a thought which gives it easiest admittance into minds not prepared for it by habit; while I became practically conversant with the difficulties of moving bodies of men, the necessities of compromise, the art of sacrificing the non-essential to preserve the essential. I learnt how to obtain the best I could, when I could not obtain everything; instead of being indignant or dispirited because I could not have entirely my own way, to be pleased and encouraged when I could have the smallest part of it; and when even that could not be, to bear with complete equanimity the being overruled altogether. I have found, through life, these acquisitions to be of the greatest possible importance for personal happiness, and they are also a very necessary condition for enabling any one, either as theorist or as practical man, to effect the greatest amount of good compatible with his opportunities.

CHAPTER IV

YOUTHFUL PROPAGANDISM. THE WESTMINSTER REVIEW

THE occupation of so much of my time by office work did not relax my attention to my own pursuits, which were never carried on more vigorously. It was about this time that I began to write in newspapers. The first writings of mine which got into print were two letters published towards the end of 1822, in the Traveller evening newspaper. The Traveller (which afterwards grew into the "Globe and Traveller," by the purchase and incorporation of the Globe) was then the property of the well-known political economist, Colonel Torrens, and under the editorship of an able man, Mr. Walter Coulson (who, after being an amanuensis of Mr. Bentham, became a reporter, then an editor, next a barrister and conveyancer, and died Counsel to the Home Office), it had become one of the most important newspaper organs of Liberal politics. Colonel Torrens himself wrote much of the political economy of his paper; and had at this time made an attack upon some opinion of Ricardo and my father, to which, at my father's instigation, I attempted an answer, and Coulson, out of consideration for my father and goodwill to me, inserted it. There was a reply by Torrens, to which I again rejoined. I soon after attempted something considerably more ambitious. The prosecutions of Richard Carlile and his wife and sister for publications hostile to Christianity, were then exciting much attention, and nowhere more than among the people I frequented. Freedom of discussion even in politics, much more in religion, was at that time far from being, even in theory, the conceded point which it at least seems to be now; and the holders of obnoxious opinions had to be always ready to argue and re-argue for the liberty of expressing them. I wrote a series of five letters, under the signature of Wickliffe, going over the whole length and breadth of the question of free publication of all opinions on religion, and offered them to the Morning Chronicle. Three of them were published in January and February, 1823; the other two, containing things too outspoken for that journal, never appeared at all. But a paper which I wrote soon after on the same subject, à propos of a debate in the House of Commons, was inserted as a leading article; and during the whole of this year, 1823, a considerable number of my contributions were printed in the Chronicle and Traveller: sometimes notices of books but oftener letters, commenting on some nonsense talked in Parliament, or some defect of the law, or misdoings of the magistracy or the courts of justice. In this last department the Chronicle was now rendering signal service. After the death of Mr. Perry, the editorship and management of the paper had devolved on Mr. John Black, long a reporter on its establishment; a man of most extensive reading and information, great honesty and simplicity of mind; a particular friend of my father, imbued with many of his and Bentham's ideas, which he reproduced in his articles, among other valuable thoughts, with great facility and skill. From this time the Chronicle ceased to be the merely Whig organ it was before, and during the next ten years became to a considerable extent a vehicle of the opinions of the Utilitarian Radicals. This was mainly by what Black himself wrote, with some assistance from Fonblanque, who first showed his eminent qualities as a writer by articles and *jeux d'esprit* in the Chronicle. The defects of the law, and of the administration of justice, were the subject on which that paper rendered most service to improvement. Up to that time hardly a word had been said, except by Bentham and my father, against that most peccant part of English institutions and of their administration. It was the almost universal creed of Englishmen, that the law of England, the judicature of England, the unpaid magistracy of England, were models of excellence. I do not go beyond the mark in saying, that after Bentham, who supplied the principal materials, the greatest share of the merit of breaking down this wretched superstition belongs to Black, as editor of the Morning Chronicle. He kept up an incessant fire against

it, exposing the absurdities and vices of the law and the
courts of justice, paid and unpaid, until he forced some
sense of them into people's minds. On many other questions he became the organ of opinions much in advance of
any which had ever before found regular advocacy in the
newspaper press. Black was a frequent visitor of my
father, and Mr. Grote used to say that he always knew by
the Monday morning's article, whether Black had been with
my father on the Sunday. Black was one of the most influential of the many channels through which my father's
conversation and personal influence made his opinions tell
on the world; co-operating with the effect of his writings in
making him a power in the country, such as it has rarely
been the lot of an individual in a private station to be,
through the mere force of intellect and character: and a
power which was often acting the most efficiently where it
was least seen and suspected. I have already noticed how
much of what was done by Ricardo, Hume, and Grote, was
the result, in part, of his prompting and persuasion. He
was the good genius by the side of Brougham in most of
what he did for the public, either on education, law reform,
or any other subject. And his influence flowed in minor
streams too numerous to be specified. This influence was
now about to receive a great extension by the foundation
of the Westminster Review.

Contrary to what may have been supposed, my father was
in no degree a party to setting up the Westminster Review.
The need of a Radical organ to make head against the Edinburgh and Quarterly (then in the period of their greatest
reputation and influence), had been a topic of conversation
between him and Mr. Bentham many years earlier, and it
had been a part of their *Château en Espagne* that my father
should be the editor; but the idea had never assumed any
practical shape. In 1823, however, Mr. Bentham determined to establish the Review at his own cost, and offered
the editorship to my father, who declined it as incompatible
with his India House appointment. It was then entrusted
to Mr. (now Sir John) Bowring, at that time a merchant in
the City. Mr. Bowring had been for two or three years previous an assiduous frequenter of Mr. Bentham, to whom he

was recommended by many personal good qualities, by an
ardent admiration for Bentham, a zealous adoption of many,
though not all of his opinions, and, not least, by an extensive acquaintanceship and correspondence with Liberals of
all countries, which seemed to qualify him for being a powerful agent in spreading Bentham's fame and doctrines through
all quarters of the world. My father had seen little of Bowring, but knew enough of him to have formed a strong opinion, that he was a man of an entirely different type from
what my father considered suitable for conducting a political
and philosophical Review: and he augured so ill of the enterprise that he regretted it altogether, feeling persuaded not
only that Mr. Bentham would lose his money, but that discredit would probably be brought upon Radical principles.
He could not, however, desert Mr. Bentham, and he consented to write an article for the first number. As it had
been a favourite portion of the scheme formerly talked of,
that part of the work should be devoted to reviewing the
other Reviews, this article of my father's was to be a general criticism of the Edinburgh Review from its commencement. Before writing it he made me read through all the
volumes of the Review, or as much of each as seemed of any
importance (which was not so arduous a task in 1823 as
it would be now), and make notes for him of the articles
which I thought he would wish to examine, either on account of their good or their bad qualities. This paper of my
father's was the chief cause of the sensation which the
Westminster Review produced at its first appearance, and is,
both in conception and in execution, one of the most striking
of all his writings. He began by an analysis of the tendencies of periodical literature in general; pointing out, that it
cannot, like books, wait for success, but must succeed immediately, or not at all, and is hence almost certain to profess and inculcate the opinions already held by the public to
which it addresses itself, instead of attempting to rectify or
improve those opinions. He next, to characterize the position of the Edinburgh Review as a political organ, entered
into a complete analysis, from the Radical point of view, of
the British Constitution. He held up to notice its thoroughly
aristocratic character: the nomination of a majority of the

House of Commons by a few hundred families; the entire identification of the more independent portion, the county members, with the great landholders; the different classes whom this narrow oligarchy was induced, for convenience, to admit to a share of power; and finally, what he called its two props, the Church, and the legal profession. He pointed out the natural tendency of an aristocratic body of this composition, to group itself into two parties, one of them in possession of the executive, the other endeavouring to supplant the former and become the predominant section by the aid of public opinion, without any essential sacrifice of the aristocratical predominance. He described the course likely to be pursued, and the political ground occupied, by an aristocratic party in opposition, coquetting with popular principles for the sake of popular support. He showed how this idea was realized in the conduct of the Whig party, and of the Edinburgh Review as its chief literary organ. He described, as their main characteristic, what he termed " seesaw;" writing alternately on both sides of every question which touched the power or interest of the governing classes; sometimes in different articles, sometimes in different parts of the same article: and illustrated his position by copious specimens. So formidable an attack on the Whig party and policy had never before been made; nor had so great a blow been ever struck, in this country, for Radicalism; nor was there, I believe, any living person capable of writing that article, except my father.[1]

In the meantime the nascent Review had formed a junction with another project, of a purely literary periodical, to be edited by Mr. Henry Southern, afterwards a diplomatist, then a literary man by profession. The two editors agreed to unite their corps, and divide the editorship, Bowring taking the political, Southern the literary department. Southern's Review was to have been published by Longman, and that firm, though part proprietors of the Edinburgh, were willing to be the publishers of the new journal. But when all the arrangements had been made, and the pros-

---

[1] The continuation of this article in the second number of the Review was written by me under my father's eye, and (except as practice in composition, in which respect it was, to me, more useful than anything else I ever wrote) was of little or no value.

pectuses sent out, the Longmans saw my father's attack on the Edinburgh, and drew back. My father was now appealed to for his interest with his own publisher, Baldwin, which was exerted with a successful result. And so, in April, 1824, amidst anything but hope on my father's part, and that of most of those who afterwards aided in carrying on the Review, the first number made its appearance.

That number was an agreeable surprise to most of us. The average of the articles was of much better quality than had been expected. The literary and artistic department had rested chiefly on Mr. Bingham, a barrister (subsequently a police magistrate), who had been for some years a frequenter of Bentham, was a friend of both the Austins, and had adopted with great ardour Mr. Bentham's philosophical opinions. Partly from accident, there were in the first number as many as five articles by Bingham; and we were extremely pleased with them. I well remember the mixed feeling I myself had about the Review; the joy at finding, what we did not at all expect, that it was sufficiently good to be capable of being made a creditable organ of those who held the opinions it professed; and extreme vexation, since it was so good on the whole, at what we thought the blemishes of it. When, however, in addition to our generally favourable opinion of it, we learned that it had an extraordinary large sale for a first number, and found that the appearance of a Radical Review, with pretensions equal to those of the established organs of parties, had excited much attention, there could be no room for hesitation, and we all became eager in doing everything we could to strengthen and improve it.

My father continued to write occasional articles. The Quarterly Review received its exposure, as a sequel to that of the Edinburgh. Of his other contributions, the most important were an attack on Southey's Book of the Church, in the fifth number, and a political article in the twelfth. Mr. Austin only contributed one paper, but one of great merit, an argument against primogeniture, in reply to an article then lately published in the Edinburgh Review by M'Culloch. Grote also was a contributor only once; all the time he could spare being already taken up with his History of Greece. The article he wrote was on his own subject, and was a very complete exposure and castigation of Mitford. Bingham and Charles Austin continued to write for some time; Fonblanque was a frequent contributor from the third number. Of my particular associates, Ellis was a regular writer up to the ninth number; and about the time when he left off, others of the set began; Eyton, Tooke, Graham, and Roebuck. I was myself the most frequent writer of all, having contributed, from the second number to the eighteenth, thirteen articles; reviews of books on history and political economy, or discussions on special political topics, as corn laws, game laws, law of libel. Occasional articles of merit came in from other acquaintances of my father's, and, in time, of mine; and some of Mr. Bowring's writers turned out well. On the whole, however, the conduct of the Review was never satisfactory to any of the persons strongly interested in its principles, with whom I came in contact. Hardly ever did a number come out without containing several things extremely offensive to us, either in point of opinion, of taste, or by mere want of ability. The unfavourable judgments passed by my father, Grote, the two Austins, and others, were re-echoed with exaggeration by us younger people; and as our youthful zeal rendered us by no means backward in making complaints, we led the two editors a sad life. From my knowledge of what I then was, I have no doubt that we were at least as often wrong as right; and I am very certain that if the Review had been carried on according to our notions (I mean those of the juniors), it would have been no better, perhaps not even so good as it was. But it is worth noting as a fact in the history of Benthamism, that the periodical organ, by which it was best known, was from the first extremely unsatisfactory to those whose opinions on all subjects it was supposed specially to represent.

Meanwhile, however, the Review made considerable noise in the world, and gave a recognised *status,* in the arena of opinion and discussion, to the Benthamic type of Radicalism, out of all proportion to the number of its adherents, and to the personal merits and abilities, at that time, of most of those who could be reckoned among them. It was a time, as is known, of rapidly rising Liberalism. When the fears and animosities accompanying the war with France had been brought to an end, and people had once more a place in their thoughts for home politics, the tide began to set towards reform. The renewed oppression of the Continent by the old reigning families, the countenance apparently given by the English Government to the conspiracy against liberty called the Holy Alliance, and the enormous weight of the national debt and taxation occasioned by so long and costly a war, rendered the government and parliament very unpopular. Radicalism, under the leadership of the Burdetts and Cobbetts, had assumed a character and importance which seriously alarmed the administration: and their alarm had scarcely been temporarily assuaged by the celebrated Six Acts, when the trial of Queen Caroline roused a still wider and deeper feeling of hatred. Though the outward signs of this hatred passed away with its exciting cause, there arose on all sides a spirit which had never shown itself before, of opposition to abuses in detail. Mr. Hume's persevering scrutiny of the public expenditure, forcing the House of Commons to a division on every objectionable item in the estimates, had begun to tell with great force on public opinion, and had extorted many minor retrenchments from an unwilling administration. Political economy had asserted itself with great vigour in public affairs, by the petition of the merchants of London for free trade, drawn up in 1820 by Mr. Tooke and presented by Mr. Alexander Baring; and by the noble exertions of Ricardo during the few years of his parliamentary life. His writings, following up the impulse given by the Bullion controversy, and followed up in their turn by the expositions and comments of my father and M'Culloch (whose writings in the Edinburgh Review during those years were most valuable), had drawn general attention to the subject, making at least partial converts in the Cabinet itself; and Huskisson, supported by Canning, had commenced that gradual demolition of the protective system, which one of their colleagues virtually completed in 1846, though the last vestiges were only swept away by Mr. Gladstone in 1860. Mr. Peel, then Home Secretary, was entering cautiously into the untrodden and peculiarly Benthamic path of Law Reform. At this period when Liberalism seemed to be becoming the tone of the time, when improvement of institutions was preached from the highest places, and a complete change of the constitution of parliament was loudly demanded in the lowest, it is not strange that attention should have been roused by the regular appearance in controversy of what seemed a new school of writers, claiming to be the legislators and theorists of this new tendency. The air of strong conviction with which they wrote, when scarcely any one else seemed to have an equally strong faith in as definite a creed; the boldness with which they tilted against the very front of both the existing political parties; their uncompromising profession of opposition to many of the generally received opinions, and the suspicion they lay under of holding others still more heterodox than they professed; the talent and verve of at least my father's articles, and the appearance of a corps behind him sufficient to carry on a Review; and finally, the fact that the Review was bought and read, made the so-called Bentham school in philosophy and politics fill a greater place in the public mind than it had held before, or has ever again held since other equally earnest schools of thought have arisen in England. As I was in the headquarters of it, knew of what it was composed, and as one of the most active of its very small number, might say without undue assumption, *quorum pars magna fui,* it belongs to me more than to most others, to give some account of it.

This supposed school, then, had no other existence than what was constituted by the fact, that my father's writings and conversation drew round him a certain number of young men who had already imbibed, or who imbibed from him, a greater or smaller portion of his very decided political and philosophical opinions. The notion that Bentham was surrounded by a band of disciples who received their opinions from his lips, is a fable to which my father did justice in his " Fragment on Mackintosh," and which, to all who knew Mr. Bentham's habits of life and manner of conversation, is simply ridiculous. The influence which Bentham exercised was by his writings. Through them he has produced, and is producing, effects on the condition of mankind, wider and deeper, no doubt, than any which can be attributed to my father. He is a much greater name in history. But my father exercised a far greater personal ascendancy. He *was* sought for the vigour and instructiveness of his conversation, and did use it largely as an instrument for the diffusion of his opinions. I have never known any man who could do such ample justice to his best thoughts in colloquial discussion. His perfect command over his great mental resources, the terseness and expressiveness of his language and the moral earnestness as well as intellectual force of his delivery, made him one of the most striking of all argumentative conversers: and he was full of anecdote, a hearty laugher, and, when with people whom he liked, a most lively and amusing companion. It was not solely, or even chiefly, in diffusing his merely intellectual convictions that his power showed itself: it was still more through the influence of a quality, of which I have only since learnt to appreciate the extreme rarity: that exalted public spirit, and regard above all things to the good of the whole, which warmed into life and activity every germ of similar virtue that existed in the minds he came in contact with: the desire he made them feel for his approbation, the shame at his disapproval; the moral support which his conversation and his very existence gave to those who were aiming at the same objects, and the encouragement he afforded to the fainthearted or desponding among them, by the firm confidence which (though the reverse of sanguine as to the results to be expected in any one particular case) he always felt in the power of reason, the general progress of improvement, and the good which individuals could do by judicious effort.

It was my father's opinions which gave the distinguishing character to the Benthamic or utilitarian propagandism of that time. They fell singly, scattered from him, in many directions, but they flowed from him in a continued stream principally in three channels. One was through me, the only mind directly formed by his instructions, and through whom considerable influence was exercised over various young men, who became, in their turn, propagandists. A second was through some of the Cambridge contemporaries of

Charles Austin, who, either initiated by him or under the
general mental impulse which he gave, had adopted many
opinions allied to those of my father, and some of the more
considerable of whom afterwards sought my father's acquaintance and frequented his house. Among these may
be mentioned Strutt, afterwards Lord Belper, and the present Lord Romilly, with whose eminent father, Sir Samuel,
my father had of old been on terms of friendship. The third
channel was that of a younger generation of Cambridge
undergraduates, contemporary, not with Austin, but with
Eyton Tooke, who were drawn to that estimable person by
affinity of opinions, and introduced by him to my father:
the most notable of these was Charles Buller. Various other
persons individually received and transmitted a considerable
amount of my father's influence: for example, Black (as before mentioned) and Fonblanque: most of these, however,
we accounted only partial allies; Fonblanque, for instance,
was always divergent from us on many important points.
But indeed there was by no means complete unanimity
among any portion of us, nor had any of us adopted implicitly all my father's opinions. For example, although his
Essay on Government was regarded probably by all of us
as a masterpiece of political wisdom, our adhesion by no
means extended to the paragraph of it, in which he maintains that women may consistently with good government,
be excluded from the suffrage, because their interest is the
same with that of men. From this doctrine, I, and all those
who formed my chosen associates, most positively dissented.
It is due to my father to say that he denied having intended
to affirm that women *should* be excluded any more than men
under the age of forty, concerning whom he maintained, in
the very next paragraph, an exactly similar thesis. He was,
as he truly said, not discussing whether the suffrage had
better be restricted, but only (assuming that it is to be restricted) what is the utmost limit of restriction, which does
not necessarily involve a sacrifice of the securities for good
government. But I thought then, as I have always thought
since, that the opinion which he acknowledged, no less than
that which he disclaimed, is as great an error as any of
those against which the Essay was directed; that the in-

terest of women is included in that of men exactly as much and no more, as the interest of subjects is included in that of kings; and that every reason which exists for giving the suffrage to anybody, demands that it should not be withheld from women. This was also the general opinion of the younger proselytes; and it is pleasant to be able to say that Mr. Bentham, on this important point, was wholly on our side.

But though none of us, probably, agreed in every respect with my father, his opinions, as I said before, were the principal element which gave its colour and character to the little group of young men who were the first propagators of what was afterwards called "Philosophic Radicalism." Their mode of thinking was not characterized by Benthamism in any sense which has relation to Bentham as a chief or guide, but rather by a combination of Bentham's point of view with that of the modern political economy, and with the Hartleian metaphysics. Malthus's population principle was quite as much a banner, and point of union among us, as any opinion specially belonging to Bentham. This great doctrine, originally brought forward as an argument against the indefinite improvability of human affairs, we took up with ardent zeal in the contrary sense, as indicating the sole means of realizing that improvability by securing full employment at high wages to the whole labouring population through a voluntary restriction of the increase of their numbers. The other leading characteristics of the creed, which we held in common with my father, may be stated as follows:

In politics, an almost unbounded confidence in the efficacy of two things: representative government, and complete freedom of discussion. So complete was my father's reliance on the influence of reason over the minds of mankind, whenever it is allowed to reach them, that he felt as if all would be gained if the whole population were taught to read, if all sorts of opinions were allowed to be addressed to them by word and in writing, and if by means of the suffrage they could nominate a legislature to give effect to the opinions they adopted. He thought that when the legislature no longer represented a class interest, it would aim at the general interest honestly, and with adequate wisdom; since the people would be sufficiently under the guidance of educated intelligence, to make in general a good choice of persons to represent them, and having done so, to leave to those whom they had chosen a liberal discretion. Accordingly aristocratic rule, the government of the Few in any of its shapes, being in his eyes the only thing which stood between mankind and an administration of their affairs by the best wisdom to be found among them, was the object of his sternest disapprobation, and a democratic suffrage the principal article of his political creed, not on the ground of liberty, Rights of Man, or any of the phrases, more or less significant, by which, up to that time, democracy had usually been defended, but as the most essential of " securities for good government." In this, too, he held fast only to what he deemed essentials; he was comparatively indifferent to monarchical or republican forms—far more so than Bentham, to whom a king, in the character of " corrupter-general," appeared necessarily very noxious. Next to aristocracy, an established church, or corporation of priests, as being by position the great depravers of religion, and interested in opposing the progress of the human mind, was the object of his greatest detestation; though he disliked no clergyman personally who did not deserve it, and was on terms of sincere friendship with several. In ethics, his moral feelings were energetic and rigid on all points which he deemed important to human well being, while he was supremely indifferent in opinion (though his indifference did not show itself in personal conduct) to all those doctrines of the common morality, which he thought had no foundation but in asceticism and priest-craft. He looked forward, for example, to a considerable increase of freedom in the relations between the sexes, though without pretending to define exactly what would be, or ought to be, the precise conditions of that freedom. This opinion was connected in him with no sensuality either of a theoretical or of a practical kind. He anticipated, on the contrary, as one of the beneficial effects of increased freedom, that the imagination would no longer dwell upon the physical relation and its adjuncts, and swell this into one of the principal objects of life; a perversion of the imagination and feelings, which he regarded as one of the deepest seated and most pervading evils in the human mind. In psychology, his fundamental doctrine was the formation of all human character by circumstances, through the universal Principle of Association, and the consequent unlimited possibility of improving the moral and intellectual condition of mankind by education. Of all his doctrines none was more important than this, or needs more to be insisted on: unfortunately there is none which is more contradictory to the prevailing tendencies of speculation, both in his time and since.

These various opinions were seized on with youthful fanaticism by the little knot of young men of whom I was one: and we put into them a sectarian spirit, from which, in intention at least, my father was wholly free. What we (or rather a phantom substituted in the place of us) were sometimes by a ridiculous exaggeration, called by others, namely a " school," some of us for a time really hoped and aspired to be. The French *philosophes* of the eighteenth century were the example we sought to imitate, and we hoped to accomplish no less results. No one of the set went to so great excesses in this boyish ambition as I did; which might be shown by many particulars, were it not an useless waste of space and time.

All this, however, is properly only the outside of our existence; or, at least, the intellectual part alone, and no more than one side of that. In attempting to penetrate inward, and give any indication of what we were as human beings, I must be understood as speaking only of myself, of whom alone I can speak, from sufficient knowledge; and I do not believe that the picture would suit any of my companions without many and great modifications.

I conceive that the description so often given of a Benthamite, as a mere reasoning machine, though extremely inapplicable to most of those who have been designated by that title, was during two or three years of my life not altogether untrue of me. It was perhaps as applicable to me as it can well be to any one just entering into life, to whom the common objects of desire must in general have at least the attraction of novelty. There is nothing very extraordinary in this fact; no youth of the age I then was, can be expected to be more than one thing, and this was the thing I happened to be. Ambition and desire of distinction, I had in abundance; and zeal for what I thought the good of mankind was my strongest sentiment, mixing with and colouring all others. But my zeal was as yet little else, at that period of my life, than zeal for speculative opinions. It had not its root in genuine benevolence, or sympathy with mankind; though these qualities held their due place in my ethical standard. Nor was it connected with any high enthusiasm for ideal nobleness. Yet of this feeling I was imaginatively very susceptible; but there was at that time an intermission of its natural aliment, poetical culture, while there was a superabundance of the discipline antagonistic to it, that of mere logic and analysis. Add to this that, as already mentioned, my father's teachings tended to the undervaluing of feeling. It was not that he was himself cold-hearted or insensible; I believe it was rather from the contrary quality; he thought that feeling could take care of itself; that there was sure to be enough of it if actions were properly cared about. Offended by the frequency with which, in ethical and philosophical controversy, feeling is made the ultimate reason and justification of conduct, instead of being itself called on for a justification, while, in practice, actions the effect of which on human happiness is mischievous, are defended as being required by feeling, and the character of a person of feeling obtains a credit for desert, which he thought only due to actions, he had a real impatience of attributing praise to feeling, or of any but the most sparing reference to it, either in the estimation of persons or in the discussion of things. In addition to the influence which this characteristic in him, had on me and others, we found all the opinions to which we attached most importance, constantly attacked on the ground of feeling. Utility was denounced as cold calculation; political economy as hard-hearted; anti-population doctrines as repulsive to the natural feelings of mankind. We retorted by the word "sentimentality," which, along with "declamation" and "vague generalities," served us as common terms of opprobrium. Although we were generally in the right, as against those who were opposed to us, the effect was that the cultivation of feeling (except the feelings of public and private duty), was not in much esteem among us, and had very little place in the thoughts of most of us, myself in particular. What we principally thought of, was to alter people's opinions; to make them believe according to evidence, and know what was their real interest, which when they once knew, they would, we thought, by the instrument of opinion, enforce a regard to it upon one another. While fully recognising the superior excellence of unselfish benevolence and love of justice, we did not expect the regeneration of mankind from any direct action on those sentiments, but from the effect of educated intellect, enlightening the selfish feelings. Although this last is prodigiously important as a means of improvement in the hands of those who are themselves impelled by nobler principles of action, I do not believe that any one of the survivors of the Benthamites or Utilitarians of that day, now relies mainly upon it for the general amendment of human conduct.

From this neglect both in theory and in practice of the cultivation of feeling, naturally resulted, among other things, an undervaluing of poetry, and of Imagination generally, as an element of human nature. It is, or was, part of the popular notion of Benthamites, that they are enemies of poetry: this was partly true of Bentham himself; he used to say that "all poetry is misrepresentation:" but in the sense in which he said it, the same might have been said of all impressive speech; of all representation or inculcation more oratorical in its character than a sum in arithmetic. An article of Bingham's in the first number of the Westminster Review, in which he offered as an explanation of something which he disliked in Moore, that "Mr. Moore *is* a poet, and therefore is *not* a reasoner," did a good deal to attach the notion of hating poetry to the writers in the Review. But the truth was that many of us were great readers of poetry; Bingham himself had been a writer of it, while as regards me (and the same thing might be said of my father), the correct statement would be, not that I disliked poetry, but that I was theoretically indifferent to it. I disliked any sentiments in poetry which I should have disliked in prose; and that included a great deal. And I was wholly blind to its place in human culture, as a means of educating the feelings. But I was always personally very susceptible to some kinds of it. In the most sectarian period of my Benthamism, I happened to look into Pope's Essay on Man, and though every opinion in it was contrary to mine, I well remember how powerfully it acted on my imagination. Perhaps at that time poetical composition of any higher type than eloquent discussion in verse, might not have produced a similar effect on me: at all events I seldom gave it an opportunity. This, however, was a mere passive state. Long before I had enlarged in any considerable degree, the basis of my intellectual creed, I had obtained in the natural course of my mental progress, poetic culture of the most valuable kind, by means of reverential admiration for the lives and characters of heroic persons; especially the heroes of philosophy. The same inspiring effect which so many of the benefactors of mankind have left on record that they had experienced from Plutarch's Lives, was produced on me by Plato's pictures of Socrates, and by some modern biographies, above all by Condorcet's Life of Turgot; a book well calculated to rouse the best sort of enthusiasm, since it contains one of the wisest and noblest of lives, delineated by one of the wisest and noblest of men. The heroic virtue of these glorious representatives of the opinions with which I sympathized, deeply affected me, and I perpetually recurred to them as others do to a favourite poet, when needing to be carried up into the more elevated regions of feeling and thought. I may observe by the way that this book cured me of my sectarian follies. The two or three pages beginning "Il regardait toute secte comme nuisible," and explaining why Turgot always kept himself perfectly distinct from the Encyclopedists, sank deeply into my mind. I left off designating myself and others as Utilitarians, and by the pronoun "we" or any other collective designation, I ceased to *afficher* sectarianism. My real inward sectarianism I did not get rid of till later, and much more gradually.

About the end of 1824, or beginning of 1825, Mr. Bentham, having lately got back his papers on Evidence from

M. Dumont (whose Traité des Preuves Judiciaires, grounded on them, was then first completed and published) resolved to have them printed in the original, and bethought himself of me as capable of preparing them for the press; in the same manner as his Book of Fallacies had been recently edited by Bingham. I gladly undertook this task, and it occupied nearly all my leisure for about a year, exclusive of the time afterwards spent in seeing the five large volumes through the press. Mr. Bentham had begun this treatise three times, at considerable intervals, each time in a different manner, and each time without reference to the preceding: two of the three times he had gone over nearly the whole subject.

These three masses of manuscript it was my business to condense into a single treatise; adopting the one last written as the groundwork, and incorporating with it as much of the two others as it had not completely superseded. I had also to unroll such of Bentham's involved and parenthetical sentences, as seemed to overpass by their complexity the measure of what readers were likely to take the pains to understand. It was further Mr. Bentham's particular desire that I should, from myself, endeavour to supply any *lacunæ* which he had left; and at his instance I read, for this purpose, the most authoritative treatises on the English Law of Evidence, and commented on a few of the objectionable points of the English rules, which had escaped Bentham's notice. I also replied to the objections which had been made to some of his doctrines by reviewers of Dumont's book, and added a few supplementary remarks on some of the more abstract parts of the subject, such as the theory of improbability and impossibility. The controversial part of these editorial additions was written in a more assuming tone than became one so young and inexperienced as I was: but indeed I had never contemplated coming forward in my own person; and as an anonymous editor of Bentham, I fell into the tone of my author, not thinking it unsuitable to him or to the subject, however it might be so to me. My name as editor was put to the book after it was printed, at Mr. Bentham's positive desire, which I in vain attempted to persuade him to forego.

The time occupied in this editorial work was extremely
well employed in respect to my own improvement. The
"Rationale of Judicial Evidence" is one of the richest in
matter of all Bentham's productions. The theory of evidence being in itself one of the most important of his subjects, and ramifying into most of the others, the book contains, very fully developed, a great proportion of all his best
thoughts: while, among more special things, it comprises
the most elaborate exposure of the vices and defects of
English law, as it then was, which is to be found in his
works; not confined to the law of evidence, but including,
by way of illustrative episode, the entire procedure or practice of Westminster Hall. The direct knowledge, therefore,
which I obtained from the book, and which was imprinted
upon me much more thoroughly than it could have been by
mere reading, was itself no small acquisition. But this
occupation did for me what might seem less to be expected;
it gave a great start to my powers of composition. Everything which I wrote subsequently to this editorial employment, was markedly superior to anything that I had written
before it. Bentham's later style, as the world knows, was
heavy and cumbersome, from the excess of a good quality,
the love of precision, which made him introduce clause
within clause into the heart of every sentence, that the
reader might receive into his mind all the modifications and
qualifications simultaneously with the main proposition: and
the habit grew on him until his sentences became, to those
not accustomed to them, most laborious reading. But his
earlier style, that of the Fragment on Government, Plan of
a Judicial Establishment, &c., is a model of liveliness and
ease combined with fulness of matter, scarcely ever surpassed: and of this earlier style there were many striking
specimens in the manuscripts on Evidence, all of which I
endeavoured to preserve. So long a course of this admirable writing had a considerable effect upon my own; and I
added to it by the assiduous reading of other writers, both
French and English, who combined in a remarkable degree,
ease with force, such as Goldsmith, Fielding, Pascal, Voltaire, and Courier. Through these influences my writing
lost the jejuneness of my early compositions; the bones and

cartilages began to clothe themselves with flesh, and the style became, at times, lively and almost light.

This improvement was first exhibited in a new field. Mr. Marshall, of Leeds, father of the present generation of Marshalls, the same who was brought into Parliament for Yorkshire, when the representation forfeited by Grampound was transferred to it, an earnest parliamentary reformer, and a man of large fortune, of which he made a liberal use, had been much struck with Bentham's Book of Fallacies; and the thought had occurred to him that it would be useful to publish annually the Parliamentary Debates, not in the chronological order of Hansard, but classified according to subjects, and accompanied by a commentary pointing out the fallacies of the speakers. With this intention, he very naturally addressed himself to the editor of the Book of Fallacies; and Bingham, with the assistance of Charles Austin, undertook the editorship. The work was called "Parliamentary History and Review." Its sale was not sufficient to keep it in existence, and it only lasted three years. It excited, however, some attention among parliamentary and political people. The best strength of the party was put forth in it; and its execution did them much more credit than that of the Westminster Review had ever done. Bingham and Charles Austin wrote much in it; as did Strutt, Romilly, and several other Liberal lawyers. My father wrote one article in his best style; the elder Austin another. Coulson wrote one of great merit. It fell to my lot to lead off the first number by an article on the principal topic of the session (that of 1825), the Catholic Association and the Catholic Disabilities. In the second number I wrote an elaborate Essay on the Commercial Crisis of 1825 and the Currency Debates. In the third I had two articles, one on a minor subject, the other on the Reciprocity principle in commerce, à propos of a celebrated diplomatic correspondence between Canning and Gallatin. These writings were no longer mere reproductions and applications of the doctrines I had been taught; they were original thinking, as far as that name can be applied to old ideas in new forms and connexions: and I do not exceed the truth in saying that there was a maturity, and a well-digested character about them, which there had not been in any of my previous performances. In execution, therefore, they were not at all juvenile; but their subjects, had either gone by, or have been so much better treated since, that they are entirely superseded, and should remain buried in the same oblivion with my contributions to the first dynasty of the Westminster Review.

While thus engaged in writing for the public, I did not neglect other modes of self-cultivation. It was at this time that I learnt German; beginning it on the Hamiltonian method, for which purpose I and several of my companions formed a class. For several years from this period, our social studies assumed a shape which contributed very much to my mental progress. The idea occurred to us of carrying on, by reading and conversation, a joint study of several of the branches of science which we wished to be masters of. We assembled to the number of a dozen or more. Mr. Grote lent a room of his house in Threadneedle Street for the purpose, and his partner, Prescott, one of the three original members of the Utilitarian Society, made one among us. We met two mornings in every week, from half-past eight till ten, at which hour most of us were called off to our daily occupations. Our first subject was Political Economy. We chose some systematic treatise as our text-book; my father's " Elements " being our first choice. One of us read aloud a chapter, or some smaller portion of the book. The discussion was then opened, and any one who had an objection, or other remark to make, made it. Our rule was to discuss thoroughly every point raised, whether great or small, prolonging the discussion until all who took part were satisfied with the conclusion they had individually arrived at; and to follow up every topic of collateral speculation which the chapter or the conversation suggested, never leaving it until we had untied every knot which we found. We repeatedly kept up the discussion of some one point for several weeks, thinking intently on it during the intervals of our meetings, and contriving solutions of the new difficulties which had risen up in the last morning's discussion. When we had finished in this way my father's Elements, we went in the same manner through Ricardo's Principles of Political Economy, and Bailey's Dissertations on Value. These close and vigorous discussions were not only improving in a high degree to those who took part in them, but brought out new views of some topics of abstract Political Economy. The theory of International Values which I afterwards published, emanated from these conversations, as did also the modified form of Ricardo's theory of Profits, laid down in my Essay on Profits and Interest. Those among us with whom new speculations chiefly originated, were Ellis, Graham, and I; though others gave valuable aid to the discussions, especially Prescott and Roebuck, the one by his knowledge, the other by his dialectical acuteness. The theories of International Values and of Profits were excogitated and worked out in about equal proportions by myself and Graham: and if our original project had been executed, my "Essays on Some Unsettled Questions of Political Economy" would have been brought out along with some papers of his, under our joint names. But when my exposition came to be written, I found that I had so much over-estimated my agreement with him, and he dissented so much from the most original of the two Essays, that on International Values, that I was obliged to consider the theory as now exclusively mine, and it came out as such when published many years later. I may mention that among the alterations which my father made in revising his Elements for the third edition, several were founded on criticisms elicited by these conversations; and in particular he modified his opinions (though not to the extent of our new speculations) on both the points to which I have adverted.

When we had enough of political economy, we took up the syllogistic logic in the same manner, Grote now joining us. Our first text-book was Aldrich, but being disgusted with its superficiality, we reprinted one of the most finished among the many manuals of the school logic, which my father, a great collector of such books, possessed, the Manuductio ad Logicam of the Jesuit Du Trieu. After finishing this, we took up Whately's Logic, then first republished from the Encyclopædia Metropolitana, and finally the "Computatio sive Logica" of Hobbes. These books, dealt with in our manner, afforded a wide range for original metaphysical speculation: and most of what has been done in the First Book of my System of Logic, to rationalize and correct the principles and distinctions of the school logicians, and to improve the theory of the Import of Propositions, had its origin in these discussions; Graham and I originating most of the novelties, while Grote and others furnished an excellent tribunal or test. From this time I formed the project of writing a book on Logic, though on a much humbler scale than the one I ultimately executed.

Having done with Logic, we launched into Analytic Psychology, and having chosen Hartley for our text-book, we raised Priestley's edition to an extravagant price by searching through London to furnish each of us with a copy. When we had finished Hartley, we suspended our meetings; but my father's Analysis of the Mind being published soon after, we reassembled for the purpose of reading it. With this our exercises ended. I have always dated from these conversations my own real inauguration as an original and independent thinker. It was also through them that I acquired, or very much strengthened, a mental habit to which I attribute all that I have ever done, or ever shall do, in speculation; that of never accepting half-solutions of difficulties as complete; never abandoning a puzzle, but again and again returning to it until it was cleared up; never allowing obscure corners of a subject to remain unexplored, because they did not appear important; never thinking that I perfectly understood any part of a subject until I understood the whole.

Our doings from 1825 to 1830 in the way of public speaking, filled a considerable place in my life during those years, and as they had important effects on my development, something ought to be said of them.

There was for some time in existence a society of Owenites, called the Co-operation Society, which met for weekly public discussions in Chancery Lane. In the early part of 1825, accident brought Roebuck in contact with several of its members, and led to his attending one or two of the meetings and taking part in the debate in opposition to Owenism. Some one of us started the notion of going there in a body and having a general battle: and Charles Austin and some

of his friends who did not usually take part in our joint
exercises, entered into the project. It was carried out by
concert with the principal members of the Society, themselves nothing loth, as they naturally preferred a controversy
with opponents to a tame discussion among their own body.
The question of population was proposed as the subject of
debate: Charles Austin led the case on our side with a brilliant speech, and the fight was kept up by adjournment
through five or six weekly meetings before crowded audi-
tories, including along with the members of the Society and
their friends, many hearers and some speakers from the
Inns of Court. When this debate was ended, another was
commenced on the general merits of Owen's system: and
the contest altogether lasted about three months. It was
a *lutte corps à corps* between Owenites and political economists, whom the Owenites regarded as their most inveterate
opponents: but it was a perfectly friendly dispute. We who
represented political economy, had the same objects in view
as they had, and took pains to show it; and the principal
champion on their side was a very estimable man, with
whom I was well acquainted, Mr. William Thompson, of
Cork, author of a book on the Distribution of Wealth, and
of an " Appeal " in behalf of women against the passage
relating to them in my father's Essay on Government. Ellis,
Roebuck, and I took an active part in the debate, and among
those from the Inns of Court who joined in it, I remember
Charles Villiers. The other side obtained also, on the population question, very efficient support from without. The
well-known Gale-Jones, then an elderly man, made one of
his florid speeches; but the speaker with whom I was most
struck, though I dissented from nearly every word he said,
was Thirlwall, the historian, since Bishop of St. David's,
then a Chancery barrister, unknown except by a high reputation for eloquence acquired at the Cambridge Union before the era of Austin and Macaulay. His speech was in
answer to one of mine. Before he had uttered ten sentences,
I set him down as the best speaker I had ever heard, and I
have never since heard any one whom I placed above him.

The great interest of these debates predisposed some of
those who took part in them, to catch at a suggestion thrown

out by M'Culloch, the political economist, that a Society was wanted in London similar to the Speculative Society of Edinburgh, in which Brougham, Horner, and others first cultivated public speaking. Our experience at the Co-operative Society seemed to give cause for being sanguine as to the sort of men who might be brought together in London for such a purpose. M'Culloch mentioned the matter to several young men of influence, to whom he was then giving private lessons in political economy. Some of these entered warmly into the project, particularly George Villiers, afterwards Earl of Clarendon. He and his brothers, Hyde and Charles, Romilly, Charles Austin and I, with some others, met and agreed on a plan. We determined to meet once a fortnight from November to June, at the Freemasons' Tavern, and we had soon a fine list of members, containing, along with several members of Parliament, nearly all the most noted speakers of the Cambridge Union and of the Oxford United Debating Society. It is curiously illustrative of the tendencies of the time, that our principal difficulty in recruiting for the Society was to find a sufficient number of Tory speakers. Almost all whom we could press into the service were Liberals, of different orders and degrees. Besides those already named, we had Macaulay, Thirlwall, Praed, Lord Howick, Samuel Wilberforce (afterwards Bishop of Oxford), Charles Poulett Thomson (afterwards Lord Sydenham), Edward and Henry Lytton Bulwer, Fonblanque, and many others whom I cannot now recollect, but who made themselves afterwards more or less conspicuous in public or literary life. Nothing could seem more promising. But when the time for action drew near, and it was necessary to fix on a President, and find somebody to open the first debate, none of our celebrities would consent to perform either office. Of the many who were pressed on the subject, the only one who could be prevailed on was a man of whom I knew very little, but who had taken high honours at Oxford and was said to have acquired a great oratorical reputation there; who some time afterwards became a Tory member of Parliament. He accordingly was fixed on, both for filling the President's chair and for making the first speech. The important day arrived; the benches

were crowded; all our great speakers were present, to judge
of, but not to help our efforts. The Oxford orator's speech
was a complete failure. This threw a damp on the whole
concern: the speakers who followed were few, and none
of them did their best; the affair was a complete *fiasco;*
and the oratorical celebrities we had counted on went away
never to return, giving to me at least a lesson in knowledge
of the world. This unexpected breakdown altered my whole
relation to the project. I had not anticipated taking a prominent part, or speaking much or often, particularly at first,
but I now saw that the success of the scheme depended on
the new men, and I put my shoulder to the wheel. I opened
the second question, and from that time spoke in nearly
every debate. It was very uphill work for some time. The
three Villiers and Romilly stuck to us for some time longer,
but the patience of all the founders of the Society was at
last exhausted, except me and Roebuck. In the season following, 1826-7, things began to mend. We had acquired two
excellent Tory speakers, Hayward and Shee (afterwards
Sergeant Shee) : the Radical side was reinforced by Charles
Buller, Cockburn, and others of the second generation of
Cambridge Benthamites; and with their and other occasional
aid, and the two Tories as well as Roebuck and me for
regular speakers, almost every debate was a *bataille rangée*
between the " philosophic Radicals " and the Tory lawyers;
until our conflicts were talked about, and several persons of
note and consideration came to hear us. This happened still
more in the subsequent seasons, 1828 and 1829, when the
Coleridgians, in the persons of Maurice and Sterling, made
their appearance in the Society as a second Liberal and even
Radical party, on totally different grounds from Benthamism
and vehemently opposed to it; bringing into these discussions the general doctrines and modes of thought of the
European reaction against the philosophy of the eighteenth
century; and adding a third and very important belligerent
party to our contests, which were now no bad exponent of
the movement of opinion among the most cultivated part
of the new generation. Our debates were very different
from those of common debating societies, for they habitually
consisted of the strongest arguments and most philosophic

principles which either side was able to produce, thrown
often into close and *serré* confutations of one another.
The practice was necessarily very useful to us, and eminently so to me. I never, indeed, acquired real fluency, and
had always a bad and ungraceful delivery; but I could make
myself listened to: and as I always wrote my speeches when,
from the feelings involved, or the nature of the ideas to be
developed, expression seemed important, I greatly increased
my power of effective writing; acquiring not only an ear
for smoothness and rhythm, but a practical sense for *telling*
sentences, and an immediate criterion of their telling property, by their effect on a mixed audience.

The Society, and the preparation for it, together with the
preparation for the morning conversations which were going
on simultaneously, occupied the greater part of my leisure;
and made me feel it a relief when, in the spring of 1828, I
ceased to write for the Westminster. The Review had fallen
into difficulties. Though the sale of the first number had
been very encouraging, the permanent sale had never, I
believe, been sufficient to pay the expenses, on the scale on
which the Review was carried on. Those expenses had been
considerably, but not sufficiently, reduced. One of the editors, Southern, had resigned; and several of the writers, including my father and me, who had been paid like other
contributors for our earlier articles, had latterly written
without payment. Nevertheless, the original funds were
nearly or quite exhausted, and if the Review was to be continued some new arrangement of its affairs had become indispensable. My father and I had several conferences with
Bowring on the subject. We were willing to do our utmost
for maintaining the Review as an organ of our opinions, but
not under Bowring's editorship: while the impossibility of
its any longer supporting a paid editor, afforded a ground on
which, without affront to him, we could propose to dispense
with his services. We and some of our friends were prepared to carry on the Review as unpaid writers, either finding among ourselves an unpaid editor, or sharing the editorship among us. But while this negotiation was proceeding
with Bowring's apparent acquiescence, he was carrying on
another in a different quarter (with Colonel Perronet Thomp-

son)', of which we received the first intimation in a letter from Bowring as editor, informing us merely that an arrangement had been made, and proposing to us to write for the next number, with promise of payment. We did not dispute Bowring's right to bring about, if he could, an arrangement more favourable to himself than the one we had proposed; but we thought the concealment which he had practised towards us, while seemingly entering into our own project, an affront: and even had we not thought so, we were indisposed to expend any more of our time and trouble in attempting to write up the Review under his management. Accordingly my father excused himself from writing; though two or three years later, on great pressure, he did write one more political article. As for me, I positively refused. And thus ended my connexion with the original Westminster. The last article which I wrote in it had cost me more labour than any previous; but it was a labour of love, being a defence of the early French Revolutionists against the Tory misrepresentations of Sir Walter Scott, in the introduction to his Life of Napoleon. The number of books which I read for this purpose, making notes and extracts— even the number I had to buy (for in those days there was no public or subscription library from which books of reference could be taken home), far exceeded the worth of the immediate object; but I had at that time a half-formed intention of writing a History of the French Revolution; and though I never executed it, my collections afterwards were very useful to Carlyle for a similar purpose.

CHAPTER V

A Crisis in my Mental History. One Stage Onward

FOR some years after this time I wrote very little, and nothing regularly, for publication: and great were the advantages which I derived from the intermission. It was of no common importance to me, at this period, to be able to digest and mature my thoughts for my own mind only, without any immediate call for giving them out in print. Had I gone on writing, it would have much disturbed the important transformation in my opinions and character, which took place during those years. The origin of this transformation, or at least the process by which I was prepared for it, can only be explained by turning some distance back.

From the winter of 1821, when I first read Bentham, and especially from the commencement of the Westminster Review, I had what might truly be called an object in life: to be a reformer of the world. My conception of my own happiness was entierly identified with this object. The personal sympathies I wished for were those of fellow labourers in this enterprise. I endeavoured to pick up as many flowers as I could by the way; but as a serious and permanent personal satisfaction to rest upon, my whole reliance was placed on this; and I was accustomed to felicitate myself on the certainty of a happy life which I enjoyed, through placing my happiness in something durable and distant, in which some progress might be always making, while it could never be exhausted by complete attainment. This did very well for several years, during which the general improvement going on in the world and the idea of myself as engaged with others in struggling to promote it, seemed enough to fill up an interesting and animated existence. But the time came when I awakened from this as from a dream. It was in the autumn of 1826. I was in a dull state of nerves, such as everybody is occasionally liable to; unsusceptible to enjoyment or pleasureable excitement; one of those moods when what is pleasure at other times, becomes insipid or indifferent; the state, I should think, in which converts to Methodism usually are, when smitten by their first " conviction of sin." In this frame of mind it occurred to me to put the question directly to myself: " Suppose that all your objects in life were realized; that all the changes in institutions and opinions which you are looking forward to, could be completely effected at this very instant: would this be a great joy and happiness to you?" And an irrepressible self-consciousness distinctly answered, " No!" At this my heart sank within me: the whole foundation on which my life was constructed fell down. All my happiness was to have been found in the continual pursuit of this end. The end had ceased to charm, and how could there ever again be any interest in the means? I seemed to have nothing left to live for.

At first I hoped that the cloud would pass away of itself; but it did not. A night's sleep, the sovereign remedy for the smaller vexations of life, had no effect on it. I awoke to a renewed consciousness of the woful fact. I carried it with me into all companies, into all occupations. Hardly anything had power to cause me even a few minutes' oblivion of it. For some months the cloud seemed to grow thicker and thicker. The lines in Coleridge's " Dejection "—I was not then acquainted with them—exactly describe my case:

> "A grief without a pang, void, dark and drear,
> A drowsy, stifled, unimpassioned grief,
> Which finds no natural outlet or relief
> In word, or sigh, or tear."

In vain I sought relief from my favourite books; those memorials of past nobleness and greatness from which I had always hitherto drawn strength and animation. I read them now without feeling, or with the accustomed feeling *minus* all its charm; and I became persuaded, that my love of mankind, and of excellence for its own sake, had worn itself out. I sought no comfort by speaking to others of what I felt. If I had loved any one sufficiently to make confiding my

griefs a necessity, I should not have been in the condition
I was. I felt, too, that mine was not an interesting, or in any
way respectable distress. There was nothing in it to attract
sympathy. Advice, if I had known where to seek it, would
have been most precious. The words of Macbeth to the
physician often occurred to my thoughts. But there was no
one on whom I could build the faintest hope of such assistance. My father, to whom it would have been natural to me
to have recourse in any practical difficulties, was the last person to whom, in such a case as this, I looked for help. Everything convinced me that he had no knowledge of any such
mental state as I was suffering from, and that even if he
could be made to understand it, he was not the physician who
could heal it. My education, which was wholly his work,
had been conducted without any regard to the possibility of
its ending in this result; and I saw no use in giving him the
pain of thinking that his plans had failed, when the failure
was probably irremediable, and, at all events, beyond the
power of *his* remedies. Of other friends, I had at that time
none to whom I had any hope of making my condition intelligible. It was however abundantly intelligible to myself; and
the more I dwelt upon it, the more hopeless it appeared.

My course of study had led me to believe, that all mental
and moral feelings and qualities, whether of a good or of a
bad kind, were the results of association; that we love one
thing, and hate another, take pleasure in one sort of action
or contemplation, and pain in another sort, through the
clinging of pleasurable or painful ideas to those things, from
the effect of education or of experience. As a corollary
from this, I had always heard it maintained by my father,
and was myself convinced, that the object of education
should be to form the strongest possible associations of the
salutary class; associations of pleasure with all things beneficial to the great whole, and of pain with all things hurtful to it. This doctrine appeared inexpugnable; but it now
seemed to me, on retrospect, that my teachers had occupied
themselves but superficially with the means of forming and
keeping up these salutary associations. They seemed to have
trusted altogether to the old familiar instruments, praise
and blame, reward and punishment. Now, I did not doubt

that by these means, begun early, and applied unremittingly, intense associations of pain and pleasure, especially of pain, might be created, and might produce desires and aversions capable of lasting undiminished to the end of life. But there must always be something artificial and casual in associations thus produced. The pains and pleasures thus forcibly associated with things, are not connected with them by any natural tie; and it is therefore, I thought, essential to the durability of these associations, that they should have become so intense and inveterate as to be practically indissoluble, before the habitual exercise of the power of analysis had commenced. For I now saw, or thought I saw, what I had always before received with incredulity—that the habit of analysis has a tendency to wear away the feelings: as indeed it has, when no other mental habit is cultivated, and the analysing spirit remains without its natural complements and correctives. The very excellence of analysis (I argued) is that it tends to weaken and undermine whatever is the result of prejudice; that it enables us mentally to separate ideas which have only casually clung together: and no associations whatever could ultimately resist this dissolving force, were it not that we owe to anlaysis our clearest knowledge of the permanent sequences in nature; the real connexions between Things, not dependent on our will and feelings; natural laws, by virtue of which, in many cases, one thing is inseparable from another in fact; which laws, in proportion as they are clearly perceived and imaginatively realized, cause our ideas of things which are always joined together in Nature, to cohere more and more closely in our thoughts. Analytic habits may thus even strengthen the associations between causes and effects, means and ends, but tend altogether to weaken those which are, to speak familiarly, a *mere* matter of feeling. They are therefore (I thought) favourable to prudence and clear-sightedness, but a perpetual worm at the root both of the passions and of the virtues; and, above all, fearfully undermine all desires, and all pleasures, which are the effects of association, that is, according to the theory I held, all except the purely physical and organic; of the entire insufficiency of which to make life desirable, no one had a stronger conviction than I had. These were the laws of human nature, by which, as it seemed to me, I had been brought to my present state. All those to whom I looked up were of opinion that the pleasure of sympathy with human beings, and the feelings which made the good of others, and especially of mankind on a large scale, the object of existence, were the greatest and surest sources of happiness. Of the truth of this I was convinced, but to know that a feeling would make me happy if I had it, did not give me the feeling. My education, I thought, had failed to create these feelings in sufficient strength to resist the dissolving influence of analysis, while the whole course of my intellectual cultivation had made precocious and premature analysis the inveterate habit of my mind. I was thus, as I said to myself, left stranded at the commencement of my voyage, with a well-equipped ship and a rudder, but no sail; without any real desire for the ends which I had been so carefully fitted out to work for: no delight in virtue, or the general good, but also just as little in anything else. The fountains of vanity and ambition seemed to have dried up within me, as completely as those of benevolence. I had had (as I reflected) some gratification of vanity at too early an age: I had obtained some distinction, and felt myself of some importance, before the desire of distinction and of importance had grown into a passion: and little as it was which I had attained, yet having been attained too early, like all pleasures enjoyed too soon, it had made me *blasé* and indifferent to the pursuit. Thus neither selfish nor unselfish pleasures were pleasures to me. And there seemed no power in nature sufficient to begin the formation of my character anew, and create in a mind now irretrievably analytic, fresh associations of pleasure with any of the objects of human desire.

These were the thoughts which mingled with the dry heavy dejection of the melancholy winter of 1826-7. During this time I was not incapable of my usual occupations. I went on with them mechanically, by the mere force of habit. I had been so drilled in a certain sort of mental exercise, that I could still carry it on when all the spirit had gone out of it. I even composed and spoke several speeches at the debating society, how, or with what degree of success, I know not. Of four years continual speaking at that society, this is the only year of which I remember next to nothing. Two lines of Coleridge, in whom alone of all writers I have found a true description of what I felt, were often in my thoughts, not at this time (for I had never read them), but in a later period of the same mental malady:

> " Work without hope draws nectar in a sieve,
> And hope without an object cannot live."

In all probability my case was by no means so peculiar as I fancied it, and I doubt not that many others have passed through a similar state; but the idiosyncrasies of my education had given to the general phenomenon a special character, which made it seem the natural effect of causes that it was hardly possible for time to remove. I frequently asked myself, if I could, or if I was bound to go on living, when life must be passed in this manner. I generally answered to myself, that I did not think I could possibly bear it beyond a year. When, however, not more than half that duration of time had elapsed, a small ray of light broke in upon my gloom. I was reading, accidentally, Marmontel's " Memoires," and came to the passage which relates his father's death, the distressed position of the family, and the sudden inspiration by which he, then a mere boy, felt and made them feel that he would be everything to them—would supply the place of all that they had lost. A vivid conception of the scene and its feelings came over me, and I was moved to tears. From this moment my burden grew lighter. The oppression of the thought that all feeling was dead within me, was gone. I was no longer hopeless: I was not a stock or a stone. I had still, it seemed, some of the material out of which all worth of character, and all capacity for happiness, are made. Relieved from my ever present sense of irremediable wretchedness, I gradually found that the ordinary incidents of life could again give me some pleasure; that I could again find enjoyment, not intense, but sufficient for cheerfulness, in sunshine and sky, in books, in conversation, in public affairs; and that there was, once more, excitement, though of a moderate kind, in exerting myself for my opinions, and for the public good. Thus the cloud gradually drew off, and I again enjoyed life: and though I had several relapses, some of which lasted many months, I never again was as miserable as I had been.

The experiences of this period had two very marked effects on my opinions and character. In the first place, they led me to adopt a theory of life, very unlike that on which I had before acted, and having much in common with what at that time I certainly had never heard of, the anti-self-consciousness theory of Carlyle. I never, indeed, wavered in the conviction that happiness is the test of all rules of conduct, and the end of life. But I now thought that this end was only to be attained by not making it the direct end. Those only are happy (I thought) who have their minds fixed on some object other than their own happiness; on the happiness of others, on the improvement of mankind, even on some art or pursuit, followed not as a means, but as itself an ideal end. Aiming thus at something else, they find happiness by the way. The enjoyments of life (such was now my theory) are sufficient to make it a pleasant thing, when they are taken *en passant,* without being made a principal object. Once make them so, and they are immediately felt to be insufficient. They will not bear a scrutinizing examination. Ask yourself whether you are happy, and you cease to be so. The only chance is to treat, not happiness, but some end external to it, as the purpose of life. Let your self-consciousness, your scrutiny, your self-interrogation, exhaust themselves on that; and if otherwise fortunately circumstanced you will inhale happiness with the air you breathe, without dwelling on it or thinking about it, without either forestalling it in imagination, or putting it to flight by fatal questioning. This theory now became the basis of my philosophy of life. And I still hold to it as the best theory for all those who have but a moderate degree of sensibility and of capacity for enjoyment, that is, for the great majority of mankind.

The other important change which my opinions at this time underwent, was that I, for the first time, gave its proper place, among the prime necessities of human wellbeing, to the internal culture of the individual. I ceased to attach almost exclusive importance to the ordering of outward circumstances, and the training of the human being for speculation and for action.

I had now learnt by experience that the passive susceptibilities needed to be cultivated as well as the active capacities, and required to be nourished and enriched as well as
guided. I did not, for an instant, lose sight of, or undervalue, that part of the truth which I had seen before; I never
turned recreant to intellectual culture, or ceased to consider
the power and practice of analysis as an essential condition
both of individual and of social improvement. But I thought
that it had consequences which required to be corrected, by
joining other kinds of cultivation with it. The maintenance
of a due balance among the faculties, now seemed to me of
primary importance. The cultivation of the feelings became
one of the cardinal points in my ethical and philosophical
creed. And my thoughts and inclinations turned in an increasing degree towards whatever seemed capable of being
instrumental to that object.

I now began to find meaning in the things which I had
read or heard about the importance of poetry and art as instruments of human culture. But it was some time longer
before I began to know this by personal experience. The
only one of the imaginative arts in which I had from childhood taken great pleasure, was music; the best effect of
which (and in this it surpasses perhaps every other art)
consists in exciting enthusiasm; in winding up to a high
pitch those feelings of an elevated kind which are already in
the character, but to which this excitement gives a glow and
a fervor, which, though transitory at its utmost height, is
precious for sustaining them at other times. This effect
of music I had often experienced; but like all my pleasurable
susceptibilities it was suspended during the gloomy period.
I had sought relief again and again from this quarter, but
found none. After the tide had turned, and I was in process
of recovery, I had been helped forward by music, but in a
much less elevated manner. I at this time first became
acquainted with Weber's Oberon, and the extreme pleasure
which I drew from its delicious melodies did me good, by
showing me a source of pleasure to which I was as susceptible as ever. The good, however, was much impaired by
the thought, that the pleasure of music (as is quite true of
such pleasure as this was, that of mere tune) fades with

familiarity, and requires either to be revived by intermittence, or fed by continual novelty. And it is very characteristic both of my then state, and of the general tone of my mind at this period of my life, that I was seriously tormented by the thought of the exhaustibility of musical combinations. The octave consists only of five tones and two semitones, which can be put together in only a limited number of ways, of which but a small proportion are beautiful: most of these, it seemed to me, must have been already discovered, and there could not be room for a long succession of Mozarts and Webers, to strike out, as these had done, entirely new and surpassingly rich veins of musical beauty. This source of anxiety may, perhaps, be thought to resemble that of the philosophers of Laputa, who feared lest the sun should be burnt out. It was, however, connected with the best feature in my character, and the only good point to be found in my very unromantic and in no way honourable distress. For though my dejection, honestly looked at, could not be called other than egotistical, produced by the ruin, as I thought, of my fabric of happiness, yet the destiny of mankind in general was ever in my thoughts, and could not be separated from my own. I felt that the flaw in my life, must be a flaw in life itself; that the question was, whether, if the reformers of society and government could succeed in their objects, and every person in the community were free and in a state of physical comfort, the pleasures of life, being no longer kept up by struggle and privation, would cease to be pleasures. And I felt that unless I could see my way to some better hope than this for human happiness in general, my dejection must continue; but that if I could see such an outlet, I should then look on the world with pleasure; content as far as I was myself concerned, with any fair share of the general lot.

This state of my thoughts and feelings made the fact of my reading Wordsworth for the first time (in the autumn of 1828), an important event in my life. I took up the collection of his poems from curiosity, with no expectation of mental relief from it, though I had before resorted to poetry with that hope. In the worst period of my depression, I had read through the whole of Byron (then new to me), to try whether a poet, whose peculiar department was supposed to be that of the intenser feelings, could rouse any feeling in me. As might be expected, I got no good from this reading, but the reverse. The poet's state of mind was too like my own. His was the lament of a man who had worn out all pleasures, and who seemed to think that life, to all who possess the good things of it, must necessarily be the vapid, uninteresting thing which I found it. His Harold and Manfred had the same burden on them which I had; and I was not in a frame of mind to desire any comfort from the vehement sensual passion of his Giaours, or the sullenness of his Laras. But while Byron was exactly what did not suit my condition, Wordsworth was exactly what did. I had looked into the Excursion two or three years before, and found little in it; and I should probably have found as little, had I read it at this time. But the miscellaneous poems, in the two-volume edition of 1815 (to which little of value was added in the latter part of the author's life) proved to be the precise thing for my mental wants at that particular juncture.

In the first place, these poems addressed themselves powerfully to one of the strongest of my pleasurable susceptibilities, the love for rural objects and natural scenery; to which I had been indebted not only for much of the pleasure of my life, but quite recently for relief from one of my longest relapses into depression. In this power of rural beauty over me, there was a foundation laid for taking pleasure in Wordsworth's poetry; the more so, as his scenery lies mostly among mountains, which, owing to my early Pyrenean excursion, were my ideal of natural beauty. But Wordsworth would never have had any great effect on me, if he had merely placed before me beautiful pictures of natural scenery. Scott does this still better than Wordsworth, and a very second-rate landscape does it more effectually than any poet. What made Wordsworth's poems a medicine for my state of mind, was that they expressed, not mere outward beauty, but states of feeling, and of thought coloured by feeling, under the excitement of beauty. They seemed to be the very culture of the feelings, which I was in quest of. In them I seemed to draw from a source of inward joy, of sympathetic and imaginative pleasure, which could be shared in by all human beings; which had no connexion with struggle or imperfection, but would be made richer by every improvement in the physical or social condition of mankind. From them I seemed to learn what would be the perennial sources of happiness, when all the greater evils of life shall have been removed. And I felt myself at once better and happier as I came under their influence. There have certainly been, even in our own age, greater poets than Wordsworth; but poetry of deeper and loftier feeling could not have done for me at that time what his did. I needed to be made to feel that there was real, permanent happiness in tranquil contemplation. Wordsworth taught me this, not only without turning away from, but with a greatly increased interest in the common feelings and common destiny of human beings. And the delight which these poems gave me, proved that with culture of this sort, there was nothing to dread from the most confirmed habit of analysis. At the conclusion of the Poems came the famous Ode, falsely called Platonic, "Intimations of Immortality:" in which, along with more than his usual sweetness of melody and rhythm, and along with the two passages of grand imagery but bad philosophy so often quoted, I found that he too had had similar experience to mine; that he also had felt that the first freshness of youthful enjoyment of life was not lasting; but that he had sought for compensation, and found it, in the way in which he was now teaching me to find it. The result was that I gradually, but completely, emerged from my habitual depression, and was never again subject to it. I long continued to value Wordsworth less according to his intrinsic merits, than by the measure of what he had done for me. Compared with the greatest poets, he may be said to be the poet of unpoetical natures, possessed of quiet and contemplative tastes. But unpoetical natures are precisely those which require poetic cultivation. This cultivation Wordsworth is much more fitted to give, than poets who are intrinsically far more poets than he.

It so fell out that the merits of Wordsworth were the occasion of my first public declaration of my new way of thinking, and separation from those of my habitual companions who had not undergone a similar change. The person with whom at that time I was most in the habit of comparing notes on such subjects was Roebuck, and I induced him to read Wordsworth, in whom he also at first seemed to find much to admire: but I, like most Wordsworthians, threw myself into strong antagonism to Byron, both as a poet and as to his influence on the character. Roebuck, all whose instincts were those of action and struggle, had, on the contrary, a strong relish and great admiration of Byron, whose writings he regarded as the poetry of human life, while Wordsworth's, according to him, was that of flowers and butterflies. We agreed to have the fight out at our Debating Society, where we accordingly discussed for two evenings the comparative merits of Byron and Wordsworth, propounding and illustrating by long recitations our respective theories of poetry: Sterling also, in a brilliant speech, putting forward his particular theory. This was the first debate on any weighty subject in which Roebuck and I had been on opposite sides. The schism between us widened from this time more and more, though we continued for some years longer to be companions. In the beginning, our chief divergence related to the cultivation of the feelings. Roebuck was in many respects very different from the vulgar notion of a Benthamite or Utilitarian. He was a lover of poetry and of most of the fine arts. He took great pleasure in music, in dramatic performances, especially in painting, and himself drew and designed landscapes with great facility and beauty. But he never could be made to see that these things have any value as aids in the formation of character. Personally, instead of being, as Benthamites are supposed to be, void of feeling, he had very quick and strong sensibilities. But, like most Englishmen who have feelings, he found his feelings stand very much in his way. He was much more susceptible to the painful sympathies than to the pleasurable, and looking for his happiness elsewhere, he wished that his feelings should be deadened rather than quickened. And, in truth, the English character, and English social circumstances, make it so seldom possible to derive happiness from the exercise of the sympathies, that it is not wonderful if they count for little in an Englishman's scheme of life. In most other countries the paramount importance of the sympathies as a constituent of individual happiness is an axiom, taken for granted rather than needing any formal statement; but most English thinkers almost seem to regard them as necessary evils, required for keeping men's actions benevolent and compassionate. Roebuck was, or appeared to be, this kind of Englishman. He saw little good in any cultivation of the feelings, and none at all in cultivating them through the imagination, which he thought was only cultivating illusions. It was in vain I urged on him that the imaginative emotion which an idea, when vividly conceived, excites in us, is not an illusion but a fact, as real as any of the other qualities of objects; and far from implying anything erroneous and delusive in our mental apprehension of the object, is quite consistent with the most accurate knowledge and most perfect practical recognition of all its physical and intellectual laws and relations. The intense feeling of the beauty of a cloud lighted by the setting sun, is no hindrance to my knowing that the cloud is vapour of water, subject to all the laws of vapours in a state of suspension; and I am just as likely to allow for, and act on, these physical laws whenever there is occasion to do so, as if I had been incapable of perceiving any distinction between beauty and ugliness.

While my intimacy with Roebuck diminished, I fell more and more into friendly intercourse with our Coleridgian adversaries in the Society, Frederick Maurice and John Sterling, both subsequently so well known, the former by his writings, the latter through the biographies by Hare and Carlyle. Of these two friends, Maurice was the thinker, Sterling the orator, and impassioned expositor of thoughts which, at this period, were almost entirely formed for him by Maurice.

With Maurice I had for some time been acquainted through Eyton Tooke, who had known him at Cambridge, and although my discussions with him were almost always disputes, I had carried away from them much that helped to build up my new fabric of thought, in the same way as I was deriving much from Coleridge, and from the writings of Goethe and other German authors which I read during these years. I have so deep a respect for Maurice's character and purposes, as well as for his great mental gifts, that it is with some unwillingness I say anything which may seem to place him on a less high eminence than I would gladly be able to accord to him. But I have always thought that there was more intellectual power wasted in Maurice than in any other of my contemporaries. Few of them certainly have had so much waste. Great powers of generalization, rare ingenuity and subtlety, and a wide perception of important and unobvious truths, served him not for putting something better into the place of the worthless heap of received opinions on the great subjects of thought, but for proving to his own mind that the Church of England had known everything from the first, and that all the truths on the ground of which the Church and orthodoxy have been attacked (many of which he saw as clearly as any one) are not only consistent with the Thirty-nine Articles, but are better understood and expressed in those Articles than by any one who rejects them. I have never been able to find any other explanation of this, than by attributing it to that timidity of conscience, combined with original sensitiveness of temperament, which has so often driven highly gifted men into Romanism from the need of a firmer support than they can find in the independent conclusions of their own judgment. Any more vulgar kind of timidity no one who knew Maurice would ever think of imputing to him, even if he had not given public proof of his freedom from it, by his ultimate collision with some of the opinions commonly regarded as orthodox, and by his noble origination of the Christian Socialist movement. The nearest parallel to him, in a moral point of view, is Coleridge, to whom, in merely intellectual power, apart from poetical genius, I think him decidedly superior. At this time, however, he might be described as a disciple of Coleridge, and Sterling as a disciple of Coleridge and of him. The modifications which were taking place in my old opinions gave me some points of contact with them; and both Maurice and Sterling were of considerable use to my development. With Sterling I soon became very intimate, and was more attached to him than I have ever been to any other man. He was indeed one of the most loveable of men. His frank, cordial, af-

fectionate, and expansive character; a love of truth alike
conspicuous in the highest things and the humblest; a generous and ardent nature which threw itself with impetuosity
into the opinions it adopted, but was as eager to do justice
to the doctrines and the men it was opposed to, as to make
war on what it thought their errors; and an equal devotion
to the two cardinal points of Liberty and Duty, formed a
combination of qualities as attractive to me, as to all others
who knew him as well as I did. With his open mind and
heart, he found no difficulty in joining hands with me across
the gulf which as yet divided our opinions. He told me how
he and others had looked upon me (from hearsay information), as a "made" or manufactured man, having had a
certain impress of opinion stamped on me which I could
only reproduce; and what a change took place in his feelings when he found, in the discussion on Wordsworth and
Byron, that Wordsworth, and all which that name implies,
"belonged" to me as much as to him and his friends. The
failure of his health soon scattered all his plans of life, and
compelled him to live at a distance from London, so that
after the first year or two of our acquaintance, we only saw
each other at distant intervals. But (as he said himself in
one of his letters to Carlyle) when we did meet it was like
brothers. Though he was never, in the full sense of the
word, a profound thinker, his openness of mind, and the
moral courage in which he greatly surpassed Maurice, made
him outgrow the dominion which Maurice and Coleridge
had once exercised over his intellect; though he retained to
the last a great but discriminating admiration of both, and
towards Maurice a warm affection. Except in that short
and transitory phasis of his life, during which he made the
mistake of becoming a clergyman, his mind was ever progressive: and the advance he always seemed to have made
when I saw him after an interval, made me apply to him
what Goethe said of Schiller, "er hatte eine furchtliche
Fortschreitung." He and I started from intellectual points
almost as wide apart as the poles, but the distance between
us was always diminishing: if I made steps towards some of
his opinions, he, during his short life, was constantly ap-
proximating more and more to several of mine: and if he

had lived, and had health and vigour to prosecute his ever assiduous self-culture, there is no knowing how much further this spontaneous assimilation might have proceeded.

After 1829 I withdrew from attendance on the Debating Society. I had had enough of speechmaking, and was glad to carry on my private studies and meditations without any immediate call for outward assertion of their results. I found the fabric of my old and taught opinions giving way in many fresh places, and I never allowed it to fall to pieces, but was incessantly occupied in weaving it anew. I never, in the course of my transition, was content to remain, for ever so short a time, confused and unsettled. When I had taken in any new idea, I could not rest till I had adjusted its relation to my old opinions, and ascertained exactly how far its effect ought to extend in modifying or superseding them.

The conflicts which I had so often had to sustain in defending the theory of government laid down in Bentham's and my father's writings, and the acquaintance I had obtained with other schools of political thinking, made me aware of many things which that doctrine, professing to be a theory of government in general, ought to have made room for, and did not. But these things, as yet, remained with me rather as corrections to be made in applying the theory to practice, than as defects in the theory. I felt that politics could not be a science of specific experience; and that the accusations against the Benthamic theory of *being* a theory, of proceeding *à priori* by way of general reasoning, instead of Baconian experiment, showed complete ignorance of Bacon's principles, and of the necessary conditions of experimental investigation. At this juncture appeared in the Edinburgh Review, Macaulay's famous attack on my father's Essay on Government. This gave me much to think about. I saw that Macaulay's conception of the logic of politics was erroneous; that he stood up for the empirical mode of treating political phenomena, against the philosophical; that even in physical science his notions of philosophizing might have recognized Kepler, but would have excluded Newton and Laplace. But I could not help feeling, that though the tone was unbecoming (an error for which the writer, at a later period, made the most ample and honourable amends), there was truth in several of his strictures on my father's treatment of the subject; that my father's premises were really too narrow, and included but a small number of the general truths, on which, in politics, the important consequences depend. Identity of interest between the governing body and the community at large, is not, in any practical sense which can be attached to it, the only thing on which good government depends; neither can this identity of interest be secured by the mere conditions of election. I was not at all satisfied with the mode in which my father met the criticisms of Macaulay. He did not, as I thought he ought to have done, justify himself by saying, " I was not writing a scientific treatise on politics, I was writing an argument for parliamentary reform." He treated Macaulay's argument as simply irrational; an attack upon the reasoning faculty; an example of the saying of Hobbes, that when reason is against a man, a man will be against reason. This made me think that there was really something more fundamentally erroneous in my father's conception of philosophical method, as applicable to politics, than I had hitherto supposed there was. But I did not at first see clearly what the error might be. At last it flashed upon me all at once in the course of other studies. In the early part of 1830 I had begun to put on paper the ideas of Logic (chiefly on the distinctions among Terms, and the import of Propositions) which had been suggested and in part worked out in the morning conversations already spoken of. Having secured these thoughts from being lost, I pushed on into the other parts of the subject, to try whether I could do anything further towards clearing up the theory of logic generally. I grappled at once with the problem of Induction, postponing that of Reasoning, on the ground that it is necessary to obtain premises before we can reason from them. Now, Induction is mainly a process for finding the causes of effects: and in attempting to fathom the mode of tracing causes and effects in physical science, I soon saw that in the more perfect of the sciences, we ascend, by generalization from particulars, to the tendencies of causes considered singly, and then reason downward from those separate tendencies, to the effect of the same causes when combined.

I then asked myself, what is the ultimate analysis of this deductive process; the common theory of the syllogism evidently throwing no light upon it. My practice (learnt from Hobbes and my father) being to study abstract principles by means of the best concrete instances I could find, the Composition of Forces, in dynamics, occurred to me as the most complete example of the logical process I was investigating. On examining, accordingly, what the mind does when it applies the principle of the Composition of Forces, I found that it performs a simple act of addition. It adds the separate effect of the one force to the separate effect of the other, and puts down the sum of these separate effects as the joint effect. But is this a legitimate process? In dynamics, and in all the mathematical branches of physics, it is; but in some other cases, as in chemistry, it is not; and I then recollected that something not unlike this was pointed out as one of the distinctions between chemical and mechanical phenomena, in the introduction to that favourite of my boyhood, Thompson's System of Chemistry. This distinction at once made my mind clear as to what was perplexing me in respect to the philosophy of politics. I now saw, that a science is either deductive or experimental, according as, in the province it deals with, the effects of causes when conjoined, are or are not the sums of the effects which the same causes produce when separate. It followed that politics must be a deductive science. It thus appeared, that both Macaulay and my father were wrong; the one in assimilating the method of philosophizing in politics to the purely experimental method of chemistry; while the other, though right in adopting a deductive method, had made a wrong selection of one, having taken as the type of deduction, not the appropriate process, that of the deductive branches of natural philosophy, but the inappropriate one of pure geometry, which, not being a science of causation at all, does not require or admit of any summing-up of effects. A foundation was thus laid in my thoughts for the principal chapters of what I afterwards published on the Logic of the Moral Sciences; and my new position in respect to my old political creed, now became perfectly definite.

If I am asked, what system of political philosophy I sub-

stituted for that which, as a philosophy, I had abandoned,
I answer, No system: only a conviction that the true system
was something much more complex and many-sided than I
had previously had any idea of, and that its office was to
supply, not a set of model institutions, but principles from
which the institutions suitable to any given circumstances
might be deduced. The influences of European, that is to
say, Continental, thought, and especially those of the reaction of the nineteenth century against the eighteenth, were
now streaming in upon me. They came from various quarters; from the writings of Coleridge, which I had begun to
read with interest even before the change in my opinions;
from the Coleridgians with whom I was in personal intercourse; from what I had read of Goethe; from Carlyle's
early articles in the Edinburgh and Foreign Reviews, though
for a long time I saw nothing in these (as my father saw
nothing in them to the last) but insane rhapsody. From
these sources, and from the acquaintance I kept up with the
French literature of the time, I derived, among other ideas
which the general turning upside down of the opinions of
European thinkers had brought uppermost, these in particular: That the human mind has a certain order of possible
progress, in which some things must precede others, an
order which governments and public instructors can modify
to some, but not to an unlimited extent: that all questions
of political institutions are relative, not absolute, and that
different stages of human progress not only *will* have, but
ought to have, different institutions: that government is always either in the hands, or passing into the hands, of whatever is the strongest power in society, and that what this
power is, does not depend on institutions, but institutions on
it: that any general theory of philosophy of politics supposes a previous theory of human progress, and that this is
the same thing with a philosophy of history. These opinions, true in the main, were held in an exaggerated and violent manner by the thinker with whom I was now most
accustomed to compare notes, and who, as usual with a reaction, ignored that half of the truth which the thinkers of
the eighteenth century saw. But though, at one period of
my progress, I for some time undervalued that great century,

I never joined in the reaction against it but kept as firm hold of one side of the truth as I took of the other. The fight between the nineteenth century and the eighteenth always reminded me of the battle about the shield, one side of which was white and the other black. I marvelled at the blind rage with which the combatants rushed against one another. I applied to them, and to Coleridge himself, many of Coleridge's sayings about half truths; and Goethe's device, "many-sidedness," was one which I would most willingly, at this period, have taken for mine.

The writers by whom, more than by any others, a new mode of political thinking was brought home to me, were those of the St. Simonian school in France. In 1829 and 1830 I became acquainted with some of their writings. They were then only in the earlier stages of their speculations. They had not yet dressed out their philosophy as a religion, nor had they organized their scheme of Socialism. They were just beginning to question the principle of hereditary property. I was by no means prepared to go with them even this length; but I was greatly struck with the connected view which they for the first time presented to me, of the natural order of human progress; and especially with their division of all history into organic periods and critical periods. During the organic periods (they said) mankind accept with firm conviction some positive creed, claiming jurisdiction over all their actions, and containing more or less of truth and adaptation to the needs of humanity. Under its influence they make all the progress compatible with the creed, and finally outgrow it; when a period follows of criticism and negation, in which mankind lose their old convictions without acquiring any new ones, of a general or authoritative character, except the conviction that the old are false. The period of Greek and Roman polytheism, so long as really believed in by instructed Greeks and Romans, was an organic period, succeeded by the critical or sceptical period of the Greek philosophers. Another organic period came in with Christianity. The corresponding critical period began with the Reformation, has lasted ever since, still lasts, and cannot altogether cease until a new organic period has been inaugurated by the triumph of a yet more advanced creed. These ideas, I knew, were not peculiar to the St. Simonians; on the contrary, they were the general property of Europe, or at least of Germany and France, but they had never, to my knowledge, been so completely systematized as by these writers, nor the distinguishing characteristics of a critical period so powerfully set forth; for I was not then acquainted with Fichte's Lectures on "The Characteristics of the Present Age." In Carlyle, indeed, I found bitter denunciations of an "age of unbelief," and of the present age as such, which I, like most people at that time, supposed to be passionate protests in favour of the old modes of belief. But all that was true in these denunciations, I thought that I found more calmly and philosophically stated by the St. Simonians. Among their publications, too, there was one which seemed to me far superior to the rest; in which the general idea was matured into something much more definite and instructive. This was an early work of Auguste Comte, who then called himself, and even announced himself in the title-page, as a pupil of Saint Simon. In this tract M. Comte first put forth the doctrine, which he afterwards so copiously illustrated, of the natural succession of three stages in every department of human knowledge: first, the theological, next the metaphysical, and lastly, the positive stage; and contended, that social science must be subject to the same law; that the feudal and Catholic system was the concluding phasis of the theological state of the social science, Protestantism the commencement, and the doctrines of the French Revolution the consummation, of the metaphysical; and that its positive state was yet to come. This doctrine harmonized well with my existing notions, to which it seemed to give a scientific shape. I already regarded the methods of physical science as the proper models for political. But the chief benefit which I derived at this time from the trains of thought suggested by the St. Simonians and by Comte, was, that I obtained a clearer conception than ever before of the peculiarities of an era of transition in opinion, and ceased to mistake the moral and intellectual characteristics of such an era, for the normal attributes of humanity. I looked forward, through the present age of loud disputes but generally weak convictions, to a future which shall unite the best qualities of the critical with the best qualities of the organic periods; unchecked liberty of thought, unbounded freedom of individual action in all modes not hurtful to others; but also, convictions as to what is right and wrong, useful and pernicious, deeply engraven on the feelings by early education and general unanimity of sentiment, and so firmly grounded in reason and in the true exigencies of life, that they shall not, like all former and present creeds, religious, ethical, and political, require to be periodically thrown off and replaced by others.

M. Comte soon left the St. Simonians, and I lost sight of him and his writings for a number of years. But the St. Simonians I continued to cultivate. I was kept *au courant* of their progress by one of their most enthusiastic disciples, M. Gustave d'Eichthal, who about that time passed a considerable interval in England. I was introduced to their chiefs, Bazard and Enfantin, in 1830; and as long as their public teachings and proselytism continued, I read nearly every thing they wrote. Their criticisms on the common doctrines of Liberalism seemed to me full of important truth; and it was partly by their writings that my eyes were opened to the very limited and temporary value of the old political economy, which assumes private property and inheritance as indefeasible facts, and freedom of production and exchange as the *dernier mot* of social improvement. The scheme gradually unfolded by the St. Simonians, under which the labour and capital of society would be managed for the general account of the community, every individual being required to take a share of labour, either as thinker, teacher, artist or producer, all being classed according to their capacity, and remunerated according to their work, appeared to me a far superior description of Socialism to Owen's. Their aim seemed to me desirable and rational, however their means might be inefficacious; and though I neither believed in the practicability, nor in the beneficial operation of their social machinery, I felt that the proclamation of such an ideal of human society could not but tend to give a beneficial direction to the efforts of others to bring society, as at present constituted, nearer to some ideal standard. I honoured them most of all for what they have been most cried down for—the boldness and freedom from prejudice with which they treated the subject of family, the most important of any, and needing more fundamental alterations than remain to be made in any other great social institution, but on which scarcely any reformer has the courage to touch. In proclaiming the perfect equality of men and women, an entirely new order of things in regard to their relations with one another, the St. Simonians, in common with Owen and Fourier, have entitled themselves to the grateful remembrance of future generations.

In giving an account of this period of my life, I have only specified such of my new impressions as appeared to me, both at the time and since, to be a kind of turning points, marking a definite progress in my mode of thought. But these few selected points give a very insufficient idea of the quantity of thinking which I carried on respecting a host of subjects during these years of transition. Much of this, it is true, consisted in rediscovering things known to all the world, which I had previously disbelieved, or disregarded. But the rediscovery was to me a discovery, giving me plenary possession of the truths, not as traditional platitudes, but fresh from their source: and it seldom failed to place them in some new light, by which they were reconciled with, and seemed to confirm while they modified the truths less generally known which lay in my early opinions, and in no essential part of which I at any time wavered. All my new thinking only laid the foundation of these more deeply and strongly, while it often removed misapprehension and confusion of ideas which had perverted their effect. For example, during the later returns of my dejection, the doctrine of what is called Philosophical Necessity weighed on my existence like an incubus. I felt as if I was scientifically proved to be the helpless slave of antecedent circumstances: as if my character and that of all others had been formed for us by agencies beyond our control, and was wholly out of our own power. I often said to myself, what a relief it would be if I could disbelieve the doctrine of the formation of character by circumstances; and remembering the wish of Fox respecting the doctrine of resistance to governments, that it might never be forgotten by kings, nor remembered

by subjects, I said that it would be a blessing if the doctrine
of necessity could be believed by all *quoad* the characters
of others, and disbelieved in regard to their own. I pon-
dered painfully on the subject, till gradually I saw light
through it. I perceived, that the word Necessity, as a name
for the doctrine of Cause and Effect applied to human
action, carried with it a misleading association; and that
this association was the operative force in the depressing
and paralysing influence which I had experienced: I saw that
though our character is formed by circumstances, our own
desires can do much to shape those circumstances; and that
what is really inspiriting and ennobling in the doctrine of
freewill, is the conviction that we have real power over the
formation of our own character; that our will, by influencing some of our circumstances, can modify our future
habits or capabilities of willing. All this was entirely consistent with the doctrine of circumstances, or rather, was
that doctrine itself, properly understood. From that time
I drew in my own mind, a clear distinction between the
doctrine of circumstances, and Fatalism; discarding altogether the misleading word Necessity. The theory, which
I now for the first time rightly apprehended, ceased altogether to be discouraging, and besides the relief to my
spirits, I no longer suffered under the burden, so heavy to
one who aims at being a reformer in opinions, of thinking
one doctrine true, and the contrary doctrine morally beneficial. The train of thought which had extricated me from
this dilemma, seemed to me, in after years, fitted to render
a similar service to others; and it now forms the chapter
on Liberty and Necessity in the concluding Book of my
System of Logic.

Again in politics, though I no longer accepted the doctrine of the Essay on Government as a scientific theory;
though I ceased to consider representative democracy as
an absolute principle, and regarded it as a question of time,
place, and circumstance; though I now looked upon the
choice of political institutions as a moral and educational
question more than one of material interests, thinking that it
ought to be decided mainly by the consideration, what
great improvement in life and culture stands next in order

for the people concerned, as the condition of their further progress, and what institutions are most likely to promote that; nevertheless, this change in the premises of my political philosophy did not alter my practical political creed as to the requirements of my own time and country. I was as much as ever a Radical and Democrat for Europe, and especially for England. I thought the predominance of the aristocratic classes, the noble and the rich, in the English constitution, an evil worth any struggle to get rid of; not on account of taxes, or any such comparatively small inconvenience, but as the great demoralizing agency in the country. Demoralizing, first, because it made the conduct of the Government an example of gross public immorality, through the predominance of private over public interests in the State, and the abuse of the powers of legislation for the advantage of classes. Secondly, and in a still greater degree, because the respect of the multitude always attaching itself principally to that which, in the existing state of society, is the chief passport to power; and under English institutions, riches, hereditary or acquired, being the almost exclusive source of political importance; riches, and the signs of riches, were almost the only things really respected, and the life of the people was mainly devoted to the pursuit of them. I thought, that while the higher and richer classes held the power of government, the instruction and improvement of the mass of the people were contrary to the self-interest of those classes, because tending to render the people more powerful for throwing off the yoke: but if the democracy obtained a large, and perhaps the principal share, in the governing power, it would become the interest of the opulent classes to promote their education, in order to ward off really mischievous errors, and especially those which would lead to unjust violations of property. On these grounds I was not only as ardent as ever for democratic institutions, but earnestly hoped that Owenite, St. Simonian, and all other anti-property doctrines might spread widely among the poorer classes; not that I thought those doctrines true, or desired that they should be acted on, but in order that the higher classes might be made to see that they had more to fear from the poor when uneducated, than when educated.

In this frame of mind the French Revolution of July found me. It roused my utmost enthusiasm, and gave me, as it were, a new existence. I went at once to Paris, was introduced to Lafayette, and laid the groundwork of the intercourse I afterwards kept up with several of the active chiefs of the extreme popular party. After my return I entered warmly, as a writer, into the political discussions of the time; which soon became still more exciting, by the coming in of Lord Grey's Ministry, and the proposing of the Reform Bill. For the next few years I wrote copiously in newspapers. It was about this time that Fonblanque, who had for some time written the political articles in the Examiner, became the proprietor and editor of the paper. It is not forgotten with what verve and talent, as well as fine wit, he carried it on, during the whole period of Lord Grey's Ministry, and what importance it assumed as the principal representative in the newspaper press, of Radical opinions. The distinguishing character of the paper was given to it entirely by his own articles, which formed at least three-fourths of all the original writing contained in it: but of the remaining fourth I contributed during those years a much larger share than any one else. I wrote nearly all the articles on French subjects, including a weekly summary of French politics, often extending to considerable length; together with many leading articles on general politics, commercial and financial legislation, and any miscellaneous subjects in which I felt interested, and which were suitable to the paper, including occasional reviews of books. Mere newspaper articles on the occurrences or questions of the moment, gave no opportunity for the development of any general mode of thought; but I attempted, in the beginning of 1831, to embody in a series of articles, headed " The Spirit of the Age," some of my new opinions, and especially to point out in the character of the present age, the anomalies and evils characteristic of the transition from a system of opinions which had worn out, to another only in process of being formed. These articles were, I fancy, lumbering in style, and not lively or striking enough to be, at any time, acceptable to newspaper readers; but had they been far more attractive, still, at that particular moment,

when great political changes were impending, and engrossing all minds, these discussions were ill-timed, and missed
fire altogether. The only effect which I know to have been
produced by them, was that Carlyle, then living in a secluded part of Scotland, read them in his solitude, and saying to himself (as he afterwards told me) " Here is a new
Mystic," inquired on coming to London that autumn
respecting their authorship; an inquiry which was the immediate cause of our becoming personally acquainted.

I have already mentioned Carlyle's earlier writings as
one of the channels through which I received the influences
which enlarged my early narrow creed; but I do not think
that those writings, by themselves, would ever have had
any effect on my opinions. What truths they contained,
though of the very kind which I was already receiving from
other quarters, were presented in a form and vesture less
suited than any other to give them access to a mind trained
as mine had been. They seemed a haze of poetry and
German metaphysics, in which almost the only clear thing
was a strong animosity to most of the opinions which were
the basis of my mode of thought: religious scepticism, utilitarianism, the doctrine of circumstances, and the attaching
any importance to democracy, logic, or political economy.
Instead of my having been taught anything, in the first instance, by Carlyle, it was only in proportion as I came to see
the same truths through media more suited to my mental
constitution, that I recognised them in his writings. Then,
indeed, the wonderful power with which he put them forth
made a deep impression upon me, and I was during a long
period one of his most fervent admirers; but the good his
writings did me, was not as philosophy to instruct, but as
poetry to animate. Even at the time when our acquaintance
commenced, I was not sufficiently advanced in my new
modes of thought to appreciate him fully; a proof of which
is, that on his showing me the manuscript of Sartor Resartus, his best and greatest work, which he had just then
finished, I made little of it; though when it came out about
two years afterwards in Fraser's Magazine I read it with
enthusiastic admiration and the keenest delight. I did not
seek and cultivate Carlyle less on account of the funda-

mental differences in our philosophy. He soon found out that I was not "another mystic," and when for the sake of my own integrity I wrote to him a distinct profession of all those of my opinions which I knew he most disliked, he replied that the chief difference between us was that I "was as yet consciously nothing of a mystic." I do not know at what period he gave up the expectation that I was destined to become one; but though both his and my opinions underwent in subsequent years considerable changes, we never approached much nearer to each other's modes of thought than we were in the first years of our acquaintance. I did not, however, deem myself a competent judge of Carlyle. I felt that he was a poet, and that I was not; that he was a man of intuition, which I was not; and that as such, he not only saw many things long before me, which I could only when they were pointed out to me, hobble after and prove, but that it was highly probable he could see many things which were not visible to me even after they were pointed out. I knew that I could not see round him, and could never be certain that I saw over him; and I never presumed to judge him with any definiteness, until he was interpreted to me by one greatly the superior of us both—who was more a poet than he, and more a thinker than I—whose own mind and nature included his, and infinitely more.

Among the persons of intellect whom I had known of old, the one with whom I had now most points of agreement was the elder Austin. I have mentioned that he always set himself in opposition to our early sectarianism; and latterly he had, like myself, come under new influences. Having been appointed Professor of Jurisprudence in the London University (now University College), he had lived for some time at Bonn to study for his Lectures; and the influences of German literature and of the German character and state of society had made a very perceptible change in his views of life. His personal disposition was much softened; he was less militant and polemic; his tastes had begun to turn themselves towards the poetic and contemplative. He attached much less importance than formerly to outward changes; unless accompanied by a better cultivation of the inward nature. He had a strong distaste for the general meanness of English life, the absence of enlarged thoughts and unselfish desires, the low objects on which the faculties of all classes of the English are intent. Even the kind of public interests which Englishmen care for, he held in very little esteem. He thought that there was more practical good government, and (which is true enough) infinitely more care for the education and mental improvement of all ranks of the people, under the Prussian monarchy, than under the English representative government: and he held, with the French *Economistes,* that the real security for good government is " un peuple éclairé," which is not always the fruit of popular institutions, and which if it could be had without them, would do their work better than they. Though he approved of the Reform Bill, he predicted, what in fact occurred, that it would not produce the great immediate improvements in government, which many expected from it. The men, he said, who could do these great things, did not exist in the country. There were many points of sympathy between him and me, both in the new opinions he had adopted and in the old ones which he retained. Like me, he never ceased to be an utilitarian, and with all his love of the Germans, and enjoyment of their literature, never became in the smallest degree reconciled to the innate-principle metaphysics. He cultivated more and more a kind of German religion, a religion of poetry and feeling with little, if anything, of positive dogma; while, in politics (and here it was that I most differed with him) he acquired an indifference, bordering on contempt, for the progress of popular institutions: though he rejoiced in that of Socialism, as the most effectual means of compelling the powerful classes to educate the people, and to impress on them the only real means of permanently improving their material condition, a limitation of their numbers. Neither was he, at this time, fundamentally opposed to Socialism in itself as an ultimate result of improvement. He professed great disrespect for what he called " the universal principles of human nature of the political economists," and insisted on the evidence which history and daily experience afford of the " extraordinary pliability of human nature " (a phrase which I have somewhere borrowed from him) ; nor did he think it possible to set any positive bounds to the moral capabilities which might unfold themselves in mankind, under an enlightened direction of social and educational influences. Whether he retained all these opinions to the end of life I know not. Certainly the modes of thinking of his later years, and especially of his last publication, were much more Tory in their general character than those which he held at this time.

My father's tone of thought and feeling, I now felt myself at a great distance from: greater, indeed, than a full and calm explanation and reconsideration on both sides, might have shown to exist in reality. But my father was not one with whom calm and full explanations on fundamental points of doctrine could be expected, at least with one whom he might consider as, in some sort, a deserter from his standard.

Fortunately we were almost always in strong agreement on the political questions of the day, which engrossed a large part of his interest and of his conversation. On those matters of opinion on which we differed, we talked little. He knew that the habit of thinking for myself, which his mode of education had fostered, sometimes led me to opinions different from his, and he perceived from time to time that I did not always tell him *how* different. I expected no good, but only pain to both of us, from discussing our differences: and I never expressed them but when he gave utterance to some opinion or feeling repugnant to mine, in a manner which would have made it disingenuousness on my part to remain silent.

It remains to speak of what I wrote during these years, which, independently of my contributions to newspapers, was considerable. In 1830 and 1831 I wrote the five Essays since published under the title of " Essays on some Unsettled Questions of Political Economy," almost as they now stand, except that in 1833 I partially rewrote the fifth Essay. They were written with no immediate purpose of publication; and when, some years later, I offered them to a publisher, he declined them. They were only printed in 1844, after the success of the "System of Logic."   I also resumed my speculations on this last subject, and puzzled myself, like others before me, with the great paradox of the discovery of new truths by general reasoning. As to the fact, there could be no doubt. As little could it be doubted, that all reasoning is resolvable into syllogisms, and that in every syllogism the conclusion is actually contained and implied in the premises. How, being so contained and implied, it could be new truth, and how the theorems of geometry, so different in appearance from the definitions and axioms, could be all contained in these, was a difficulty which no one, I thought, had sufficiently felt, and which, at all events, no one had succeeded in clearing up. The explanations offered by Whately and others, though they might give a temporary satisfaction, always, in my mind, left a mist still hanging over the subject. At last, when reading a second or third time the chapters on Reasoning in the second volume of Dugald Stewart, interrogating myself on every point, and following out, as far as I knew how, every topic of thought which the book suggested, I came upon an idea of his respecting the use of axioms in ratiocination, which I did not remember to have before noticed, but which now, in meditating on it, seemed to me not only true of axioms, but of all general propositions whatever, and to be the key of the whole perplexity. From this germ grew the theory of the Syllogism propounded in the Second Book of the Logic; which I immediately fixed by writing it out. And now, with greatly increased hope of being able to produce a work on Logic, of some originality and value, I proceeded to write the First Book, from the rough and imperfect draft I had already made. What I now wrote became the basis of that part of the subsequent Treatise; except that it did not contain the Theory of Kinds, which was a later addition, suggested by otherwise inextricable difficulties which met me in my first attempt to work out the subject of some of the concluding chapters of the Third Book. At the point which I had now reached I made a halt, which lasted five years. I had come to the end of my tether; I could make nothing satisfactory of Induction, at this time. I continued to read any book which seemed to promise light on the subject, and appropriated, as well as I could, the results;

but for a long time I found nothing which seemed to open to me any very important vein of meditation.

In 1832 I wrote several papers for the first series of Tait's Magazine, and one for a quarterly periodical called the Jurist, which had been founded, and for a short time carried on, by a set of friends, all lawyers and law reformers, with several of whom I was acquainted. The paper in question is the one on the rights and duties of the State respecting Corporation and Church Property, now standing first among the collected " Dissertations and Discussions; " where one of my articles in " Tait," " The Currency Juggle," also appears. In the whole mass of what I wrote previous to these, there is nothing of sufficient permanent value to justify reprinting. The paper in the Jurist, which I still think a very complete discussion of the rights of the State over Foundations, showed both sides of my opinions, asserting as firmly as I should have done at any time, the doctrine that all endowments are national property, which the government may and ought to control; but not, as I should once have done, condemning endowments in themselves, and proposing that they should be taken to pay off the national debt. On the contrary, I urged strenuously the importance of having a provision for education, not dependent on the mere demand of the market, that is, on the knowledge and discernment of average parents, but calculated to establish and keep up a higher standard of instruction than is likely to be spontaneously demanded by the buyers of the article. All these opinions have been confirmed and strengthened by the whole course of my subsequent reflections.

CHAPTER VI

Commencement of the Most Valuable Friendship of My Life. My Father's Death. Writings and Other Proceedings Up to 1840.

IT was at the period of my mental progress which I have now reached that I formed the friendship which has been the honour and chief blessing of my existence, as well as the source of a great part of all that I have attempted to do, or hope to effect hereafter, for human improvement. My first introduction to the lady who, after a friendship of twenty years, consented to become my wife, was in 1830, when I was in my twenty-fifth and she in her twenty-third year. With her husband's family it was the renewal of an old acquaintanceship. His grandfather lived in the next house to my father's in Newington Green, and I had, sometimes when a boy, been invited to play in the old gentleman's garden. He was a fine specimen of the old Scotch Puritan; stern, severe, and powerful, but very kind to children, on whom such men make a lasting impression. Although it was years after my introduction to Mrs. Taylor before my acquaintance with her became at all intimate or confidential, I very soon felt her to be the most admirable person I had ever known. It is not to be supposed that she was, or that any one, at the age at which I first saw her, could be, all that she afterwards became. Least of all could this be true of her, with whom self-improvement, progress in the highest and in all senses, was a law of her nature; a necessity equally from the ardour with which she sought it, and from the spontaneous tendency of faculties which could not receive an impression or an experience without making it the source or the occasion of an accession of wisdom. Up to the time when I first saw her, her rich and powerful nature had chiefly unfolded itself according to the received type of feminine genius. To her outer circle she was a beauty and a wit, with an air of natural distinction, felt by all who approached her: to the inner, a woman of deep and strong feeling, of penetrating and intuitive intelligence, and of an eminently meditative and poetic nature. Married at an early age, to a most upright, brave, and honourable man, of liberal opinions and good education, but without the intellectual or artistic tastes which would have made him a companion for her, though a steady and affectionate friend, for whom she had true esteem and the strongest affection through life, and whom she most deeply lamented when dead; shut out by the social disabilities of women from any adequate exercise of her highest faculties in action on the world without; her life was one of inward meditation, varied by familiar intercourse with a small circle of friends, of whom one only (long since deceased) was a person of genius, or of capacities of feeling or intellect kindred with her own, but all had more or less of alliance with her in sentiments and opinions. Into this circle I had the good fortune to be admitted, and I soon perceived that she possessed in combination, the qualities which in all other persons whom I had known I had been only too happy to find singly. In her, complete emancipation from every kind of superstition (including that which attributes a pretended perfection to the order of nature and the universe), and an earnest protest against many things which are still part of the established constitution of society, resulted not from the hard intellect, but from strength of noble and elevated feeling, and co-existed with a highly reverential nature. In general spiritual characteristics, as well as in temperament and organization, I have often compared her, as she was at this time, to Shelley: but in thought and intellect, Shelley, so far as his powers were developed in his short life, was but a child compared with what she ultimately became. Alike in the highest regions of speculation and in the smaller practical concerns of daily life, her mind was the same perfect instrument, piercing to the very heart and marrow of the matter; always seizing the essential idea or principle. The same exactness and rapidity of operation, pervading as it did her sensitive as well as her mental faculties, would,

with her gifts of feeling and imagination, have fitted her
to be a consummate artist, as her fiery and tender soul and
her vigorous eloquence would certainly have made her a
great orator, and her profound knowledge of human nature
and discernment and sagacity in practical life, would, in
the times when such a *carrière* was open to women, have
made her eminent among the rulers of mankind. Her intellectual gifts did but minister to a moral character at once the
noblest and the best balanced which I have ever met with
in life. Her unselfishness was not that of a taught system
of duties, but of a heart which thoroughly identified itself
with the feelings of others, and often went to excess in
consideration for them by imaginatively investing their feelings with the intensity of its own. The passion of justice
might have been thought to be her strongest feeling, but
for her boundless generosity, and a lovingness ever ready to
pour itself forth upon any or all human beings who were
capable of giving the smallest feeling in return. The rest
of her moral characteristics were such as naturally accompany these qualities of mind and heart: the most genuine
modesty combined with the loftiest pride; a simplicity and
sincerity which were absolute, towards all who were fit to
receive them; the utmost scorn of whatever was mean and
cowardly, and a burning indignation at everything brutal or
tyrannical, faithless or dishonourable in conduct and character, while making the broadest distinction between *mala
in se* and mere *mala prohibita*—between acts giving evidence
of intrinsic badness in feeling and character, and those
which are only violations of conventions either good or bad,
violations which whether in themselves right or wrong, are
capable of being committed by persons in every other respect loveable or admirable.

To be admitted into any degree of mental intercourse
with a being of these qualities, could not but have a most
beneficial influence on my development; though the effect
was only gradual, and many years elapsed before her mental progress and mine went forward in the complete com-
panionship they at last attained. The benefit I received was
far greater than any which I could hope to give; though to
her, who had at first reached her opinions by the moral

intuition of a character of strong feeling, there was doubtless help as well as encouragement to be derived from one
who had arrived at many of the same results by study and
reasoning: and in the rapidity of her intellectual growth,
her mental activity, which converted everything into knowledge, doubtless drew from me, as it did from other sources,
many of its materials. What I owe, even intellectually, to
her, is in its detail, almost infinite; of its general character
a few words will give some, though a very imperfect, idea.

With those who, like all the best and wisest of mankind,
are dissatisfied with human life as it is, and whose feelings
are wholly identified with its radical amendment, there are
two main regions of thought. One is the region of ultimate
aims; the constituent elements of the highest realizable ideal
of human life. The other is that of the immediately useful
and practically attainable. In both these departments, I
have acquired more from her teaching, than from all other
sources taken together. And, to say truth, it is in these two
extremes principally, that real certainty lies. My own
strength lay wholly in the uncertain and slippery intermediate region, that of theory, on moral and political
science: respecting the conclusions of which, in any of the
forms in which I have received or originated them, whether
as political economy, analytic psychology, logic, philosophy of history, or anything else, it is not the least of my
intellectual obligations to her that I have derived from her
a wise scepticism, which, while it has not hindered me from
following out the honest exercise of my thinking faculties
to whatever conclusions might result from it, has put me
on my guard against holding or announcing these conclusions with a degree of confidence which the nature of such
speculations does not warrant, and has kept my mind not only
open to admit, but prompt to welcome and eager to seek,
even on the questions on which I have most meditated, any
prospect of clearer perceptions and better evidence. I have
often received praise, which in my own right I only partially deserve, for the greater practicality which is supposed to be found in my writings, compared with those of
most thinkers who have been equally addicted to large generalizations. The writings in which this quality has been

observed, were not the work of one mind, but of the fusion
of two, one of them as pre-eminently practical in its judgments and perceptions of things present, as it was high and
bold in its anticipations for a remote futurity.

At the present period, however, this influence was only
one among many which were helping to shape the character
of my future development: and even after it became, I may
truly say, the presiding principle of my mental progress, it
did not alter the path, but only made me move forward more
boldly, and, at the same time, more cautiously, in the same
course.   The only actual revolution which has ever taken
place in my modes of thinking, was already complete.   My
new tendencies had to be confirmed in some respects, mod-
erated in others: but the only substantial changes of opinion
that were yet to come, related to politics, and consisted, on
one hand, in a greater approximation, so far as regards the
ultimate prospects of humanity, to a qualified Socialism, and
on the other, a shifting of my political ideal from pure
democracy, as commonly understood by its partizans, to the
modified form of it, which is set forth in my "Considerations on Representative Government."

This last change, which took place very gradually, dates
its commencement from my reading, or rather study, of
M. de Tocqueville's "Democracy in America," which fell
into my hands immediately after its first appearance.   In
that remarkable work, the excellences of democracy were
pointed out in a more conclusive, because a more specific
manner than I had ever known them to be, even by the most
enthusiastic democrats; while the specific dangers which
beset democracy, considered as the government of the numerical majority, were brought into equally strong light,
and subjected to a masterly analysis, not as reasons for
resisting what the author considered as an inevitable result
of human progress, but as indications of the weak points of
popular government, the defences by which it needs to be
guarded, and the correctives which must be added to it in
order that while full play is given to its beneficial tendencies,
those which are of a different nature may be neutralized or
mitigated.   I was now well prepared for speculations of this
character, and from this time onward my own thoughts

moved more and more in the same channel, though the consequent modifications in my practical political creed were
spread over many years, as would be shown by comparing
my first review of "Democracy in America," written and
published in 1835, with the one in 1840 (reprinted in the
"Dissertations"), and this last, with the "Considerations
on Representative Government."

A collateral subject on which also I derived great benefit
from the study of Tocqueville, was the fundamental question
of centralization. The powerful philosophic analysis which
he applied to American and to French experience, led him
to attach the utmost importance to the performance of as
much of the collective business of society, as can safely be
so performed, by the people themselves, without any inter-
vention of the executive government, either to supersede
their agency, or to dictate the manner of its exercise.   He
viewed this practical political activity of the individual citizen, not only as one of the most effectual means of training
the social feelings and practical intelligence of the people,
so important in themselves, and so indispensable to good
government, but also as the specific counteractive to some
of the characteristic infirmities of democracy, and a necessary protection against its degenerating into the only despotism of which, in the modern world, there is real danger—
the absolute rule of the head of the executive over a congre-
gation of isolated individuals, all equals but all slaves. There
was, indeed, no immediate peril from this source on the
British side of the channel, where nine-tenths of the internal business which elsewhere devolves on the government,
was transacted by agencies independent of it; where centralization was, and is, the subject not only of national
disapprobation, but of unreasoning prejudice; where jealousy of government interference was a blind feeling
preventing or resisting even the most beneficial exertion of
legislative authority to correct the abuses of what pretends
to be local self-government, but is, too often, selfish mismanagement of local interests, by a jobbing and *borné*
local oligarchy. But the more certain the public were to
go wrong on the side opposed to centralization, the greater
danger was there lest philosophic reformers should fall into

the contrary error, and overlook the mischiefs of which they had been spared the painful experience. I was myself, at this very time, actively engaged in defending important measures, such as the great Poor Law Reform of 1834, against an irrational clamour grounded on the anti-centralization prejudice: and had it not been for the lessons of Tocqueville, I do not know that I might not, like many reformers before me, have been hurried into the excess opposite to that, which, being the one prevalent in my own country, it was generally my business to combat. As it is, I have steered carefully between the two errors, and whether I have or have not drawn the line between them exactly in the right place, I have at least insisted with equal emphasis upon the evils on both sides, and have made the means of reconciling the advantages of both, a subject of serious study.

In the meanwhile had taken place the election of the first Reformed Parliament, which included several of the most notable of my Radical friends and acquaintances—Grote, Roebuck, Buller, Sir William Molesworth, John and Edward Romilly, and several more; besides Warburton, Strutt, and others, who were in Parliament already. Those who thought themselves, and were called by their friends, the philosophic Radicals, had now, it seemed, a fair opportunity, in a more advantageous position than they had ever before occupied, for showing what was in them; and I, as well as my father, founded great hopes on them. These hopes were destined to be disappointed. The men were honest, and faithful to their opinions, as far as votes were concerned; often in spite of much discouragement. When measures were proposed, flagrantly at variance with their principles, such as the Irish Coercion Bill, or the Canada Coercion in 1837, they came forward manfully, and braved any amount of hostility and prejudice rather than desert the right. But on the whole they did very little to promote any opinions; they had little enterprise, little activity: they left the lead of the Radical portion of the House to the old hands, to Hume and O'Connell. A partial exception must be made in favour of one or two of the younger men; and in the case of Roebuck, it is his title to permanent remembrance, that in the very first year during which he sat in Parliament, he originated (or re-originated after the unsuccessful attempt of Mr. Brougham) the parliamentary movement for National Education; and that he was the first to commence, and for years carried on almost alone, the contest for the self-government of the Colonies. Nothing, on the whole equal to these two things, was done by any other individual, even of those from whom most was expected. And now, on a calm retrospect, I can perceive that the men were less in fault than we supposed, and that we had expected too much from them. They were in unfavourable circumstances. Their lot was cast in the ten years of inevitable reaction, when, the Reform excitement being over, and the few legislative improvements which the public really called for having been rapidly effected, power gravitated back in its natural direction, to those who were for keeping things as they were; when the public mind desired rest, and was less disposed than at any other period since the peace, to let itself be moved by attempts to work up the Reform feeling into fresh activity in favour of new things. It would have required a great political leader, which no one is to be blamed for not being, to have effected really great things by parliamentary discussion when the nation was in this mood. My father and I had hoped that some competent leader might arise; some man of philosophic attainments and popular talents, who could have put heart into the many younger or less distinguished men that would have been ready to join him—could have made them available, to the extent of their talents, in bringing advanced ideas before the public—could have used the House of Commons as a rostra or a teacher's chair for instructing and impelling the public mind; and would either have forced the Whigs to receive their measures from him, or have taken the lead of the Reform party out of their hands. Such a leader there would have been, if my father had been in Parliament. For want of such a man, the instructed Radicals sank into a mere *Côté Gauche* of the Whig party. With a keen, and as I now think, an exaggerated sense of the possibilities which were open to the Radicals if they made even ordinary exertion for their opinions, I laboured from this time till 1839, both by personal influence with some of them, and by writings, to put ideas into their heads, and purpose into their hearts. I did some good with Charles Buller, and some with Sir William Molesworth; both of whom did valuable service, but were unhappily cut off almost in the beginning of their usefulness. On the whole, however, my attempt was vain. To have had a chance of succeeding in it, required a different position from mine. It was a task only for one who, being himself in Parliament, could have mixed with the Radical members in daily' consultation, could himself have taken the initiative, and instead of urging others to lead, could have summoned them to follow.

What I could do by writing, I did. During the year 1833 I continued working in the Examiner with Fonblanque, who at that time was zealous in keeping up the fight for Radicalism against the Whig ministry. During the session of 1834 I wrote comments on passing events, of the nature of newspaper articles (under the title of " Notes on the Newspapers "), in the Monthly Repository, a magazine conducted by Mr. Fox, well known as a preacher and political orator, and subsequently as member of Parliament for Oldham; with whom I had lately become acquainted, and for whose sake chiefly I wrote in his magazine. I contributed several other articles to this periodical, the most considerable of which (on the theory of Poetry), is reprinted in the " Dissertations." Altogether, the writings (independently of those in newspapers) which I published from 1832 to 1834, amount to a large volume. This, however, includes abstracts of several of Plato's Dialogues, with introductory remarks, which, though not published until 1834, had been written several years earlier; and which I afterwards, on various occasions, found to have been read, and their authorship known, by more people than were aware of anything else which I had written, up to that time. To complete the tale of my writings at this period, I may add that in 1833, at the request of Bulwer, who was just then completing his " England and the English " (a work, at that time, greatly in advance of the public mind), I wrote for him a critical account of Bentham's philosophy, a small part of which he incorporated in his text, and printed the rest (with an honourable acknowledgment), as an appendix. In this, along with the favourable, a part also of the unfavourable side of my estimation of Bentham's doctrines, considered as a complete philosophy, was for the first time put into print.

But an opportunity soon offered, by which, as it seemed, I might have it in my power to give more effectual aid, and, at the same time, stimulus, to the "philosophic Radical" party, than I had done hitherto. One of the projects occasionally talked of between my father and me, and some of the parliamentary and other Radicals who frequented his house, was the foundation of a periodical organ of philosophic radicalism, to take the place which the Westminster Review had been intended to fill: and the scheme had gone so far as to bring under discussion the pecuniary contributions which could be looked for, and the choice of an editor. Nothing, however, came of it for some time: but in the summer of 1834 Sir William Molesworth, himself a laborious student, and a precise and metaphysical thinker, capable of aiding the cause by his pen as well as by his purse, spontaneously proposed to establish a Review, provided I would consent to be the real, if I could not be the ostensible editor. Such a proposal was not to be refused; and the Review was founded, at first under the title of the London Review, and afterwards under that of the London and Westminster, Molesworth having bought the Westminster from its proprietor, General Thompson, and merged the two into one. In the years between 1834 and 1840 the conduct of this Review occupied the greater part of my spare time. In the beginning, it did not, as a whole, by any means represent my opinions. I was under the necessity of conceding much to my inevitable associates. The Review was established to be the representative of the "philosophic Radicals," with most of whom I was not at issue on many essential points, and among whom I could not even claim to be the most important individual. My father's co-operation as a writer we all deemed indispensable, and he wrote largely in it until prevented by his last illness. The subjects of his articles, and the strength and decision with which his opinions were expressed in them, made the Review at first derive its tone and colouring from him much more than from any of the other writers. I could not exercise editorial control over his articles, and I was sometimes obliged to sacrifice to him portions of my own. The old Westminster Review doctrines, but little modified, thus formed the staple of the Review; but I hoped, by the side of these, to introduce other ideas and another tone, and to obtain for my own shade of opinion a fair representation, along with those of other members of the party. With this end chiefly in view, I made it one of the peculiarities of the work that every article should bear an initial, or some other signature, and be held to express the opinions solely of the individual writer; the editor being only responsible for its being worth publishing, and not in conflict with the objects for which the Review was set on foot. I had an opportunity of putting in practice my scheme of conciliation between the old and the new "philosophic radicalism," by the choice of a subject for my own first contribution. Professor Sedgwick, a man of eminence in a particular walk of natural science, but who should not have trespassed into philosophy, had lately published his Discourse on the Studies of Cambridge, which had as its most prominent feature an intemperate assault on analytic psychology and utilitarian ethics, in the form of an attack on Locke and Paley. This had excited great indignation in my father and others, which I thought it fully deserved. And here, I imagined, was an opportunity of at the same time repelling an unjust attack, and inserting into my defence of Hartleianism and Utilitarianism a number of the opinions which constituted my view of those subjects, as distinguished from that of my old associates. In this I partially succeeded, though my relation to my father would have made it painful to me in any case, and impossible in a Review for which he wrote, to speak out my whole mind on the subject at this time.

I am, however, inclined to think that my father was not so much opposed as he seemed, to the modes of thought in which I believed myself to differ from him; that he did injustice to his own opinions by the unconscious exaggerations of an intellect emphatically polemical; and that when thinking without an adversary in view, he was willing to make room for a great portion of the truths he seemed to deny.

I have frequently observed that he made large allowance in practice for considerations which seemed to have no place in his theory. His "Fragment on Mackintosh," which he wrote and published about this time, although I greatly admired some parts of it, I read as a whole with more pain than pleasure; yet on reading it again, long after, I found little in the opinions it contains, but what I think in the main just; and I can even sympathize in his disgust at the *verbiage* of Mackintosh, though his asperity towards it went not only beyond what was judicious, but beyond what was even fair. One thing, which I thought, at the time, of good augury, was the very favourable reception he gave to Tocqueville's "Democracy in America." It is true, he said and thought much more about what Tocqueville said in favour of democracy, than what he said of its disadvantages. Still, his high appreciation of a book which was at any rate an example of a mode of treating the question of government almost the reverse of his—wholly inductive and analytical, instead of purely ratiocinative—gave me great encouragement. He also approved of an article which I published in the first number following the junction of the two reviews, the essay reprinted in the "Dissertations," under the title "Civilization;" into which I threw many of my new opinions, and criticised rather emphatically the mental and moral tendencies of the time, on grounds and in a manner which I certainly had not learnt from him.

All speculation, however, on the possible future developments of my father's opinions, and on the probabilities of permanent co-operation between him and me in the promulgation of our thoughts, was doomed to be cut short. During the whole of 1835 his health had been declining: his symptoms became unequivocally those of pulmonary consumption, and after lingering to the last stage of debility, he died on the 23rd of June, 1836. Until the last few days of his life there was no apparent abatement of intellectual vigour; his interest in all things and persons that had interested him through life was undiminished, nor did the approach of death cause the smallest wavering (as in so strong and firm a mind it was impossible that it should) in his convictions on the subject of religion. His principal satisfaction, after he knew that his end was near, seemed to be the thought of what he had done to make the world better than he found it; and his chief regret in not living longer, that he had not had time to do more.

His place is an eminent one in the literary, and even in the political history of his country; and it is far from honourable to the generation which has benefited by his worth, that he is so seldom mentioned, and, compared with men far his inferiors, so little remembered. This is probably to be ascribed mainly to two causes. In the first place, the thought of him merges too much in the deservedly superior fame of Bentham. Yet he was anything but Bentham's mere follower or disciple. Precisely because he was himself one of the most original thinkers of his time, he was one of the earliest to appreciate and adopt the most important mass of original thought which had been produced by the generation preceding him. His mind and Bentham's were essentially of different construction. He had not all Bentham's high qualities, but neither had Bentham all his. It would, indeed, be ridiculous to claim for him the praise of having accomplished for mankind such splendid services as Bentham's. He did not revolutionize, or rather create, one of the great departments of human thought. But, leaving out of the reckoning all that portion of his labours in which he benefited by what Bentham had done, and counting only what he achieved in a province in which Bentham had done nothing, that of analytic psychology, he will be known to posterity as one of the greatest names in that most important branch of speculation, on which all the moral and political sciences ultimately rest, and will mark one of the essential stages in its progress. The other reason which has made his fame less than he deserved, is that notwithstanding the great number of his opinions which, partly through his own efforts, have now been generally adopted, there was, on the whole, a marked opposition between his spirit and that of the present time. As Brutus was called the last of the Romans, so was he the last of the eighteenth century: he continued its tone of thought and sentiment into the nineteenth (though not unmodified nor unimproved), partaking neither in the good nor in the bad influences of the reaction against the eighteenth century, which was the great characteristic of the first half of the nineteenth. The eighteenth century was a great age, an age of strong and brave men, and he was a fit companion for its strongest and bravest. By his writings and his personal influence he was a great centre of light to his generation. During his later years he was quite as much the head and leader of the intellectual radicals in England, as Voltaire was of the *philosophes* of France. It is only one of his minor merits, that he was the originator of all sound statesmanship in regard to the subject of his largest work, India. He wrote on no subject which he did not enrich with valuable thought, and excepting the " Elements of Political Economy," a very useful book when first written, but which has now for some time finished its work, it will be long before any of his books will be wholly superseded, or will cease to be instructive reading to students of their subjects. In the power of influencing by mere force of mind and character, the convictions and purposes of others, and in the strenuous exertion of that power to promote freedom and progress, he left, as my knowledge extends, no equal among men and but one among women.

Though acutely sensible of my own inferiority in the qualities by which he acquired his personal ascendancy, I had now to try what it might be possible for me to accomplish without him: and the Review was the instrument on which I built my chief hopes of establishing a useful influence over the liberal and democratic section of the public mind. Deprived of my father's aid, I was also exempted from the restraints and reticences by which that aid had been purchased. I did not feel that there was any other radical writer or politician to whom I was bound to defer, further than consisted with my own opinions: and having the complete confidence of Molesworth, I resolved henceforth to give full scope to my own opinions and modes of thought, and to open the Review widely to all writers who were in sympathy with Progress as I understood it, even though I should lose by it the support of my former associates. Carlyle, consequently, became from this time a frequent writer in the Review; Sterling, soon after, an occasional one; and though each individual article continued to

be the expression of the private sentiments of its writer, the
general tone conformed in some tolerable degree to my
opinions. For the conduct of the Review, under, and in
conjunction with me, I associated with myself a young
Scotchman of the name of Robertson, who had some ability
and information, much industry, and an active scheming
head, full of devices for making the Review more saleable,
and on whose capacities in that direction I founded a good
deal of hope: insomuch, that when Molesworth, in the beginning of 1837, became tired of carrying on the Review
at a loss, and desirous of getting rid of it (he had done his
part honourably, and at no small pecuniary cost), I, very
imprudently for my own pecuniary interest, and very much
from reliance on Robertson's devices, determined to continue it at my own risk, until his plans should have had a
fair trial. The devices were good, and I never had any
reason to change my opinion of them. But I do not believe
that any devices would have made a radical and democratic
review defray its own expenses, including a paid editor or
sub-editor, and a liberal payment to writers. I myself and
several frequent contributors gave our labour gratuitously,
as we had done for Molesworth; but the paid contributors
continued to be remunerated on the usual scale of the Edinburgh and Quarterly Reviews; and this could not be done
from the proceeds of the sale.

In the same year, 1837, and in the midst of these occupations, I resumed the Logic. I had not touched my pen on the
subject for five years, having been stopped and brought to a
halt on the threshold of Induction. I had gradually discovered that what was mainly wanting, to overcome the difficulties of that branch of the subject, was a comprehensive,
and, at the same time, accurate view of the whole circle of
physical science, which I feared it would take me a long
course of study to acquire; since I knew not of any book,
or other guide, that would spread out before me the generalities and processes of the sciences, and I apprehended that
I should have no choice but to extract them for myself, as I
best could, from the details. Happily for me, Dr. Whewell,
early in this year, published his History of the Inductive
Sciences. I read it with eagerness, and found in it a consid-

erable approximation to what I wanted. Much, if not most, of the philosophy of the work appeared open to objection; but the materials were there, for my own thoughts to work upon: and the author had given to those materials that first degree of elaboration, which so greatly facilitates and abridges the subsequent labour. I had now obtained what I had been waiting for. Under the impulse given me by the thoughts excited by Dr. Whewell, I read again Sir J. Herschel's discourse on the Study of Natural Philosophy: and I was able to measure the progress my mind had made, by the great help I now found in this work—though I had read and even reviewed it several years before with little profit. I now set myself vigorously to work out the subject in thought and in writing. The time I bestowed on this had to be stolen from occupations more urgent. I had just two months to spare, at this period, in the intervals of writing for the Review. In these two months I completed the first draft of about a third, the most difficult third, of the book. What I had before written, I estimate at another third, so that only one-third remained. What I wrote at this time consisted of the remainder of the doctrine of Reasoning (the theory of Trains of Reasoning, and Demonstrative Science), and the greater part of the Book on Induction. When this was done, I had, as it seemed to me, untied all the really hard knots, and the completion of the book had become only a question of time. Having got thus far, I had to leave off in order to write two articles for the next number of the Review. When these were written, I returned to the subject, and now for the first time fell in with Comte's Cour de Philosophie Positive, or rather with the two volumes of it which were all that had at that time been published.

My theory of Induction was substantially completed before I knew of Comte's book; and it is perhaps well that I came to it by a different road from his, since the consequence has been that my treatise contains, what his certainly does not, a reduction of the inductive process to strict rules and to a scientific test, such as the syllogism is for ratiocination. Comte is always precise and profound on the method of investigation, but he does not even attempt any exact definition of the conditions of proof: and his writings show that he never attained a just conception of them. This, however, was specifically the problem which, in treating of Induction, I had proposed to myself. Nevertheless, I gained much from Comte, with which to enrich my chapters in the subsequent rewriting; and his book was of essential service to me in some of the parts which still remained to be thought out. As his subsequent volumes successively made their appearance, I read them with avidity, but, when he reached the subject of Social Science, with varying feelings. The fourth volume disappointed me: it contained those of his opinions on social subjects with which I most disagree. But the fifth, containing the connected view of history, rekindled all my enthusiasm; which the sixth (or concluding) volume did not materially. abate. In a merely logical point of view, the only leading conception for which I am indebted to him is that of the Inverse Deductive Method, as the one chiefly applicable to the complicated subjects of History and Statistics: a process differing from the more common form of the deductive method in this—that instead of arriving at its conclusions by general reasoning, and verifying them by specific experience (as is the natural order in the deductive branches of physical science), it obtains its generalizations by a collation of specific experience, and verifies them by ascertaining whether they are such as would follow from known general principles. This was an idea entirely new to me when I found it in Comte: and but for him I might not soon (if ever) have arrived at it.

I had been long an ardent admirer of Comte's writings before I had any communication with himself; nor did I ever, to the last, see him in the body. But for some years we were frequent correspondents, until our correspondence became controversial, and our zeal cooled. I was the first to slacken correspondence; he was the first to drop it. I found, and he probably found likewise, that I could do no good to his mind, and that all the good he could do to mine, he did by his books. This would never have led to discontinuance of intercourse, if the differences between us had been on matters of simple doctrine. But they were chiefly on those points of opinion which blended in both of us with our strongest feelings, and determined the entire direction of our aspirations. I had fully agreed with him when he maintained that the mass of mankind, including even their rulers in all the practical departments of life, must, from the necessity of the case, accept most of their opinions on political and social matters, as they do on physical, from the authority of those who have bestowed more study on those subjects than they generally have it in their power to do. This lesson had been strongly impressed on me by the early work of Comte, to which I have adverted. And there was nothing in his great Treatise which I admired more than his remarkable exposition of the benefits which the nations of modern Europe have historically derived from the separation, during the Middle Ages, of temporal and spiritual power, and the distinct organization of the latter. I agreed with him that the moral and intellectual ascendancy, once exercised by priests, must in time pass into the hands of philosophers, and will naturally do so when they become sufficiently unanimous, and in other respects worthy to possess it. But when he exaggerated this line of thought into a practical system, in which philosophers were to be organized into a kind of corporate hierarchy, invested with almost the same spiritual supremacy (though without any secular power) once possessed by the Catholic Church; when I found him relying on this spiritual authority as the only security for good government, the sole bulwark against practical oppression, and expecting that by it a system of despotism in the state and despotism in the family would be rendered innocuous and beneficial; it is not surprising, that while as logicians we were nearly at one, as sociologists we could travel together no further. M. Comte lived to carry out these doctrines to their extremest consequences, by planning, in his last work, the "Système de Politique Positive," the completest system of spiritual and temporal despotism which ever yet emanated from a human brain, unless possibly that of Ignatius Loyola: a system by which the yoke of general opinion, wielded by an organized body of spiritual teachers and rulers, would be made supreme over every action, and as far as is in human possibility, every thought, of every member of the community, as well in the things which regard only himself, as in those which concern the interests of others. It is but just to say that this work is a considerable improvement, in many points of feeling, over Comte's previous writings on the same subjects: but as an accession to social philosophy, the only value it seems to me to possess, consists in putting an end to the notion that no effectual moral authority can be maintained over society without the aid of religious belief; for Comte's work recognizes no religion except that of Humanity, yet it leaves an irresistible conviction that any moral beliefs concurred in by the community generally, may be brought to bear upon the whole conduct and lives of its individual members, with an energy and potency truly alarming to think of. The book stands a monumental warning to thinkers on society and politics, of what happens when once men lose sight in their speculations, of the value of Liberty and of Individuality.

To return to myself. The Review engrossed, for some time longer, nearly all the time I could devote to authorship, or to thinking with authorship in view. The articles from the London and Westminster Review which are reprinted in the " Dissertations," are scarcely a fourth part of those I wrote. In the conduct of the Review I had two principal objects. One was to free philosophic radicalism from the reproach of sectarian Benthamism. I desired, while retaining the precision of expression, the definiteness of meaning, the contempt of declamatory phrases and vague generalities, which were so honourably characteristic both of Bentham and of my father, to give a wider basis and a more free and genial character to Radical speculations; to show that there was a Radical philosophy, better and more complete than Bentham's, while recognizing and incorporating all of Bentham's which is permanently valuable. In this first object I, to a certain extent, succeeded. The other thing I attempted, was to stir up the educated Radicals, in and out of Parliament, to exertion, and induce them to make themselves, what I thought by using the proper means they might become—a powerful party capable of taking the government of the country, or at least of dictating the terms on which they should share it with the Whigs. This attempt was from the first chimerical: partly because the time was unpropitious, the Reform fervour being in its period of ebb, and the Tory influences powerfully rallying; but still more, because, as Austin so truly said, "the country did not contain the men." Among the Radicals in Parliament there were several qualified to be useful members of an enlightened Radical party, but none capable of forming and leading such a party. The exhortations I addressed to them found no response. One occasion did present itself when there seemed to be room for a bold and successful stroke for Radicalism. Lord Durham had left the Ministry, by reason, as was thought, of their not being sufficiently Liberal; he afterwards accepted from them the task of ascertaining and removing the causes of the Canadian rebellion; he had shown a disposition to surround himself at the outset with Radical advisers; one of his earliest measures, a good measure both in intention and in effect, having been disapproved and reversed by the Government at home, he had resigned his post, and placed himself openly in a position of quarrel with the Ministers. Here was a possible chief for a Radical party in the person of a man of importance, who was hated by the Tories and had just been injured by the Whigs. Any one who had the most elementary notions of party tactics, must have attempted to make something of such an opportunity. Lord Durham was bitterly attacked from all sides, inveighed against by enemies, given up by timid friends; while those who would willingly have defended him did not know what to say. He appeared to be returning a defeated and discredited man. I had followed the Canadian events from the beginning; I had been one of the prompters of his prompters; his policy was almost exactly what mine would have been, and I was in a position to defend it. I wrote and published a manifesto in the Review, in which I took the very highest ground in his behalf, claiming for him not mere acquittal, but praise and honour. Instantly a number of other writers took up the tone: I believe there was a portion of truth in what Lord Durham, soon after, with polite exaggeration, said to me—that to this article might be ascribed the almost triumphant reception which he met with on his arrival in England. I believe it to have been the word in season, which, at a critical moment, does much to decide the result; the touch which determines whether a stone, set in motion at the top of an eminence, shall roll down on one side or on the other. All hopes connected with Lord Durham as a politician soon vanished; but with regard to Canadian, and generally to colonial policy, the cause was gained: Lord Durham's report, written by Charles Buller, partly under the inspiration of Wakefield, began a new era; its recommendations, extending to complete internal self-government, were in full operation in Canada within two or three years, and have been since extended to nearly all the other colonies, of European race, which have any claim to the character of important communities. And I may say that in successfully upholding the reputation of Lord Durham and his advisers at the most important moment, I contributed materially to this result.

One other case occurred during my conduct of the Review, which similarly illustrated the effect of taking a prompt initiative. I believe that the early success and reputation of Carlyle's French Revolution, were considerably accelerated by what I wrote about it in the Review. Immediately on its publication, and before the commonplace critics, all whose rules and modes of judgment it set at defiance, had time to pre-occupy the public with their disapproval of it, I wrote and published a review of the book, hailing it as one of those productions of genius which are above all rules, and are a law to themselves. Neither in this case nor in that of Lord Durham do I ascribe the impression, which I think was produced by what I wrote, to any particular merit of execution: indeed, in at least one of the cases (the article on Carlyle) I do not think the execution was good. And in both instances, I am persuaded that anybody, in a position to be read, who had expressed the same opinion at the same precise time, and had made any tolerable statement of the just grounds for it, would have produced the same effect. But, after the complete failure of my hopes of putting a new life into Radical politics by means of the Review, I am glad to look back on these two instances of success in an honest attempt to do immediate service to things and persons that deserved it.

After the last hope of the formation of a Radical party had disappeared, it was time for me to stop the heavy expenditure of time and money which the Review cost me. It had to some extent answered my personal purpose as a vehicle for my opinions. It had enabled me to express in print much of my altered mode of thought, and to separate myself in a marked manner from the narrower Benthamism of my early writings. This was done by the general tone of all I wrote, including various purely literary articles, but especially by the two papers (reprinted in the Dissertations) which attempted a philosophical estimate of Bentham and of Coleridge. In the first of these, while doing full justice to the merits of Bentham, I pointed out what I thought the errors and deficiencies of his philosophy. The substance of this criticism I still think perfectly just; but I have sometimes doubted whether it was right to publish it at that time. I have often felt that Bentham's philosophy, as an instrument of progress, has been to some extent discredited before it had done its work, and that to lend a hand towards lowering its reputation was doing more harm than service to improvement. Now, however, when a counter-reaction appears to be setting in towards what is good in Benthamism, I can look with more satisfaction on this criticism of its defects, especially as I have myself balanced it by vindications of the fundamental principles of Bentham's philosophy, which are reprinted along with it in the same collection. In the essay on Coleridge I attempted to characterize the European reaction against the negative philosophy of the eighteenth century: and here, if the effect only of this one paper were to be considered, I might be thought to have erred by giving undue prominence to the favourable side, as I had done in the case of Bentham to the unfavourable. In both cases, the impetus with which I had detached myself from what was untenable in the doctrines of Bentham and of the eighteenth century, may have carried me, though in appearance rather than in reality, too far on the contrary side. But as far as relates to the article on Coleridge, my defence is, that I was writing for Radicals and Liberals, and it was my business to dwell most on that, in writers of a different school, from the knowledge of which, they might derive most improvement.

The number of the Review which contained the paper on

Coleridge, was the last which was published during my proprietorship. In the spring of 1840 I made over the Review to Mr. Hickson, who had been a frequent and very useful unpaid contributor under my management: only stipulating that the change should be marked by a resumption of the old name, that of Westminster Review. Under that name Mr. Hickson conducted it for ten years, on the plan of dividing among contributors only the net proceeds of the Review, giving his own labour as writer and editor gratuitously. Under the difficulty in obtaining writers, which arose from this low scale of payment, it is highly creditable to him that he was able to maintain, in some tolerable degree, the character of the Review as an organ of radicalism and progress. I did not cease altogether to write for the Review, but continued to send it occasional contributions, not, however, exclusively; for the greater circulation of the Edinburgh Review induced me from this time to offer articles to it also when I had anything to say for which it appeared to be a suitable vehicle. And the concluding volumes of "Democracy in America," having just then come out, I inaugurated myself as a contributor to the Edinburgh, by the article on that work, which heads the second volume of the "Dissertations."

CHAPTER VII

GENERAL VIEW OF THE REMAINDER OF MY LIFE

FROM this time, what is worth relating of my life will come into a very small compass; for I have no further mental changes to tell of, but only, as I hope, a continued mental progress; which does not admit of a consecutive history, and the results of which, if real, will be best found in my writings. I shall, therefore, greatly abridge the chronicle of my subsequent years.

The first use I made of the leisure which I gained by disconnecting myself from the Review, was to finish the Logic. In July and August, 1838, I had found an interval in which to execute what was still undone of the original draft of the Third Book. In working out the logical theory of those laws of nature which are not laws of Causation, nor corollaries from such laws, I was led to recognise kinds as realities in nature, and not mere distinctions for convenience; a light which I had not obtained when the First Book was written, and which made it necessary for me to modify and enlarge several chapters of that Book. The Book on Language and Classification, and the chapter on the Classification of Fallacies, were drafted in the autumn of the same year; the remainder of the work, in the summer and autumn of 1840. From April following, to the end of 1841, my spare time was devoted to a complete re-writing of the book from its commencement. It is in this way that all my books have been composed. They were always written at least twice over; a first draft of the entire work was completed to the very end of the subject, then the whole begun again *de novo;* but incorporating, in the second writing, all sentences and parts of sentences of the old draft, which appeared as suitable to my purpose as anything which I could write in lieu of them. I have found great advantages in this system of double rédaction. It combines, better than any other mode of composition, the freshness and vigour of the first conception, with the superior precision and completeness resulting from prolonged thought. In my own case, moreover, I have found that the patience necessary for a careful elaboration of the details of composition and expression, costs much less effort after the entire subject has been once gone through, and the substance of all that I find to say has in some manner, however imperfect, been got upon paper. The only thing which I am careful, in the first draft, to make as perfect as I am able, is the arrangement. If that is bad, the whole thread on which the ideas string themselves becomes twisted; thoughts placed in a wrong connexion are not expounded in a manner that suits the right, and a first draft with this original vice is next to useless as a foundation for the final treatment.

During the re-writing of the Logic, Dr. Whewell's Philosophy of the Inductive Sciences made its appearance; a circumstance fortunate for me, as it gave me what I greatly desired, a full treatment of the subject by an antagonist, and enabled me to present my ideas with greater clearness and emphasis as well as fuller and more varied development, in defending them against definite objections, or confronting them distinctly with an opposite theory. The controversies with Dr. Whewell, as well as much matter derived from Comte, were first introduced into the book in the course of the re-writing.

At the end of 1841, the book being ready for the press, I offered it to Murray, who kept it until too late for publication that season, and then refused it, for reasons which could just as well have been given at first. But I have had no cause to regret a rejection which led to my offering it to Mr. Parker, by whom it was published in the spring of 1843. My original expectations of success were extremely limited. Archbishop Whately had, indeed, rehabilitated the name of Logic, and the study of the forms, rules, and fallacies of Ratiocination; and Dr. Whewell's writings had begun to excite an interest in the other part of my subject, the theory of Induction. A treatise, however, on a matter so abstract, could not be expected to be popular; it could only be a book for students, and students on such subjects were not only (at least in England) few, but addicted chiefly to the opposite school of metaphysics, the ontological and "innate principles" school. I therefore did not expect that the book would have many readers, or approvers; and looked for little practical effect from it, save that of keeping the tradition unbroken of what I thought a better philosophy. What hopes I had of exciting any immediate attention, were mainly grounded on the polemical propensities of Dr. Whewell; who, I thought, from observation of his conduct in other cases, would probably do something to bring the book into notice, by replying, and that promptly, to the attack on his opinions. He did reply, but not till 1850, just in time for me to answer him in the third edition. How the book came to have, for a work of the kind, so much success, and what sort of persons compose the bulk of those who have bought, I will not venture to say read, it, I have never thoroughly understood. But taken in conjunction with the many proofs which have since been given of a revival of speculation, speculation too of a free kind, in many quarters, and above all (where at one time I should have least expected it) in the Universities, the fact becomes partially intelligible. I have never indulged the illusion that the book had made any considerable impression on philosophical opinion. The German, or *à priori* view of human knowledge, and of the knowing faculties, is likely for some time longer (though it may be hoped in a diminishing degree) to predominate among those who occupy themselves with such inquiries, both here and on the Continent. But the "System of Logic" supplies what was much wanted, a text-book of the opposite doctrine—that which derives all knowledge from experience, and all moral and intellectual qualities principally from the direction given to the associations. I make as humble an estimate as anybody of what either an analysis of logical processes, or any possible canons of evidence, can do by themselves, towards guiding or rectifying the operations of the understanding. Combined with other requisites, I certainly do think them of great use; but whatever may be the practical value of a true philosophy of these matters, it is hardly possible to exaggerate the mischiefs of a false one. The notion that truths external to the mind may be known by intuition or consciousness, independently of observation and experience, is, I am persuaded, in these times, the great intellectual support of false doctrines and bad institutions. By the aid of this theory, every inveterate belief and every intense feeling, of which the origin is not remembered, is enabled to dispense with the obligation of justifying itself by reason, and is erected into its own all-sufficient voucher and justification. There never was such an instrument devised for consecrating all deep-seated prejudices. And the chief strength of this false philosophy in morals, politics, and religion, lies in the appeal which it is accustomed to make to the evidence of mathematics and of the cognate branches of physical science. To expel it from these, is to drive it from its stronghold: and because this had never been effectually done, the intuitive school, even after what my father had written in his Analysis of the Mind, had in appearance, and as far as published writings were concerned, on the whole the best of the argument. In attempting to clear up the real nature of the evidence of mathematical and physical truths, the "System of Logic" met the intuitive philosophers on ground on which they had previously been deemed unassailable; and gave its own explanation, from experience and association, of that peculiar character of what are called necessary truths, which is adduced as proof that their evidence must come from a deeper source than experience. Whether this has been done effectually, is still *sub judice;* and even then, to deprive a mode of thought so strongly rooted in human prejudices and partialities, of its mere speculative support, goes but a very little way towards overcoming it; but though only a step, it is a quite indispensable one; for since, after all, prejudice can only be successfully combated by philosophy, no way can really be made against it permanently until it has been shown not to have philosophy on its side.

Being now released from any active concern in temporary politics, and from any literary occupation involving personal communication with contributors and others, I was enabled to indulge the inclination, natural to thinking persons when **the** age of boyish vanity is once past, for limiting my own society to a very few persons. General society, as now carried on in England, is so insipid an affair, even to the persons who make it what it is, that it is kept up for any reason rather than the pleasure it affords. All serious discussion on matters on which opinions differ, being considered ill-bred, and the national deficiency in liveliness and sociability having prevented the cultivation of the art of talking agreeably on trifles, in which the French of the last century so much excelled, the sole attraction of what is called society to those who are not at the top of the tree, is the hope of being aided to climb a little higher in it; while to those who are already at the top, it is chiefly a compliance with custom, and with the supposed requirements of their station. To a person of any but a very common order in thought or feeling, such society, unless he has personal objects to serve by it, must be supremely unattractive: and most people, in the present day, of any really high class of intellect, make their contact with it so slight, and at such long intervals, as to be almost considered as retiring from it altogether. Those persons of any mental superiority who do otherwise, are, almost without exception, greatly deteriorated by it. Not to mention loss of time, the tone of their feelings is lowered: they become less in earnest about those of their opinions respecting which they must remain silent in the society they frequent: they come to look upon their most elevated objects as unpractical, or, at least, too remote from realization to be more than a vision, or a theory; and if, more fortunate than most, they retain their higher principles unimpaired, yet with respect to the persons and affairs of their own day they insensibly adopt the modes of feeling and judgment in which they can hope for sympathy from the company they keep. A person of high intellect should never go into unintellectual society unless he can enter it as an apostle; yet he is the only person with high objects who can safely enter it at all. Persons even of intellectual aspirations had much better, if they can, make their habitual associates of at least their equals, and, as far as possible, their superiors, in knowledge, intellect, and elevation of sentiment. Moreover, if the character is formed, and the mind made up, on the few cardinal points of human opinion, agreement of conviction and feeling on these, has been felt in all times to be an essential requisite of anything worthy the name of friendship, in a really earnest mind. All these circumstances united, made the number very small of those whose society, and still more whose intimacy, I now voluntarily sought.

Among these, the principal was the incomparable friend of whom I have already spoken. At this period she lived mostly with one young daughter, in a quiet part of the country, and only occasionally in town, with her first husband, Mr. Taylor. I visited her equally in both places; and was greatly indebted to the strength of character which enabled her to disregard the false interpretations liable to be put on the frequency of my visits to her while living generally apart from Mr. Taylor, and on our occasionally travelling together, though in all other respects our conduct during those years gave not the slightest ground for any other supposition than the true one, that our relation to each other at that time was one of strong affection and confidential intimacy only. For though we did not consider the ordinances of society binding on a subject so entirely personal, we did feel bound that our conduct should be such as in no degree to bring discredit on her husband, nor therefore on herself.

In this third period (as it may be termed) of my mental progress, which now went hand in hand with hers, my opinions gained equally in breadth and depth, I understood more things, and those which I had understood before, I now understood more thoroughly. I had now completely turned back from what there had been of excess in my reaction against Benthamism. I had, at the height of that reaction, certainly become much more indulgent to the common opinions of society and the world, and more willing to be content with seconding the superficial improvement which had begun to take place in those common opinions, than became one whose convictions, on so many points, differed fundamentally from them. I was much more inclined, than I can now approve, to put in abeyance the more decidedly heretical part of my opinions, which I now look upon as almost the only ones, the assertion of which tends in any way to regenerate society. But in addition to this, our opinions were far *more* heretical than mine had been in the days of my most extreme Benthamism. In those days I had seen little further than the old school of political economists into the possibilities of fundamental improvement in social arrangements. Private property, as now understood, and inheritance, appeared to me, as to them, the *dernier mot* of legislation: and I looked no further than to mitigating the inequalities consequent on these institutions, by getting rid of primogeniture and entails. The notion that it was possible to go further than this in removing the injustice—for injustice it is, whether admitting of a complete remedy or not—involved in the fact that some are born to riches and the vast majority to poverty, I then reckoned chimerical, and only hoped that by universal education, leading to voluntary restraint on population, the portion of the poor might be made more tolerable. In short, I was a democrat, but not the least of a Socialist. We were now much less democrats than I had been, because so long as education continues to be so wretchedly imperfect, we dreaded the ignorance and especially the selfishness and brutality of the mass: but our ideal of ultimate improvement went far beyond Democracy, and would class us decidedly under the general designation of Socialists. While we repudiated with the greatest energy that tyranny of society over the individual which most Socialistic systems are supposed to involve, we yet looked forward to a time when society will no longer be divided into the idle and the industrious; when the rule that they who do not work shall not eat, will be applied not to paupers only, but impartially to all; when the division of the produce of labour, instead of depending, as in so great a degree it now does, on the accident of birth, will be made by concert on an acknowledged principle of justice; and when it will no longer either be, or be thought to be, impossible for human beings to exert themselves strenuously in procuring benefits which are not to be exclusively their own, but to be shared with the society they belong to. The social problem of the future we considered to be, how to unite the greatest individual liberty of action, with a common ownership in the raw material of

the globe, and an equal participation of all in the benefits
of combined labour. We had not the presumption to suppose that we could already foresee, by what precise form of
institutions these objects could most effectually be attained,
or at how near or how distant a period they would become practicable. We saw clearly that to render any such
social transformation either possible or desirable, an equivalent change of character must take place both in the uncultivated herd who now compose the labouring masses, and
in the immense majority of their employers. Both these
classes must learn by practice to labour and combine for
generous, or at all events for public and social purposes, and
not, as hitherto, solely for narrowly interested ones. But
the capacity to do this has always existed in mankind, and
is not, nor is ever likely to be, extinct. Education, habit,
and the cultivation of the sentiments, will make a common
man dig or weave for his country, as readily as fight for
his country. True enough, it is only by slow degrees, and a
system of culture prolonged through successive generations,
that men in general can be brought up to this point. But the
hindrance is not in the essential constitution of human
nature. Interest in the common good is at present so weak a
motive in the generality, not because it can never be otherwise, but because the mind is not accustomed to dwell on it
as it dwells from morning till night on things which tend
only to personal advantage. When called into activity, as
only self-interest now is, by the daily course of life, and
spurred from behind by the love of distinction and the fear
of shame, it is capable of producing, even in common men,
the most strenuous exertions as well as the most heroic sacrifices. The deep-rooted selfishness which forms the general
character of the existing state of society, is *so* deeply rooted,
only because the whole course of existing institutions tends
to foster it; and modern institutions in some respects more
than ancient, since the occasion on which the individual is
called on to do anything for the public without receiving
its pay, are far less frequent in modern life, than in the
smaller commonwealths of antiquity. These considerations
did not make us overlook the folly of premature attempts to
dispense with the inducement of private interest in social

affairs, while no substitute for them has been or can be provided: but we regarded all existing institutions and social arrangements as being (in a phrase I once heard from Austin) "merely provisional," and we welcomed with the greatest pleasure and interest all socialistic experiments by select individuals (such as the Co-operative Societies), which, whether they succeeded or failed, could not but operate as a most useful education of those who took part in them, by cultivating their capacity of acting upon motives pointing directly to the general good, or making them aware of the defects which render them and others incapable of doing so.

In the "Principles of Political Economy," these opinions were promulgated, less clearly and fully in the first edition, rather more so in the second, and quite unequivocally in the third. The difference arose partly from the change of times, the first edition having been written and sent to press before the French Revolution of 1848, after which the public mind became more open to the reception of novelties in opinion, and doctrines appeared moderate which would have been thought very startling a short time before. In the first edition the difficulties of socialism were stated so strongly, that the tone was on the whole that of opposition to it. In the year or two which followed, much time was given to the study of the best Socialistic writers on the Continent, and to meditation and discussion on the whole range of topics involved in the controversy: and the result was that most of what had been written on the subject in the first edition was cancelled, and replaced by arguments and reflections which represent a more advanced opinion.

The Political Economy was far more rapidly executed than the Logic, or indeed than anything of importance which I had previously written. It was commenced in the autumn of 1845, and was ready for the press before the end of 1847. In this period of little more than two years there was an interval of six months during which the work was laid aside, while I was writing articles in the Morning Chronicle (which unexpectedly entered warmly into my purpose) urging the formation of peasant properties on the waste lands of Ireland. This was during the period of the

Famine, the winter of 1846-47, when the stern necessities of the time seemed to afford a chance of gaining attention for what appeared to me the only mode of combining relief to immediate destitution with permanent improvement of the social and economical condition of the Irish people. But the idea was new and strange; there was no English precedent for such a proceeding: and the profound ignorance of English politicians and the English public concerning all social phenomena not generally met with in England (however common elsewhere,) made my endeavours an entire failure. Instead of a great operation on the waste lands, and the conversion of cottiers into proprietors, Parliament passed a Poor Law for maintaining them as paupers: and if the nation has not since found itself in inextricable difficulties from the joint operation of the old evils and the quack remedy, it is indebted for its deliverance to that most unexpected and surprising fact, the depopulation of Ireland, commenced by famine, and continued by emigration.

The rapid success of the Political Economy showed that the public wanted, and were prepared for such a book. Published early in 1848, an edition of a thousand copies was sold in less than a year. Another similar edition was published in the spring of 1849; and a third, of 1250 copies, early in 1852. It was, from the first, continually cited and referred to as an authority, because it was not a book merely of abstract science, but also of application, and treated Political Economy not as a thing by itself, but as a fragment of a greater whole; a branch of Social Philosophy, so interlinked with all the other branches, that its conclusions, even in its own peculiar province, are only true conditionally, subject to interference and counteraction from causes not directly within its scope: while to the character of a practical guide it has no pretension, apart from other classes of considerations. Political Economy, in truth, has never pretended to give advice to mankind with no lights but its own; though people who knew nothing but political economy (and therefore knew that ill) have taken upon themselves to advise, and could only do so by such lights as they had. But the numerous sentimental enemies of political economy, and its still more numerous interested enemies in-

sentimental guise, have been very successful in gaining belief for this among other unmerited imputations against
it, and the "Principles" having, in spite of the freedom of
many of its opinions, become for the present the most
popular treatise on the subject, has helped to disarm the
enemies of so important a study. The amount of its worth
as an exposition of the science, and the value of the different applications which it suggests, others, of course must
judge.

For a considerable time after this, I published no work
of magnitude; though I still occasionally wrote in periodicals,
and my correspondence (much of it with persons quite unknown to me), on subjects of public interest, swelled to a
considerable bulk. During these years I wrote or commenced various Essays, for eventual publication, on some of
the fundamental questions of human and social life, with
regard to several of which I have already much exceeded
the severity of the Horatian precept. I continued to watch
with keen interest the progress of public events. But it was
not, on the whole, very encouraging to me. The European
reaction after 1848, and the success of an unprincipled
usurper in December, 1851, put an end, as it seemed, to all
present hope of freedom or social improvement in France
and the Continent. In England, I had seen and continued
to see many of the opinions of my youth obtain general
recognition, and many of the reforms in institutions, for
which I had through life contended, either effected or in
course of being so. But these changes had been attended
with much less benefit to human well-being than I should
formerly have anticipated, because they had produced very
little improvement in that which all amelioration in the
lot of mankind depends on, their intellectual and moral
state: and it might even be questioned if the various causes
of deterioration which had been at work in the meanwhile,
had not more than counterbalanced the tendencies to improvement. I had learnt from experience that many false
opinions may be changed for true ones, without in the
least altering the habits of mind of which false opinions
are the result. The English public, for example, are quite
as raw and undiscerning on subjects of political economy

since the nation has been converted to free-trade, as they were before; and are still further from having acquired better habits of thought or feeling, or being in any way better fortified against error, on subjects of a more elevated character. For, though they have thrown off certain errors, the general discipline of their minds, intellectually and morally, is not altered. I am now convinced, that no great improvements in the lot of mankind are possible, until a great change takes place in the fundamental constitution of their modes of thought. The old opinions in religion, morals, and politics, are so much discredited in the more intellectual minds as to have lost the greater part of their efficacy for good, while they have still life enough in them to be a powerful obstacle to the growing up of any better opinions on those subjects. When the philosophic minds of the world can no longer believe its religion, or can only believe it with modifications amounting to an essential change of its character, a transitional period commences, of weak convictions, paralysed intellects, and growing laxity of principle, which cannot terminate until a renovation has been effected in the basis of their belief leading to the evolution of some faith, whether religious or merely human, which they can really believe: and when things are in this state, all thinking or writing which does not tend to promote such a renovation, is of very little value beyond the moment. Since there was little in the apparent condition of the public mind, indicative of any tendency in this direction, my view of the immediate prospects of human improvement was not sanguine. More recently a spirit of free speculation has sprung up, giving a more encouraging prospect of the gradual mental emancipation of England; and concurring with the renewal under better auspices, of the movement for political freedom in the rest of Europe, has given to the present condition of human affairs a more hopeful aspect.[1]

Between the time of which I have now spoken, and the present, took place the most important events of my private life. The first of these was my marriage, in April, 1851, to the lady whose incomparable worth had made her friendship the greatest source to me both of happiness and of improve-

[1] Written about 1861.

ment during many years in which we never expected to be
in any closer relation to one another. Ardently as I should
have aspired to this complete union of our lives at any time
in the course of my existence at which it had been practicable, I, as much as my wife, would far rather have foregone
that privilege for ever, than have owed it to the premature
death of one for whom I had the sincerest respect, and she
the strongest affection. That event, however, having taken
place in July, 1849, it was granted to me to derive from that
evil my own greatest good, by adding to the partnership of
thought, feeling, and writing which had long existed, a
partnership of our entire existence. For seven and a half
years that blessing was mine; for seven and a half only! I
can say nothing which could describe, even in the faintest
manner, what that loss was and is. But because I know
that she would have wished it, I endeavour to make the best
of what life I have left, and to work on for her purposes with
such diminished strength as can be derived from thoughts
of her, and communion with her memory.

When two persons have their thoughts and speculations
completely in common; when all subjects of intellectual or
moral interest are discussed between them in daily life, and
probed to much greater depths than are usually or conveni-
ently sounded in writings intended for general readers;
when they set out from the same principles, and arrive at
their conclusions by processes pursued jointly, it is of little
consequence in respect to the question of originality, which
of them holds the pen; the one who contributes least to the
composition may contribute most to the thought; the writings which result are the joint product of both, and it must
often be impossible to disentangle their respective parts, and
affirm that this belongs to one and that to the other. In this
wide sense, not only during the years of our married life,
but during many of the years of confidential friendship
which preceded, all my published writings were as much her
work as mine; her share in them constantly increasing as
years advanced. But in certain cases, what belongs to her
can be distinguished, and specially identified. Over and
above the general influence which her mind had over mine,
the most valuable ideas and features in these joint produc-

tions—those which have been most fruitful of important
results, and have contributed most to the success and reputation of the works themselves—originated with her, were
emanations from her mind, my part in them being no greater
than in any of the thoughts which I found in previous
writers, and made my own only by incorporating them with
my own system of thought. During the greater part of
my literary life I have performed the office in relation to her,
which from a rather early period I had considered as the
most useful part that I was qualified to take in the domain
of thought, that of an interpreter of original thinkers, and
mediator between them and the public; for I had always a
humble opinion of my own powers as an original thinker,
except in abstract science (logic, metaphysics, and the theoretic principles of political economy and politics), but
thought myself much superior to most of my contemporaries
in willingness and ability to learn from everybody; as I
found hardly any one who made such a point of examining
what was said in defence of all opinions, however new or
however old, in the conviction that even if they were errors
there might be a substratum of truth underneath them, and
that in any case the discovery of what it was that made them
plausible, would be a benefit to truth. I had, in consequence,
marked this out as a sphere of usefulness in which I was
under a special obligation to make myself active: the more
so, as the acquaintance I had formed with the ideas of the
Coleridgians, of the German thinkers, and of Carlyle, all of
them fiercely opposed to the mode of thought in which I had
been brought up, had convinced me that along with much
error they possessed much truth, which was veiled from
minds otherwise capable of receiving it by the transcendental and mystical phraseology in which they were accustomed
to shut it up, and from which they neither cared, nor knew
how, to disengage it; and I did not despair of separating the
truth from the error, and exposing it in terms which would
be intelligible and not repulsive to those on my own side
in philosophy. Thus prepared, it will easily be believed
that when I came into close intellectual communion with a
person of the most eminent faculties, whose genius, as it
grew and unfolded itself in thought, continually struck out

truths far in advance of me, but in which I could not, as I
had done in those others, detect any mixture of error, the
greatest part of my mental growth consisted in the assimilation of those truths, and the most valuable part of my intellectual work was in building the bridges and clearing the
paths which connected them with my general system of
thought.[1]

The first of my books in which her share was conspicuous
was the " Principles of Political Economy." The " System
of Logic " owed little to her except in the minuter matters
of composition, in which respect my writings, both great and
small, have largely benefited by her accurate and clear-
sighted criticism.[2] The chapter of the Political Economy

[1] The steps in my mental growth for which I was indebted to her were
far from being those which a person wholly uninformed on the subject
would probably suspect. It might be supposed, for instance, that my
strong convictions on the complete equality in all legal, political, social
and domestic relations, which ought to exist between men and women,
may have been adopted or learnt from her. This was so far from being
the fact, that those convictions were among the earliest results of the
application of my mind to political subjects, and the strength with which
I held them was, as I believe, more than anything else, the originating
cause of the interest she felt in me. What is true is, that until I knew
her, the opinion was in my mind, little more than an abstract principle.
I saw no more reason why women should be held in legal subjection to
other people, than why men should. I was certain that their interests
required fully as much protection as those of men, and were quite as
little likely to obtain it without an equal voice in making the laws by
which they were to be bound. But that perception of the vast practical
bearings of women's disabilities which found expression in the book on
the " Subjection of Women " was acquired mainly through her teaching.
But for her rare knowledge of human nature and comprehension of moral
and social influences, though I should doubtless have held my present opinions, I should have had a very insufficient perception of the mode in which
the consequences of the inferior position of women intertwine themselves
with all the evils of existing society and with all the difficulties of human
improvement. I am indeed painfully conscious of how much of her best
thoughts on the subject I have failed to reproduce, and how greatly that
little treatise falls short of what would have been if she had put on paper
her entire mind on this question, or had lived to revise and improve, as
she certainly would have done, my imperfect statement of the case.

[2] The only person from whom I received any direct assistance in the
preparation of the System of Logic was Mr. Bain, since so justly celebrated
for his philosophical writings. He went carefully through the manuscript
before it was sent to press, and enriched it with a great number of additional examples and illustrations from science; many of which, as well as
some detached remarks of his own in confirmation of my logical views,
I inserted nearly in his own words.

My obligations to Comte were only to his writings—to the part which
had then been published of his " Système de Philosophie Positive: " and,
as has been seen from what I have already said in this narrative, the
amount of these obligations is far less than has sometimes been asserted.
The first volume, which contains all the fundamental doctrines of the book,
was substantially complete before I had seen Comte's treatise. I derived
from him many valuable thoughts, conspicuously in the chapter on Hypotheses and in the view taken of the logic of Algebra: but it is only in
the concluding Book, on the Logic of the Moral Sciences, that I owe to

which has had a greater influence on opinion than all the rest, that on "The Probable Future of the Labouring Classes," is entirely due to her: in the first draft of the book, that chapter did not exist. She pointed out the need of such a chapter, and the extreme imperfection of the book without it: she was the cause of my writing it; and the more general part of the chapter, the statement and discussion of the two opposite theories respecting the proper condition of the labouring classes, was wholly an exposition of her thoughts, often in words taken from her own lips. The purely scientific part of the Political Economy I did not learn from her; but it was chiefly her influence that gave to the book that general tone by which it is distinguished from all previous expositions of Political Economy that had any pretension to being scientific, and which has made it so useful in conciliating minds which those previous expositions had repelled. This tone consisted chiefly in making the proper distinction between the laws of the Production of Wealth, which are real laws of nature, dependent on the properties of objects, and the modes of its Distribution, which, subject to certain conditions, depend on human will. The common run of political economists confuse these together, under the resignation of economic laws, which they deem incapable of being defeated or modified by human effort; ascribing the same necessity to things dependent on the unchangeable conditions of our earthly existence, and to those which, being but the necessary consequences of particular social arrangements, are merely co-extensive with these: given certain institutions and customs, wages, profits, and rent will be determined by certain causes; but this class of political economists drop the indispensable presupposition, and argue that these causes must, by an inherent necessity against which no human means can avail, determine the shares which fall, in the division of the produce, to labourers, capitalists, and landlords. The "Principles of Political Economy" yielded to none of its predecessors in aiming at the scientific appreciation of the action of these causes, under the conditions which they presuppose; but it set the

him any radical improvement in my conception of the application of logical method. This improvement I have stated and characterized in a former part of the present Memoir.

example of not treating those conditions as final. The economic generalizations which depend, not on necessities of nature but on those combined with the existing arrangements of society, it deals with only as provisional, and as liable to be much altered by the progress of social improvement. I had indeed partially learnt this view of things from the thoughts awakened in me by the speculations of the St. Simonians; but it was made a living principle pervading and animating the book by my wife's promptings. This example illustrates well the general character of what she contributed to my writings. What was abstract and purely scientific was generally mine; the properly human element came from her: in all that concerned the application of philosophy to the exigencies of human society and progress, I was her pupil, alike in boldness of speculation and cautiousness of practical judgment. For, on the one hand, she was much more courageous and far-sighted than without her I should have been, in anticipations of an order of things to come, in which many of the limited generalizations now so often confounded with universal principles will cease to be applicable. Those parts of my writings, and especially of the Political Economy, which contemplate possibilities in the future such as, when affirmed by socialists, have in general been fiercely denied by political economists, would, but for her, either have been absent, or the suggestions would have been made much more timidly and in a more qualified form. But while she thus rendered me bolder in speculation on human affairs, her practical turn of mind, and her almost unerring estimate of practical obstacles, repressed in me all tendencies that were really visionary. Her mind invested all ideas in a concrete shape, and formed to itself a conception of how they would actually work: and her knowledge of the existing feelings and conduct of mankind was so seldom at fault, that the weak point in any unworkable suggestion seldom escaped her.[1]

During the years which intervened between the commencement of my married life and the catastrophe which closed it,

[1] A few dedicatory lines acknowledging what the book owed to her, were prefixed to some of the presentation copies of the Political Economy on its first publication. Her dislike of publicity alone prevented their insertion in the other copies of the work.

the principal occurrences of my outward existence (unless I count as such a first attack of the family disease, and a consequent journey of more than six months for the recovery of health, in Italy, Sicily, and Greece) had reference to my position in the India House. In 1856 I was promoted to the rank of chief of the office in which I had served for upwards of thirty-three years. The appointment, that of Examiner of India Correspondence, was the highest, next to that of Secretary, in the East India Company's home service, involving the general superintendence of all the correspondence with the Indian Governments, except the military, naval, and financial. I held this office as long as it continued to exist, being a little more than two years; after which it pleased Parliament, in other words, Lord Palmerston, to put an end to the East India Company as a branch of the Government of India under the Crown, and convert the administration of that country into a thing to be scrambled for by the second and third class of English parliamentary politicians. I was the chief manager of the resistance which the Company made to their own political extinction, and to the letters and petitions I wrote for them, and the concluding chapter of my treatise on Representative Government, I must refer for my opinions on the folly and mischief of this ill-considered change. Personally I considered myself a gainer by it, as I had given enough of my life to India, and was not unwilling to retire on the liberal compensation granted. After the change was consummated, Lord Stanley, the First Secretary of State for India, made me the honourable offer of a seat in the Council, and the proposal was subsequently renewed by the Council itself, on the first occasion of its having to supply a vacancy in its own body. But the conditions of Indian Government under the new system made me anticipate nothing but useless vexation and waste of effort from any participation in it: and nothing that has since happened has had any tendency to make me regret my refusal.

During the two years which immediately preceded the cessation of my official life, my wife and I were working together at the "Liberty." I had first planned and written it as a short essay in 1854. It was in mounting the steps of

the Capitol, in January, 1855, that the thought first arose
of converting it into a volume. None of my writings have
been either so carefully composed, or so sedulously corrected as this. After it had been written as usual twice
over, we kept it by us, bringing it out from time to time,
and going through it *de novo,* reading, weighing, and criticising every sentence. Its final revision was to have been a
work of the winter of 1858-9, the first after my retirement, which we had arranged to pass in the South of Europe.
That hope and every other were frustrated by the most
unexpected and bitter calamity of her death—at Avignon,
on our way to Montpellier, from a sudden attack of pulmonary congestion.

Since then I have sought for such alleviation as my state
admitted of, by the mode of life which most enabled me to
feel her still near me. I bought a cottage as close as possible to the place where she is buried, and there her daughter
(my fellow-sufferer and now my chief comfort) and I,
live constantly during a great portion of the year. My
objects in life are solely those which were hers; my pursuits and occupations those in which she shared, or sympathized, and which are indissolubly associated with her. Her
memory is to me a religion, and her approbation the standard by which, summing up as it does all worthiness, I endeavour to regulate my life.[1]

After my irreparable loss, one of my earliest cares was to
print and publish the treatise, so much of which was the
work of her whom I had lost, and consecrate it to her memory. I have made no alteration or addition to it, nor shall I
ever. Though it wants the last touch of her hand, no substitute for that touch shall ever be attempted by mine.

The "Liberty" was more directly and literally our joint
production than anything else which bears my name, for
there was not a sentence of it which was not several times
gone through by us together, turned over in many ways,
and carefully weeded of any faults, either in thought or
expression, that we detected in it. It is in consequence of
this that, although it never underwent her final revision, it

---

[1] What precedes was written or revised previous to, or during the year
1861. What follows was written in 1870.

far surpasses, as a mere specimen of composition, anything which has proceeded from me either before or since. With regard to the thoughts, it is difficult to identify any particular part or element as being more hers than all the rest. The whole mode of thinking of which the book was the expression, was emphatically hers. But I also was so thoroughly imbued with it, that the same thoughts naturally occurred to us both. That I was thus penetrated with it, however, I owe in a great degree to her. There was a moment in my mental progress when I might easily have fallen into a tendency towards over-government, both social and political; as there was also a moment when, by reaction from a contrary excess, I might have become a less thorough radical and democrat than I am. In both these points, as in many others, she benefited me as much by keeping me right where I was right, as by leading me to new truths, and ridding me of errors. My great readiness and eagerness to learn from everybody, and to make room in my opinions for every new acquisition by adjusting the old and the new to one another, might, but for her steadying influence, have seduced me into modifying my early opinions too much. She was in nothing more valuable to my mental development than by her just measure of the relative importance of different considerations, which often protected me from allowing to truths I had only recently learnt to see, a more important place in my thoughts than was properly their due.

The "Liberty" is likely to survive longer than anything else that I have written (with the possible exception of the "Logic"), because the conjunction of her mind with mine has rendered it a kind of philosophic text-book of a single truth, which the changes progressively taking place in modern society tend to bring out into ever stronger relief: the importance, to man and society, of a large variety in types of character, and of giving full freedom to human nature to expand itself in innumerable and conflicting directions. Nothing can better show how deep are the foundations of this truth, than the great impression made by the exposition of it at a time which, to superficial observation, did not seem to stand much in need of such a lesson. The fears we expressed, lest the inevitable growth of social equality and of the government of public opinion, should impose on mankind an oppressive yoke of uniformity in opinion and practice, might easily have appeared chimerical to those who looked more at present facts than at tendencies; for the gradual revolution that is taking place in society and institutions has, thus far, been decidedly favourable to the development of new opinions, and has procured for them a much more unprejudiced hearing than they previously met with. But this is a feature belonging to periods of transition, when old notions and feelings have been unsettled, and no new doctrines have yet succeeded to their ascendancy. At such times people of any mental activity, having given up their old beliefs, and not feeling quite sure that those they still retain can stand unmodified, listen eagerly to new opinions. But this state of thing; is necessarily transitory: some particular body of doctrine in time rallies the majority round it, organizes social institutions and modes of action conformably to itself, education impresses this new creed upon the new generations without the mental processes that have led to it, and by degrees it acquires the very same power of compression, so long exercised by the creeds of which it had taken the place. Whether this noxious power will be exercised, depends on whether mankind have by that time become aware that it cannot be exercised without stunt· ing and dwarfing human nature. It is then that the teachings of the " Liberty " will have their greatest value. And it is to be feared that they will retain that value a long time.

As regards originality, it has of course no other than that which every thoughtful mind gives to its own mode of conceiving and expressing truths which are common property. The leading thought of the book is one which though in many ages confined to insulated thinkers, mankind have probably at no time since the beginning of civilization been entirely without. To speak only of the last few generations, it is distinctly contained in the vein of important thought respecting education and culture, spread through the European mind by the labours and genius of Pestalozzi. The unqualified championship of it by Wilhelm von Humboldt is referred to in the book; but he by no means stood alone in his own

country. During the early part of the present century the
doctrine of the rights of individuality, and the claim of the
moral nature to develop itself in its own way, was pushed
by a whole school of German authors even to exaggeration;
and the writings of Goethe, the most celebrated of all German authors, though not belonging to that or to any other
school, are penetrated throughout by views of morals and
of conduct in life, often in my opinion not defensible,
but which are incessantly seeking whatever defence they
admit of in the theory of the right and duty of self-development. In our own country, before the book " On Liberty "
was written, the doctrine of Individuality had been enthusi-
astically asserted, in a style of vigorous declamation sometimes reminding one of Fichte, by Mr. William Maccall,
in a series of writings of which the most elaborate is entitled " Elements of Individualism:" and a remarkable
American, Mr. Warren, had formed a System of Society, on
the foundation of the " Sovereignty of the Individual," had
obtained a number of followers, and had actually commenced
the formation of a Village Community (whether it now
exists I know not), which, though bearing a superficial resemblance to some of the projects of Socialists, is diamet-
rically opposite to them in principle, since it recognises no
authority whatever in Society over the individual, except to
enforce equal freedom of development for all individualities.
As the book which bears my name claimed no originality
for any of its doctrines, and was not intended to write their
history, the only author who had preceded me in their assertion, of whom I thought it appropriate to say anything, was
Humboldt, who furnished the motto to the work; although
in one passage I borrowed from the Warrenites their phrase,
the sovereignty of the individual. It is hardly necessary
here to remark that there are abundant differences in detail,
between the conception of the doctrine by any of the predecessors I have mentioned, and that set forth in the book.

The political circumstances of the time induced me,
shortly after, to complete and publish a pamphlet
(" Thoughts on Parliamentary Reform "), part of which
had been written some years previously, on the occasion of
one of the abortive Reform Bills, and had at the time been

approved and revised by her. Its principal features were, hostility to the Ballot (a change of opinion in both of us, in which she rather preceded me), and a claim of representation for minorities; not, however, at that time going beyond the cumulative vote proposed by Mr. Garth Marshall. In finishing the pamphlet for publication, with a view to the discussions on the Reform Bill of Lord Derby's and Mr. Disraeli's government in 1859, I added a third feature, a plurality of votes to be given, not to property, but to proved superiority of education. This recommended itself to me as a means of reconciling the irresistible claim of every man or woman to be consulted, and to be allowed a voice, in the regulation of affairs which vitally concern them, with the superiority of weight justly due to opinions grounded on superiority of knowledge. The suggestion, however, was one which I had never discussed with my almost infallible counsellor, and I have no evidence that she would have concurred in it. As far as I have been able to observe, it has found favour with nobody; all who desire any sort of inequality in the electoral vote, desiring it in favour of property and not of intelligence or knowledge. If it ever overcomes the strong feeling which exists against it, this will only be after the establishment of a systematic National Education by which the various grades of politically valuable acquirement may be accurately defined and authenticated. Without this it will always remain liable to strong, possibly conclusive, objections; and with this, it would perhaps not be needed.

It was soon after the publication of " Thoughts on Parliamentary Reform," that I became acquainted with Mr. Hare's admirable system of Personal Representation, which, in its present shape, was then for the first time published. I saw in this great practical and philosophical idea, the greatest improvement of which the system of representative government is susceptible; an improvement which, in the most felicitous manner, exactly meets and cures the grand, and what before seemed the inherent, defect of the representative system; that of giving to a numerical majority all power, instead of only a power proportional to its numbers, and enabling the strongest party to exclude all weaker parties from making their opinions heard in the assembly of the nation, except through such opportunity as may be given to them by the accidentally unequal distribution of opinions in different localities. To these great evils nothing more than very imperfect palliations had seemed possible; but Mr. Hare's system affords a radical cure. This great discovery, for it is no less, in the political art, inspired me, as I believe it has inspired all thoughtful persons who have adopted it, with new and more sanguine hopes respecting the prospects of human society; by freeing the form of political institutions towards which the whole civilized world is manifestly and irresistibly tending, from the chief part of what seemed to qualify, or render doubtful, its ultimate benefits. Minorities, so long as they remain minorities, are, and ought to be, outvoted; but under arrangements which enable any assemblage of voters, amounting to a certain number, to place in the legislature a representative of its own choice, minorities cannot be suppressed. Independent opinions will force their way into the council of the nation and make themselves heard there, a thing which often cannot happen in the existing forms of representative democracy; and the legislature, instead of being weeded of individual peculiarities and entirely made up of men who simply represent the creed of great political or religious parties, will comprise a large proportion of the most eminent individual minds in the country, placed there, without reference to party, by voters who appreciate their individual eminence. I can understand that persons, otherwise intelligent, should, for want of sufficient examination, be repelled from Mr. Hare's plan by what they think the complex nature of its machinery. But any one who does not feel the want which the scheme is intended to supply; any one who throws it over as a mere theoretical subtlety or crotchet, tending to no valuable purpose, and unworthy of the attention of practical men, may be pronounced an incompetent statesman, unequal to the politics of the future. I mean, unless he is a minister or aspires to become one: for we are quite accustomed to a minister continuing to profess unqualified hostility to an improvement almost to the very day when his conscience, or his interest, induces him to take it up as a public measure, and **carry it.**

Had I met with Mr. Hare's system before the publication of my pamphlet, I should have given an account of it there. Not having done so, I wrote an article in Fraser's Magazine (reprinted in my miscellaneous writings) principally for that purpose, though I included in it, along with Mr. Hare's book, a review of two other productions on the question of the day; one of them a pamphlet by my early friend, Mr. John Austin, who had in his old age become an enemy to all further Parliamentary reform; the other an able and vigorous, though partially erroneous work by Mr. Lorimer.

In the course of the same summer I fulfilled a duty particularly incumbent upon me, that of helping (by an article in the Edinburgh Review) to make known Mr. Bain's profound treatise on the Mind, just then completed by the publication of its second volume. And I carried through the press a selection of my minor writings, forming the first two volumes of " Dissertations and Discussions." The selection had been made during my wife's lifetime, but the revision, in concert with her, with a view to republication, had been barely commenced; and when I had no longer the guidance of her judgment I despaired of pursuing it further, and republished the papers as they were, with the exception of striking out such passages as were no longer in accordance with my opinions. My literary work of the year was terminated with an essay in Fraser's Magazine, (afterwards republished in the third volume of " Dissertations and Discussions,") entitled " A Few Words on Non-Intervention." I was prompted to write this paper by a desire, while vindicating England from the imputations commonly brought against her on the Continent, of a peculiar selfishness in matters of foreign policy, to warn Englishmen of the colour given to this imputation by the low tone in which English statesmen are accustomed to speak of English policy as concerned only with English interests, and by the conduct of Lord Palmerston at that particular time in opposing the Suez Canal: and I took the opportunity of expressing ideas which had long been in my mind (some of them generated by my Indian experience, and others by the international questions which then greatly occupied the European public), respecting the true principles of international morality, and the legitimate modifications made in it by difference of times and circumstances; a subject I had already, to some extent, discussed in the vindication of the French Provisional Government of 1848 against the attacks of Lord Brougham and others, which I published at the time in the Westminster Review, and which is reprinted in the " Dissertations."

I had now settled, as I believed, for the remainder of my existence into a purely literary life: if that can be called literary which continued to be occupied in a pre-eminent degree with politics, and not merely with theoretical, but practical politics, although a great part of the year was spent at a distance of many hundred miles from the chief seat of the politics of my own country, to which, and primarily for which, I wrote. But, in truth, the modern facilities of communication have not only removed all the disadvantages, to a political writer in tolerably easy circumstances, of distance from the scene of political action, but have converted them into advantages. The immediate and regular receipt of newspapers and periodicals keeps him *au courant* of even the most temporary politics, and gives him a much more correct view of the state and progress of opinion than he could acquire by personal contact with individuals: for every one's social intercourse is more or less limited to particular sets or classes, whose impressions and no others reach him through that channel; and experience has taught me that those who give their time to the absorbing claims of what is called society, not having leisure to keep up a large acquaintance with the organs of opinion, remain much more ignorant of the general state either of the public mind, or of the active and instructed part of it, than a recluse who reads the newspapers need be. There are, no doubt, disadvantages in too long a separation from one's country—in not occasionally renewing one's impressions of the light in which men and things appear when seen from a position in the midst of them; but the deliberate judgment formed at a distance, and undisturbed by inequalities of perspective, is the most to be depended on, even for application to practice. Alternating between the two positions, I combined the advantages of both. And, though the inspirer of my best thoughts was

no longer with me, I was not alone: she had left a daughter
my step-daughter,   *   *   *   *   *
*   *   *   *   *   *   *   *
*   *   *   *   * whose ever growing and
ripening talents from that day to this have been devoted
to the same great purposes   *   *   *   *
*   *   *   *   *   *   *   *
Surely no one ever before was so fortunate, as, after such
a loss as mine, to draw another prize in the lottery of life.
*   *   *   *   *   *   *   *
*   *   *   Whoever, either now or hereafter,
may think of me and of the work I have done, must never
forget that it is the product not of one intellect and conscience, but of three   *   *   *   *   *
*   *   *   *   *   *   *   *
*   *   *   *   *   *   *   *

The work of the years 1860 and 1861 consisted chiefly of
two treatises, only one of which was intended for immediate
publication. This was the " Considerations on Representative Government; " a connected exposition of what, by the
thoughts of many years, I had come to regard as the best
form of a popular constitution. Along with as much of the
general theory of government as is necessary to support
this particular portion of its practice, the volume contains
my matured views of the principal questions which occupy
the present age, within the province of purely organic institutions, and raises, by anticipation, some other questions to
which growing necessities will sooner or later compel the
attention both of theoretical and of practical politicians. The
chief of these last, is the distinction between the function of
making laws, for which a numerous popular assembly is
radically unfit, and that of getting good laws made, which is
its proper duty and cannot be satisfactorily fulfilled by any
other authority: and the consequent need of a Legislative
Commission, as a permanent part of the constitution of a
free country; consisting of a small number of highly trained
political minds, on whom, when Parliament has determined
that a law shall be made, the task of making it should be
devolved: Parliament retaining the power of passing or rejecting the bill when drawn up, but not of altering it other-

wise than by sending proposed amendments to be dealt with
by the Commission. The question here raised respecting the
most important of all public functions, that of legislation, is
a particular case of the great problem of modern political
organization, stated, I believe, for the first time in its full
extent by Bentham, though in my opinion not always satisfactorily resolved by him; the combination of complete
popular control over public affairs, with the greatest attainable perfection of skilled agency.

The other treatise written at this time is the one which
was published some years later[1] under the title of " The
Subjection of Women." It was written   *   *
*   *   *   *   *   that there might, in
any event, be in existence a written exposition of my opinions on that great question, as full and conclusive as I could
make it. The intention was to keep this among other unpublished papers, improving it from time to time if I was able,
and to publish it at the time when it should seem likely
to be most useful. As ultimately published   *   *
*   *   *   *   *   *   *   *
in what was of my own composition, all that is most striking
and profound belongs to my wife; coming from the fund of
thought which had been made common to us both, by our
innumerable conversations and discussions on a topic which
filled so large a place in our minds.

Soon after this time I took from their repository a portion
of the unpublished papers which I had written during the
last years of our married life, and shaped them, with some
additional matter, into the little work entitled " Utilitarianism; " which was first published, in three parts, in successive numbers of Fraser's Magazine, and afterwards reprinted in a volume.

Before this, however, the state of public affairs had become
extremely critical, by the commencement of the American
civil war. My strongest feelings were engaged in this
struggle, which, I felt from the beginning, was destined to
be a turning point, for good or evil, of the course of human
affairs for an indefinite duration. Having been a deeply interested observer of the slavery quarrel in America, during

[1] In 1869.

the many years that preceded the open breach, I knew that it was in all its stages an aggressive enterprise of the slave-owners to extend the territory of slavery; under the combined influences of pecuniary interest, domineering temper, and the fanaticism of a class for its class privileges, influences so fully and powerfully depicted in the admirable work of my friend Professor Cairnes, " The Slave Power." Their success, if they succeeded, would be a victory of the powers of evil which would give courage to the enemies of progress and damp the spirits of its friends all over the civilized world, while it would create a formidable military power, grounded on the worst and most anti-social form of the tyranny of men over men, and, by destroying for a long time the prestige of the great democratic republic, would give to all the privileged classes of Europe a false confidence, probably only to be extinguished in blood. On the other hand, if the spirit of the North was sufficiently roused to carry the war to a successful termination, and if that termination did not come too soon and too easily, I foresaw, from the laws of human nature, and the experience of revolutions, that when it did come it would in all probability be thorough: that the bulk of the Northern population, whose conscience had as yet been awakened only to the point of resisting the further extension of slavery, but whose fidelity to the Constitution of the United States made them disapprove of any attempt by the Federal Government to interfere with slavery in the States where it already existed, would acquire feelings of another kind when the Constitution had been shaken off by armed rebellion, would determine to have done for ever with the accursed thing, and would join their banner with that of the noble body of Abolitionists, of whom Garrison was the courageous and single-minded apostle, Wendell Phillips the eloquent orator, and John Brown the voluntary martyr.[1] Then, too, the whole mind of the United States would be let loose from its bonds, no longer corrupted by the supposed necessity of apologizing to foreigners for the most flagrant of all possible violations of the free principles of their Constitution; while the tendency of a fixed state of

[1] The saying of this true hero, after his capture, that he was worth more for hanging than for any other purpose, reminds one, by its combination of wit, wisdom, and self-devotion, of Sir Thomas More.

society to stereotype a set of national opinions would be at least temporarily checked, and the national mind would become more open to the recognition of whatever was bad in either the institutions or the customs of the people. These hopes, so far as related to slavery, have been completely, and in other respects are in course of being progressively realized. Foreseeing from the first this double set of consequences from the success or failure of the rebellion, it may be imagined with what feelings I contemplated the rush of nearly the whole upper and middle classes of my own country, even those who passed for Liberals, into a furious pro-Southern partisanship: the working classes, and some of the literary and scientific men, being almost the sole exceptions to the general frenzy. I never before felt so keenly how little permanent improvement had reached the minds of our influential classes, and of what small value were the Liberal opinions they had got into the habit of professing. None of the Continental Liberals committed the same frightful mistake. But the generation which had extorted negro emancipation from our West India planters had passed away; another had succeeded which had not learnt by many years of discussion and exposure to feel strongly the enormities of slavery; and the inattention habitual with Englishmen to whatever is going on in the world outside their own island, made them profoundly ignorant of all the antecedents of the struggle, insomuch that it was not generally believed in England, for the first year or two of the war, that the quarrel was one of slavery. There were men of high principle and unquestionable liberality of opinion, who thought it a dispute about tariffs, or assimilated it to the cases in which they were accustomed to sympathize, of a people struggling for independence.

It was my obvious duty to be one of the small minority who protested against this perverted state of public opinion. I was not the first to protest. It ought to be remembered to the honour of Mr. Hughes and of Mr. Ludlow, that they, by writings published at the very beginning of the struggle, began the protestation. Mr. Bright followed in one of the most powerful of his speeches, followed by others not less striking. I was on the point of adding my word to theirs, when there occurred, towards the end of 1861, the seizure of the Southern envoys on board a British vessel, by an officer of the United States. Even English forgetfulness has not yet had time to lose all remembrance of the explosion of feeling in England which then burst forth, the expectation, which prevailed for some weeks, of war with the United States, and the warlike preparations actually commenced on this side. While this state of things lasted, there was no chance of a hearing for anything favourable to the American cause; and, moreover, I agreed with those who thought the act unjustifiable, and such as to require that England should demand its disavowal. When the disavowal came, and the alarm of war was over, I wrote, in January, 1862, the paper, in Fraser's Magazine, entitled "The Contest in America." * * * * * Written and published when it was, this paper helped to encourage those Liberals who had felt overborne by the tide of illiberal opinion, and to form in favour of the good cause a nucleus of opinion which increased gradually, and, after the success of the North began to seem probable, rapidly. When we returned from our journey I wrote a second article, a review of Professor Cairnes' book, published in the Westminster Review. England is paying the penalty, in many uncomfortable ways, of the durable resentment which her ruling classes stirred up in the United States by their ostentatious wishes for the ruin of America as a nation: they have reason to be thankful that a few, if only a few, known writers and speakers, standing firmly by the Americans in the time of their greatest difficulty, effected a partial diversion of these bitter feelings, and made Great Britain not altogether odious to the Americans.

This duty having been performed, my principal occupation for the next two years was on subjects not political. The publication of Mr. Austin's Lectures on Jurisprudence after his decease, gave me an opportunity of paying a deserved tribute to his memory, and at the same time expressing some thoughts on a subject on which, in my old days of Benthamism, I had bestowed much study. But the chief product of those years was the Examination of Sir William Hamilton's Philosophy. His Lectures, published in 1860 and 1861, I had read towards the end of the latter year, with a half-formed intention of giving an account of them in a Review, but I soon found that this would be idle, and that justice could not be done to the subject in less than a volume. I had then to consider whether it would be advisable that I myself should attempt such a performance. On consideration, there seemed to be strong reasons for doing so. I was greatly disappointed with the Lectures. I read them, certainly, with no prejudice against Sir William Hamilton. I had up to that time deferred the study of his Notes to Reid on account of their unfinished state, but I had not neglected his " Discussions in Philosophy; " and though I knew that his general mode of treating the facts of mental philosophy differed from that of which I most approved, yet his vigorous polemic against the later Transcendentalists, and his strenuous assertion of some important principles, especially the Relativity of human knowledge, gave me many points of sympathy with his opinions, and made me think that genuine psychology had considerably more to gain than to lose by his authority and reputation. His Lectures and the Dissertations on Reid dispelled this illusion: and even the Discussions, read by the light which these throw on them, lose much of their value. I found that the points of apparent agreement between his opinions and mine were more verbal than real; that the important philosophical principles which I had thought he recognized, were so explained away by him as to mean little or nothing, or were continually lost sight of, and doctrines entirely inconsistent with them were taught in nearly every part of his philosophical writings. My estimation of him was therefore so far altered, that instead of regarding him as occupying a kind of intermediate position between the two rival philosophies, holding some of the principles of both, and supplying to both powerful weapons of attack and defence, I now looked upon him as one of the pillars, and in this country from his high philosophical reputation the chief pillar, of that one of the two which seemed to me to be erroneous.

Now, the difference between these two schools of philosophy, that of Intuition, and that of Experience and Association, is not a mere matter of abstract speculation; it is full of practical consequences, and lies at the foundation of all the greatest differences of practical opinion in an age of progress. The practical reformer has continually to demand that changes be made in things which are supported by powerful and widely-spread feelings, or to question the apparent necessity and indefeasibleness of established facts; and it is often an indispensable part of his argument to show, how those powerful feelings had their origin, and how those facts came to seem necessary and indefeasible. There is therefore a natural hostility between him and a philosophy which discourages the explanation of feelings and moral facts by circumstances and association, and prefers to treat them as ultimate elements of human nature; a philosophy which is addicted to holding up favourite doctrines as intuitive truths, and deems intuition to be the voice of Nature and of God, speaking with an authority higher than that of our reason.

In particular, I have long felt that the prevailing tendency to regard all the marked distinctions of human character as innate, and in the main indelible, and to ignore the irresistible proofs that by far the greater part of those differences, whether between individuals, races, or sexes, are such as not only might but naturally would be produced by differences in circumstances, is one of the chief hindrances to the rational treatment of great social questions, and one of the greatest stumbling blocks to human improvement. This tendency has its source in the intuitional metaphysics which characterized the reaction of the nineteenth century against the eighteenth, and it is a tendency so agreeable to human indolence, as well as to conservative interests generally, that unless attacked at the very root, it is sure to be carried to even a greater length than is really justified by the more moderate forms of the intuitional philosophy. That philosophy, not always in its moderate forms, had ruled the thought of Europe for the greater part of a century. My father's Analysis of the Mind, my own Logic, and Professor Bain's great treatise, had attempted to re-introduce a better mode of philosophizing, latterly with quite as much success as could be expected; but I had for some time felt that the mere contrast of the two philosophies was not enough, that there ought to be a hand-to-hand fight between them, that controversial as well as expository writings were needed, and that the time was come when such controversy would be useful. Considering then the writings and fame of Sir W. Hamilton as the great fortress of the intuitional philosophy in this country, a fortress the more formidable from the imposing character, and the in many respects great personal merits and mental endowments, of the man, I thought it might be a real service to philosophy to attempt a thorough examination of all his most important doctrines, and an estimate of his general claims to eminence as a philosopher, and I was confirmed in this resolution by observing that in the writings of at least one, and him one of the ablest, of Sir W. Hamilton's followers, his peculiar doctrines were made the justification of a view of religion which I hold to be profoundly immoral—that it is our duty to bow down in worship before a Being whose natural attributes are affirmed to be unknowable by us, and to be perhaps extremely different from those which, when we are speaking of our fellow creatures, we call by the same names.

As I advanced in my task, the damage to Sir W. Hamilton's reputation became greater than I at first expected, through the almost incredible multitude of inconsistencies which showed themselves on comparing different passages with one another. It was my business, however, to show things exactly as they were, and I did not flinch from it. I endeavoured always to treat the philosopher whom I criticised with the most scrupulous fairness; and I knew that he had abundance of disciples and admirers to correct me if I ever unintentionally did him injustice. Many of them accordingly have answered me, more or less elaborately; and they have pointed out oversights and misunderstandings, though few in number, and mostly very unimportant in substance. Such of those as had (to my knowledge) been pointed out before the publication of the latest edition (at present the third) have been corrected there, and the remainder of the criticisms have been, as far as seemed necessary, replied to. On the whole, the book has done its work: it has shown the weak side of Sir William Hamilton, and has reduced his too great philosophical reputation within more moderate bounds; and by some of its discussions, as well as by two expository chapters, on the notions of Matter and of Mind, it has perhaps thrown additional light on some of the disputed questions in the domain of psychology and metaphysics.

After the completion of the book on Hamilton, I applied myself to a task which a variety of reasons seemed to render specially incumbent upon me; that of giving an account, and forming an estimate, of the doctrines of Auguste Comte. I had contributed more than any one else to make his speculations known in England, and, in consequence chiefly of what I had said of him in my Logic, he had readers and admirers among thoughtful men on this side of the Channel at a time when his name had not yet in France emerged from obscurity. So unknown and unappreciated was he at the time when my Logic was written and published, that to criticise his weak points might well appear superfluous, while it was a duty to give as much publicity as one could to the important contributions he had made to philosophic thought. At the time, however, at which I have now arrived, this state of affairs had entirely changed. His name, at least, was known almost universally, and the general character of his doctrines very widely. He had taken his place in the estimation both of friends and opponents, as one of the conspicuous figures in the thought of the age. The better parts of his speculations had made great progress in working their way into those minds, which, by their previous culture and tendencies, were fitted to receive them: under cover of those better parts those of a worse character, greatly developed and added to in his later writings, had also made some way, having obtained active and enthusiastic adherents, some of them of no inconsiderable personal merit, in England, France, and other countries. These causes not only made it desirable that some one should undertake the task of sifting what is good from what is bad in M. Comte's speculations, but seemed to impose on myself in particular a special obligation to make the attempt. This I accordingly did in two essays, published in successive numbers of the Westminster Review, and reprinted in a small volume under the title " Auguste Comte and Positivism."

The writings which I have now mentioned, together with a small number of papers in periodicals which I have not deemed worth preserving, were the whole of the products of my activity as a writer during the years from 1859 to 1865. In the early part of the last-mentioned year, in compliance with a wish frequently expressed to me by working men, I published cheap People's Editions of those of my writings which seemed the most likely to find readers among the working classes: viz., Principles of Political Economy, Liberty, and Representative Government. This was a considerable sacrifice of my pecuniary interest, especially as I resigned all idea of deriving profit from the cheap editions, and after ascertaining from my publishers the lowest price which they thought would remunerate them on the usual terms of an equal division of profits, I gave up my half share to enable the price to be fixed still lower. To the credit of Messrs. Longman they fixed, unasked, a certain number of years after which the copyright and stereotype plates were to revert to me, and a certain number of copies after the sale of which I should receive half of any further profit. This number of copies (which in the case of the Political Economy was 10,000) has for some time been exceeded, and the People's Editions have begun to yield me a small but unexpected pecuniary return, though very far from an equivalent for the diminution of profit from the Library Editions.

In this summary of my outward life I have now arrived at the period at which my tranquil and retired existence as a writer of books was to be exchanged for the less congenial occupation of a member of the House of Commons. The proposal made to me early in 1865, by some electors of Westminster, did not present the idea to me for the first time. It was not even the first offer I had received, for, more than ten years previous, in consequence of my opinions on the Irish Land Question, Mr. Lucas and Mr. Duffy, in the name of the popular party in Ireland, offered to bring me into Parliament for an Irish county, which they could easily have done: but the incompatibility of a seat in Parliament with the office I then held in the India House, precluded even consideration of the proposal. After I had quitted the India House, several of my friends would gladly have seen me a member of Parliament; but there seemed no probability that the idea would ever take any practical shape. I was con-

vinced that no numerous or influential portion of any electoral body, really wished to be represented by a person of
my opinions; and that one who possessed no local connexion
or popularity, and who did not choose to stand as the mere
organ of a party, had small chance of being elected anywhere unless through the expenditure of money. Now it
was, and is, my fixed conviction, that a candidate ought not
to incur one farthing of expense for undertaking a public
duty. Such of the lawful expenses of an election as have no
special reference to any particular candidate, ought to be
borne as a public charge, either by the State or by the locality. What has to be done by the supporters of each candidate in order to bring his claims properly before the constituency, should be done by unpaid agency, or by voluntary
subscription. If members of the electoral body, or others,
are willing to subscribe money of their own for the purpose
of bringing, by lawful means, into Parliament some one
who they think would be useful there, no one is entitled to
object: but that the expense, or any part of it, should fall
on the candidate, is fundamentally wrong; because it
amounts in reality to buying his seat. Even on the most
favourable supposition as to the mode in which the money
is expended, there is a legitimate suspicion that any one who
gives money for leave to undertake a public trust, has other
than public ends to promote by it; and (a consideration of
the greatest importance) the cost of elections, when borne
by the candidates, deprives the nation of the services, as
members of Parliament, of all who cannot or will not afford
to incur a heavy expense. I do not say that, so long as
there is scarcely .. chance for an independent candidate to
come into Parliament without complying with this vicious
practice, it must always be morally wrong in him to spend
money, provided that no part of it is either directly or indirectly employed in corruption. But, to justify it, he ought
to be very certain that he can be of more use to his country
as a member of Parliament than in any other mode which
is open to him; and this assurance, in my own case, I did
not feel. It was by no means clear to me that I could do
more to advance the public objects which had a claim on my
exertions, from the benches of the House of Commons, than

from the simple position of a writer. I felt, therefore, that I ought not to seek election to Parliament, much less to expend any money in procuring it.

But the conditions of the question were considerably altered when a body of electors sought me out, and spontaneously offered to bring me forward as their candidate. If it should appear, on explanation, that they persisted in this wish, knowing my opinions, and accepting the only conditions on which I could conscientiously serve, it was questionable whether this was not one of those calls upon a member of the community by his fellow-citizens, which he was scarcely justified in rejecting. I therefore put their disposition to the proof by one of the frankest explanations ever tendered, I should think, to an electoral body by a candidate. I wrote, in reply to the offer, a letter for publication, saying that I had no personal wish to be a member of Parliament, that I thought a candidate ought neither to canvass nor to incur any expense, and that I could not consent to do either. I said further, that if elected, I could not undertake to give any of my time and labour to their local interests. With respect to general politics, I told them without reserve, what I thought on a number of important subjects on which they had asked my opinion; and one of these being the suffrage, I made known to them, among other things, my conviction (as I was bound to do, since I intended, if elected, to act on it), that women were entitled to representation in Parliament on the same terms with men. It was the first time, doubtless, that such a doctrine had ever been mentioned to English electors; and the fact that I was elected after proposing it, gave the start to the movement which has since become so vigorous, in favour of women's suffrage. Nothing, at the time, appeared more unlikely than that a candidate (if candidate I could be called) whose professions and conduct set so completely at defiance all ordinary notions of electioneering, should nevertheless be elected. A well-known literary man was heard to say that the Almighty himself would have no chance of being elected on such a programme. I strictly adhered to it, neither spending money nor canvassing, nor did I take any personal part in the election, until about a week preceding the day of nomination, when I attended a few public meetings to state my principles and give answers to any questions which the electors might exercise their just right of putting to me for their own guidance; answers as plain and unreserved as my address. On one subject only, my religious opinions, I announced from the beginning that I would answer no questions; a determination which appeared to be completely approved by those who attended the meetings. My frankness on all other subjects on which I was interrogated, evidently did me far more good than my answers, whatever they might be, did harm. Among the proofs I received of this, one is too remarkable not to be recorded. In the pamphlet, " Thoughts on Parliamentary Reform," I had said, rather bluntly, that the working classes, though differing from those of some other countries, in being ashamed of lying, are yet generally liars. This passage some opponent got printed in a placard, which was handed to me at a meeting, chiefly composed of the working classes, and I was asked whether I had written and published it. I at once answered " I did." Scarcely were these two words out of my mouth, when vehement applause resounded through the whole meeting. It was evident that the working people were so accustomed to expect equivocation and evasion from those who sought their suffrages, that when they found, instead of that, a direct avowal of what was likely to be disagreeable to them, instead of being affronted, they concluded at once that this was a person whom they could trust. A more striking instance never came under my notice of what, I believe, is the experience of those who best know the working classes, that the most essential of all recommendations to their favour is that of complete straightforwardness; its presence outweighs in their minds very strong objections, while no amount of other qualities will make amends for its apparent absence. The first working man who spoke after the incident I have mentioned (it was Mr. Odger) said, that the working classes had no desire not to be told of their faults; they wanted friends, not flatterers, and felt under obligation to any one who told them anything in themselves which he sincerely believed to require amendment. And to this the meeting heartily responded.

Had I been defeated in the election, I should still have had no reason to regret the contact it had brought me into with large bodies of my countrymen; which not only gave me much new experience, but enabled me to scatter my political opinions more widely, and, by making me known in many quarters where I had never before been heard of, increased the number of my readers, and the presumable influence of my writings. These latter effects were of course produced in a still greater degree, when, as much to my surprise as to that of any one, I was returned to Parliament by a majority of some hundreds over my Conservative competitor.

I was a member of the House during the three sessions of the Parliament which passed the Reform Bill; during which time Parliament was necessarily my main occupation except during the recess. I was a tolerably frequent speaker, sometimes of prepared speeches, sometimes extemporaneously. But my choice of occasions was not such as I should have made if my leading object had been Parliamentary influence. When I had gained the ear of the House, which I did by a successful speech on Mr. Gladstone's Reform Bill, the idea I proceeded on was that when anything was likely to be as well done, or sufficiently well done, by other people, there was no necessity for me to meddle with it. As I, therefore, in general reserved myself for work which no others were likely to do, a great proportion of my appearances were on points on which the bulk of the Liberal party, even the advanced portion of it, either were of a different opinion from mine, or were comparatively indifferent. Several of my speeches, especially one against the motion for the abolition of capital punishment, and another in favour of resuming the right of seizing enemies' goods in neutral vessels, were opposed to what then was, and probably still is, regarded as the advanced Liberal opinion. My advocacy of women's suffrage and of Personal Representation, were at the time looked upon by many as whims of my own; but the great progress since made by those opinions, and especially the response made from almost all parts of the kingdom to the demand for women's suffrage, fully justified the timeliness of those movements, and have made what was undertaken as a moral and social duty, a personal success. Another duty which was particularly incumbent on me as one of the metropolitan members, was the attempt to obtain a Municipal Government for the Metropolis: but on that subject the indifference of the House of Commons was such that I found hardly any help or support within its walls. On this subject, however, I was the organ of an active and intelligent body of persons outside, with whom, and not with me, the scheme originated, and who carried on all the agitation on the subject and drew up the Bills. My part was to bring in Bills already prepared, and to sustain the discussion of them during the short time they were allowed to remain before the House; after having taken an active part in the work of a Committee presided over by Mr. Ayrton, which sat through the greater part of the session of 1866, to take evidence on the subject. The very different position in which the question now stands (1870) may justly be attributed to the preparation which went on during those years, and which produced but little visible effect at the time; but all questions on which there are strong private interests on one side, and only the public good on the other, have a similar period of incubation to go through.

The same idea, that the use of my being in Parliament was to do work which others were not able or not willing to do, made me think it my duty to come to the front in defence of advanced Liberalism on occasions when the obloquy to be encountered was such as most of the advanced Liberals in the House, preferred not to incur. My first vote in the House was in support of an amendment in favour of Ireland, moved by an Irish member, and for which only five English and Scotch votes were given, including my own: the other four were Mr. Bright, Mr. M'Laren, Mr. T. B. Potter, and Mr. Hadfield. And the second speech I delivered[1] was on the Bill to prolong the suspension of the Habeas Corpus in Ireland. In denouncing, on this occasion, the English mode of governing Ireland, I did no more than the general opinion of England now admits to have been just; but the anger

---

[1] The first was in answer to Mr. Lowe's reply to Mr. Bright on the Cattle Plague Bill, and was thought at the time to have helped to get rid of a provision in the Government measure which would have given to landholders a second indemnity, after they had already been once indemnified for the loss of some of their cattle by the increased selling price of the remainder.

against Fenianism was then in all its freshness; any attack
on what Fenians attacked was looked upon as an apology
for them; and I was so unfavourably received by the House,
that more than one of my friends advised me (and my own
judgment agreed with the advice) to wait, before speaking
again, for the favourable opportunity that would be given
by the first great debate on the Reform Bill. During this
silence, many flattered themselves that I had turned out a
failure, and that they should not be troubled with me any
more. Perhaps their uncomplimentary comments may, by
the force of reaction, have helped to make my speech
on the Reform Bill the success it was. My position in the
House was further improved by a speech in which I insisted
on the duty of paying off the National Debt before our coal
supplies are exhausted, and by an ironical reply to some of
the Tory leaders who had quoted against me certain passages
of my writings, and called me to account for others, especially for one in my "Considerations on Representative
Government," which said that the Conservative party was,
by the law of its composition, the stupidest party. They
gained nothing by drawing attention to the passage, which
up to that time had not excited any notice, but the *sobriquet*
of "the stupid party" stuck to them for a considerable time
afterwards. Having now no longer any apprehension of not
being listened to, I confined myself, as I have since thought
too much, to occasions on which my services seemed specially needed, and abstained more than enough from speaking on the great party questions. With the exception of
Irish questions, and those which concerned the working
classes, a single speech on Mr. Disraeli's Reform Bill was
nearly all that I contributed to the great decisive debates of
the last two of my three sessions.

I have, however, much satisfaction in looking back to the
part I took on the two classes of subjects just mentioned.
With regard to the working classes, the chief topic of my
speech on Mr. Gladstone's Reform Bill was the assertion
of their claims to the suffrage. A little later, after the
resignation of Lord Russell's Ministry and the succession
of a Tory Government, came the attempt of the working
classes to hold a meeting in Hyde Park, their exclusion by

the police, and the breaking down of the park railing by the crowd. Though Mr. Beales and the leaders of the working men had retired under protest when this took place, a scuffle ensued in which many innocent persons were maltreated by the police, and the exasperation of the working men was extreme. They showed a determination to make another attempt at a meeting in the Park, to which many of them would probably have come armed; the Government made military preparations to resist the attempt, and something very serious seemed impending. At this crisis I really believe that I was the means of preventing much mischief. I had in my place in Parliament taken the side of the working men, and strongly censured the conduct of the Government. I was invited, with several other Radical members, to a conference with the leading members of the Council of the Reform League; and the task fell chiefly upon myself, of persuading them to give up the Hyde Park project, and hold their meeting elsewhere. It was not Mr. Beales and Colonel Dickson who needed persuading; on the contrary, it was evident that these gentlemen had already exerted their influence in the same direction, thus far without success. It was the working men who held out, and so bent were they on their original scheme, that I was obliged to have recourse to *les grands moyens*. I told them that a proceeding which would certainly produce a collision with the military, could only be justifiable on two conditions: if the position of affairs had become such that a revolution was desirable, and if they thought themselves able to accomplish one. To this argument, after considerable discussion, they at last yielded: and I was able to inform Mr. Walpole that their intention was given up. I shall never forget the depth of his relief or the warmth of his expressions of gratitude. After the working men had conceded so much to me, I felt bound to comply with their request that I would attend and speak at their meeting at the Agricultural Hall; the only meeting called by the Reform League which I ever attended. I had always declined being a member of the League, on the avowed ground that I did not agree in its programme of manhood suffrage and the ballot: from the ballot I dissented entirely; and I could not consent to hoist the flag of man-

hood suffrage, even on the assurance that the exclusion of
women was not intended to be implied; since if one goes
beyond what can be immediately carried, and professes to
take one's stand on a principle, one should go the whole
length of the principle. I have entered thus particularly
into this matter because my conduct on this occasion gave
great displeasure to the Tory and Tory-Liberal press, who
have charged me ever since with having shown myself, in
the trials of public life, intemperate and passionate. I do
not know what they expected from me; but they had reason
to be thankful to me if they knew from what I had, in all
probability, preserved them. And I do not believe it could
have been done, at that particular juncture, by any one else.
No other person, I believe, had at that moment the necessary
influence for restraining the working classes, except Mr.
Gladstone and Mr. Bright, neither of whom was available:
Mr. Gladstone for obvious reasons; Mr. Bright because he
was out of town.

When, some time later, the Tory Government brought in
a Bill to prevent public meetings in the Parks, I not only
spoke strongly in opposition to it, but formed one of a number of advanced Liberals, who, aided by the very late period
of the session, succeeded in defeating the Bill by what is
called talking it out. It has not since been renewed.

On Irish affairs also I felt bound to take a decided part.
I was one of the foremost in the deputation of members of
Parliament who prevailed on Lord Derby to spare the life
of the condemned Fenian insurgent, General Burke. The
Church question was so vigorously handled by the leaders
of the party, in the session of 1868, as to require no more
from me than an emphatic adhesion: but the land question
was by no means in so advanced a position: the superstitions of landlordism had up to that time been little chal-
lenged, especially in Parliament, and the backward state of
the question, so far as concerned the Parliamentary mind,
was evidenced by the extremely mild measure brought in
by Lord Russell's Government in 1866, which nevertheless
could not be carried. On that Bill I delivered one of my
most careful speeches, in which I attempted to lay down
some of the principles of the subject, in a manner calcu-

lated less to stimulate friends, than to conciliate and convince opponents. The engrossing subject of Parliamentary Reform prevented either this Bill, or one of a similar character brought in by Lord Derby's Government, from being carried through. They never got beyond the second reading. Meanwhile the signs of Irish disaffection had become much more decided; the demand for complete separation between the two countries had assumed a menacing aspect, and there were few who did not feel that if there was still any chance of reconciling Ireland to the British connexion, it could only be by the adoption of much more thorough reforms in the territorial and social relations of the country, than had yet been contemplated. The time seemed to me to have come when it would be useful to speak out my whole mind; and the result was my pamphlet " England and Ireland," which was written in the winter of 1867, and published shortly before the commencement of the session of 1868. The leading features of the pamphlet were, on the one hand, an argument to show the undesirableness, for Ireland as well as for England, of separation between the countries, and on the other, a proposal for settling the land question by giving to the existing tenants a permanent tenure, at a fixed rent, to be assessed after due inquiry by the State.

The pamphlet was not popular, except in Ireland, as I did not expect it to be. But, if no measure short of that which I proposed would do full justice to Ireland, or afford a prospect of conciliating the mass of the Irish people, the duty of proposing it was imperative; while if, on the other hand, there was any intermediate course which had a claim to a trial, I well knew that to propose something which would be called extreme, was the true way not to impede but to facilitate a more moderate experiment. It is most improbable that a measure conceding so much to the tenantry as Mr. Gladstone's Irish Land Bill, would have been proposed by a Government, or could have been carried through Parliament, unless the British public had been led to perceive that a case might be made, and perhaps a party formed, for a measure considerably stronger. It is the character of the British people, or at least of the higher and middle classes who pass muster for the British people, that to induce them to approve of any change, it is necessary that they should look upon it as a middle course: they think every proposal extreme and violent unless they hear of some other proposal going still farther, upon which their antipathy to extreme views may discharge itself. So it proved in the present instance; my proposal was condemned, but any scheme for Irish Land reform, short of mine, came to be thought moderate by comparison. I may observe that the attacks made on my plan usually gave a very incorrect idea of its nature. It was usually discussed as a proposal that the State should buy up the land and become the universal landlord; though in fact it only offered to each individual landlord this as an alternative, if he liked better to sell his estate than to retain it on the new conditions; and I fully anticipated that most landlords would continue to prefer the position of land-owners to that of Government annuitants, and would retain their existing relation to their tenants, often on more indulgent terms than the full rents on which the compensation to be given them by Government would have been based. This and many other explanations I gave in a speech on Ireland, in the debate on Mr. Maguire's resolution, early in the session of 1868. A corrected report of this speech, together with my speech on Mr. Fortescue's Bill, has been published (not by me, but with my permission) in Ireland.

Another public duty, of a most serious kind, it was my lot to have to perform, both in and out of Parliament, during these years. A disturbance in Jamaica, provoked in the first instance by injustice, and exaggerated by rage and panic into a premeditated rebellion, had been the motive or excuse for taking hundreds of innocent lives by military violence, or by sentence of what were called courts-martial, continuing for weeks after the brief disturbance had been put down; with many added atrocities of destruction of property, flogging women as well as men, and a general display of the brutal recklessness which usually prevails when fire and sword are let loose. The perpetrators of those deeds were defended and applauded in England by the same kind of people who had so long upheld negro slavery: and it seemed at first as if the British nation was about to incur the disgrace of letting pass without even a protest, excesses of authority as revolting as any of those for which, when perpetrated by the instruments of other Governments, Englishmen can hardly find terms sufficient to express their abhorrence. After a short time, however, an indignant feeling was roused: a voluntary Association formed itself under the name of the Jamaica Committee, to take such deliberation and action as the case might admit of, and adhesions poured in from all parts of the country. I was abroad at the time, but I sent in my name to the Committee as soon as I heard of it, and took an active part in the proceedings from the time of my return. There was much more at stake than only justice to the Negroes, imperative as was that consideration. The question was, whether the British dependencies, and eventually, perhaps, Great Britain itself, were to be under the government of law, or of military license; whether the lives and persons of British subjects are at the mercy of any two or three officers however raw and inexperienced or reckless and brutal, whom a panic-stricken Governor, or other functionary, may assume the right to constitute into a so-called court-martial. This question could only be decided by an appeal to the tribunals; and such an appeal the Committee determined to make. Their determination led to a change in the chairmanship of the Committee, as the chairman, Mr. Charles Buxton, thought it not unjust indeed, but inexpedient, to prosecute Governor Eyre and his principal subordinates in a criminal court; but a numerously attended general meeting of the Association having decided this point against him, Mr. Buxton withdrew from the Committee, though continuing to work in the cause, and I was, quite unexpectedly on my own part, proposed and elected chairman. It became, in consequence, my duty to represent the Committee in the House of Commons, sometimes by putting questions to the Government, sometimes as the recipient of questions, more or less provocative, addressed by individual members to myself; but especially as speaker in the important debate originated in the session of 1866 by Mr. Buxton: and the speech I then delivered is that which I should

probably select as the best of my speeches in Parliament.[1]
For more than two years we carried on the combat, trying every avenue legally open to us, to the Courts of Criminal Justice.   A bench of magistrates in one of the most
Tory counties in England dismissed our case: we were
more successful before the magistrates at Bow Street;
which gave an opportunity to the Lord Chief Justice of the
Queen's Bench, Sir Alexander Cockburn, for delivering
his celebrated charge, which settled the law of the question
in favour of liberty, as far as it is in the power of a judge's
charge to settle it.   There, however, our success ended, for
the Old Bailey Grand Jury by throwing out our Bill prevented the case from coming to trial.   It was clear that to
bring English functionaries to the bar of a criminal court
for abuses of power committed against negroes and mulat-
toes was not a popular proceeding with the English middle
classes.   We had, however, redeemed, so far as lay in us,
the character of our country, by showing that there was at
any rate a body of persons determined to use all the means
which the law afforded to obtain justice for the injured.   We
had elicited from the highest criminal judge in the nation
an authoritative declaration that the law was what we maintained it to be; and we had given an emphatic warning to
those who might be tempted to similar guilt hereafter, that,
though they might escape the actual sentence of a criminal
tribunal, they were not safe against being put to some
trouble and expense in order to avoid it.   Colonial governors and other persons in authority, will have a considerable motive to stop short of such extremities in future.

As a matter of curiosity, I kept some specimens of the
abusive letters, almost all of them anonymous, which I
received while these proceedings were going on.   They are
evidence of the sympathy felt with the brutalities in Jamaica by the brutal part of the population at home.   They
graduated from coarse jokes, verbal and pictorial, up to
threats of assassination.

---

[1] Among the most active members of the Committee were Mr. P. A.
Taylor, M.P., always faithful and energetic in every assertion of the
principles of liberty; Mr. Goldwin Smith, Mr. Frederick Harrison, Mr.
Slack, Mr. Chamerovzow, Mr. Shaen, and Mr. Chesson, the Honorary
Secretary of the Association.

Among other matters of importance in which I took an active part, but which excited little interest in the public, two deserve particular mention. I joined with several other independent Liberals in defeating an Extradition Bill introduced at the very end of the session of 1866, and by which, though surrender avowedly for political offences was not authorized, political refugees, if charged by a foreign Government with acts which are necessarily incident to all attempts at insurrection, would have been surrendered to be dealt with by the criminal courts of the Government against which they had rebelled: thus making the British Government an accomplice in the vengeance of foreign despotisms. The defeat of this proposal led to the appointment of a Select Committee (in which I was included), to examine and report on the whole subject of Extradition Treaties; and the result was, that in the Extradition Act which passed through Parliament after I had ceased to be a member, opportunity, is given to any one whose extradition is demanded, of being heard before an English court of justice to prove that the offence with which he is charged, is really political. The cause of European freedom has thus been saved from a serious misfortune, and our own country from a great iniquity. The other subject to be mentioned is the fight kept up by a body of advanced Liberals in the session of 1868, on the Bribery Bill of Mr. Disraeli's Government, in which I took a very active part. I had taken counsel with several of those who had applied their minds most carefully to the details of the subject—Mr. W. D. Christie, Serjeant Pulling, Mr. Chadwick—as well as bestowed much thought of my own, for the purpose of framing such amendments and additional clauses as might make the Bill really effective against the numerous modes of corruption, direct and indirect, which might otherwise, as there was much reason to fear, be increased instead of diminished by the Reform Act. We also aimed at engrafting on the Bill, measures for diminishing the mischievous burden of what are called the legitimate expenses of elections. Among our many amendments, was that of Mr. Fawcett for making the returning officer's expenses a charge on the rates, instead of on the candidates; another was the prohibition of paid canvassers, and the limitation of paid agents to one for each candidate; a third was the extension of the precautions and penalties against bribery, to municipal elections, which are well known to be not only a preparatory school for bribery at Parliamentary elections, but an habitual cover for it. The Conservative Government, however, when once they had carried the leading provision of their Bill (for which I voted and spoke), the transfer of the jurisdiction in elections from the House of Commons to the Judges, made a determined resistance to all other improvements; and after one of the most important proposals, that of Mr. Fawcett, had actually obtained a majority, they summoned the strength of their party and threw out the clause in a subsequent stage. The Liberal party in the House was greatly dishonoured by the conduct of many of its members in giving no help whatever to this attempt to secure the necessary conditions of an honest representation of the people. With their large majority in the House they could have carried all the amendments, or better ones if they had better to propose. But it was late in the session; members were eager to set about their preparations for the impending General Election: and while some (such as Sir Robert Anstruther), honourably remained at their post, though rival candidates were already canvassing their constituency, a much greater number placed their electioneering interests before their public duty. Many Liberals also looked with indifference on legislation against bribery, thinking that it merely diverted public interest from the Ballot, which they considered, very mistakenly as I expect it will turn out, to be a sufficient, and the only, remedy. From these causes our fight, though kept up with great vigour for several nights, was wholly unsuccessful, and the practices which we sought to render more difficult, prevailed more widely than ever in the first General Election held under the new electoral law.

In the general debates on Mr. Disraeli's Reform Bill, my participation was limited to the one speech already mentioned; but I made the Bill an occasion for bringing the two greatest improvements which remain to be made in Representative Government, formally before the House and the nation. One of them was Personal, or, as it is called with equal propriety, Proportional Representation. I brought this under the consideration of the House, by an expository and argumentative speech on Mr. Hare's plan; and subsequently I was active in support of the very imperfect substitute for that plan, which, in a small number of constituencies, Parliament was induced to adopt. This poor makeshift had scarcely any recommendation, except that it was a partial recognition of the evil which it did so little to remedy. As such, however, it was attacked by the same fallacies, and required to be defended on the same principles, as a really good measure; and its adoption in a few Parliamentary elections, as well as the subsequent introduction of what is called the Cumulative Vote in the elections for the London School Board, have had the good effect of converting the equal claim of all electors to a proportional share in the representation, from a subject of merely speculative discussion, into a question of practical politics, much sooner than would otherwise have been the case.

This assertion of my opinions on Personal Representation cannot be credited with any considerable or visible amount of practical result. It was otherwise with the other motion which I made in the form of an amendment to the Reform Bill, and which was by far the most important, perhaps the only really important, public service I performed in the capacity of a member of Parliament; a motion to strike out the words which were understood to limit the electoral franchise to males, and thereby to admit to the suffrage all women who, as householders or otherwise, possessed the qualification required of male electors. For women not to make their claim to the suffrage, at the time when the elective franchise was being largely extended, would have been to abjure the claim altogether; and a movement on the subject was begun in 1866, when I presented a petition for the suffrage, signed by a considerable number of distinguished women. But it was as yet uncertain whether the proposal would obtain more than a few stray votes in the House: and when, after a debate in which the speakers on the contrary side were conspicuous by their feebleness, the votes recorded in favour of the motion amounted to 73—made up

by pairs and tellers to above 80—the surprise was general
and the encouragement great: the greater, too, because one
of those who voted for the motion was Mr. Bright, a fact
which could only be attributed to the impression made on
him by the debate, as he had previously made no secret of
his non-concurrence in the proposal   *   *   *   *   *

I believe I have mentioned all that is worth remembering
of my proceedings in the House. But their enumeration,
even if complete, would give but an inadequate idea of my
occupations during that period, and especially of the time
taken up by correspondence. For many years before my
election to Parliament, I had been continually receiving letters from strangers, mostly addressed to me as a writer on
philosophy, and either propounding difficulties or communicating thoughts on subjects connected with logic or political economy. In common, I suppose, with all who are known
as political economists, I was a recipient of all the shallow
theories and absurd proposals by which people are perpetually endeavouring to show the way to universal wealth and
happiness by some artful reorganization of the currency.
When there were signs of sufficient intelligence in the
writers to make it worth while attempting to put them right,
I took the trouble to point out their errors, until the growth
of my correspondence made it necessary to dismiss such
persons with very brief answers. Many, however, of the
communications I received were more worthy of attention
than these, and in some, over-sights of detail were pointed
out in my writings, which I was thus enabled to correct. Correspondence of this sort naturally multiplied with the mul-
tiplication of the subjects on which I wrote, especially those
of a metaphysical character. But when I became a member
of Parliament, I began to receive letters on private griev-
ances and on every imaginable subject that related to any
kind of public affairs, however remote from my knowledge
or pursuits. It was not my constituents in Westminster who
laid this burden on me: they kept with remarkable
fidelity to the understanding on which I had consented to
serve. I received, indeed, now and then an application from
some ingenuous youth to procure for him a small Government appointment; but these were few, and how simple and

ignorant the writers were, was shown by the fact that the applications came in about equally whichever party was in power. My invariable answer was, that it was contrary to the principles on which I was elected to ask favours of any Government. But, on the whole, hardly any part of the country gave me less trouble than my own constituents. The general mass of correspondence, however, swelled into an oppressive burden.   *   *   *   *   *   *

*   *   *   *   *   *   *   *   *

*   *   *   *   *   *   *   *

While I remained in Parliament my work as an author was unavoidably limited to the recess. During that time I wrote (besides the pamphlet on Ireland, already mentioned), the Essay on Plato, published in the Edinburgh Review, and reprinted in the third volume of " Dissertations and Discussions;" and the address which, conformably to custom, I delivered to the University of St. Andrew's, whose students had done me the honour of electing me to the office of Rector. In this discourse I gave expression to many thoughts and opinions which had been accumulating in me through life, respecting the various studies which belong to a liberal education, their uses and influences, and the mode in which they should be pursued to render their influences most beneficial. The position taken up, vindicating the high educational value alike of the old classic and the new scientific studies, on even stronger grounds than are urged by most of their advocates, and insisting that it is only the stupid inefficiency of the usual teaching which makes those studies be regarded as competitors instead of allies, was, I think, calculated, not only to aid and stimulate the improvement which has happily commenced in the national institutions for higher education, but to diffuse juster ideas than we often find, even in highly educated men, on the conditions of the highest mental cultivation.

During this period also I commenced (and completed soon after I had left Parliament) the performance of a duty to philosophy and to the memory of my father, by preparing and publishing an edition of the " Analysis of the Phenomena of the Human Mind," with notes bringing up the doctrines of that admirable book to the latest improvements in science and in speculation. This was a joint undertaking: the psychological notes being furnished in about equal proportions by Mr. Bain and myself, while Mr. Grote supplied some valuable contributions on points in the history of philosophy incidently raised, and Dr. Andrew Findlater supplied the deficiencies in the book which had been occasioned by the imperfect philological knowledge of the time when it was written. Having been originally published at a time when the current of metaphysical speculation ran in a quite opposite direction to the psychology of Experience and Association, the "Analysis" had not obtained the amount of immediate success which it deserved, though it had made a deep impression on many individual minds, and had largely contributed, through those minds, to create that more favourable atmosphere for the Association Psychology of which we now have the benefit. Admirably adapted for a class-book of the Experience Metaphysics, it only required to be enriched, and in some cases corrected, by the results of more recent labours in the same school of thought, to stand, as it now does, in company with Mr. Bain's treatise, at the head of the systematic works on Analytic Psychology.

In the Autumn of 1868 the Parliament which passed the Reform Act was dissolved, and at the new election for Westminster I was thrown out; not to my surprise, nor, I believe, to that of my principal supporters, though in the few days preceding the election they had become more sanguine than before. That I should not have been elected at all would not have required any explanation; what excites curiosity is that I should have been elected the first time, or, having been elected then, should have been defeated afterwards. But the efforts made to defeat me were far greater on the second occasion than on the first. For one thing, the Tory Government was now struggling for existence, and success in any contest was of more importance to them. Then, too, all persons of Tory feelings were far more embittered against me individually than on the previous occasion; many who had at first been either favourable or indifferent, were vehemently opposed to my re-election. As I had shown in my political writings that I was aware of the weak points

in democratic opinions, some Conservatives, it seems, had
not been without hopes of finding me an opponent of democracy: as I was able to see the Conservative side of the
question, they presumed that, like them, I could not see any
other side.   Yet if they had really read my writings, they
would have known that after giving full weight to all that
appeared to me well grounded in the arguments against
democracy, I unhesitatingly decided in its favour, while
recommending that it should be accompanied by such institutions as were consistent with its principle and calculated
to ward off its inconveniences: one of the chief of these
remedies being Proportional Representation, on which
scarcely any of the Conservatives gave me any support.
Some Tory expectations appear to have been founded on
the approbation I had expressed of plural voting, under
certain conditions: and it has been surmised that the suggestion of this sort made in one of the resolutions which
Mr. Disraeli introduced into the House preparatory to his
Reform Bill (a suggestion which meeting with no favour
he did not press), may have been occasioned by what I
had written on the point: but if so, it was forgotten that I
had made it an express condition that the privilege of a
plurality of votes should be annexed to education, not to
property, and even so, had approved of it only on the supposition of universal suffrage.   How utterly inadmissible
such plural voting would be under the suffrage given by the
present Reform Act, is proved, to any who could otherwise doubt it, by the very small weight which the working
classes are found to possess in elections, even under the
law which gives no more votes to any one elector than to
any other.

While I thus was far more obnoxious to the Tory interest,
and to many Conservative Liberals than I had formerly
been, the course I pursued in Parliament had by no means
been such as to make Liberals generally at all enthusiastic
in my support.   It has already been mentioned, how large a
proportion of my prominent appearances had been on questions on which I differed from most of the Liberal party, or
about which they cared little, and how few occasions there
had been on which the line I took was such as could lead

them to attach any great value to me as an organ of their opinions. I had moreover done things which had excited, in many minds, a personal prejudice against me. Many were offended by what they called the persecution of Mr. Eyre: and still greater offence was taken at my sending a subscription to the election expenses of Mr. Bradlaugh. Having refused to be at any expense for my own election, and having had all its expenses defrayed by others, I felt under a peculiar obligation to subscribe in my turn where funds were deficient for candidates whose election was desirable. I accordingly sent subscriptions to nearly all the working class candidates, and among others to Mr. Bradlaugh. He had the support of the working classes; having heard him speak, I knew him to be a man of ability, and he had proved that he was the reverse of a demagogue, by placing himself in strong opposition to the prevailing opinion of the democratic party on two such important subjects as Malthusianism and Personal Representation. Men of this sort, who, while sharing the democratic feelings of the working classes, judged political questions for themselves, and had courage to assert their individual convictions against popular opposition, were needed, as it seemed to me, in Parliament, and I did not think that Mr. Bradlaugh's anti-religious opinions (even though he had been intemperate in the expression of them) ought to exclude him. In subscribing, however, to his election, I did what would have been highly imprudent if I had been at liberty to consider only the interests of my own re-election; and, as might be expected, the utmost possible use, both fair and unfair, was made of this act of mine to stir up the electors of Westminster against me. To these various causes, combined with an unscrupulous use of the usual pecuniary and other influences on the side of my Tory competitor, while none were used on my side, it is to be ascribed that I failed at my second election after having succeeded at the first. No sooner was the result of the election known than I received three or four invitations to become a candidate for other constituencies, chiefly counties; but even if success could have been expected, and this without expense, I was not disposed to deny myself the relief of returning to private life.

I had no cause to feel humiliated at my rejection by the electors; and if I had, the feeling would have been far out-weighed by the numerous expressions of regret which I received from all sorts of persons and places, and in a most marked degree from those members of the Liberal party in Parliament, with whom I had been accustomed to act.

Since that time little has occurred which there is need to commemorate in this place. I returned to my old pursuits and to the enjoyment of a country life in the south of Europe, alternating twice a year with a residence of some few weeks or months in the neighbourhood of London. I have written various articles in periodicals (chiefly in my friend Mr. Morley's Fortnightly Review), have made a small number of speeches on public occasions, have published the "Subjection of Women," written some years before, with some additions * * * * * * *
* * * and have commenced the preparation of matter for future books, of which it will be time to speak more particularly if I live to finish them. Here therefore, for the present, this memoir may close.

ON LIBERTY
BY
JOHN STUART MILL

ON LIBERTY

CHAPTER I

INTRODUCTORY

THE subject of this Essay is not the so-called Liberty of the Will, so unfortunately opposed to the mis-named doctrine of Philosophical Necessity; but Civil, or Social Liberty: the nature and limits of the power which can be legitimately exercised by society over the individual. A question seldom stated, and hardly ever discussed, in general terms, but which profoundly influences the practical controversies of the age by its latent presence, and is likely soon to make itself recognized as the vital question of the future. It is so far from being new, that, in a certain sense, it has divided mankind, almost from the remotest ages, but in the stage of progress into which the more civilized portions of the species have now entered, it presents itself under new conditions, and requires a different and more fundamental treatment.

The struggle between Liberty and Authority is the most conspicuous feature in the portions of history with which we are earliest familiar, particularly in that of Greece, Rome, and England. But in old times this contest was between subjects, or some classes of subjects, and the government. By liberty, was meant protection against the tyranny of the political rulers. The rulers were conceived (except in some of the popular governments of Greece) as in a necessarily antagonistic position to the people whom they ruled. They consisted of a governing One, or a governing tribe or caste, who derived their authority from inheritance or conquest; who, at all events, did not hold it at the pleasure of the governed, and whose supremacy men did not venture, perhaps did not desire, to contest, whatever precautions might be taken against its oppressive exercise. Their power was regarded as necessary, but also as highly dangerous; as a weapon which they would attempt to use against their subjects, no less than against external enemies. To prevent the weaker members of the community from being preyed upon by innumerable vultures, it was needful that there should be an animal of prey stronger than the rest, commissioned to keep them down. But as the king of the vultures would be no less bent upon preying upon the flock than any of the minor harpies, it was indispensable to be in a perpetual attitude of defence against his beak and claws. The aim, therefore, of patriots, was to set limits to the power which the ruler should be suffered to exercise over the community; and this limitation was what they meant by liberty. It was attempted in two ways. First, by obtaining a recognition of certain immunities, called political liberties or rights, which it was to be regarded as a breach of duty in the ruler to infringe, and which, if he did infringe, specific resistance, or general rebellion, was held to be justifiable. A second, and generally a later expedient, was the establishment of constitutional checks; by which the consent of the community, or of a body of some sort supposed to represent its interests, was made a necessary condition to some of the more important acts of the governing power. To the first of these modes of limitation, the ruling power, in most European countries, was compelled, more or less, to submit. It was not so with the second; and to attain this, or when already in some degree possessed, to attain it more completely, became everywhere the principal object of the lovers of liberty. And so long as mankind were content to combat one enemy by another, and to be ruled by a master, on condition of being guaranteed more or less efficaciously against his tyranny, they did not carry their aspirations beyond this point.

A time, however, came in the progress of human affairs, when men ceased to think it a necessity of nature that their governors should be an independent power, opposed in interest to themselves. It appeared to them much better that the various magistrates of the State should be their tenants or delegates, revocable at their pleasure. In that way alone, it seemed, could they have complete security that the powers of government would never be abused to their disadvantage. By degrees, this new demand for elective and temporary rulers became the prominent object of the exertions of the popular party, wherever any such party existed; and superseded, to a considerable extent, the previous efforts to limit the power of rulers. As the struggle proceeded for making the ruling power emanate from the periodical choice of the ruled, some persons began to think that too much importance had been attached to the limitation of the power itself. *That* (it might seem) was a resource against rulers whose interests were habitually opposed to those of the people. What was now wanted was, that the rulers should be identified with the people; that their interest and will should be the interest and will of the nation. The nation did not need to be protected against its own will. There was no fear of its tyrannizing over itself. Let the rulers be effectually responsible to it, promptly removable by it, and it could afford to trust them with power of which it could itself dictate the use to be made. Their power was but the nation's own power, concentrated, and in a form convenient for exercise. This mode of thought, or rather perhaps of feeling, was common among the last generation of European liberalism, in the Continental section of which, it still apparently predominates. Those who admit any limit to what a government may do, except in the case of such governments as they think ought not to exist, stand out as brilliant exceptions among the political thinkers of the Continent. A similar tone of sentiment might by this time have been prevalent in our own country, if the circumstances which for a time encouraged it had continued unaltered.

But, in political and philosophical theories, as well as in persons, success discloses faults and infirmities which failure might have concealed from observation. The notion, that the people have no need to limit their power over themselves, might seem axiomatic, when popular government was a thing only dreamed about, or read of as having existed at some distant period of the past. Neither was that notion necessarily disturbed by such temporary aberrations as those of the French Revolution, the worst of which were the work of an usurping few, and which, in any case, belonged, not to the permanent working of popular institutions, but to a sudden and convulsive outbreak against monarchical and aristocratic despotism. In time, however, a democratic republic came to occupy a large portion of the earth's surface, and made itself felt as one of the most powerful members of the community of nations; and elective and responsible government became subject to the observations and criticisms which wait upon a great existing fact. It was now perceived that such phrases as " self-government," and " the power of the people over themselves," do not express the true state of the case. The " people " who exercise the power, are not always the same people with those over whom it is exercised, and the " self-government " spoken of, is not the government of each by himself, but of each by all the rest. The will of the people, moreover, practically means, the will of the most numerous or the most active *part* of the people; the majority, or those who succeed in making themselves accepted as the majority: the people, consequently, *may* desire to oppress a part of their number; and precautions are as much needed against this, as against any other abuse of power. The limitation, therefore, of the power of government over individuals, loses none of its importance when the holders of power are regularly accountable to the community, that is, to the strongest party therein. This view of things, recommending itself equally to the intelligence of thinkers and to the inclination of those important classes in European society to whose real or supposed interests democracy is adverse, has had no difficulty in establishing itself; and in political speculations " the tyranny of the majority " is now generally included among the evils against which society requires to be on its guard.

Like other tyrannies, the tyranny of the majority was at first, and is still vulgarly, held in dread, chiefly as operating through the acts of the public authorities. But reflecting persons perceived that when society is itself the tyrant —society collectively, over the separate individuals who compose it—its means of tyrannizing are not restricted to the acts which it may do by the hands of its political functionaries. Society can and does execute its own mandates: and

If it issues wrong mandates instead of right, or any mandates at all in things with which it ought not to meddle, it practises a social tyranny more formidable than many kinds of political oppression, since, though not usually upheld by such extreme penalties, it leaves fewer means of escape, penetrating much more deeply into the details of life, and enslaving the soul itself. Protection, therefore, against the tyranny of the magistrate is not enough; there needs protection also against the tyranny of the prevailing opinion and feeling; against the tendency of society to impose, by other means than civil penalties, its own ideas and practices as rules of conduct on those who dissent from them; to fetter the development, and, if possible, prevent the formation, of any individuality not in harmony with its ways, and compel all characters to fashion themselves upon the model of its own. There is a limit to the legitimate interference of collective opinion with individual independence; and to find that limit, and maintain it against encroachment, is as indispensable to a good condition of human affairs, as protection against political despotism.

But though this proposition is not likely to be contested in general terms, the practical question, where to place the limit—how to make the fitting adjustment between individual independence and social control—is a subject on which nearly everything remains to be done. All that makes existence valuable to any one, depends on the enforcement of restraints upon the actions of other people. Some rules of conduct, therefore, must be imposed, by law in the first place, and by opinion on many things which are not fit subjects for the operation of law. What these rules should be, is the principal question in human affairs; but if we except a few of the most obvious cases, it is one of those which least progress has been made in resolving. No two ages, and scarcely any two countries, have decided it alike; and the decision of one age or country is a wonder to another. Yet the people of any given age and country no more suspect any difficulty in it, than if it were a subject on which mankind had always been agreed. The rules which obtain among themselves appear to them self-evident and self-justifying. This all but universal illusion is one of the examples of the magical influence of custom, which is not only, as the proverb says a second nature, but is continually mistaken for the first. The effect of custom, in preventing any misgiving respecting the rules of conduct which mankind impose on one another, is all the more complete because the subject is one on which it is not generally considered necessary that reasons should be given, either by one person to others, or by each to himself. People are accustomed to believe and have been encouraged in the belief by some who aspire to the character of philosophers, that their feelings, on subjects of this nature, are better than reasons, and render reasons unnecessary. The practical principle which guides them to their opinions on the regulation of human conduct, is the feeling in each person's mind that everybody should be required to act as he, and those with whom he sympathizes, would like them to act. No one, indeed, acknowledges to himself that his standard of judgment is his own liking; but an opinion on a point of conduct, not supported by reasons, can only count as one person's preference; and if the reasons, when given, are a mere appeal to a similar preference felt by other people, it is still only many people's liking instead of one. To an ordinary man, however, his own preference, thus supported, is not only a perfectly satisfactory reason, but the only one he generally has for any of his notions of morality, taste, or propriety, which are not expressly written in his religious creed; and his chief guide in the interpretation even of that. Men's opinions, accordingly, on what is laudable or blamable, are affected by all the multifarious causes which influence their wishes in regard to the conduct of others, and which are as numerous as those which determine their wishes on any other subject. Sometimes their reason—at other times their prejudices or superstitions: often their social affections, not seldom their antisocial ones, their envy or jealousy, their arrogance or contemptuousness: but most commonly, their desires or fears for themselves—their legitimate or illegitimate self-interest. Wherever there is an ascendant class, a large portion of the morality of the country emanates from its class interests, and its feelings of class superiority. The morality between Spartans and Helots, between planters and negroes, between princes and subjects, between nobles and roturiers, between men and women, has been for the most part the creation of these class interests and feelings: and the sentiments thus generated, react in turn upon the moral feelings of the members of the ascendant class, in their relations among themselves. Where, on the other hand, a class, formerly ascendant, has lost its ascendency, or where its ascendency is unpopular, the prevailing moral sentiments frequently bear the impress of an impatient dislike of superiority. Another grand determining principle of the rules of conduct, both in act and forbearance which have been enforced by law or opinion, has been the servility of mankind towards the supposed preferences or aversions of their temporal masters, or of their gods. This servility though essentially selfish, is not hypocrisy; it gives rise to perfectly genuine sentiments of abhorrence; it made men burn magicians and heretics. Among so many baser influences, the general and obvious interests of society have of course had a share, and a large one, in the direction of the moral sentiments: less, however, as a matter of reason, and on their own account, than as a consequence of the sympathies and antipathies which grew out of them: and sympathies and antipathies which had little or nothing to do with the interests of society, have made themselves felt in the establishment of moralities with quite as great force.

The likings and dislikings of society, or of some powerful portion of it, are thus the main thing which has practically determined the rules laid down for general observance, under the penalties of law or opinion. And in general, those who have been in advance of society in thought and feeling, have left this condition of things unassailed in principle, however they may have come into conflict with it in some of its details. They have occupied themselves rather in inquiring what things society ought to like or dislike, than in questioning whether its likings or dislikings should be a law to individuals. They preferred endeavouring to alter the feelings of mankind on the particular points on which they were themselves heretical, rather than make common cause in defence of freedom, with heretics generally. The only case in which the higher ground has been taken on principle and

maintained with consistency, by any but an individual here
and there, is that of religious belief: a case instructive in
many ways, and not least so as forming a most striking instance of the fallibility of what is called the moral sense:
for the *odium theologicum,* in a sincere bigot, is one of the
most unequivocal cases of moral feeling. Those who first
broke the yoke of what called itself the Universal Church,
were in general as little willing to permit difference of religious opinion as that church itself. But when the heat of
the conflict was over, without giving a complete victory to
any party, and each church or sect was reduced to limit its
hopes to retaining possession of the ground it already occupied; minorities, seeing that they had no chance of becoming majorities, were under the necessity of pleading to
those whom they could not convert, for permission to
differ. It is accordingly on this battle-field, almost solely,
that the rights of the individual against society have been asserted on broad grounds of principle, and the claim of
society to exercise authority over dissentients openly controverted. The great writers to whom the world owes what
religious liberty it possesses, have mostly asserted freedom
of conscience as an indefeasible right, and denied absolutely
that a human being is accountable to others for his religious belief. Yet so natural to mankind is intolerance in whatever they really care about, that religious freedom has hardly
anywhere been practically realized, except where religious
indifference, which dislikes to have its peace disturbed by
theological quarrels, has added its weight to the scale.
In the minds of almost all religious persons, even in the most
tolerant countries, the duty of toleration is admitted with
tacit reserves. One person will bear with dissent in matters
of church government, but not of dogma; another can
tolerate everybody, short of a Papist or an Unitarian; another, every one who believes in revealed religion; a few
extend their charity a little further, but stop at the belief
in a God and in a future state. Wherever the sentiment of
the majority is still genuine and intense, it is found to have
abated little of its claim to be obeyed.

In England, from the peculiar circumstances of our
political history, though the yoke of opinion is perhaps

heavier, that of law is lighter, than in most other countries of Europe; and there is considerable jealousy of direct interference, by the legislative or the executive power with private conduct; not so much from any just regard for the independence of the individual, as from the still subsisting habit of looking on the government as representing an opposite interest to the public. The majority have not yet learnt to feel the power of the government their power, or its opinions their opinions. When they do so, individual liberty will probably be as much exposed to invasion from the government, as it already is from public opinion. But, as yet, there is a considerable amount of feeling ready to be called forth against any attempt of the law to control individuals in things in which they have not hitherto been accustomed to be controlled by it; and this with very little discrimination as to whether the matter is, or is not, within the legitimate sphere of legal control; insomuch that the feeling, highly salutary on the whole, is perhaps quite as often misplaced as well grounded in the particular instances of its application.

There is, in fact, no recognized principle by which the propriety or impropriety of government interference is customarily tested. People decide according to their personal preferences. Some, whenever they see any good to be done, or evil to be remedied, would willingly instigate the government to undertake the business; while others prefer to bear almost any amount of social evil, rather than add one to the departments of human interests amenable to governmental control. And men range themselves on one or the other side in any particular case, according to this general direction of their sentiments; or according to the degree of interest which they feel in the particular thing which it is proposed that the government should do; or according to the belief they entertain that the government would, or would not, do it in the manner they prefer; but very rarely on account of any opinion to which they consistently adhere, as to what things are fit to be done by a government. And it seems to me that, in consequence of this absence of rule or principle, one side is at present as often wrong as the other; the interference of government is, with about

equal frequency, improperly invoked and improperly condemned.

The object of this Essay is to assert one very simple
principle, as entitled to govern absolutely the dealings of
society with the individual in the way of compulsion and
control, whether the means used be physical force in the
form of legal penalties, or the moral coercion of public
opinion. That principle is, that the sole end for which mankind are warranted, individually or collectively in interfering with the liberty of action of any of their number, is
self-protection. That the only purpose for which power can
be rightfully exercised over any member of a civilized community, against his will, is to prevent harm to others. His
own good, either physical or moral, is not a sufficient warrant. He cannot rightfully be compelled to do or forbear
because it will be better for him to do so, because it will
make him happier, because, in the opinions of others, to do
so would be wise, or even right. These are good reasons
for remonstrating with him, or reasoning with him, or persuading him, or entreating him, but not for compelling him,
or visiting him with any evil, in case he do otherwise. To
justify that, the conduct from which it is desired to deter
him must be calculated to produce evil to some one else.
The only part of the conduct of any one, for which he is
amenable to society, is that which concerns others. In the
part which merely concerns himself, his independence is, of
right, absolute. Over himself, over his own body and mind,
the individual is sovereign.

It is, perhaps, hardly necessary to say that this doctrine
is meant to apply only to human beings in the maturity of
their faculties. We are not speaking of children, or of
young persons below the age which the law may fix as that
of manhood or womanhood. Those who are still in a state
to require being taken care of by others, must be protected
against their own actions as well as against external injury. For the same reason, we may leave out of consideration those backward states of society in which the race
itself may be considered as in its nonage. The early difficulties in the way of spontaneous progress are so great, that
there is seldom any choice of means for overcoming them;

and a ruler full of the spirit of improvement is warranted in the use of any expedients that will attain an end, perhaps otherwise unattainable. Despotism is a legitimate mode of government in dealing with barbarians, provided the end be their improvement, and the means justified by actually effecting that end. Liberty, as a principle, has no application to any state of things anterior to the time when mankind have become capable of being improved by free and equal discussion. Until then, there is nothing for them but implicit obedience to an Akbar or a Charlemagne, if they are so fortunate as to find one. But as soon as mankind have attained the capacity of being guided to their own improvement by conviction or persuasion (a period long since reached in all nations with whom we need here concern ourselves), compulsion, either in the direct form or in that of pains and penalties for non-compliance, is no longer admissible as a means to their own good, and justifiable only for the security of others.

It is proper to state that I forego any advantage which could be derived to my argument from the idea of abstract right as a thing independent of utility. I regard utility as the ultimate appeal on all ethical questions; but it must be utility in the largest sense, grounded on the permanent interests of man as a progressive being. Those interests, I contend, authorize the subjection of individual spontaneity to external control, only in respect to those actions of each, which concern the interest of other people. If any one does an act hurtful to others, there is a *primâ facie* case for punishing him, by law, or, where legal penalties are not safely applicable, by general disapprobation. There are also many positive acts for the benefit of others, which he may rightfully be compelled to perform; such as, to give evidence in a court of justice; to bear his fair share in the common defence, or in any other joint work necessary to the interest of the society of which he enjoys the protection; and to perform certain acts of individual beneficence, such as saving a fellow-creature's life, or interposing to protect the defenceless against ill-usage, things which whenever it is obviously a man's duty to do, he may rightfully be made responsible to society for not doing. A person may cause evil to others not only by his actions but by his inaction, and in neither case he is justly accountable to them for the injury. The latter case, it is true, requires a much more cautious exercise of compulsion than the former. To make any one answerable for doing evil to others, is the rule; to make him answerable for not preventing evil, is, comparatively speaking, the exception. Yet there are many cases clear enough and grave enough to justify that exception. In all things which regard the external relations of the individual, he is *de jure* amenable to those whose interests are concerned, and if need be, to society as their protector. There are often good reasons for not holding him to the responsibility; but these reasons must arise from the special expediencies of the case: either because it is a kind of case in which he is on the whole likely to act better, when left to his own discretion, than when controlled in any way in which society have it in their power to control him; or because the attempt to exercise control would produce other evils, greater than those which it would prevent. When such reasons as these preclude the enforcement of responsibility, the conscience of the agent himself should step into the vacant judgment-seat, and protect those interests of others which have no external protection; judging himself all the more rigidly, because the case does not admit of his being made accountable to the judgment of his fellow-creatures.

But there is a sphere of action in which society, as distinguished from the individual, has, if any, only an indirect interest; comprehending all that portion of a person's life and conduct which affects only himself, or, if it also affects others, only with their free, voluntary, and undeceived consent and participation. When I say only himself, I mean directly, and in the first instance: for whatever affects himself, may affect others *through* himself; and the objection which may be grounded on this contingency, will receive consideration in the sequel. This, then, is the appropriate region of human liberty. It comprises, first, the inward domain of consciousness; demanding liberty of conscience, in the most comprehensive sense; liberty of thought and feeling; absolute freedom of opinion and sentiment on all subjects, practical or speculative, scientific, moral, or theological. The liberty of expressing and publishing opinions may seem to fall under a different principle, since it belongs to that part of the conduct of an individual which concerns other people; but, being almost of as much importance as the liberty of thought itself, and resting in great part on the same reasons, is practically inseparable from it. Secondly, the principle requires liberty of tastes and pursuits; of framing the plan of our life to suit our own character; of doing as we like, subject to such consequences as may follow; without impediment from our fellow-creatures, so long as what we do does not harm them even though they should think our conduct foolish, perverse, or wrong. Thirdly, from this liberty of each individual, follows the liberty, within the same limits, of combination among individuals; freedom to unite, for any purpose not involving harm to others: the persons combining being supposed to be of full age, and not forced or deceived.

No society in which these liberties are not, on the whole, respected, is free, whatever may be its form of government; and none is completely free in which they do not exist absolute and unqualified. The only freedom which deserves the name, is that of pursuing our own good in our own way, so long as we do not attempt to deprive others of theirs, or impede their efforts to obtain it. Each is the proper guardian of his own health, whether bodily, or mental or spiritual. Mankind are greater gainers by suffering each other to live as seems good to themselves, than by compelling each to live as seems good to the rest.

Though this doctrine is anything but new, and, to some persons, may have the air of a truism, there is no doctrine which stands more directly opposed to the general tendency of existing opinion and practice. Society has expended fully as much effort in the attempt (according to its lights) to compel people to conform to its notions of personal, as of social excellence. The ancient commonwealths thought themselves entitled to practise, and the ancient philosophers countenanced, the regulation of every part of private conduct by public authority, on the ground that the State had a deep interest in the whole bodily and mental discipline of every one of its citizens, a mode of thinking which may have been admissible in small republics surrounded by powerful enemies, in constant peril of being subverted by foreign attack or internal commotion, and to which even a short interval of relaxed energy and self-command might so easily be fatal, that they could not afford to wait for the salutary permanent effects of freedom. In the modern world, the greater size of political communities, and above all, the separation between the spiritual and temporal authority (which placed the direction of men's consciences in other hands than those which controlled their worldly affairs), prevented so great an interference by law in the details of private life; but the engines of moral repression have been wielded more strenuously against divergence from the reigning opinion in self-regarding, than even in social matters; religion, the most powerful of the elements which have entered into the formation of moral feeling, having almost always been governed either by the ambition of a hierarchy, seeking control over every department of human conduct, or by the spirit of Puritanism. And some of those modern reformers who have placed themselves in strongest opposition to the religions of the past, have been noway behind either churches or sects in their assertion of the right of spiritual domination: M. Comte, in particular, whose social system, as unfolded in his *Traité de Politique Positive,* aims at establishing (though by moral more than by legal appliances) a despotism of society over the individual, surpassing anything contemplated in the political ideal of the most rigid disciplinarian among the ancient philosophers.

Apart from the peculiar tenets of individual thinkers, there is also in the world at large an increasing inclination to stretch unduly the powers of society over the individual, both by the force of opinion and even by that of legislation: and as the tendency of all the changes taking place in the world is to strengthen society, and diminish the power of the individual, this encroachment is not one of the evils which tend spontaneously to disappear, but, on the contrary, to grow more and more formidable. The disposition of mankind, whether as rulers or as fellow-citizens, to impose their own opinions and inclinations as a rule of conduct on others, is so energetically supported by some of the best and by some of the worst feelings incident to human nature, that it is hardly ever kept under restraint by anything but want of power; and as the power is not declining, but growing, unless a strong barrier of moral conviction can be raised against the mischief, we must expect, in the present circumstances of the world, to see it increase.

It will be convenient for the argument, if, instead of at once entering upon the general thesis, we confine ourselves in the first instance to a single branch of it, on which the principle here stated is, if not fully, yet to a certain point, recognized by the current opinions. This one branch is the Liberty of Thought: from which it is impossible to separate the cognate liberty of speaking and of writing. Although these liberties, to some considerable amount, form part of the political morality of all countries which profess religious toleration and free institutions, the grounds, both philosophical and practical, on which they rest, are perhaps not so familiar to the general mind, nor so thoroughly appreciated by many even of the leaders of opinion, as might have been expected. Those grounds, when rightly understood, are of much wider application than to only one division of the subject, and a thorough consideration of this part of the question will be found the best introduction to the remainder. Those to whom nothing which I am about to say will be new, may therefore, I hope, excuse me, if on a subject which for now three centuries has been so often discussed, I venture on one discussion more.

CHAPTER II

OF THE LIBERTY OF THOUGHT AND DISCUSSION

THE time, it is to be hoped, is gone by when any defence would be necessary of the "liberty of the press" as one of the securities against corrupt or tyrannical government. No argument, we may suppose, can now be needed, against permitting a legislature or an executive, not identified in interest with the people, to prescribe opinions to them, and determine what doctrines or what arguments they shall be allowed to hear. This aspect of the question, besides, has been so often and so triumphantly enforced by preceding writers, that it needs not be specially insisted on in this place. Though the law of England, on the subject of the press, is as servile to this day as it was in the time of the Tudors, there is little danger of its being actually put in force against political discussion, except during some temporary panic, when fear of insurrection drives ministers and judges from their propriety;[1]

[1] These words had scarcely been written, when, as if to give them an emphatic contradiction, occurred the Government Press Prosecutions of 1858. That ill-judged interference with the liberty of public discussion has not, however, induced me to alter a single word in the text, nor has it at all weakened my conviction that, moments of panic excepted, the era of pains and penalties for political discussion has, in our own country, passed away. For, in the first place, the prosecutions were not persisted in; and, in the second, they were never, properly speaking, political prosecutions. The offence charged was not that of criticizing institutions, or the acts or persons of rulers, but of circulating what was deemed an immoral doctrine, the lawfulness of Tyrannicide.

If the arguments of the present chapter are of any validity, there ought to exist the fullest liberty of professing and discussing, as a matter of ethical conviction, any doctrine, however immoral it may be considered. It would, therefore, be irrelevant and out of place to examine here, whether the doctrine of Tyrannicide deserves that title. I shall content myself with saying, that the subject has been at all times one of the open questions of morals; that the act of a private citizen in striking down a criminal, who, by raising himself above the law, has placed himself beyond the reach of legal punishment or control, has been accounted by whole nations, and by some of the best and wisest of men, not a crime, but an act of exalted virtue; and that, right or wrong, it is not of the nature of assassination, but of civil war. As such, I hold that the instigation to it, in a specific case, may be a proper subject of punishment, but only if an overt act has and, speaking generally, it is not, in constitutional countries, to be apprehended that the government, whether completely responsible to the people or not, will often attempt to control the expression of opinion, except when in doing so it makes itself the organ of the general intolerance of the public. Let us suppose, therefore, that the government is entirely at one with the people, and never thinks of exerting any power of coercion unless in agreement with what it conceives to be their voice. But I deny the right of the people to exercise such coercion, either by themselves or by their government. The power itself is illegitimate. The best government has no more title to it than the worst. It is as noxious, or more noxious, when exerted in accordance with public opinion, than when in opposition to it. If all mankind minus one, were of one opinion, and only one person were of the contrary opinion, mankind would be no more justified in silencing that one person, than he, if he had the power, would be justified in silencing mankind. Were an opinion a personal possession of no value except to the owner; if to be obstructed in the enjoyment of it were simply a private injury, it would make some difference whether the injury was inflicted only on a few persons or on many. But the peculiar evil of silencing the expression of an opinion is, that it is robbing the human race; posterity as well as the existing generation; those who dissent from the opinion, still more than those who hold it. If the opinion is right, they are deprived of the opportunity of exchanging error for truth: if wrong, they lose, what is almost as great a benefit, the clearer perception and livelier impression of truth, produced by its collision with error.

It is necessary to consider separately these two hypotheses, each of which has a distinct branch of the argument corresponding to it. We can never be sure that the opinion we are endeavouring to stifle is a false opinion; and if we were sure, stifling it would be an evil still.

First: the opinion which it is attempted to suppress by authority may possibly be true. Those who desire to sup-

followed, and at least a probable connection can be established between the act and the instigation. Even then, it is not a foreign government, but the very government assailed, which alone, in the exercise of self-defence, can legitimately punish attacks directed against its own existence.

press it, of course deny its truth; but they are not infallible. They have no authority to decide the question for all mankind, and exclude every other person from the means of judging. To refuse a hearing to an opinion, because they are sure that it is false, is to assume that *their* certainty is the same thing as *absolute* certainty. All silencing of discussion is an assumption of infallibility. Its condemnation may be allowed to rest on this common argument, not the worse for being common.

Unfortunately for the good sense of mankind, the fact of their fallibility is far from carrying the weight in their practical judgment, which is always allowed to it in theory; for while every one well knows himself to be fallible, few think it necessary to take any precautions against their own fallibility, or admit the supposition that any opinion of which they feel very certain, may be one of the examples of the error to which they acknowledge themselves to be liable. Absolute princes, or others who are accustomed to unlimited deference, usually feel this complete confidence in their own opinions on nearly all subjects. People more happily situated, who sometimes hear their opinions disputed, and are not wholly unused to be set right when they are wrong, place the same unbounded reliance only on such of their opinions as are shared by all who surround them, or to whom they habitually defer: for in proportion to a man's want of confidence in his own solitary judgment, does he usually repose, with implicit trust, on the infallibility of "the world" in general. And the world, to each individual, means the part of it with which he comes in contact; his party, his sect, his church, his class of society: the man may be called, by comparison, almost liberal and large-minded to whom it means anything so comprehensive as his own country or his own age. Nor is his faith in this collective authority at all shaken by his being aware that other ages, countries, sects, churches, classes, and parties have thought, and even now think, the exact reverse. He devolves upon his own world the responsibility of being in the right against the dissentient worlds of other people; and it never troubles him that mere accident has decided which of these numerous worlds is the object of his reliance, and that the same causes which make him a Churchman in London, would have made him a Buddhist or a Confucian in Pekin. Yet it is as evident in itself as any amount of argument can make it, that ages are no more infallible than individuals; every age having held many opinions which subsequent ages have deemed not only false but absurd; and it is as certain that many opinions, now general, will be rejected by future ages, as it is that many, once general, are rejected by the present.

The objection likely to be made to this argument, would probably take some such form as the following. There is no greater assumption of infallibility in forbidding the propagation of error, than in any other thing which is done by public authority on its own judgment and responsibility. Judgment is given to men that they may use it. Because it may be used erroneously, are men to be told that they ought not to use it at all? To prohibit what they think pernicious, is not claiming exemption from error, but fulfilling the duty incumbent on them, although fallible, of acting on their conscientious conviction. If we were never to act on our opinions, because those opinions may be wrong, we should leave all our interests uncared for, and all our duties unperformed. An objection which applies to all conduct can be no valid objection to any conduct in particular.

It is the duty of governments, and of individuals, to form the truest opinions they can; to form them carefully, and never impose them upon others unless they are quite sure of being right. But when they are sure (such reasoners may say), it is not conscientiousness but cowardice to shrink from acting on their opinions, and allow doctrines which they honestly think dangerous to the welfare of mankind, either in this life or in another, to be scattered abroad without restraint, because other people, in less enlightened times, have persecuted opinions now believed to be true. Let us take care, it may be said, not to make the same mistake: but governments and nations have made mistakes in other things, which are not denied to be fit subjects for the exercise of authority: they have laid on bad taxes, made unjust wars. Ought we therefore to lay on no taxes, and,

under whatever provocation, make no wars? Men, and
governments, must act to the best of their ability. There
is no such thing as absolute certainty, but there is assurance
sufficient for the purposes of human life. We may, and
must, assume our opinion to be true for the guidance of our
own conduct: and it is assuming no more when we forbid
bad men to pervert society by the propagation of opinions
which we regard as false and pernicious.

I answer, that it is assuming very much more. There is
the greatest difference between presuming an opinion to be
true, because, with every opportunity for contesting it, it
has not been refuted, and assuming its truth for the purpose
of not permitting its refutation. Complete liberty of con-
tradicting and disproving our opinion, is the very condition
which justifies us in assuming its truth for purposes of
action; and on no other terms can a being with human
faculties have any rational assurance of being right.

When we consider either the history of opinion, or the
ordinary conduct of human life, to what is it to be ascribed
that the one and the other are no worse than they are? Not
certainly to the inherent force of the human understanding;
for, on any matter not self-evident, there are ninety-nine persons totally incapable of judging of it, for one who is capable;
and the capacity of the hundredth person is only comparative; for the majority of the eminent men of every past
generation held many opinions now known to be erroneous, ·
and did or approved numerous things which no one will now
justify. Why is it, then, that there is on the whole a preponderance among mankind of rational opinions and rational
conduct? If there really is this preponderance—which there
must be, unless human affairs are, and have always been,
in an almost desperate state—it is owing to a quality of the
human mind, the source of everything respectable in man,
either as an intellectual or as a moral being, namely, that
his errors are corrigible. He is capable of rectifying his
mistakes by discussion and experience. Not by experience
alone. There must be discussion, to show how experience is
to be interpreted. Wrong opinions and practices gradually
yield to fact and argument: but facts and arguments, to produce any effect on the mind, must be brought before it.

Very few facts are able to tell their own story, without comments to bring out their meaning. The whole strength and value, then, of human judgment, depending on the one property, that it can be set right when it is wrong, reliance can be placed on it only when the means of setting it right are kept constantly at hand. In the case of any person whose judgment is really deserving of confidence, how has it become so? Because he has kept his mind open to criticism of his opinions and conduct. Because it has been his practice to listen to all that could be said against him; to profit by as much of it as was just, and expound to himself, and upon occasion to others, the fallacy of what was fallacious. Because he has felt, that the only way in which a human being can make some approach to knowing the whole of a subject, is by hearing what can be said about it by persons of every variety of opinion, and studying all modes in which it can be looked at by every character of mind. No wise man ever acquired his wisdom in any mode but this; nor is it in the nature of human intellect to become wise in any other manner. The steady habit of correcting and completing his own opinion by collating it with those of others, so far from causing doubt and hesitation in carrying it into practice, is the only stable foundation for a just reliance on it: for, being cognizant of all that can, at least obviously, be said against him, and having taken up his position against all gainsayers knowing that he has sought for objections and difficulties, instead of avoiding them, and has shut out no light which can be thrown upon the subject from any quarter—he has a right to think his judgment better than that of any person, or any multitude, who have not gone through a similar process.

It is not too much to require that what the wisest of mankind, those who are best entitled to trust their own judgment, find necessary to warrant their relying on it, should be submitted to by that miscellaneous collection of a few wise and many foolish individuals, called the public. The most intolerant of churches, the Roman Catholic Church, even at the canonization of a saint, admits, and listens patiently to, a " devil's advocate." The holiest of men, it appears, cannot be admitted to posthumous honors, until all that the devil could say against him is known and weighed. If even the Newtonian philosophy were not permitted to be questioned, mankind could not feel as complete assurance of its truth as they now do. The beliefs which we have most warrant for, have no safeguard to rest on, but a standing invitation to the whole world to prove them unfounded. If the challenge is not accepted, or is accepted and the attempt fails, we are far enough from certainty still; but we have done the best that the existing state of human reason admits of; we have neglected nothing that could give the truth a chance of reaching us: if the lists are kept open, we may hope that if there be a better truth, it will be found when the human mind is capable of receiving it; and in the meantime we may rely on having attained such approach to truth, as is possible in our own day. This is the amount of certainty attainable by a fallible being, and this the sole way of attaining it.

Strange it is, that men should admit the validity of the arguments for free discussion, but object to their being "pushed to an extreme;" not seeing that unless the reasons are good for an extreme case, they are not good for any case. Strange that they should imagine that they are not assuming infallibility when they acknowledge that there should be free discussion on all subjects which can possibly be *doubtful,* but think that some particular principle or doctrine should be forbidden to be questioned because it is *so certain,* that is, because *they are certain* that it is certain. To call any proposition certain, while there is any one who would deny its certainty if permitted, but who is not permitted, is to assume that we ourselves, and those who agree with us, are the judges of certainty, and judges without hearing the other side.

In the present age—which has been described as "destitute of faith, but terrified at scepticism,"—in which people feel sure, not so much that their opinions are true, as that they should not know what to do without them—the claims of an opinion to be protected from public attack are rested not so much on its truth, as on its importance to society. There are, it is alleged, certain beliefs, so useful, not to say indispensable to well-being, that it is as much the duty of governments to uphold those beliefs, as to protect any other of the interests of society. In a case of such necessity, and so directly in the line of their duty, something less than infallibility may, it is maintained, warrant, and even bind, governments, to act on their own opinion, confirmed by the general opinion of mankind. It is also often argued, and still oftener thought, that none but bad men would desire to weaken these salutary beliefs; and there can be nothing wrong, it is thought, in restraining bad men, and prohibiting what only such men would wish to practise. This mode of thinking makes the justification of restraints on discussion not a question of the truth of doctrines, but of their usefulness; and flatters itself by that means to escape the responsibility of claiming to be an infallible judge of opinions. But those who thus satisfy themselves, do not perceive that the assumption of infallibility is merely shifted from one point to another. The usefulness of an opinion is itself matter of opinion: as disputable, as open to discussion and requiring discussion as much, as the opinion itself. There is the same need of an infallible judge of opinions to decide an opinion to be noxious, as to decide it to be false, unless the opinion condemned has full opportunity of defending itself. And it will not do to say that the heretic may be allowed to maintain the utility or harmlessness of his opinion, though forbidden to maintain its truth. The truth of an opinion is part of its utility. If we would know whether or not it is desirable that a proposition should be believed, is it possible to exclude the consideration of whether or not it is true? In the opinion, not of bad men, but of the best men, no belief which is contrary to truth can be really useful: and can you prevent such men from urging that plea, when they are charged with culpability for denying some doctrine which they are told is useful, but which they believe to be false? Those who are on the side of received opinions, never fail to take all possible advantage of this plea; you do not find *them* handling the question of utility as if it could be completely abstracted from that of truth: on the contrary, it is, above all, because their doctrine is "the truth," that the knowledge or the belief of it is held to be so indispensable. There can be no fair discussion of the question of usefulness, when an argument so vital may be employed on one side, but not on the other. And in point of fact, when law or public feeling do not permit the truth of an opinion to be disputed, they are just as little tolerant of a denial of its usefulness. The utmost they allow is an extenuation of its absolute necessity or of the positive guilt of rejecting it.

In order more fully to illustrate the mischief of denying a hearing to opinions because we, in our own judgment, have condemned them, it will be desirable to fix down the discussion to a concrete case; and I choose, by preference, the cases which are least favourable to me—in which the argument against freedom of opinion, both on the score of truth and on that of utility, is considered the strongest. Let the opinions impugned be the belief in a God and in a future state, or any of the commonly received doctrines of morality. To fight the battle on such ground, gives a great advantage to an unfair antagonist; since he will be sure to say (and many who have no desire to be unfair will say it internally), Are these the doctrines which you do not deem sufficiently certain to be taken under the protection of law? Is the belief in a God one of the opinions, to feel sure of which, you hold to be assuming infallibility? But I must be permitted to observe, that it is not the feeling sure of a doctrine (be it what it may) which I call an assumption of infallibility. It is the undertaking to decide that question *for others*, without allowing them to hear what can be said on the contrary side. And I denounce and reprobate this pretension not the less, if put forth on the side of my most solemn convictions. However positive any one's persuasion may be, not only of the falsity, but of the pernicious consequences—not only of the pernicious consequences, but (to adopt expressions which I altogether condemn) the immorality and impiety of an opinion; yet if, in pursuance of that private judgment, though backed by the public judgment of his country or his cotemporaries, he prevents the opinion from being heard in its defence, he assumes infallibility. And so far from the assumption being less objectionable or less dangerous because the opinion is called immoral or impious, this is the case of all others in which it is most fatal. These are exactly the occasions on which the men of one generation commit those dreadful mistakes which excite the astonishment and horror of posterity. It is among such that we find the instances memorable in history, when the arm of the law has been employed to root out the best men and the noblest doctrines; with deplorable success as to the men, though some of the doctrines have survived to be (as if in mockery) invoked, in defence of similar conduct towards those who dissent from *them*, or from their received interpretation.

Mankind can hardly be too often reminded, that there was once a man named Socrates, between whom and the legal authorities and public opinion of his time, there took place a memorable collision. Born in an age and country abounding in individual greatness, this man has been handed down to us by those who best knew both him and the age, as the most virtuous man in it; while *we* know him as the head and prototype of all subsequent teachers of virtue, the source equally of the lofty inspiration of Plato and the judicious utilitarianism of Aristotle, "*i maëstri di color che sanno*," the two headsprings of ethical as of all other philosophy. This acknowledged master of all the eminent thinkers who have since lived—whose fame, still growing after more than two thousand years, all but outweighs the whole remainder of the names which make his native city illustrious—was put to death by his countrymen, after a judicial conviction, for impiety and immorality. Impiety, in denying the gods recognized by the State; indeed his accuser asserted (see the "Apologia") that he believed in no gods at all. Immorality, in being, by his doctrines and instructions, a "corrupter of youth." Of these charges the tribunal, there is every ground for believing, honestly found him guilty, and condemned the man who probably of all then born had deserved best of mankind, to be put to death as a criminal.

To pass from this to the only other instance of judicial iniquity, the mention of which, after the condemnation of Socrates, would not be an anti-climax: the event which took place on Calvary rather more than eighteen hundred years ago. The man who left on the memory of those who witnessed his life and conversation, such an impression of his moral grandeur, that eighteen subsequent centuries have done homage to him as the Almighty in person, was ignominiously put to death, as what? As a blasphemer. Men did not merely mistake their benefactor; they mistook him for the exact contrary of what he was, and treated him as that prodigy of impiety, which they themselves are now held to be, for their treatment of him. The feelings with which mankind now regard these lamentable transactions, especially the latter of the two, render them extremely unjust in their judgment of the unhappy actors. These were, to all appearance, not bad men—not worse than men most commonly are, but rather the contrary; men who possessed in a full, or somewhat more than a full measure, the religious, moral, and patriotic feelings of their time and people: the very kind of men who, in all times, our own included, have every chance of passing through life blameless and respected. The high-priest who rent his garments when the words were pronounced, which, according to all the ideas of his country, constituted the blackest guilt, was in all probability quite as sincere in his horror and indignation, as the generality of respectable and pious men now are in the religious and moral sentiments they profess; and most of those who now shudder at his conduct, if they had lived in his time and been born Jews, would have acted precisely as he did. Orthodox Christians who are tempted to think that those who stoned to death the first martyrs must have been worse men than they themselves are, ought to remember that one of those persecutors was Saint Paul.

Let us add one more example, the most striking of all, if the impressiveness of an error is measured by the wisdom and virtue of him who falls into it. If ever any one, possessed of power, had grounds for thinking himself the best and most enlightened among his cotemporaries, it was the Emperor Marcus Aurelius. Absolute monarch of the whole civilized world, he preserved through life not only the most unblemished justice, but what was less to be expected from his Stoical breeding, the tenderest heart. The few failings which are attributed to him, were all on the side of indulgence: while his writings, the highest ethical product of the ancient mind, differ scarcely perceptibly, if they differ at all, from the most characteristic teachings of Christ. This man, a better Christian in all but the dogmatic sense of the word, than almost any of the ostensibly Christian sovereigns who have since reigned, persecuted Christianity. Placed at the summit of all the previous attainments of humanity, with an open, unfettered intellect, and a character which led him of himself to embody in his moral writings the Christian ideal, he yet failed to see that Christianity was to be a good and not an evil to the world, with his duties to which he was so deeply penetrated. Existing society he knew to be in a deplorable state. But such as it was, he saw or thought he saw, that it was held together and prevented from being worse, by belief and reverence of the received divinities. As a ruler of mankind, he deemed it his duty not to suffer society to fall in pieces; and saw not how, if its existing ties were removed, any others could be formed which could again knit it together. The new religion openly aimed at dissolving these ties: unless, therefore, it was his duty to adopt that religion, it seemed to be his duty to put it down. Inasmuch then as the theology of Christianity did not appear to him true or of divine origin; inasmuch as this strange history of a crucified God was not credible to him, and a system which purported to rest entirely upon a foundation to him so wholly unbelievable, could not be foreseen by him to be that renovating agency which, after all abatements, it has in fact proved to be; the gentlest and most amiable of philosophers and rulers, under a solemn sense of duty, authorized the persecution of Christianity. To my mind this is one of the most tragical facts in all history. It is a bitter thought, how different a thing the Christianity of the world might have been, if the Christian faith had been adopted as the religion of the empire under the auspices of Marcus Aurelius instead of those of Constantine. But it would be equally unjust to him and false to truth, to deny that no one plea which can be urged for punishing anti-Christian teaching, was wanting to Marcus Aurelius for punishing, as he did, the propagation of Christianity. No Christian more firmly believes that Atheism is false, and tends to the dissolution of society, than Marcus Aurelius believed the same things of Christianity; he who, of all men then living, might have been thought the most capable of appreciating it. Unless any one who approves of punishment for the promulgation of opinions, flatters himself that he is a wiser and better man than Marcus Aurelius—more deeply versed in the wisdom of his time, more elevated in his intellect above it—more earnest in his search for truth, or more single-minded in his devotion to it when found;—let him abstain from that assumption of the joint infallibility of himself and the multitude, which the great Antoninus made with so unfortunate a result.

Aware of the impossibility of defending the use of punishment for restraining irreligious opinions, by any argument which will not justify Marcus' Antoninus, the enemies of religious freedom, when hard pressed, occasionally accept this consequence, and say, with Dr. Johnson, that the persecutors of Christianity were in the right; that persecution is an ordeal through which truth ought to pass, and always passes successfully, legal penalties being, in the end, powerless against truth, though sometimes beneficially effective against mischievous errors. This is a form of the argument for religious intolerance, sufficiently remarkable not to be passed without notice.

A theory which maintains that truth may justifiably be persecuted because persecution cannot possibly do it any harm, cannot be charged with being intentionally hostile to the reception of new truths; but we cannot commend the generosity of its dealing with the persons to whom mankind are indebted for them. To discover to the world something which deeply concerns it, and of which it was previously ignorant; to prove to it that it had been mistaken on some vital point of temporal or spiritual interest, is as important a service as a human being can render to his fellow-creatures, and in certain cases, as in those of the early Christians and of the Reformers, those who think with Dr. Johnson believe it to have been the most precious gift which could be bestowed on mankind. That the authors of such splendid benefits should be requited by martyrdom; that their reward should be to be dealt with as the vilest of criminals, is not, upon this theory, a deplorable error and misfortune, for which humanity should mourn in sackcloth and ashes, but the normal and justifiable state of things. The propounder of a new truth, according to this doctrine, should stand, as stood, in the legislation of the Locrians, the proposer of a new law, with a halter round his neck, to be instantly tightened if the public assembly did not, on hearing his reasons, then and there adopt his proposition. People who defend this mode of treating benefactors, can not be supposed to set much value on the benefit; and I believe this view of the subject is mostly confined to the sort of persons who think that new truths may have been desirable once, but that we have had enough of them now.

But, indeed, the dictum that truth always triumphs over persecution, is one of those pleasant falsehoods which men repeat after one another till they pass into commonplaces, but which all experience refutes. History teems with instances of truth put down by persecution. If not suppressed forever, it may be thrown back for centuries. To speak only of religious opinions: the Reformation broke out at least twenty times before Luther, and was put down. Arnold of Brescia was put down. Fra Dolcino was put down. Savonarola was put down. The Albigeois were put down. The Vaudois were put down. The Lollards were put down. The Hussites were put down. Even after the era of Luther, wherever persecution was persisted in, it was successful. In Spain, Italy, Flanders, the Austrian empire, Protestantism was rooted out; and, most likely, would have been so in England, had Queen Mary lived, or Queen Elizabeth died. Persecution has always succeeded, save where the heretics were too strong a party to be effectually persecuted. No reasonable person can doubt that Christianity might have been extirpated in the Roman empire. It spread, and became predominant, because the persecutions were only occasional, lasting but a short time, and separated by long intervals of almost undisturbed propagandism. It is a piece of idle sentimentality that truth, merely as truth, has any inherent power denied to error, of prevailing against the dungeon and the stake. Men are not more zealous for truth than they often are for error, and a sufficient application of legal or even of social penalties will generally succeed in stopping the propagation of either. The real advantage which truth has, consists in this, that when an opinion is true, it may be extinguished once, twice, or many times, but in the course of ages there will generally be found persons to rediscover it, until some one of its reappearances falls on a time when from favourable circumstances it escapes persecution until it has made such head as to withstand all subsequent attempts to suppress it.

It will be said, that we do not now put to death the introducers of new opinions: we are not like our fathers who slew the prophets, we even build sepulchres to them. It is true we no longer put heretics to death; and the amount of penal infliction which modern feeling would probably tolerate, even against the most obnoxious opinions, is not sufficient to extirpate them. But let us not flatter ourselves that we are yet free from the stain even of legal persecution. Penalties for opinion, or at least for its expression, still exist by law; and their enforcement is not, even in these times, so unexampled as to make it at all incredible that they may some day be revived in full force. In the year 1857, at the summer assizes of the county of Cornwall, an unfortunate man,[2] said to be of unexceptionable conduct in all relations of life, was sentenced to twenty-one months imprisonment, for uttering, and writing on a gate, some offensive words concerning Christianity. Within a month of the same time, at the Old Bailey, two persons, on two separate occasions,[3] were rejected as jurymen, and one of them grossly insulted by the judge and one of the counsel, because they honestly declared that they had no theological belief; and a third, a foreigner,[4] for the same reason, was denied justice against a thief. This refusal of redress took place in virtue of the legal doctrine, that no person can be allowed to give evidence in a court of justice, who does not profess belief in a God (any god is sufficient) and in a future state; which is equivalent to declaring such persons to be outlaws, excluded from the protection of the tribunals; who may not only be robbed or assaulted with impunity, if no one

[2] Thomas Pooley, Bodmin Assizes, July 31, 1857. In December following, he received a free pardon from the Crown.
[3] George Jacob Holyoake, August 17, 1857; Edward Truelove, July, 1857.
[4] Baron de Gleichen, Marlborough Street Police Court, August 4, 1857.

but themselves, or persons of similar opinions, be present, but any one else may be robbed or assaulted with impunity, if the proof of the fact depends on their evidence. The assumption on which this is grounded, is that the oath is worthless, of a person who does not believe in a future state; a proposition which betokens much ignorance of history in those who assent to it (since it is historically true that a large proportion of infidels in all ages have been persons of distinguished integrity and honor); and would be maintained by no one who had the smallest conception how many of the persons in greatest repute with the world, both for virtues and for attainments, are well known, at least to their intimates, to be unbelievers. The rule, besides, is suicidal, and cuts away its own foundation. Under pretence that atheists must be liars, it admits the testimony of all atheists who are willing to lie, and rejects only those who brave the obloquy of publicly confessing a detested creed rather than affirm a falsehood. A rule thus self-convicted of absurdity so far as regards its professed purpose, can be kept in force only as a badge of hatred, a relic of persecution; a persecution, too, having the peculiarity that the qualification for undergoing it is the being clearly proved not to deserve it. The rule, and the theory it implies, are hardly less insulting to believers than to infidels. For if he who does not believe in a future state necessarily lies, it follows that they who do believe are only prevented from lying, if prevented they are, by the fear of hell. We will not do the authors and abettors of the rule the injury of supposing, that the conception which they have formed of Christian virtue is drawn from their own consciousness.

These, indeed, are but rags and remnants of persecution, and may be thought to be not so much an indication of the wish to persecute, as an example of that very frequent infirmity of English minds, which makes them take a preposterous pleasure in the assertion of a bad principle, when they are no longer bad enough to desire to carry it really into practice. But unhappily there is no security in the state of the public mind, that the suspension of worse forms of legal persecution, which has lasted for about the space of a generation, will continue. In this age the quiet surface of routine is as often ruffled by attempts to resuscitate past evils, as to introduce new benefits. What is boasted of at the present time as the revival of religion, is always, in narrow and uncultivated minds, at least as much the revival of bigotry; and where there is the strongest permanent leaven of intolerance in the feelings of a people, which at all times abides in the middle classes of this country, it needs but little to provoke them into actively persecuting those whom they have never ceased to think proper objects of persecution.[5] For it is this—it is the opinions men entertain, and the feelings they cherish, respecting those who disown the beliefs they deem important, which makes this country not a place of mental freedom. For a long time past, the chief mischief of the legal penalties is that they strengthen the social stigma. It is that stigma which is really effective, and so effective is it, that the profession of opinions which are under the ban of society is much less common in England, than is, in many other countries, the avowal of those which incur risk of judicial punishment. In respect to all persons but those whose pecuniary circumstances make them independent of the good will of other people, opinion, on this subject, is as efficacious as law; men might as well be imprisoned, as excluded from the means of earning their bread. Those whose bread is already secured, and who

[5] Ample warning may be drawn from the large infusion of the passions of a persecutor, which mingled with the general display of the worst parts of our national character on the occasion of the Sepoy insurrection. The ravings of fanatics or charlatans from the pulpit may be unworthy of notice; but the heads of the Evangelical party have announced as their principle, for the government of Hindoos and Mahomedans, that no schools be supported by public money in which the Bible is not taught, and by necessary consequence that no public employment be given to any but real or pretended Christians. An Under-Secretary of State, in a speech delivered to his constituents on the 12th of November, 1857, is reported to have said: "Toleration of their faith" (the faith of a hundred millions of British subjects), "the superstition which they called religion, by the British Government, had had the effect of retarding the ascendency of the British name, and preventing the salutary growth of Christianity. . . . Toleration was the great corner-stone of the religious liberties of this country; but do not let them abuse that precious word toleration. As he understood it, it meant the complete liberty to all, freedom of worship, *among Christians, who worshipped upon the same foundation.* It meant toleration of all sects and denominations of *Christians who believed in the one mediation.*" I desire to call attention to the fact, that a man who has been deemed fit to fill a high office in the government of this country, under a liberal Ministry, maintains the doctrine that all who do not believe in the divinity of Christ are beyond the pale of toleration. Who, after this imbecile display, can indulge the illusion that religious persecution has passed away, never to return?

desire no favors from men in power, or from bodies of men, or from the public, have nothing to fear from the open avowal of any opinions, but to be ill-thought of and ill-spoken of, and this it ought not to require a very heroic mould to enable them to bear. There is no room for any appeal *ad misericordiam* in behalf of such persons. But though we do not now inflict so much evil on those who think differently from us, as it was formerly our custom to do, it may be that we do ourselves as much evil as ever by our treatment of them. Socrates was put to death, but the Socratic philosophy rose like the sun in heaven, and spread its illumination over the whole intellectual firmament. Christians were cast to the lions, but the Christian Church grew up a stately and spreading tree, overtopping the older and less vigorous growths, and stifling them by its shade. Our merely social intolerance, kills no one, roots out no opinions, but induces men to disguise them, or to abstain from any active effort for their diffusion. With us, heretical opinions do not perceptibly gain or even lose, ground in each decade or generation; they never blaze out far and wide, but continue to smoulder in the narrow circles of thinking and studious persons among whom they originate, without ever lighting up the general affairs of mankind with either a true or a deceptive light. And thus is kept up a state of things very satisfactory to some minds, because, without the unpleasant process of fining or imprisoning anybody, it maintains all prevailing opinions outwardly undisturbed, while it does not absolutely interdict the exercise of reason by dissentients afflicted with the malady of thought. A convenient plan for having peace in the intellectual world, and keeping all things going on therein very much as they do already. But the price paid for this sort of intellectual pacification, is the sacrifice of the entire moral courage of the human mind. A state of things in which a large portion of the most active and inquiring intellects find it advisable to keep the genuine principles and grounds of their convictions within their own breasts, and attempt, in what they address to the public, to fit as much as they can of their own conclusions to premises which they have internally renounced, cannot send forth the open, fearless characters, and logical, consistent intellects who once adorned the thinking world. The sort of men who can be looked for under it, are either mere conformers to commonplace, or time-servers for truth whose arguments on all great subjects are meant for their hearers, and are not those which have convinced themselves. Those who avoid this alternative, do so by narrowing their thoughts and interests to things which can be spoken of without venturing within the region of principles, that is, to small practical matters, which would come right of themselves, if but the minds of mankind were strengthened and enlarged, and which will never be made effectually right until then; while that which would strengthen and enlarge men's minds, free and daring speculation on the highest subjects, is abandoned.

Those in whose eyes this reticence on the part of heretics is no evil, should consider in the first place, that in consequence of it there is never any fair and thorough discussion of heretical opinions; and that such of them as could not stand such a discussion, though they may be prevented from spreading, do not disappear. But it is not the minds of heretics that are deteriorated most, by the ban placed on all inquiry which does not end in the orthodox conclusions. The greatest harm done is to those who are not heretics, and whose whole mental development is cramped, and their reason cowed, by the fear of heresy. Who can compute what the world loses in the multitude of promising intellects combined with timid characters, who dare not follow out any bold, vigorous, independent train of thought, lest it should land them in something which would admit of being comsidered irreligious or immoral? Among them we may occasionally see some man of deep conscientiousness, and subtile and refined understanding, who spends a life in sophisticating with an intellect which he cannot silence, and exhausts the resources of ingenuity in attempting to reconcile the promptings of his conscience and reason with orthodoxy, which yet he does not, perhaps, to the end succeed in doing. No one can be a great thinker who does not recognize, that as a thinker it is his first duty to follow his intellect to whatever conclusions it may lead. Truth gains more even by the errors of one who, with due study and preparation, thinks for himself, than by the true opinions of those who only hold them because they do not suffer themselves to think. Not that it is solely, or chiefly, to form great thinkers, that freedom of thinking is required. On the contrary, it is as much, and even more indispensable, to enable average human beings to attain the mental stature which they are capable of. There have been, and may again be, great individual thinkers, in a general atmosphere of mental slavery. But there never has been, nor ever will be, in that atmosphere, an intellectually active people. Where any people has made a temporary approach to such a character, it has been because the dread of heterodox speculation was for a time suspended. Where there is a tacit convention that principles are not to be disputed; where the discussion of the greatest questions which can occupy humanity is considered to be closed, we cannot hope to find that generally high scale of mental activity which has made some periods of history so remarkable. Never when controversy avoided the subjects which are large and important enough to kindle enthusiasm, was the mind of a people stirred up from its foundations, and the impulse given which raised even persons of the most ordinary intellect to something of the dignity of thinking beings. Of such we have had an example in the condition of Europe during the times immediately following the Reformation; another, though limited to the Continent and to a more cultivated class, in the speculative movement of the latter half of the eighteenth century; and a third, of still briefer duration, in the intellectual fermentation of Germany during the Goethian and Fichtean period. These periods differed widely in the particular opinions which they developed; but were alike in this, that during all three the yoke of authority was broken. In each, an old mental despotism had been thrown off, and no new one had yet taken its place. The impulse given at these three periods has made Europe what it now is. Every single improvement which has taken place either in the human mind or in institutions, may be traced distinctly to one or other of them. Appearances have for some time indicated that all three impulses are well-nigh spent; and we can expect no fresh start, until we again assert our mental freedom.

Let us now pass to the second division of the argument, and dismissing the supposition that any of the received opinions may be false, let us assume them to be true, and examine into the worth of the manner in which they are likely to be held, when their truth is not freely and openly canvassed. However unwillingly a person who has a strong opinion may admit the possibility that his opinion may be false, he ought to be moved by the consideration that however true it may be, if it is not fully, frequently, and fearlessly discussed, it will be held as a dead dogma, not a living truth.

There is a class of persons (happily not quite so numerous as formerly) who think it enough if a person assents undoubtingly to what they think true, though he has no knowledge whatever of the grounds of the opinion, and could not make a tenable defence of it against the most superficial objections. Such persons, if they can once get their creed taught from authority, naturally think that no good, and some harm, comes of its being allowed to be questioned. Where their influence prevails, they make it nearly impossible for the received opinion to be rejected wisely and considerately, though it may still be rejected rashly and ignorantly; for to shut out discussion entirely is seldom possible, and when it once gets in, beliefs not grounded on conviction are apt to give way before the slightest semblance of an argument. Waiving, however, this possibility—assuming that the true opinion abides in the mind, but abides as a prejudice, a belief independent of, and proof against, argument—this is not the way in which truth ought to be held by a rational being. This is not knowing the truth. Truth, thus held, is but one superstition the more, accidentally clinging to the words which enunciate a truth.

If the intellect and judgment of mankind ought to be cultivated, a thing which Protestants at least do not deny, on what can these faculties be more appropriately exercised by any one, than on the things which concern him so much that it is considered necessary for him to hold opinions on them? If the cultivation of the understanding consists in one thing more than in another, it is surely in learning the grounds of one's own opinions. Whatever people believe, on subjects on which it is of the first importance to believe rightly, they ought to be able to defend against at least the common objections. But, some one may say, " Let them be *taught* the grounds of their opinions. It does not follow that opinions must be merely parroted because they are never heard controverted. Persons who learn geometry do not simply commit the theorems to memory, but understand and learn likewise the demonstrations; and it would be absurd to say that they remain ignorant of the grounds of geometrical truths, because they never hear any one deny, and attempt to disprove them." Undoubtedly: and such teaching suffices on a subject like mathematics, where there is nothing at all to be said on the wrong side of the question. The peculiarity of the evidence of mathematical truths is, that all the argument is on one side. There are no objections, and no answers to objections. But on every subject on which difference of opinion is possible, the truth depends on a balance to be struck between two sets of conflicting reasons. Even in natural philosophy, there is always some other explanation possible of the same facts; some geocentric theory instead of heliocentric, some phlogiston instead of oxygen; and it has to be shown why that other theory cannot be the true one: and until this is shown and until we know how it is shown, we do not understand the grounds of our opinion. But when we turn to subjects infinitely more complicated, to morals, religion, politics, social relations, and the business of life, three-fourths of the arguments for every disputed opinion consist in dispelling the appearances which favor some opinion different from it. The greatest orator, save one, of antiquity, has left it on record that he always studied his adversary's case with as great, if not with still greater, intensity than even his own. What Cicero practised as the means of forensic success, requires to be imitated by all who study any subject in order to arrive at the truth. He who knows only his own side of the case, knows little of that. His reasons may be good, and no one may have been able to refute them. But if he is equally unable to refute the reasons on the opposite side; if he does not so much as know what they are, he has no ground for preferring either opinion. The rational position for him would be suspension of judgment, and unless he contents himself with that, he is either led by authority, or adopts, like the generality of the world, the side to which he feels most inclination. Nor is it enough that he should hear the arguments of adversaries from his own teachers, presented as they state them, and accompanied by what they offer as refutations. This is not the way to do justice to the arguments, or bring them into real contact with his own mind. He must be able to hear them from persons who actually believe them; who defend them in earnest, and do their very utmost for them. He must know them in their most plausible and persuasive form; he must feel the whole force of the difficulty which the true view of the subject has to encounter and dispose of, else he will never really possess himself of the portion of truth which meets and removes that difficulty. Ninety-nine in a hundred of what are called educated men are in this condition, even of those who can argue fluently for their opinions. Their conclusion may be true, but it might be false for anything they know: they have never thrown themselves into the mental position of those who think differently from them, and considered what such persons may have to say; and consequently they do not, in any proper sense of the word, know the doctrine which they themselves profess. They do not know those parts of it which explain and justify the remainder; the considerations which show that a fact which seemingly conflicts with another is reconcilable with it, or that, of two apparently strong reasons, one and not the other ought to be preferred. All that part of the truth which turns the scale, and decides the judgment of a completely informed mind, they are strangers to; nor is it ever really known, but to those who have attended equally and impartially to both sides, and endeavored to see the reasons of both in the strongest light. So essential is this discipline to a real understanding of moral and human subjects, that if opponents of all important truths do not exist, it is indispensable to imagine them and supply them with the strongest arguments which the most skilful devil's advocate can conjure up.

To abate the force of these considerations, an enemy

of free discussion may be supposed to say, that there is no necessity for mankind in general to know and understand all that can be said against or for their opinions by philosophers and theologians. That it is not needful for common men to be able to expose all the misstatements or fallacies of an ingenious opponent. That it is enough if there is always somebody capable of answering them, so that nothing likely to mislead uninstructed persons remains unrefuted. That simple minds, having been taught the obvious grounds of the truths inculcated on them, may trust to authority for the rest, and being aware that they have neither knowledge nor talent to resolve every difficulty which can be raised, may repose in the assurance that all those which have been raised have been or can be answered, by those who are specially trained to the task.

Conceding to this view of the subject the utmost that can be claimed for it by those most easily satisfied with the amount of understanding of truth which ought to accompany the belief of it; even so, the argument for free discussion is no way weakened. For even this doctrine acknowledges that mankind ought to have a rational assurance that all objections have been satisfactorily answered; and how are they to be answered if that which requires to be answered is not spoken? or how can the answer be known to be satisfactory, if the objectors have no opportunity of showing that it is unsatisfactory? If not the public, at least the philosophers and theologians who are to resolve the difficulties, must make themselves familiar with those difficulties in their most puzzling form; and this cannot be accomplished unless they are freely stated, and placed in the most advantageous light which they admit of. The Catholic Church has its own way of dealing with this embarrassing problem. It makes a broad separation between those who can be permitted to receive its doctrines on conviction, and those who must accept them on trust. Neither, indeed, are allowed any choice as to what they will accept; but the clergy, such at least as can be fully confided in, may admissibly and meritoriously make themselves acquainted with the arguments of opponents, in order to answer them, and may, therefore, read heretical books; the laity, not unless by special permission, hard to be obtained. This discipline recognizes a knowledge of the enemy's case as beneficial to the teachers, but finds means, consistent with this, of denying it to the rest of the world: thus giving to the *élite* more mental culture, though not more mental freedom, than it allows to the mass. By this device it succeeds in obtaining the kind of mental superiority which its purposes require; for though culture without freedom never made a large and liberal mind, it can make a clever *nisi prius* advocate of a cause. But in countries professing Protestantism, this resource is denied; since Protestants hold, at least in theory, that the responsibility for the choice of a religion must be borne by each for himself, and cannot be thrown off upon teachers. Besides, in the present state of the world, it is practically impossible that writings which are read by the instructed can be kept from the uninstructed. If the teachers of mankind are to be cognizant of all that they ought to know, everything must be free to be written and published without restraint.

If, however, the mischievous operation of the absence of free discussion, when the received opinions are true, were confined to leaving men ignorant of the grounds of those opinions, it might be thought that this, if an intellectual, is no moral evil, and does not affect the worth of the opinions, regarded in their influence on the character. The fact, however, is, that not only the grounds of the opinion are forgotten in the absence of discussion, but too often the meaning of the opinion itself. The words which convey it, cease to suggest ideas, or suggest only a small portion of those they were originally employed to communicate. Instead of a vivid conception and a living belief, there remain only a few phrases retained by rote; or, if any part, the shell and husk only of the meaning is retained, the finer essence being lost. The great chapter in human history which this fact occupies and fills, cannot be too earnestly studied and meditated on.

It is illustrated in the experience of almost all ethical doctrines and religious creeds. They are all full of meaning and vitality to those who originate them, and to the direct disciples of the originators. Their meaning continues to be felt in undiminished strength, and is perhaps brought out into even fuller consciousness, so long as the struggle lasts to give the doctrine or creed an ascendency over other creeds. At last it either prevails, and becomes the general opinion, or its progress stops; it keeps possession of the ground it has gained, but ceases to spread further. When either of these results has become apparent, controversy on the subject flags, and gradually dies away. The doctrine has taken its place, if not as a received opinion, as one of the admitted sects or divisions of opinion: those who hold it have generally inherited, not adopted it; and conversion from one of these doctrines to another, being now an exceptional fact, occupies little place in the thoughts of their professors. Instead of being, as at first, constantly on the alert either to defend themselves against the world, or to bring the world over to them, they have subsided into acquiescence, and neither listen, when they can help it, to arguments against their creed, nor trouble dissentients (if there be such) with arguments in its favor. From this time may usually be dated the decline in the living power of the doctrine. We often hear the teachers of all creeds lamenting the difficulty of keeping up in the minds of believers a lively apprehension of the truth which they nominally recognize, so that it may penetrate the feelings, and acquire a real mastery over the conduct. No such difficulty is complained of while the creed is still fighting for its existence: even the weaker combatants then know and feel what they are fighting for, and the difference between it and other doctrines; and in that period of every creed's existence, not a few persons may be found, who have realized its fundamental principles in all the forms of thought, have weighed and considered them in all their important bearings, and have experienced the full effect on the character, which belief in that creed ought to produce in a mind thoroughly imbued with it. But when it has come to be an hereditary creed, and to be received passively, not actively—when the mind is no longer compelled, in the same degree as at first, to exercise its vital powers on the questions which its belief presents to it, there is a progressive tendency to forget all of the belief except the formularies, or to give it a dull and torpid assent, as if accepting it on trust dispensed with the necessity of realizing it in consciousness, or testing it by personal experience; until it almost ceases to connect itself at all with the inner life of the human being. Then are seen the cases, so frequent in this age of the world as almost to form the majority, in which the creed remains as it were outside the mind, encrusting and petrifying it against all other influences addressed to the higher parts of our nature; manifesting its power by not suffering any fresh and living conviction to get in, but itself doing nothing for the mind or heart, except standing sentinel over them to keep them vacant.

To what an extent doctrines intrinsically fitted to make the deepest impression upon the mind may remain in it as dead beliefs, without being ever realized in the imagination, the feelings, or the understanding, is exemplified by the manner in which the majority of believers hold the doctrines of Christianity. By Christianity I here mean what is accounted such by all churches and sects—the maxims and precepts contained in the New Testament. These are considered sacred, and accepted as laws, by all professing Christians. Yet it is scarcely too much to say that not one Christian in a thousand guides or tests his individual conduct by reference to those laws. The standard to which he does refer it, is the custom of his nation, his class, or his religious profession. He has thus, on the one hand, a collection of ethical maxims, which he believes to have been vouchsafed to him by infallible wisdom as rules for his government; and on the other, a set of every-day judgments and practices, which go a certain length with some of those maxims, not so great a length with others, stand in direct opposition to some, and are, on the whole, a compromise between the Christian creed and the interests and suggestions of worldly life. To the first of these standards he gives his homage; to the other his real allegiance. All Christians believe that the blessed are the poor and humble, and those who are ill-used by the world; that it is easier for a camel to pass through the eye of a needle than for a rich man to enter the kingdom of heaven; that they should judge not, lest they be judged; that they should swear not at all; that they should love their neighbor as themselves; that if one take their cloak, they should give him their coat also; that they should take no thought for the morrow; that if they would be perfect, they should sell all that they have and give it to the poor. They are not insincere when they say that they believe these things. They do believe them, as people believe what they have always heard lauded and never discussed. But in the sense of that living belief which regulates conduct, they believe these doctrines just up to the point to which it is usual to act upon them. The doctrines in their integrity are serviceable to pelt adversaries with; and it is understood that they are to be put forward (when possible) as the reasons for whatever people do that they think laudable. But any one who reminded them that the maxims require an infinity of things which they never even think of doing would gain nothing but to be classed among those very unpopular characters who affect to be better than other people. The doctrines have no hold on ordinary believers—are not a power in their minds. They have an habitual respect for the sound of them, but no feeling which spreads from the words to the things signified, and forces the mind to take *them* in, and make them conform to the formula. Whenever conduct is concerned, they look round for Mr. A and B to direct them how far to go in obeying Christ.

Now we may be well assured that the case was not thus, but far otherwise, with the early Christians. Had it been thus, Christianity never would have expanded from an obscure sect of the despised Hebrews into the religion of the Roman empire. When their enemies said, " See how these Christians love one another " (a remark not likely to be made by anybody now), they assuredly had a much livelier feeling of the meaning of their creed than they have ever had since. And to this cause, probably, it is chiefly owing that Christianity now makes so little progress in extending its domain, and after eighteen centuries, is still nearly confined to Europeans and the descendants of Europeans. Even with the strictly religious, who are much in earnest about their doctrines, and attach a greater amount of meaning to many of them than people in general, it commonly happens that the part which is thus comparatively active in their minds is that which was made by Calvin, or Knox, or some such person much nearer in character to themselves. The sayings of Christ coexist passively in their minds, producing hardly any effect beyond what is caused by mere listening to words so amiable and bland. There are many reasons, doubtless, why doctrines which are the badge of a sect retain more of their vitality than those common to all recognized sects, and why more pains are taken by teachers to keep their meaning alive; but one reason certainly is, that the peculiar doctrines are more questioned, and have to be oftener defended against open gainsayers. Both teachers and learners go to sleep at their post, as soon as there is no enemy in the field.

The same thing holds true, generally speaking, of all traditional doctrines—those of prudence and knowledge of life, as well as of morals or religion. All languages and literatures are full of general observations on life, both as to what it is, and how to conduct oneself in it; observations which everybody knows, which everybody repeats, or hears with acquiescence, which are received as truisms, yet of which most people first truly learn the meaning, when experience, generally of a painful kind, has made it a reality to them. How often, when smarting under some unforeseen misfortune or disappointment, does a person call to mind some proverb or common saying familiar to him all his life, the meaning of which, if he had ever before felt it as he does now, would have saved him from the calamity. There are indeed reasons for this, other than the absence of discussion: there are many truths of which the full meaning *cannot* be realized, until personal experience has brought it home. But much more of the meaning even of these would have been understood, and what was understood would have been far more deeply impressed on the mind, if the man had been accustomed to hear it argued *pro* and *con* by people who did understand it. The fatal tendency of mankind to leave off thinking about a thing when it is no longer doubtful, is the cause of half their errors. A contemporary author has well spoken of "' the deep slumber of a decided opinion."

But what! (it may be asked) Is the absence of unanimity

an indispensable condition of true knowledge? Is it necessary that some part of mankind should persist in error, to enable any to realize the truth? Does a belief cease to be real and vital as soon as it is generally received—and is a proposition never thoroughly understood and felt unless some doubt of it remains? As soon as mankind have unanimously accepted a truth, does the truth perish within them? The highest aim and best result of improved intelligence, it has hitherto been thought, is to unite mankind more and more in the acknowledgment of all important truths: and does the intelligence only last as long as it has not achieved its object? Do the fruits of conquest perish by the very completeness of the victory?

I affirm no such thing. As mankind improve, the number of doctrines which are no longer disputed or doubted will be constantly on the increase: and the well-being of mankind may almost be measured by the number and gravity of the truths which have reached the point of being uncontested. The cessation, on one question after another, of serious controversy, is one of the necessary incidents of the consolidation of opinion; a consolidation as salutary in the case of true opinions, as it is dangerous and noxious when the opinions are erroneous. But though this gradual narrowing of the bounds of diversity of opinion is necessary in both senses of the term, being at once inevitable and indispensable, we are not therefore obliged to conclude that all its consequences must be beneficial. The loss of so important an aid to the intelligent and living apprehension of a truth, as is afforded by the necessity of explaining it to, or defending it against, opponents, though not sufficient to outweigh, is no trifling drawback from, the benefit of its universal recognition. Where this advantage can no longer be had, I confess I should like to see the teachers of mankind endeavoring to provide a substitute for it; some contrivance for making the difficulties of the question as present to the learner's consciousness, as if they were pressed upon him by a dissentient champion, eager for his conversion.

But instead of seeking contrivances for this purpose, they have lost those they formerly had. The Socratic dialectics, so magnificently exemplified in the dialogues of Plato, were a contrivance of this description. They were essentially a negative discussion of the great questions of philosophy and life, directed with consummate skill to the purpose of convincing any one who had merely adopted the commonplaces of received opinion, that he did not understand the subject —that he as yet attached no definite meaning to the doctrines he professed; in order that, becoming aware of his ignorance, he might be put in the way to attain a stable belief, resting on a clear apprehension both of the meaning of doctrines and of their evidence. The school disputations of the Middle Ages had a somewhat similar object. They were intended to make sure that the pupil understood his own opinion, and (by necessary correlation) the opinion opposed to it, and could enforce the grounds of the one and confute those of the other. These last-mentioned contests had indeed the incurable defect, that the premises appealed to were taken from authority, not from reason; and, as a discipline to the mind, they were in every respect inferior to the powerful dialectics which formed the intellects of the "Socratici viri:" but the modern mind owes far more to both than it is generally willing to admit, and the present modes of education contain nothing which in the smallest degree supplies the place either of the one or of the other. A person who derives all his instruction from teachers or books, even if he escape the besetting temptation of contenting himself with cram, is under no compulsion to hear both sides; accordingly it is far from a frequent accomplishment, even among thinkers, to know both sides; and the weakest part of what everybody says in defence of his opinion, is what he intends as a reply to antagonists. It is the fashion of the present time to disparage negative logic —that which points out weaknesses in theory or errors in practice, without establishing positive truths. Such negative criticism would indeed be poor enough as an ultimate result; but as a means to attaining any positive knowledge or conviction worthy the name, it cannot be valued too highly; and until people are again systematically trained to it, there will be few great thinkers, and a low general average of intellect, in any but the mathematical and physical departments of speculation. On any other subject no one's opinions deserve the name of knowledge, except so far as he has either had forced upon him by others, or gone through of himself, the same mental process which would have been required of him in carrying on an active controversy with opponents. That, therefore, which when absent, it is so indispensable, but so difficult, to create, how worse than absurd is it to forego, when spontaneously offering itself! If there are any persons who contest a received opinion, or who will do so if law or opinion will let them, let us thank them for it, open our minds to listen to them, and rejoice that there is some one to do for us what we otherwise ought, if we have any regard for either the certainty or the vitality of our convictions, to do with much greater labor for ourselves.

It still remains to speak of one of the principal causes which make diversity of opinion advantageous, and will continue to do so until mankind shall have entered a stage of intellectual advancement which at present seems at an incalculable distance. We have hitherto considered only two possibilities: that the received opinion may be false, and some other opinion, consequently, true; or that, the received opinion being true, a conflict with the opposite error is essential to a clear apprehension and deep feeling of its truth. But there is a commoner case than either of these; when the conflicting doctrines, instead of being one true and the other false, share the truth between them; and the nonconforming opinion is needed to supply the remainder of the truth, of which the received doctrine embodies only a part. Popular opinions, on subjects not palpable to sense, are often true, but seldom or never the whole truth. They are a part of the truth; sometimes a greater, sometimes a smaller part, but exaggerated, distorted, and disjoined from the truths by which they ought to be accompanied and limited. Heretical opinions, on the other hand, are generally some of these suppressed and neglected truths, bursting the bonds which kept them down, and either seeking reconciliation with the truth contained in the common opinion, or fronting it as enemies, and setting themselves up, with similar exclusiveness, as the whole truth. The latter case is hitherto the most frequent, as, in the human mind, one-sidedness has always been the rule, and many-sidedness the exception. Hence, even in revolutions of opinion, one part of the truth usually sets while another rises. Even progress, which ought to superadd, for the most part only substitutes one partial and incomplete truth for another; improvement consisting chiefly in this, that the new fragment of truth is more wanted, more adapted to the needs of the time, than, that which it displaces. Such being the partial character of prevailing opinions, even when resting on a true foundation; every opinion which embodies somewhat of the portion of truth which the common opinion omits, ought to be considered precious, with whatever amount of error and confusion that truth may be blended. No sober judge of human affairs will feel bound to be indignant because those who force on our notice truths which we should otherwise have overlooked, overlook some of those which we see. Rather, he will think that so long as popular truth is one-sided, it is more desirable than otherwise that unpopular truth should have one-sided asserters too; such being usually the most energetic, and the most likely to compel reluctant attention to the fragment of wisdom which they proclaim as if it were the whole.

Thus, in the eighteenth century, when nearly all the instructed, and all those of the uninstructed who were led by them, were lost in admiration of what is called civilization, and of the marvels of modern science, literature, and philosophy, and while greatly overrating the amount of unlikeness between the men of modern and those of ancient times, indulged the belief that the whole of the difference was in their own favor; with what a salutary shock did the paradoxes of Rousseau explode like bombshells in the midst, dislocating the compact mass of one-sided opinion, and forcing its elements to recombine in a better form and with additional ingredients. Not that the current opinions were on the whole farther from the truth than Rousseau's were; on the contrary, they were nearer to it; they contained more of positive truth, and very much less of error. Nevertheless there lay in Rousseau's doctrine, and has floated down the stream of opinion along with it, a considerable amount of exactly those truths which the popular opinion wanted; and these are the deposit which was left behind when the flood subsided. The superior worth of simplicity of life, the enervating and demoralizing effect of the trammels and hypocrisies of artificial society, are ideas which have never been entirely absent from cultivated minds since Rousseau wrote; and they will in time produce their due effect, though at present needing to be asserted as much as ever, and to be asserted by deeds, for words, on this subject, have nearly exhausted their power.

In politics, again, it is almost a commonplace, that a party of order or stability, and a party of progress or reform, are both necessary elements of a healthy state of political life; until the one or the other shall have so enlarged its mental grasp as to be a party equally of order and of progress, knowing and distinguishing what is fit to be preserved from what ought to be swept away. Each of these modes of thinking derives its utility from the deficiencies of the other; but it is in a great measure the opposition of the other that keeps each within the limits of reason and sanity. Unless opinions favorable to democracy and to aristocracy, to property and to equality, to co-operation and to competition, to luxury and to abstinence, to sociality and individuality, to liberty and discipline, and all the other standing antagonisms of practical life, are expressed with equal freedom, and enforced and defended with equal talent and energy, there is no chance of both elements obtaining their due; one scale is sure to go up, and the other down. Truth, in the great practical concerns of life, is so much a question of the reconciling and combining of opposites, that very few have minds sufficiently capacious and impartial to make the adjustment with an approach to correctness, and it has to be made by the rough process of a struggle between combatants fighting under hostile banners. On any of the great open questions just enumerated, if either of the two opinions has a better claim than the other, not merely to be tolerated, but to be encouraged and countenanced, it is the one which happens at the particular time and place to be in a minority. That is the opinion which, for the time being, represents the neglected interests, the side of human well-being which is in

danger of obtaining less than its share. I am aware that
there is not, in this country, any intolerance of differences of
opinion on most of these topics. They are adduced to show,
by admitted and multiplied examples, the universality of the
fact, that only through diversity of opinion is there, in the
existing state of human intellect, a chance of fair play to all
sides of the truth. When there are persons to be found,
who form an exception to the apparent unanimity of the
world on any subject, even if the world is in the right, it
is always probable that dissentients have something worth
hearing to say for themselves, and that truth would lose
something by their silence.

It may be objected, "But *some* received principles, especially on the highest and most vital subjects, are more than
half-truths. The Christian morality, for instance, is the
whole truth on that subject and if any one teaches a morality
which varies from it, he is wholly in error." As this is of
all cases the most important in practice, none can be fitter
to test the general maxim. But before pronouncing what
Christian morality is or is not, it would be desirable to decide what is meant by Christian morality. If it means the
morality of the New Testament, I wonder that any one who
derives his knowledge of this from the book itself, can suppose that it was announced, or intended, as a complete doctrine of morals. The Gospel always refers to a preëxisting
morality, and confines its precepts to the particulars in which
that morality was to be corrected, or superseded by a wider
and higher; expressing itself, moreover, in terms most general, often impossible to be interpreted literally, and possessing rather the impressiveness of poetry or eloquence than the
precision of legislation. To extract from it a body of ethical doctrine, has never been possible without eking it out
from the Old Testament, that is, from a system elaborate
indeed, but in many respects barbarous, and intended only
for a barbarous people. St. Paul, a declared enemy to this
Judaical mode of interpreting the doctrine and filling up the
scheme of his Master, equally assumes a preëxisting morality, namely, that of the Greeks and Romans; and his
advice to Christians is in a great measure a system of accommodation to that; even to the extent of giving an ap-

parent sanction to slavery. What is called Christian, but should rather be termed theological, morality, was not the work of Christ or the Apostles, but is of much later origin, having been gradually built up by the Catholic Church of the first five centuries, and though not implicitly adopted by moderns and Protestants, has been much less modified by them than might have been expected. For the most part, indeed, they have contented themselves with cutting off the additions which had been made to it in the Middle Ages, each sect supplying the place by fresh additions, adapted to its own character and tendencies. That mankind owe a great debt to this morality, and to its early teachers, I should be the last person to deny; but I do not scruple to say of it, that it is, in many important points, incomplete and one-sided, and that unless ideas and feelings, not sanctioned by it, had contributed to the formation of European life and character, human affairs would have been in a worse condition than they now are. Christian morality (so called) has all the characters of a reaction; it is, in great part, a protest against Paganism. Its ideal is negative rather than positive; passive rather than active; Innocence rather than Nobleness; Abstinence from Evil, rather than energetic Pursuit of Good: in its precepts (as has been well said) "thou shalt not" predominates unduly over "thou shalt." In its horror of sensuality, it made an idol of asceticism, which has been gradually compromised away into one of legality. It holds out the hope of heaven and the threat of hell, as the appointed and appropriate motives to a virtuous life: in this falling far below the best of the ancients, and doing what lies in it to give to human morality an essentially selfish character, by disconnecting each man's feelings of duty from the interests of his fellow-creatures, except so far as a self-interested inducement is offered to him for consulting them. It is essentially a doctrine of passive obedience; it inculcates submission to all authorities found established; who indeed are not to be actively obeyed when they command what religion forbids, but who are not to be resisted, far less rebelled against, for any amount of wrong to ourselves. And while, in the morality of the best Pagan nations, duty to the State holds even a disproportionate place, infringing on the just liberty of the individual; in purely Christian ethics that grand department of duty is scarcely noticed or acknowledged. It is in the Koran, not the New Testament, that we read the maxim—" A ruler who appoints any man to an office, when there is in his dominions another man better qualified for it, sins against God and against the State." What little recognition the idea of obligation to the public obtains in modern morality, is derived from Greek and Roman sources, not from Christian; as, even in the morality of private life, whatever exists of magnanimity, high-mindedness, personal dignity, even the sense of honor, is derived from the purely human, not the religious part of our education, and never could have grown out of a standard of ethics in which the only worth, professedly recognized, is that of obedience.

I am as far as any one from pretending that these defects are necessarily inherent in the Christian ethics, in every manner in which it can be conceived, or that the many requisites of a complete moral doctrine which it does not contain, do not admit of being reconciled with it. Far less would I insinuate this of the doctrines and precepts of Christ himself. I believe that the sayings of Christ are all, that I can see any evidence of their having been intended to be; that they are irreconcilable with nothing which a comprehensive morality requires; that everything which is excellent in ethics may be brought within them, with no greater violence to their language than has been done to it by all who have attempted to deduce from them any practical system of conduct whatever. But it is quite consistent with this, to believe that they contain and were meant to contain, only a part of the truth; that many essential elements of the highest morality are among the things which are not provided for, nor intended to be provided for, in the recorded deliverances of the Founder of Christianity, and which have been entirely thrown aside in the system of ethics erected on the basis of those deliverances by the Christian Church. And this being so, I think it a great error to persist in attempting to find in the Christian doctrine that complete rule for our guidance, which its author intended it to sanction and enforce, but only partially to provide. I believe, too, that this narrow theory is becoming a grave practical evil, detracting greatly from the value of the moral training and instruction, which so many well-meaning persons are now at length exerting themselves to promote. I much fear that by attempting to form the mind and feelings on an exclusively religious type, and discarding those secular standards (as for want of a better name they may be called) which heretofore coexisted with and supplemented the Christian ethics, receiving some of its spirit, and infusing into it some of theirs, there will result, and is even now resulting, a low, abject, servile type of character, which, submit itself as it may to what it deems the Supreme Will, is incapable of rising to or sympathizing in the conception of Supreme Goodness. I believe that other ethics than any one which can be evolved from exclusively Christian sources, must exist side by side with Christian ethics to produce the moral regeneration of mankind; and that the Christian system is no exception to the rule that in an imperfect state of the human mind, the interests of truth require a diversity of opinions. It is not necessary that in ceasing to ignore the moral truths not contained in Christianity, men should ignore any of those which it does contain. Such prejudice, or oversight, when it occurs, is altogether an evil; but it is one from which we cannot hope to be always exempt, and must be regarded as the price paid for an inestimable good. The exclusive pretension made by a part of the truth to be the whole, must and ought to be protested against, and if a reactionary impulse should make the protestors unjust in their turn, this one-sidedness, like the other, may be lamented, but must be tolerated. If Christians would teach infidels to be just to Christianity, they should themselves be just to infidelity. It can do truth no service to blink the fact, known to all who have the most ordinary acquaintance with literary history, that a large portion of the noblest and most valuable moral teaching has been the work, not only of men who did not know, but of men who knew and rejected, the Christian faith.

I do not pretend that the most unlimited use of the freedom of enunciating all possible opinions would put an end to the evils of religious or philosophical sectarianism. Every truth which men of narrow capacity are in earnest about, is sure to be asserted, inculcated, and in many ways even acted on, as if no other truth existed in the world, or at all events none that could limit or qualify the first. I acknowledge that the tendency of all opinions to become sectarian is not cured by the freest discussion, but is often heightened and exacerbated thereby; the truth which ought to have been, but was not, seen, being rejected all the more violently because proclaimed by persons regarded as opponents. But it is not on the impassioned partisan, it is on the calmer and more disinterested bystander, that this collision of opinions works its salutary effect. Not the violent conflict between parts of the truth, but the quiet suppression of half of it, is the formidable evil: there is always hope when people are forced to listen to both sides; it is when they attend only to one that errors harden into prejudices, and truth itself ceases to have the effect of truth, by being exaggerated into falsehood. And since there are few mental attributes more rare than that judicial faculty which can sit in intelligent judgment between two sides of a question, of which only one is represented by an advocate before it, truth has no chance but in proportion as every side of it, every opinion which embodies any fraction of the truth, not only finds advocates, but is so advocated as to be listened to.

We have now recognized the necessity to the mental wellbeing of mankind (on which all their other well-being depends) of freedom of opinion, and freedom of the expression of opinion, on four distinct grounds; which we will now briefly recapitulate.

First, if any opinion is compelled to silence, that opinion may, for aught we can certainly know, be true. To deny this is to assume our own infallibility.

Secondly, though the silenced opinion be an error, it may, and very commonly does, contain a portion of truth; and since the general or prevailing opinion on any object is rarely or never the whole truth, it is only by the collision of adverse opinions that the remainder of the truth has any chance of being supplied.

Thirdly, even if the received opinion be not only true,

but the whole truth; unless it is suffered to be, and actually is, vigorously and earnestly contested, it will, by most of those who receive it, be held in the manner of a prejudice, with little comprehension or feeling of its rational grounds. And not only this, but, fourthly, the meaning of the doctrine itself will be in danger of being lost, or enfeebled, and deprived of its vital effect on the character and conduct: the dogma becoming a mere formal profession, inefficacious for good, but cumbering the ground, and preventing the growth of any real and heartfelt conviction, from reason or personal experience.

Before quitting the subject of freedom of opinion, it is fit to take notice of those who say, that the free expression of all opinions should be permitted, on condition that the manner be temperate, and do not pass the bounds of fair discussion. Much might be said on the impossibility of fixing where these supposed bounds are to be placed; for if the test be offence to those whose opinion is attacked, I think experience testifies that this offence is given whenever the attack is telling and powerful, and that every opponent who pushes them hard, and whom they find it difficult to answer, appears to them, if he shows any strong feeling on the subject, an intemperate opponent. But this, though an important consideration in a practical point of view, merges in a more fundamental objection. Undoubtedly the manner of asserting an opinion, even though it be a true one, may be very objectionable, and may justly incur severe censure. But the principal offences of the kind are such as it is mostly impossible, unless by accidental self-betrayal, to bring home to conviction. The gravest of them is, to argue sophistically, to suppress facts or arguments, to misstate the elements of the case, or misrepresent the opposite opinion. But all this, even to the most aggravated degree, is so continually done in perfect good faith, by persons who are not considered, and in many other respects may not deserve to be considered, ignorant or incompetent, that it is rarely possible on adequate grounds conscientiously to stamp the misrepresentation as morally culpable; and still less could law presume to interfere with this kind of controversial misconduct. With regard to what is commonly meant by intemperate discussion, namely, invective, sarcasm, personality, and the like, the denunciation of these weapons would deserve more sympathy if it were ever proposed to interdict them equally to both sides; but it is only desired to restrain the employment of them against the prevailing opinion: against the unprevailing they may not only be used without general disapproval, but will be likely to obtain for him who uses them the praise of honest zeal and righteous indignation. Yet whatever mischief arises from their use, is greatest when they are employed against the comparatively defenceless; and whatever unfair advantage can be derived by any opinion from this mode of asserting it, accrues almost exclusively to received opinions. The worst offence of this kind which can be committed by a polemic, is to stigmatize those who hold the contrary opinion as bad and immoral men. To calumny of this sort, those who hold any unpopular opinion are peculiarly exposed, because they are in general few and uninfluential, and nobody but themselves feels much interest in seeing justice done them; but this weapon is, from the nature of the case, denied to those who attack a prevailing opinion: they can neither use it with safety to themselves, nor if they could, would it do anything but recoil on their own cause. In general, opinions contrary to those commonly received can only obtain a hearing by studied moderation of language, and the most cautious avoidance of unnecessary offence, from which they hardly ever deviate even in a slight degree without losing ground: while unmeasured vituperation employed on the side of the prevailing opinion, really does deter people from professing contrary opinions, and from listening to those who profess them. For the interest, therefore, of truth and justice, it is far more important to restrain this employment of vituperative language than the other; and, for example, if it were necessary to choose, there would be much more need to discourage offensive attacks on infidelity, than on religion. It is, however, obvious that law and authority have no business with restraining either, while opinion ought, in every instance, to determine its verdict by the circumstances of the individual case; condemning every one, on whichever side of the argument he places himself, in whose mode of advocacy either want of candor, or malignity, bigotry or intolerance of feeling manifest themselves, but not inferring these vices from the side which a person takes, though it be the contrary side of the question to our own; and giving merited honor to every one, whatever opinion he may hold, who has calmness to see and honesty to state what his opponents and their opinions really are, exaggerating nothing to their discredit, keeping nothing back which tells, or can be supposed to tell, in their favor. This is the real morality of public discussion; and if often violated, I am happy to think that there are many controversialists who to a great extent observe it, and a still greater number who conscientiously strive towards it.

CHAPTER III

On Individuality, as One of the Elements of Wellbeing

SUCH being the reasons which make it imperative that human beings should be free to form opinions, and to express their opinions without reserve; and such the baneful consequences to the intellectual, and through that to the moral nature of man, unless this liberty is either conceded, or asserted in spite of prohibition; let us next examine whether the same reasons do not require that men should be free to act upon their opinions—to carry these out in their lives, without hindrance, either physical or moral, from their fellow-men, so long as it is at their own risk and peril. This last proviso is of course indispensable. No one pretends that actions should be as free as opinions. On the contrary, even opinions lose their immunity, when the circumstances in which they are expressed are such as to constitute their expression a positive instigation to some mischievous act. An opinion that corn-dealers are starvers of the poor, or that private property is robbery, ought to be unmolested when simply circulated through the press, but may justly incur punishment when delivered orally to an excited mob assembled before the house of a corn-dealer, or when handed about among the same mob in the form of a placard. Acts of whatever kind, which, without justifiable cause, do harm to others, may be, and in the more important cases absolutely require to be, controlled by the unfavorable sentiments, and, when needful, by the active interference of mankind. The liberty of the individual must be thus far limited; he must not make himself a nuisance to other people. But if he refrains from molesting others in what concerns them, and merely acts according to his own inclination and judgment in things which concern himself, the same reasons which show that

260

opinion should be free, prove also that he should be allowed, without molestation, to carry his opinions into practice at his own cost. That mankind are not infallible; that their truths, for the most part, are only half-truths; that unity of opinion, unless resulting from the fullest and freest comparison of opposite opinions, is not desirable, and diversity not an evil, but a good, until mankind are much more capable than at present of recognizing all sides of the truth, are principles applicable to men's modes of action, not less than to their opinions. As it is useful that while mankind are imperfect there should be different opinions, so is it that there should be different experiments of living; that free scope should be given to varieties of character, short of injury to others; and that the worth of different modes of life should be proved practically, when any one thinks fit to try them. It is desirable, in short, that in things which do not primarily concern others, individuality should assert itself. Where, not the person's own character, but the traditions of customs of other people are the rule of conduct, there is wanting one of the principal ingredients of human happiness, and quite the chief ingredient of individual and social progress.

In maintaining this principle, the greatest difficulty to be encountered does not lie in the appreciation of means towards an acknowledged end, but in the indifference of persons in general to the end itself. If it were felt that the free development of individuality is one of the leading essentials of well-being; that it is not only a coördinate element with all that is designated by the terms civilization, instruction, education, culture, but is itself a necessary part and condition of all those things; there would be no danger that liberty should be undervalued, and the adjustment of the boundaries between it and social control would present no extraordinary difficulty. But the evil is, that individual spontaneity is hardly recognized by the common modes of thinking as having any intrinsic worth, or deserving any regard on its own account. The majority, being satisfied with the ways of mankind as they now are (for it is they who make them what they are), cannot comprehend why those ways should not be good enough for everybody; and what is more,

spontaneity forms no part of the ideal of the majority of
moral and social reformers, but is rather looked on with
jealousy, as a troublesome and perhaps rebellious obstruction to the general acceptance of what these reformers, in
their own judgment, think would be best for mankind. Few
persons, out of Germany, even comprehend the meaning of
the doctrine which Wilhelm von Humboldt, so eminent both
as a *savant* and as a politician, made the text of a treatise—
that "the end of man, or that which is prescribed by the
eternal or immutable dictates of reason, and not suggested
by vague and transient desires, is the highest and most harmonious development of his powers to a complete and consistent whole;" that, therefore, the object "towards which
every human being must ceaselessly direct his efforts, and
on which especially those who design to influence their
fellow-men must ever keep their eyes, is the individuality
of power and development;" that for this there are two
requisites, "freedom, and a variety of situations;" and
that from the union of these arise "individual vigor and
manifold diversity," which combine themselves in "originality."[1]

Little, however, as people are accustomed to a doctrine
like that of Von Humboldt, and surprising as it may be to
them to find so high a value attached to individuality, the
question, one must nevertheless think, can only be one of
degree. No one's idea of excellence in conduct is that people
should do absolutely nothing but copy one another. No
one would assert that people ought not to put into their
mode of life, and into the conduct of their concerns, any
impress whatever of their own judgment, or of their own
individual character. On the other hand, it would be absurd
to pretend that people ought to live as if nothing whatever
had been known in the world before they came into it; as if
experience had as yet done nothing towards showing that
one mode of existence, or of conduct, is preferable to another. Nobody denies that people should be so taught and
trained in youth, as to know and benefit by the ascertained
results of human experience. But it is the privilege and

---

[1] *The Sphere and Duties of Government,* from the German of Baron
Wilhelm von Humboldt, pp. 11-13.

proper condition of a human being, arrived at the maturity of his faculties, to use and interpret experience in his own way. It is for him to find out what part of recorded experience is properly applicable to his own circumstances and character. The traditions and customs of other people are, to a certain extent, evidence of what their experience has taught *them;* presumptive evidence, and as such, have a claim to this deference: but, in the first place, their experience may be too narrow; or they may not have interpreted it rightly. Secondly, their interpretation of experience may be correct but unsuitable to him. Customs are made for customary circumstances, and customary characters: and his circumstances or his character may be uncustomary. Thirdly, though the customs be both good as customs, and suitable to him, yet to conform to custom, merely *as* custom, does not educate or develop in him any of the qualities which are the distinctive endowment of a human being. The human faculties of perception, judgment, discriminative feeling, mental activity, and even moral preference, are exercised only in making a choice. He who does anything because it is the custom, makes no choice. He gains no practice either in discerning or in desiring what is best. The mental and moral, like the muscular powers, are improved only by being used. The faculties are called into no exercise by doing a thing merely because others do it, no more than by believing a thing only because others believe it. If the grounds of an opinion are not conclusive to the person's own reason, his reason cannot be strengthened, but is likely to be weakened by his adopting it: and if the inducements to an act are not such as are consentaneous to his own feelings and character (where affection, or the rights of others are not concerned), it is so much done towards rendering his feelings and character inert and torpid, instead of active and energetic.

He who lets the world, or his own portion of it, choose his plan of life for him, has no need of any other faculty than the ape-like one of imitation. He who chooses his plan for himself, employs all his faculties. He must use observation to see, reasoning and judgment to foresee, activity to gather materials for decision, discrimination to

decide, and when he has decided, firmness and self-control
to hold to his deliberate decision. And these qualities he
requires and exercises exactly in proportion as the part of his
conduct which he determines according to his own judgment
and feelings is a large one. It is possible that he might be
guided in some good path, and kept out of harm's way, without any of these things. But what will be his comparative
worth as a human being? It really is of importance, not
only what men do, but also what manner of men they are
that do it. Among the works of man, which human life is
rightly employed in perfecting and beautifying, the first in
importance surely is man himself. Supposing it were possible to get houses built, corn grown, battles fought, causes
tried, and even churches erected and prayers said, by machinery—by automatons in human form—it would be a considerable loss to exchange for these automatons even the
men and women who at present inhabit the more civilized
parts of the world, and who assuredly are but starved specimens of what nature can and will produce. Human nature
is not a machine to be built after a model, and set to do
exactly the work prescribed for it, but a tree, which requires
to grow and develop itself on all sides, according to the
tendency of the inward forces which make it a living thing.

It will probably be conceded that it is desirable people
should exercise their understandings, and that an intelligent
following of custom, or even occasionally an intelligent de-
viation from custom, is better than a blind and simply
mechanical adhesion to it. To a certain extent it is admitted, that our understanding should be our own: but there
is not the same willingness to admit that our desires and
impulses should be our own likewise; or that to possess impulses of our own, and of any strength, is anything but a
peril and a snare. Yet desires and impulses are as much
a part of a perfect human being, as beliefs and restraints:
and strong impulses are only perilous when not properly
balanced; when one set of aims and inclinations is developed
into strength, while others, which ought to coexist with
them, remain weak and inactive. It is not because men's
desires are strong that they act ill; it is because their consciences are weak. There is no natural connection between

strong impulses and a weak conscience. The natural connection is the other way. To say that one person's desires and feelings are stronger and more various than those of another, is merely to say that he has more of the raw material of human nature, and is therefore capable, perhaps of more evil, but certainly of more good. Strong impulses are but another name for energy. Energy may be turned to bad uses; but more good may always be made of an energetic nature, than of an indolent and impassive one. Those who have most natural feeling, are always those whose cultivated feelings may be made the strongest. The same strong susceptibilities which make the personal impulses vivid and powerful, are also the source from whence are generated the most passionate love of virtue, and the sternest self-control. It is through the cultivation of these, that society both does its duty and protects its interests: not by rejecting the stuff of which heroes are made, because it knows not how to make them. A person whose desires and impulses are his own—are the expression of his own nature, as it has been developed and modified by his own culture—is said to have a character. One whose desires and impulses are not his own, has no character, no more than a steam-engine has a character. If, in addition to being his own, his impulses are strong, and are under the government of a strong will, he has an energetic character. Whoever thinks that individuality of desires and impulses should not be encouraged to unfold itself, must maintain that society has no need of strong natures—is not the better for containing many persons who have much character—and that a high general average of energy is not desirable.

In some early states of society, these forces might be, and were, too much ahead of the power which society then possessed of disciplining and controlling them. There has been a time when the element of spontaneity and individuality was in excess, and the social principle had a hard struggle with it. The difficulty then was, to induce men of strong bodies or minds to pay obedience to any rules which required them to control their impulses. To overcome this difficulty, law and discipline, like the Popes struggling against the Emperors, asserted a power over the whole man, claiming to control all his life in order to control his character—which society had not found any other sufficient means of binding. But society has now fairly got the better of individuality; and the danger which threatens human nature is not the excess, but the deficiency, of personal impulses and preferences. Things are vastly changed, since the passions of those who were strong by station or by personal endowment were in a state of habitual rebellion against laws and ordinances, and required to be rigorously chained up to enable the persons within their reach to enjoy any particle of security. In our times, from the highest class of society down to the lowest every one lives as under the eye of a hostile and dreaded censorship. Not only in what concerns others, but in what concerns only themselves, the individual, or the family, do not ask themselves—what do I prefer? or, what would suit my character and disposition? or, what would allow the best and highest in me to have fair play, and enable it to grow and thrive? They ask themselves, what is suitable to my position? what is usually done by persons of my station and pecuniary circumstances? or (worse still) what is usually done by persons of a station and circumstances superior to mine? I do not mean that they choose what is customary, in preference to what suits their own inclination. It does not occur to them to have any inclination, except for what is customary. Thus the mind itself is bowed to the yoke: even in what people do for pleasure, conformity is the first thing thought of; they like in crowds; they exercise choice only among things commonly done: peculiarity of taste, eccentricity of conduct, are shunned equally with crimes: until by dint of not following their own nature, they have no nature to follow: their human capacities are withered and starved: they become incapable of any strong wishes or native pleasures, and are generally without either opinions or feelings of home growth, or properly their own. Now is this, or is it not, the desirable condition of human nature?

It is so, on the Calvinistic theory. According to that, the one great offence of man is Self-will. All the good of which humanity is capable, is comprised in Obedience. You have no choice; thus you must do, and no otherwise; "whatever is not a duty is a sin." Human nature being radically corrupt, there is no redemption for any one until human nature is killed within him. To one holding this theory of life, crushing out any of the human faculties, capacities, and susceptibilities, is no evil: man needs no capacity, but that of surrendering himself to the will of God: and if he uses any of his faculties for any other purpose but to do that supposed will more effectually, he is better without them. That is the theory of Calvinism; and it is held, in a mitigated form, by many who do not consider themselves Calvinists; the mitigation consisting in giving a less ascetic interpretation to the alleged will of God; asserting it to be his will that mankind should gratify some of their inclinations; of course not in the manner they themselves prefer, but in the way of obedience, that is, in a way prescribed to them by authority; and, therefore, by the necessary conditions of the case, the same for all.

In some such insidious form there is at present a strong tendency to this narrow theory of life, and to the pinched and hidebound type of human character which it patronizes. Many persons, no doubt, sincerely think that human beings thus cramped and dwarfed, are as their Maker designed them to be; just as many have thought that trees are a much finer thing when clipped into pollards, or cut out into figures of animals, than as nature made them. But if it be any part of religion to believe that man was made by a good Being, it is more consistent with that faith to believe, that this Being gave all human faculties that they might be cultivated and unfolded, not rooted out and consumed, and that he takes delight in every nearer approach made by his creatures to the ideal conception embodied in them, every increase in any of their capabilities of comprehension, of action, or of enjoyment. There is a different type of human excellence from the Calvinistic; a conception of humanity as having its nature bestowed on it for other purposes than merely to be abnegated. "Pagan self-assertion" is one of the elements of human worth, as well as "Christian self-denial."[2] There is a Greek ideal of self-development, which the Platonic and Chris-

[2] Sterling's *Essays*.

tian ideal of self-government blends with, but does not supersede. It may be better to be a John Knox than an Alcibiades, but it is better to be a Pericles than either; nor would a Pericles, if we had one in these days, be without anything good which belonged to John Knox.

It is not by wearing down into uniformity all that is individual in themselves, but by cultivating it and calling it forth, within the limits imposed by the rights and interests of others, that human beings become a noble and beautiful object of contemplation; and as the works partake the character of those who do them, by the same process human life also becomes rich, diversified, and animating, furnishing more abundant aliment to high thoughts and elevating feelings, and strengthening the tie which binds every individual to the race, by making the race infinitely better worth belonging to. In proportion to the development of his individuality, each person becomes more valuable to himself, and is therefore capable of being more valuable to others. There is a greater fulness of life about his own existence, and when there is more life in the units there is more in the mass which is composed of them. As much compression as is necessary to prevent the stronger specimens of human nature from encroaching on the rights of others, cannot be dispensed with; but for this there is ample compensation even in the point of view of human development. The means of development which the individual loses by being prevented from gratifying his inclinations to the injury of others, are chiefly obtained at the expense of the development of other people. And even to himself there is a full equivalent in the better development of the social part of his nature, rendered possible by the restraint put upon the selfish part. To be held to rigid rules of justice for the sake of others, develops the feelings and capacities which have the good of others for their object. But to be restrained in things not affecting their good, by their mere displeasure, develops nothing valuable, except such force of character as may unfold itself in resisting the restraint. If acquiesced in, it dulls and blunts the whole nature. To give any fair play to the nature of each, it is essential that different persons should be allowed to lead different lives. In proportion as this latitude has been exercised in any age, has that age been noteworthy to posterity. Even despotism does not produce its worst effects, so long as Individuality exists under it; and whatever crushes individuality is despotism, by whatever name it may be called, and whether it professes to be enforcing the will of God or the injunctions of men.

Having said that Individuality is the same thing with development, and that it is only the cultivation of individuality which produces, or can produce, well-developed human beings, I might here close the argument: for what more or better can be said of any condition of human affairs, than that it brings human beings themselves nearer to the best thing they can be? or what worse can be said of any obstruction to good, than that it prevents this? Doubtless, however, these considerations will not suffice to convince those who most need convincing; and it is necessary further to show, that these developed human beings are of some use to the undeveloped—to point out to those who do not desire liberty, and would not avail themselves of it, that they may be in some intelligible manner rewarded for allowing other people to make use of it without hindrance.

In the first place, then, I would suggest that they might possibly learn something from them. It will not be denied by anybody, that originality is a valuable element in human affairs. There is always need of persons not only to discover new truths, and point out when what were once truths are true no longer, but also to commence new practices, and set the example of more enlightened conduct, and better taste and sense in human life. This cannot well be gainsaid by anybody who does not believe that the world has already attained perfection in all its ways and practices. It is true that this benefit is not capable of being rendered by everybody alike: there are but few persons, in comparison with the whole of mankind, whose experiments, if adopted by others, would be likely to be any improvement on established practice. But these few are the salt of the earth; without them, human life would become a stagnant pool. Not only is it they who introduce good things which did not before exist; it is they who keep the life in those which already existed. If there were nothing new to be done, would human intellect cease to be necessary? Would it be a reason why those who do the old things should forget why they are done, and do them like cattle, not like human beings? There is only too great a tendency in the best beliefs and practices to degenerate into the mechanical; and unless there were a succession of persons whose ever-recurring originality prevents the grounds of those beliefs and practices from becoming merely traditional, such dead matter would not resist the smallest shock from anything really alive, and there would be no reason why civilization should not die out, as in the Byzantine Empire. Persons of genius, it is true, are, and are always likely to be, a small minority; but in order to have them, it is necessary to preserve the soil in which they grow. Genius can only breathe freely in an *atmosphere* of freedom. Persons of genius are, *ex vi termini, more* individual than any other people—less capable, consequently, of fitting themselves, without hurtful compression, into any of the small number of moulds which society provides in order to save its members the trouble of forming their own character. If from timidity they consent to be forced into one of these moulds, and to let all that part of themselves which cannot expand under the pressure remain unexpanded, society will be little the better for their genius. If they are of a strong character, and break their fetters they become a mark for the society which has not succeeded in reducing them to common-place, to point at with solemn warning as " wild," " erratic," and the like; much as if one should complain of the Niagara river for not flowing smoothly between its banks like a Dutch canal.

I insist thus emphatically on the importance of genius, and the necessity of allowing it to unfold itself freely both in thought and in practice, being well aware that no one will deny the position in theory, but knowing also that almost every one, in reality, is totally indifferent to it. People think genius a fine thing if it enables a man to write an exciting poem, or paint a picture. But in its true sense, that of originality in thought and action, though no one says that it is not a thing to be admired, nearly all, at heart, think they can do very well without it. Unhappily this is too natural to be wondered at. Originality is the one thing which unoriginal minds cannot feel the use of. They cannot see what it is to do for them: how should they? If they could see what it would do for them, it would not be originality. The first service which originality has to render them, is that of opening their eyes: which being once fully done, they would have a chance of being themselves original. Meanwhile, recollecting that nothing was ever yet done which some one was not the first to do, and that all good things which exist are the fruits of originality, let them be modest enough to believe that there is something still left for it to accomplish, and assure themselves that they are more in need of originality, the less they are conscious of the want.

In sober truth, whatever homage may be professed, or even paid, to real or supposed mental superiority, the general tendency of things throughout the world is to render mediocrity the ascendant power among mankind. In ancient history, in the Middle Ages, and in a diminishing degree through the long transition from feudality to the present time, the individual was a power in himself; and if he had either great talents or a high social position, he was a considerable power. At present individuals are lost in the crowd. In politics it is almost a triviality to say that public opinion now rules the world. The only power deserving the name is that of masses, and of governments while they make themselves the organ of the tendencies and instincts of masses. This is as true in the moral and social relations of private life as in public transactions. Those whose opinions go by the name of public opinion, are not always the same sort of public: in America, they are the whole white population; in England, chiefly the middle class. But they are always a mass, that is to say, collective mediocrity. And what is still greater novelty, the mass do not now take their opinions from dignitaries in Church or State, from ostensible leaders, or from books. Their thinking is done for them by men much like themselves, addressing them or speaking in their name, on the spur of the moment, through the newspapers. I am not complaining of all this. I do not assert that anything better is compatible, as a general rule, with the present low state of the human mind. But that does not hinder the government of mediocrity from being mediocre government. No government by a democracy or a numerous aristocracy, either in its political acts or in the opinions, qualities, and tone of mind which it fosters, ever did or could rise above mediocrity, except in so far as the sovereign Many have let themselves be guided (which in their best times they always have done) by the counsels and influence of a more highly gifted and instructed One or Few. The initiation of all wise or noble things, comes and must come from individuals; generally at first from some one individual. The honor and glory of the average man is that he is capable of following that initiative; that he can respond internally to wise and noble things, and be led to them with his eyes open. I am not countenancing the sort of "hero-worship" which applauds the strong man of genius for forcibly seizing on the government of the world and making it do his bidding in spite of itself. All he can claim is, freedom to point out the way. The power of compelling others into it, is not only inconsistent with the freedom and development of all the rest, but corrupting to the strong man himself. It does seem, however, that when the opinions of masses of merely average men are everywhere become or becoming the dominant power, the counterpoise and corrective to that tendency would be, the more and more pronounced individuality of those who stand on the higher eminences of thought. It is in these circumstances most especially, that exceptional individuals, instead of being deterred, should be encouraged in acting differently from the mass. In other times there was no advantage in their doing so, unless they acted not only differently, but better. In this age the mere example of non-conformity, the mere refusal to bend the knee to custom, is itself a service. Precisely because the tyranny of opinion is such as to make eccentricity a reproach, it is desirable, in order to break through that tyranny, that people should be eccentric. Eccentricity has always abounded when and where strength of character has abounded; and the amount of eccentricity in a society has generally been proportional to the amount of genius, mental vigor, and moral courage which it contained. That so few now dare to be eccentric, marks the chief danger of the time.

I have said that it is important to give the freest scope possible to uncustomary things, in order that it may in time appear which of these are fit to be converted into customs. But independence of action, and disregard of custom are not solely deserving of encouragement for the chance they afford that better modes of action, and customs more worthy of general adoption, may be struck out; nor is it only persons of decided mental superiority who have a just claim to carry on their lives in their own way. There is no reason that all human existences should be constructed on some one, or some small number of patterns. If a person possesses any tolerable amount of common sense and experience, his own mode of laying out his existence is the best, not because it is the best in itself, but because it is his own mode. Human beings are not like sheep; and even sheep are not undistinguishably alike. A man cannot get a coat or a pair of boots to fit him, unless they are either made to his measure, or he has a whole warehouseful to choose from: and is it easier to fit him with a life than with a coat, or are human beings more like one another in their whole physical and spiritual conformation than in the shape of their feet? If it were only that people have diversities of taste that is reason enough for not attempting to shape them all after one model. But different persons also require different conditions for their spiritual development; and can no more exist healthily in the same moral, than all the variety of plants can in the same physical atmosphere and climate. The same things which are helps to one person towards the cultivation of his higher nature, are hindrances to another. The same mode of life is a healthy excitement to one, keeping all his faculties of action and enjoyment in their best order, while to another it is a distracting burden, which suspends or crushes all internal life. Such are the differences among human beings in their sources of pleasure, their susceptibilities of pain, and the operation on them of different physical and moral agencies, that unless there is a

corresponding diversity in their modes of life, they neither
obtain their fair share of happiness, nor grow up to the
mental, moral, and æsthetic stature of which their nature is
capable. Why then should tolerance, as far as the public
sentiment is concerned, extend only to tastes and modes of
life which extort acquiescence by the multitude of their adherents? Nowhere (except in some monastic institutions)
is diversity of taste entirely unrecognized; a person may
without blame, either like or dislike rowing, or smoking, or
music, or athletic exercises, or chess, or cards, or study, because both those who like each of these things, and those
who dislike them, are too numerous to be put down. But the
man, and still more the woman, who can be accused either
of doing " what nobody does," or of not doing " what everybody does," is the subject of as much depreciatory remark
as if he or she had committed some grave moral delinquency.
Persons require to possess a title, or some other badge of
rank, or the consideration of people of rank, to be able to
indulge somewhat in the luxury of doing as they like without detriment to their estimation. To indulge somewhat, I
repeat: for whoever allow themselves much of that indulgence, incur the risk of something worse than disparaging speeches—they are in peril of a commission *de lunatico,*
and of having their property taken from them and given to
their relations.[3]

---

[3] There is something both contemptible and frightful in the sort of evidence on which, of late years, any person can be judicially declared unfit
for the management of his affairs; and after his death, his disposal of his
property can be set aside, if there is enough of it to pay the expenses of
litigation—which are charged on the property itself. All the minute details
of his daily life are pried into, and whatever is found which, seen through
the medium of the perceiving and describing faculties of the lowest of the
low, bears an appearance unlike absolute commonplace, is laid before the
jury as evidence of insanity, and often with success; the jurors being little,
if at all, less vulgar and ignorant than the witnesses; while the judges, with
that extraordinary want of knowledge of human nature and life which continually astonishes us in English lawyers, often help to mislead them. These
trials speak volumes as to the state of feeling and opinion among the vulgar
with regard to human liberty. So far from setting any value on individuality—so far from respecting the rights of each individual to act, in things
indifferent, as seems good to his own judgment and inclinations, judges and
juries cannot even conceive that a person in a state of sanity can desire such
freedom. In former days, when it was proposed to burn atheists, charitable
people used to suggest putting them in a madhouse instead: it would be
nothing surprising now-a-days were we to see this done, and the doers
applauding themselves, because, instead of persecuting for religion, they had
adopted so humane and Christian a mode of treating these unfortunates, not
without a silent satisfaction at their having thereby obtained their deserts.

There is one characteristic of the present direction of public opinion, peculiarly calculated to make it intolerant of any marked demonstration of individuality. The general average of mankind are not only moderate in intellect, but also moderate in inclinations: they have no tastes or wishes strong enough to incline them to do anything unusual, and they consequently do not understand those who have, and class all such with the wild and intemperate whom they are accustomed to look down upon. Now, in addition to this fact which is general, we have only to suppose that a strong movement has set in towards the improvement of morals, and it is evident what we have to expect. In these days such a movement has set in; much has actually been effected in the way of increased regularity of conduct, and discouragement of excesses; and there is a philanthropic spirit abroad, for the exercise of which there is no more inviting field than the moral and prudential improvement of our fellow-creatures. These tendencies of the times cause the public to be more disposed than at most former periods to prescribe general rules of conduct, and endeavor to make every one conform to the approved standard. And that standard, express or tacit, is to desire nothing strongly. Its ideal of character is to be without any marked character; to maim by compression, like a Chinese lady's foot, every part of human nature which stands out prominently, and tends to make the person markedly dissimilar in outline to commonplace humanity.

As is usually the case with ideals which exclude one half of what is desirable, the present standard of approbation produces only an inferior imitation of the other half. Instead of great energies guided by vigorous reason, and strong feelings strongly controlled by a conscientious will, its result is weak feelings and weak energies, which therefore can be kept in outward conformity to rule without any strength either of will or of reason. Already energetic characters on any large scale are becoming merely traditional. There is now scarcely any outlet for energy in this country except business. The energy expended in that may still be regarded as considerable. What little is left from that employment, is expended on some hobby; which may be a useful, even a philanthropic hobby, but is always some one thing, and generally a thing of small dimensions. The greatness of England is now all collective: individually small, we only appear capable of anything great by our habit of combining; and with this our moral and religious philanthropists are perfectly contented. But it was men of another stamp than this that made England what it has been; and men of another stamp will be needed to prevent its decline.

The despotism of custom is everywhere the standing hindrance to human advancement, being in unceasing antagonism to that disposition to aim at something better than customary, which is called, according to circumstances, the spirit of liberty, or that of progress or improvement. The spirit of improvement is not always a spirit of liberty, for it may aim at forcing improvements on an unwilling people; and the spirit of liberty, in so far as it resists such attempts, may ally itself locally and temporarily with the opponents of improvement; but the only unfailing and permanent source of improvement is liberty, since by it there are as many possible independent centres of improvement as there are individuals. The progressive principle, however, in either shape, whether as the love of liberty or of improvement, is antagonistic to the sway of Custom, involving at least emancipation from that yoke; and the contest between the two constitutes the chief interest of the history of mankind. The greater part of the world has, properly speaking, no history, because the despotism of Custom is complete. This is the case over the whole East. Custom is there, in all things, the final appeal; justice and right mean conformity to custom; the argument of custom no one, unless some tyrant intoxicated with power, thinks of resisting. And we see the result. Those nations must once have had originality; they did not start out of the ground populous, lettered, and versed in many of the arts of life; they made themselves all this, and were then the greatest and most powerful nations in the world. What are they now? The subjects or dependents of tribes whose forefathers wandered in the forests when theirs had magnificent palaces and gorgeous temples, but over whom custom exercised only a divided rule with liberty and progress. A people, it appears, may be progressive for a certain length of time, and then stop: when does it stop? When it ceases to possess individuality. If a similar change should befall the nations of Europe, it will not be in exactly the same shape: the despotism of custom with which these nations are threatened is not precisely stationariness. It proscribes singularity, but it does not preclude change, provided all change together. We have discarded the fixed costumes of our forefathers; every one must still dress like other people, but the fashion may change once or twice a year. We thus take care that when there is change, it shall be for change's sake, and not from any idea of beauty or convenience; for the same idea of beauty or convenience would not strike all the world at the same moment, and be simultaneously thrown aside by all at another moment. But we are progressive as well as changeable: we continually make new inventions in mechanical things, and keep them until they are again superseded by better; we are eager for improvement in politics, in education, even in morals, though in this last our idea of improvement chiefly consists in persuading or forcing other people to be as good as ourselves. It is not progress that we object to; on the contrary, we flatter ourselves that we are the most progressive people who ever lived. It is individuality that we war against: we should think we had done wonders if we had made ourselves all alike; forgetting that the unlikeness of one person to another is generally the first thing which draws the attention of either to the imperfection of his own type, and the superiority of another, or the possibility, by combining the advantages of both, of producing something better than either. We have a warning example in China—a nation of much talent, and, in some respects, even wisdom, owing to the rare good fortune of having been provided at an early period with a particularly good set of customs, the work, in some measure, of men to whom even the most enlightened European must accord, under certain limitations, the title of sages and philosophers. They are remarkable, too, in the excellence of their apparatus for impressing, as far as possible, the best wisdom they possess upon every mind in the community, and securing that those who have appropriated most of it shall occupy the posts of honor and

power. Surely the people who did this have discovered the
secret of human progressiveness, and must have kept themselves steadily at the head of the movement of the world.
On the contrary, they have become stationary—have remained so for thousands of years; and if they are ever to
be farther improved, it must be by foreigners. They have
succeeded beyond all hope in what English philanthropists
are so industriously working at—in making a people all alike,
all governing their thoughts and conduct by the same
maxims and rules; and these are the fruits. The modern
régime of public opinion is, in an unorganized form, what
the Chinese educational and political systems are in an organized; and unless individuality shall be able successfully to
assert itself against this yoke, Europe, notwithstanding its
noble antecedents and its professed Christianity, will tend
to become another China.

What is it that has hitherto preserved Europe from this
lot? What has made the European family of nations an
improving, instead of a stationary portion of mankind? Not
any superior excellence in them, which when it exists, exists
as the effect, not as the cause; but their remarkable diversity
of character and culture. Individuals, classes, nations, have
been extremely unlike one another: they have struck out a
great variety of paths, each leading to something valuable;
and although at every period those who travelled in different
paths have been intolerant of one another, and each would
have thought it an excellent thing if all the rest could have
been compelled to travel his road, their attempts to thwart
each other's development have rarely had any permanent
success, and each has in time endured to receive the good
which the others have offered. Europe is, in my judgment,
wholly indebted to this plurality of paths for its progressive
and many-sided development. But it already begins to possess this benefit in a considerably less degree. It is decidedly
advancing towards the Chinese ideal of making all people
alike. M. de Tocqueville, in his last important work, remarks how much more the Frenchmen of the present day
resemble one another, than did those even of the last generation. The same remark might be made of Englishmen
in a far greater degree. In a passage already quoted from

Wilhelm von Humboldt, he points out two things as necessary conditions of human development, because necessary to
render people unlike one another; namely, freedom, and
variety of situations. The second of these two conditions is
in this country every day diminishing. The circumstances
which surround different classes and individuals, and shape
their characters, are daily becoming more assimilated. Formerly, different ranks, different neighborhoods, different
trades and professions lived in what might be called different
worlds; at present, to a great degree, in the same. Comparatively speaking, they now read the same things, listen to the
same things, see the same things, go to the same places, have
their hopes and fears directed to the same objects, have the
same rights and liberties, and the same means of asserting
them. Great as are the differences of position which remain, they are nothing to those which have ceased. And
the assimilation is still proceeding. All the political changes
of the age promote it, since they all tend to raise the low
and to lower the high. Every extension of education promotes it, because education brings people under common
influences, and gives them access to the general stock of
facts and sentiments. Improvements in the means of communication promote it, by bringing the inhabitants of distant
places into personal contact, and keeping up a rapid flow of
changes of residence between one place and another. The
increase of commerce and manufactures promotes it, by
diffusing more widely the advantages of easy circumstances,
and opening all objects of ambition, even the highest, to
general competition, whereby the desire of rising becomes
no longer the character of a particular class, but of all
classes. A more powerful agency than even all these, in
bringing about a general similarity among mankind, is the
complete establishment, in this and other free countries, of
the ascendancy of public opinion in the State. As the various
social eminences which enabled persons entrenched on them
to disregard the opinion of the multitude, gradually became
levelled; as the very idea of resisting the will of the public,
when it is positively known that they have a will, disappears
more and more from the minds of practical politicians; there
ceases to be any social support for non-conformity—any sub-

stantive power in society, which, itself opposed to the ascendancy of numbers, is interested in taking under its protection opinions and tendencies at variance with those of the public.

The combination of all these causes forms so great a mass of influences hostile to Individuality, that it is not easy to see how it can stand its ground. It will do so with increasing difficulty, unless the intelligent part of the public can be made to feel its value—to see that it is good there should be differences, even though not for the better, even though, as it may appear to them, some should be for the worse. If the claims of Individuality are ever to be asserted, the time is now, while much is still wanting to complete the enforced assimilation. It is only in the earlier stages that any stand can be successfully made against the encroachment. The demand that all other people shall resemble ourselves, grows by what it feeds on. If resistance waits till life is reduced *nearly* to one uniform type, all deviations from that type will come to be considered impious, immoral, even monstrous and contrary to nature. Mankind speedily become unable to conceive diversity, when they have been for some time unaccustomed to see it.

CHAPTER IV

Of the Limits to the Authority of Society Over the Individual

WHAT, then, is the rightful limit to the sovereignty of the individual over himself? Where does the authority of society begin? How much of human life should be assigned to individuality, and how much to society?

Each will receive its proper share, if each has that which more particularly concerns it. To individuality should belong the part of life in which it is chiefly the individual that is interested; to society, the part which chiefly interests society.

Though society is not founded on a contract, and though no good purpose is answered by inventing a contract in order to deduce social obligations from it, every one who receives the protection of society owes a return for the benefit, and the fact of living in society renders it indispensable that each should be bound to observe a certain line of conduct towards the rest. This conduct consists, first, in not injuring the interests of one another; or rather certain interests, which, either by express legal provision or by tacit understanding, ought to be considered as rights; and secondly, in each person's bearing his share (to be fixed on some equitable principle) of the labors and sacrifices incurred for defending the society or its members from injury and molestation. These conditions society is justified in enforcing, at all costs to those who endeavor to withhold fulfilment. Nor is this all that society may do. The acts of an individual may be hurtful to others, or wanting in due consideration for their welfare, without going the length of violating any of their constituted rights. The offender may then be justly punished by opinion, though not by law. As

soon as any part of a person's conduct affects prejudicially
the interests of others, society has jurisdiction over it, and
the question whether the general welfare will or will not be
promoted by interfering with it, becomes open to discussion.
But there is no room for entertaining any such question
when a person's conduct affects the interests of no persons
besides himself, or needs not affect them unless they like
(all the persons concerned being of full age, and the ordinary
amount of understanding). In all such cases there should be
perfect freedom, legal and social, to do the action and stand
the consequences.

It would be a great misunderstanding of this doctrine, to
suppose that it is one of selfish indifference, which pretends
that human beings have no business with each other's conduct in life, and that they should not concern themselves
about the well-doing or well-being of one another, unless
their own interest is involved. Instead of any diminution,
there is need of a great increase of disinterested exertion
to promote the good of others. But disinterested benevolence can find other instruments to persuade people to their
good, than whips and scourges, either of the literal or the
metaphorical sort. I am the last person to undervalue the
self-regarding virtues; they are only second in importance,
if even second, to the social. It is equally the business of
education to cultivate both. But even education works by
conviction and persuasion as well as by compulsion, and it is
by the former only that, when the period of education is
past, the self-regarding virtues should be inculcated. Human
beings owe to each other help to distinguish the better from
the worse, and encouragement to choose the former and
avoid the latter. They should be forever stimulating each
other to increased exercise of their higher faculties, and
increased direction of their feelings and aims towards wise
instead of foolish, elevating instead of degrading, objects
and contemplations. But neither one person, nor any number of persons, is warranted in saying to another human
creature of ripe years, that he shall not do with his life for
his own benefit what he chooses to do with it. He is the
person most interested in his own well-being, the interest
which any other person, except in cases of strong personal

attachment, can have in it, is trifling, compared with that
which he himself has; the interest which society has in him
individually (except as to his conduct to others) is fractional, and altogether indirect: while, with respect to his own
feelings and circumstances, the most ordinary man or woman
has means of knowledge immeasurably surpassing those that
can be possessed by any one else. The interference of
society to overrule his judgment and purposes in what only
regards himself, must be grounded on general presumptions;
which may be altogether wrong, and even if right, are as
likely as not to be misapplied to individual cases, by persons no better acquainted with the circumstances of such
cases than those are who look at them merely from without. In this department, therefore, of human affairs, Individuality has its proper field of action. In the conduct of
human beings towards one another, it is necessary that general rules should for the most part be observed, in order that
people may know what they have to expect; but in each person's own concerns, his individual spontaneity is entitled to
free exercise. Considerations to aid his judgment, exhortations to strengthen his will, may be offered to him, even
obtruded on him, by others; but he, himself, is the final
judge. All errors which he is likely to commit against advice
and warning, are far outweighed by the evil of allowing
others to constrain him to what they deem his good.

I do not mean that the feelings with which a person is
regarded by others, ought not to be in any way affected by
his self-regarding qualities or deficiencies. This is neither
possible nor desirable. If he is eminent in any of the qualities which conduce to his own good, he is, so far, a proper
object of admiration. He is so much the nearer to the ideal
perfection of human nature. If he is grossly deficient in
those qualities, a sentiment the opposite of admiration will
follow. There is a degree of folly, and a degree of what
may be called (though the phrase is not unobjectionable) low-
ness or depravation of taste, which, though it cannot justify
doing harm to the person who manifests it, renders him
necessarily and properly a subject of distaste, or, in extreme cases, even of contempt: a person could not have the
opposite qualities in due strength without entertaining these

feelings. Though doing no wrong to any one, a person may so act as to compel us to judge him, and feel to him, as a fool, or as a being of an inferior order: and since this judgment and feeling are a fact which he would prefer to avoid, it is doing him a service to warn him of it beforehand, as of any other disagreeable consequence to which he exposes himself. It would be well, indeed, if this good office were much more freely rendered than the common notions of politeness at present permit, and if one person could honestly point out to another that he thinks him in fault, without being considered unmannerly or presuming. We have a right, also, in various ways, to act upon our unfavorable opinion of any one, not to the oppression of his individuality, but in the exercise of ours. We are not bound, for example, to seek his society; we have a right to avoid it (though not to parade the avoidance), for we have a right to choose the society most acceptable to us. We have a right, and it may be our duty, to caution others against him, if we think his example or conversation likely to have a pernicious effect on those with whom he associates. We may give others a preference over him in optional good offices, except those which tend to his improvement. In these various modes a person may suffer very severe penalties at the hands of others, for faults which directly concern only himself; but he suffers these penalties only in so far as they are the natural, and, as it were, the spontaneous consequences of the faults themselves, not because they are purposely inflicted on him for the sake of punishment. A person who shows rashness, obstinacy, self-conceit—who cannot live within moderate means—who cannot restrain himself from hurtful indulgences—who pursues animal pleasures at the expense of those of feeling and intellect—must expect to be lowered in the opinion of others, and to have a less share of their favorable sentiments, but of this he has no right to complain, unless he has merited their favor by special excellence in his social relations, and has thus established a title to their good offices, which is not affected by his demerits towards himself.

What I contend for is, that the inconveniences which are strictly inseparable from the unfavorable judgment of others, are the only ones to which a person should ever be subjected for that portion of his conduct and character which concerns his own good, but which does not affect the interests of others in their relations with him. Acts injurious to others require a totally different treatment. Encroachment on their rights; infliction on them of any loss or damage not justified by his own rights; falsehood or duplicity in dealing with them; unfair or ungenerous use of advantages over them; even selfish abstinence from defending them against injury—these are fit objects of moral reprobation, and, in grave cases, of moral retribution and punishment. And not only these acts, but the dispositions which lead to them, are properly immoral, and fit subjects of disapprobation which may rise to abhorrence. Cruelty of disposition; malice and ill-nature; that most anti-social and odious of all passions, envy; dissimulation and insincerity; irascibility on insufficient cause, and resentment disproportioned to the provocation; the love of domineering over others; the desire to engross more than one's share of advantages (the πλεονεξία of the Greeks) ; the pride which derives gratification from the abasement of others; the egotism which thinks self and its concerns more important than everything else, and decides all doubtful questions in his own favor;—these are moral vices, and constitute a bad and odious moral character: unlike the self-regarding faults previously mentioned, which are not properly immoralities, and to whatever pitch they may be carried, do not constitute wickedness. They may be proofs of any amount of folly, or want of personal dignity and self-respect; but they are only a subject of moral reprobation when they involve a breach of duty to others, for whose sake the individual is bound to have care for himself. What are called duties to ourselves are not socially obligatory, unless circumstances render them at the same time duties to others. The term duty to oneself, when it means anything more than prudence, means self-respect or self-development; and for none of these is any one accountable to his fellow-creatures, because for none of them is it for the good of mankind that he be held accountable to them.

The distinction between the loss of consideration which a person may rightly incur by defect of prudence or of personal dignity, and the reprobation which is due to him for an offence against the rights of others, is not a merely nominal distinction. It makes a vast difference both in our feelings and in our conduct towards him, whether he displeases us in things in which we think we have a right to control him, or in things in which we know that we have not. If he displeases us, we may express our distaste, and we may stand aloof from a person as well as from a thing that displeases us; but we shall not therefore feel called on to make his life uncomfortable. We shall reflect that he already bears, or will bear, the whole penalty of his error; if he spoils his life by mismanagement, we shall not, for that reason, desire to spoil it still further: instead of wishing to punish him, we shall rather endeavor to alleviate his punishment, by showing him how he may avoid or cure the evils his conduct tends to bring upon him. He may be to us an object of pity, perhaps of dislike, but not of anger or resentment; we shall not treat him like an enemy of society: the worst we shall think ourselves justified in doing is leaving him to himself, if we do not interfere benevolently by showing interest or concern for him. It is far otherwise if he has infringed the rules necessary for the protection of his fellow-creatures, individually or collectively. The evil consequences of his acts do not then fall on himself, but on others; and society, as the protector of all its members, must retaliate on him; must inflict pain on him for the express purpose of punishment, and must take care that it be sufficiently severe. In the one case, he is an offender at our bar, and we are called on not only to sit in judgment on him, but, in one shape or another, to execute our own sentence: in the other case, it is not our part to inflict any suffering on him, except what may incidentally follow from our using the same liberty in the regulation of our own affairs, which we allow to him in his.

The distinction here pointed out between the part of a person's life which concerns only himself, and that which concerns others, many persons will refuse to admit. How (it may be asked) can any part of the conduct of a member of society be a matter of indifference to the other members? No person is an entirely isolated being; it is impossible for a person to do anything seriously or permanently hurtful to himself, without mischief reaching at least to his near connections, and often far beyond them. If he injures his property, he does harm to those who directly or indirectly derived support from it, and usually diminishes, by a greater or less amount, the general resources of the community. If he deteriorates his bodily or mental faculties, he not only brings evil upon all who depended on him for any portion of their happiness, but disqualifies himself for rendering the services which he owes to his fellow-creatures generally; perhaps becomes a burden on their affection or benevolence; and if such conduct were very frequent, hardly any offence that is committed would detract more from the general sum of good. Finally, if by his vices or follies a person does no direct harm to others, he is nevertheless (it may be said) injurious by his example; and ought to be compelled to control himself, for the sake of those whom the sight or knowledge of his conduct might corrupt or mislead.

And even (it will be added) if the consequences of misconduct could be confined to the vicious or thoughtless individual, ought society to abandon to their own guidance those who are manifestly unfit for it? If protection against themselves is confessedly due to children and persons under age, is not society equally bound to afford it to persons of mature years who are equally incapable of self-government? If gambling, or drunkenness, or incontinence, or idleness, or uncleanliness, are as injurious to happiness, and as great a hindrance to improvement, as many or most of the acts prohibited by law, why (it may be asked) should not law, so far as is consistent with practicability and social convenience, endeavor to repress these also? And as a supplement to the unavoidable imperfections of law, ought not opinion at least to organize a powerful police against these vices, and visit rigidly with social penalties those who are known to practise them? There is no question here (it may be said) about restricting individuality, or impeding the trial of new and original experiments in living. The only things it is sought to prevent are things which have been tried and condemned from the beginning of the world until now; things which experience has shown not to be useful or suitable to any person's individuality. There must be some length of time and amount of experience, after which a moral or prudential truth may be regarded as established, and it is merely desired to prevent generation after generation from falling over the same precipice which has been fatal to their predecessors.

I fully admit that the mischief which a person does to himself, may seriously affect, both through their sympathies and their interests, those nearly connected with him, and in a minor degree, society at large. When, by conduct of this sort, a person is led to violate a distinct and assignable obligation to any other person or persons, the case is taken out of the self-regarding class, and becomes amenable to moral disapprobation in the proper sense of the term. If, for example, a man, through intemperance or extravagance, becomes unable to pay his debts, or, having undertaken the moral responsibility of a family, becomes from the same cause incapable of supporting or educating them, he is deservedly reprobated, and might be justly punished; but it is for the breach of duty to his family or creditors, not for the extravagence. If the resources which ought to have been devoted to them, had been diverted from them for the most prudent investment, the moral culpability would have been the same. George Barnwell murdered his uncle to get money for his mistress, but if he had done it to set himself up in business, he would equally have been hanged. Again, in the frequent case of a man who causes grief to his family by addiction to bad habits, he deserves reproach for his unkindness or ingratitude; but so he may for cultivating habits not in themselves vicious, if they are painful to those with whom he passes his life, or who from personal ties are dependent on him for their comfort. Whoever fails in the consideration generally due to the interests and feelings of others, not being compelled by some more imperative duty, or justified by allowable self-preference, is a subject of moral disapprobation for that failure, but not for the cause of it, nor for the errors, merely personal to himself, which may have remotely led to it. In like manner, when a person disables himself, by conduct purely self-regarding, from the performance of some definite duty incumbent on him to the public, he is guilty of a social offence. No person ought to be punished simply for being drunk; but a soldier or a policeman should be punished for being drunk on duty. Whenever, in short, there is a definite damage, or a definite risk of damage, either to an individual or to the public, the case is taken out of the province of liberty, and placed in that of morality or law.

But with regard to the merely contingent or, as it may be called, constructive injury which a person causes to society, by conduct which neither violates any specific duty to the public, nor occasions perceptible hurt to any assignable individual except himself; the inconvenience is one which society can afford to bear, for the sake of the greater good of human freedom. If grown persons are to be punished for not taking proper care of themselves, I would rather it were for their own sake, than under pretence of preventing them from impairing their capacity of rendering to society benefits which society does not pretend it has a right to exact. But I cannot consent to argue the point as if society had no means of bringing its weaker members up to its ordinary standard of rational conduct, except waiting till they do something irrational, and then punishing them, legally or morally, for it. Society has had absolute power over them during all the early portion of their existence: it has had the whole period of childhood and nonage in which to try whether it could make them capable of rational conduct in life. The existing generation is master both of the training and the entire circumstances of the generation to come; it cannot indeed make them perfectly wise and good, because it is itself so lamentably deficient in goodness and wisdom; and its best efforts are not always, in individual cases, its most successful ones; but it is perfectly well able to make the rising generation, as a whole, as good as, and a little better than, itself. If society lets any considerable number of its members grow up mere children, incapable of being acted on by rational consideration of distant motives, society has itself to blame for the consequences. Armed not only with all the powers of education, but with the ascendency which the authority of a received opinion always exercises over the minds who are least fitted to judge for themselves; and aided by the *natural* penalties which cannot be prevented from falling on those who incur the distaste or the contempt of those who know them; let not society pretend that it needs, besides all this, the power to issue commands and enforce obedience in the personal concerns of individuals, in which, on all principles of justice and policy, the decision ought to rest with those who are to abide the consequences. Nor is there anything which tends more to discredit and frustrate the better means of influencing conduct, than a resort to the worse. If there be among those whom it is attempted to coerce into prudence or temperance, any of the material of which vigorous and independent characters are made, they will infallibly rebel against the yoke. No such person will ever feel that others have a right to control him in his concerns, such as they have to prevent him from injuring them in theirs; and it easily comes to be considered a mark of spirit and courage to fly in the face of such usurped authority, and do with ostentation the exact opposite of what it enjoins; as in the fashion of grossness which succeeded, in the time of Charles II., to the fanatical moral intolerance of the Puritans. With respect to what is said of the necessity of protecting society from the bad example set to others by the vicious or the self-indulgent; it is true that bad example may have a pernicious effect, especially the example of doing wrong to others with impunity to the wrong-doer. But we are now speaking of conduct which, while it does no wrong to others, is supposed to do great harm to the agent himself: and I do not see how those who believe this, can think otherwise than that the example, on the whole, must be more salutary than hurtful, since, if it displays the misconduct, it displays also the painful or degrading consequences which, if the conduct is justly censured, must be supposed to be in all or most cases attendant on it.

But the strongest of all the arguments against the interference of the public with purely personal conduct, is that when it does interfere, the odds are that it interferes wrongly, and in the wrong place. On questions of social morality, of duty to others, the opinion of the public, that is, of an overruling majority, though often wrong, is likely to be still oftener right; because on such questions they are only required to judge of their own interests; of the manner in which some mode of conduct, if allowed to be practised, would affect themselves. But the opinion of a similar majority, imposed as a law on the minority, on questions of self-regarding conduct, is quite as likely to be wrong as right; for in these cases public opinion means, at the best, some people's opinion of what is good or bad for other people; while very often it does not even mean that; the public, with the most perfect indifference, passing over the pleasure or convenience of those whose conduct they censure, and considering only their own preference. There are many who consider as an injury to themselves any conduct which they have a distaste for, and resent it as an outrage to their feelings; as a religious bigot, when charged with disregarding the religious feelings of others, has been known to retort that they disregard his feelings, by persisting in their abominable worship or creed. But there is no parity between the feeling of a person for his own opinion, and the feeling of another who is offended at his holding it; no more than between the desire of a thief to take a purse, and the desire of the right owner to keep it. And a person's taste is as much his own peculiar concern as his opinion or his purse. It is easy for any one to imagine an ideal public, which leaves the freedom and choice of individuals in all uncertain matters undisturbed, and only requires them to abstain from modes of conduct which universal experience has condemned. But where has there been seen a public which set any such limit to its censorship? or when does the public trouble itself about universal experience. In its interferences with personal conduct it is seldom thinking of anything but the enormity of acting or feeling differently from itself; and this standard of judgment, thinly disguised, is held up to mankind as the dictate of religion and philosophy, by nine tenths of all moralists and speculative writers. These teach that things are right because they are right; because we feel them to be so. They tell us to search in our own minds and hearts for laws of conduct binding on ourselves and on all others. What can the poor public do but apply these instructions, and make their own personal feelings of good and evil, if they are tolerably unanimous in them, obligatory on all the world?

The evil here pointed out is not one which exists only in theory; and it may perhaps be expected that I should specify the instances in which the public of this age and country improperly invests its own preferences with the character of moral laws. I am not writing an essay on the aberrations of existing moral feeling. That is too weighty a subject to be discussed parenthetically, and by way of illustration. Yet examples are necessary, to show that the principle I maintain is of serious and practical moment, and that I am not endeavoring to erect a barrier against imaginary evils. And it is not difficult to show, by abundant instances, that to extend the bounds of what may be called moral police, until it encroaches on the most unquestionably legitimate liberty of the individual, is one of the most universal of all human propensities.

As a first instance, consider the antipathies which men cherish on no better grounds than that persons whose religious opinions are different from theirs, do not practise their religious observances, especially their religious abstinences. To cite a rather trivial example, nothing in the creed or practice of Christians does more to envenom the hatred of Mahomedans against them, than the fact of their eating pork. There are few acts which Christians and Europeans regard with more unaffected disgust, than Mussulmans regard this particular mode of satisfying hunger. It is, in the first place, an offence against their religion; but this circumstance by no means explains either the degree or the kind of their repugnance; for wine also is forbidden by their religion, and to partake of it is by all Mussulmans accounted wrong, but not disgusting. Their aversion to the flesh of the "unclean beast" is, on the contrary, of that peculiar character, resembling an instinctive antipathy, which the idea of uncleanness, when once it thoroughly sinks into the feelings, seems always to excite even in those whose personal habits are anything but scrupulously cleanly and of which the sentiment of religious impurity, so intense in the Hindoos, is a remarkable example. Suppose now that in a people, of whom the majority were Mussulmans, that majority should insist upon not permitting pork to be eaten within the limits of the country. This would be nothing new in Mahomedan countries.[1] Would it be a legitimate exercise of the moral authority of public opinion? and if not, why not? The practice is really revolting to such a public. They also sincerely think that it is forbidden and abhorred by the Deity. Neither could the prohibition be censured as religious persecution. It might be religious in its origin, but it would not be persecution for religion, since nobody's religion makes it a duty to eat pork. The only tenable ground of condemnation would be, that with the personal tastes and self-regarding concerns of individuals the public has no business to interfere.

To come somewhat nearer home: the majority of Spaniards consider it a gross impiety, offensive in the highest degree to the Supreme Being, to worship him in any other manner than the Roman Catholic; and no other public worship is lawful on Spanish soil. The people of all Southern Europe look upon a married clergy as not only irreligious, but unchaste, indecent, gross, disgusting. What do Protestants think of these perfectly sincere feelings, and of the attempt to enforce them against non-Catholics? Yet, if mankind are justified in interfering with each other's liberty in things which do not concern the interests of others, on what principle is it possible consistently to exclude these cases? or who can blame people for desiring to suppress what they regard as a scandal in the sight of God and man?

No stronger case can be shown for prohibiting anything which is regarded as a personal immorality, than is made out for suppressing these practices in the eyes of those who regard them as impieties; and unless we are willing to adopt

[1] The case of the Bombay Parsees is a curious instance in point. When this industrious and enterprising tribe, the descendants of the Persian fire-worshippers, flying from their native country before the Caliphs, arrived in Western India, they were admitted to toleration by the Hindoo sovereigns, on condition of not eating beef. When those regions afterwards fell under the dominion of Mahomedan conquerors, the Parsees obtained from them a continuance of indulgence, on condition of refraining from pork. What was at first obedience to authority became a second nature, and the Parsees to this day abstain both from beef and pork. Though not required by their religion, the double abstinence has had time to grow into a custom of their tribe; and custom, in the East, is a religion.

the logic of persecutors, and to say that we may persecute others because we are right, and that they must not persecute us because they are wrong, we must beware of admitting a principle of which we should resent as a gross injustice the application to ourselves.

The preceding instances may be objected to, although unreasonably, as drawn from contingencies impossible among us: opinion, in this country, not being likely to enforce abstinence from meats, or to interfere with people for worshipping, and for either marrying or not marrying, according to their creed or inclination. The next example, however, shall be taken from an interference with liberty which we have by no means passed all danger of. Wherever the Puritans have been sufficiently powerful, as in New England, and in Great Britain at the time of the Commonwealth, they have endeavored, with considerable success, to put down all public, and nearly all private, amusements: especially music, dancing, public games, or other assemblages for purposes of diversion, and the theatre. There are still in this country large bodies of persons by whose notions of morality and religion these recreations are condemned; and those persons belonging chiefly to the middle class, who are the ascendant power in the present social and political condition of the kingdom, it is by no means impossible that persons of these sentiments may at some time or other command a majority in Parliament. How will the remaining portion of the community like to have the amusements that shall be permitted to them regulated by the religious and moral sentiments of the stricter Calvinists and Methodists? Would they not, with considerable peremptoriness, desire these intrusively pious members of society to mind their own business? This is precisely what should be said to every government and every public, who have the pretension that no person shall enjoy any pleasure which they think wrong. But if the principle of the pretension be admitted, no one can reasonably object to its being acted on in the sense of the majority, or other preponderating power in the country; and all persons must be ready to conform to the idea of a Christian commonwealth, as understood by the early settlers in New England, if a religious profession similar to theirs should ever succeed in regaining its lost ground, as religions supposed to be declining have so often been known to do.

To imagine another contingency, perhaps more likely to be realized than the one last mentioned. There is confessedly a strong tendency in the modern world towards a democratic constitution of society, accompanied or not by popular political institutions. It is affirmed that in the country where this tendency is most completely realized—where both society and the government are most democratic—the United States—the feeling of the majority, to whom any appearance of a more showy or costly style of living than they can hope to rival is disagreeable, operates as a tolerably effectual sumptuary law, and that in many parts of the Union it is really difficult for a person possessing a very large income, to find any mode of spending it, which will not incur popular disapprobation. Though such statements as these are doubtless much exaggerated as a representation of existing facts, the state of things they describe is not only a conceivable and possible, but a probable result of democratic feeling, combined with the notion that the public has a right to a veto on the manner in which individuals shall spend their incomes. We have only further to suppose a considerable diffusion of Socialist opinions, and it may become infamous in the eyes of the majority to possess more property than some very small amount, or any income not earned by manual labor. Opinions similar in principle to these, already prevail widely among the artisan class, and weigh oppressively on those who are amenable to the opinion chiefly of that class, namely, its own members. It is known that the bad workmen who form the majority of the operatives in many branches of industry, are decidedly of opinion that bad workmen ought to receive the same wages as good, and that no one ought to be allowed, through piecework or otherwise, to earn by superior skill or industry more than others can without it. And they employ a moral police, which occasionally becomes a physical one, to deter skilful workmen from receiving, and employers from giving, a larger remuneration for a more useful service. If the public have any jurisdiction over private concerns, I cannot see that these people are in fault, or that any individual's particular public can be blamed for asserting the same authority over his individual conduct, which the general public asserts over people in general.

But, without dwelling upon supposititious cases, there are, in our own day, gross usurpations upon the liberty of private life actually practised, and still greater ones threatened with some expectation of success, and opinions proposed which assert an unlimited right in the public not only to prohibit by law everything which it thinks wrong, but in order to get at what it thinks wrong, to prohibit any number of things which it admits to be innocent.

Under the name of preventing intemperance the people of one English colony, and of nearly half the United States, have been interdicted by law from making any use whatever of fermented drinks, except for medical purposes: for prohibition of their sale is in fact, as it is intended to be, prohibition of their use. And though the impracticability of executing the law has caused its repeal in several of the States which had adopted it, including the one from which it derives its name, an attempt has notwithstanding been commenced, and is prosecuted with considerable zeal by many of the professed philanthropists, to agitate for a similar law in this country. The association, or "Alliance" as it terms itself, which has been formed for this purpose, has acquired some notoriety through the publicity given to a correspondence between its Secretary and one of the very few English public men who hold that a politician's opinions ought to be founded on principles. Lord Stanley's share in this correspondence is calculated to strengthen the hopes already built on him, by those who know how rare such qualities as are manifested in some of his public appearances, unhappily are among those who figure in political life. The organ of the Alliance, who would "deeply deplore the recognition of any principle which could be wrested to justify bigotry and persecution," undertakes to point out the "broad and impassable barrier" which divides such principles from those of the association. "All matters relating to thought, opinion, conscience, appear to me," he says, "to be without the sphere of legislation; all pertaining to social act, habit, relation, subject only to a discretionary power vested in the State itself, and not in the individual, to be within it." No mention is made of a third class, different from either of these, viz., acts and habits which are not social, but individual; although it is to this class, surely, that the act of drinking fermented liquors belongs. Selling fermented liquors, however, is trading, and trading is a social act. But the infringement complained of is not on the liberty of the seller, but on that of the buyer and consumer; since the State might just as well forbid him to drink wine, as purposely make it impossible for him to obtain it. The Secretary, however, says, "I claim, as a citizen, a right to legislate whenever my social rights are invaded by the social act of another." And now for the definition of these "social rights." "If anything invades my social rights, certainly the traffic in strong drink does. It destroys my primary right of security, by constantly creating and stimulating social disorder. It invades my right of equality, by deriving a profit from the creation of a misery, I am taxed to support. It impedes my right to free moral and intellectual development, by surrounding my path with dangers, and by weakening and demoralizing society, from which I have a right to claim mutual aid and intercourse." A theory of "social rights," the like of which probably never before found its way into distinct language—being nothing short of this—that it is the absolute social right of every individual, that every other individual shall act in every respect exactly as he ought; that whosoever fails thereof in the smallest particular, violates my social right, and entitles me to demand from the legislature the removal of the grievance. So monstrous a principle is far more dangerous than any single interference with liberty; there is no violation of liberty which it would not justify; it acknowledges no right to any freedom whatever, except perhaps to that of holding opinions in secret, without ever disclosing them; for the moment an opinion which I consider noxious, passes any one's lips, it invades all the "social rights" attributed to me by the Alliance. The doctrine ascribes to all mankind a vested interest in each other's moral, intellectual, and even physical perfection, to be defined by each claimant according to his own standard.

Another important example of illegitimate interference with the rightful liberty of the individual, not simply threatened, but long since carried into triumphant effect, is Sabbatarian legislation. Without doubt, abstinence on one day in the week, so far as the exigencies of life permit, from the usual daily occupation, though in no respect religiously binding on any except Jews, is a highly beneficial custom. And inasmuch as this custom cannot be observed without a general consent to that effect among the industrious classes, therefore, in so far as some persons by working may impose the same necessity on others, it may be allowable and right that the law should guarantee to each, the observance by others of the custom, by suspending the greater operations of industry on a particular day. But this justification, grounded on the direct interest which others have in each individual's observance of the practice, does not apply to the self-chosen occupations in which a person may think fit to employ his leisure; nor does it hold good, in the smallest degree, for legal restrictions on amusements. It is true that the amusement of some is the day's work of others; but the pleasure, not to say the useful recreation, of many, is worth the labor of a few, provided the occupation is freely chosen, and can be freely resigned. The operatives are perfectly right in thinking that if all worked on Sunday, seven days' work would have to be given for six days' wages: but so long as the great mass of employments are suspended, the small number who for the enjoyment of others must still work, obtain a proportional increase of earnings; and they are not obliged to follow those occupations, if they prefer leisure to emolument. If a further remedy is sought, it might be found in the establishment by custom of a holiday on some other day of the week for those particular classes of persons. The only ground, therefore, on which restrictions on Sunday amusements can be defended, must be that they are religiously wrong; a motive of legislation which never can be too earnestly protested against. "Deorum injuriæ Diis curæ." It remains to be proved that society or any of its officers holds a commission from on high to avenge any supposed offence to Omnipotence, which is not also a wrong to our fellow-creatures. The notion that it is one man's duty that another should be religious, was the foundation of all the religious persecutions ever perpetrated, and if admitted, would fully justify them. Though the feeling which breaks out in the repeated attempts to stop railway travelling on Sunday, in the resistance to the opening of Museums, and the like, has not the cruelty of the old persecutors, the state of mind indicated by it is fundamentally the same. It is a determination not to tolerate others in doing what is permitted by their religion, because it is not permitted by the persecutor's religion. It is a belief that God not only abominates the act of the misbeliever, but will not hold us guiltless if we leave him unmolested.

I cannot refrain from adding to these examples of the little account commonly made of human liberty, the language of downright persecution which breaks out from the press of this country, whenever it feels called on to notice the remarkable phenomenon of Mormonism. Much might be said on the unexpected and instructive fact, that an alleged new revelation, and a religion, founded on it, the product of palpable imposture, not even supported by the *prestige* of extraordinary qualities in its founder, is believed by hundreds of thousands, and has been made the foundation of a society, in the age of newspapers, railways, and the electric telegraph. What here concerns us is, that this religion, like other and better religions, has its martyrs; that its prophet and founder was, for his teaching, put to death by a mob; that others of its adherents lost their lives by the same lawless violence; that they were forcibly expelled, in a body, from the country in which they first grew up; while, now that they have been chased into a solitary recess in the midst of a desert, many in this country openly declare that it would be right (only that it is not convenient) to send an expedition against them, and compel them by force to conform to the opinions of other people. The article of the Mormonite doctrine which is the chief provocative to the antipathy which thus breaks through the ordinary restraints of religious tolerance, is its sanction of polygamy; which, though permitted to Mahomedans, and Hindoos, and Chinese, seems to excite unquenchable animosity when practised by persons who speak English, and profess to be a kind of Christians. No one has a deeper disapprobation than I have of this Mormon institution; both for other reasons, and because, far from being in any way countenanced by the principle of liberty, it is a direct infraction of that principle, being a mere riveting of the chains of one half of the community, and an emancipation of the other from reciprocity of obligation towards them. Still, it must be remembered that this relation is as much voluntary on the part of the women concerned in it, and who may be deemed the sufferers by it, as is the case with any other form of the marriage institution; and however surprising this fact may appear, it has its explanation in the common ideas and customs of the world, which teaching women to think marriage the one thing needful, make it intelligible that many a woman should prefer being one of several wives, to not being a wife at all. Other countries are not asked to recognize such unions, or release any portion of their inhabitants from their own laws on the score of Mormonite opinions. But when the dissentients have conceded to the hostile sentiments of others, far more than could justly be demanded; when they have left the countries to which their doctrines were unacceptable, and established themselves in a remote corner of the earth, which they have been the first to render habitable to human beings; it is difficult to see on what principles but those of tyranny they can be prevented from living there under what laws they please, provided they commit no aggression on other nations, and allow perfect freedom of departure to those who are dissatisfied with their ways. A recent writer, in some respects of considerable merit, proposes (to use his own words,) not a crusade, but a *civilizade,* against this polygamous community, to put an end to what seems to him a retrograde step in civilization. It also appears so to me, but I am not aware that any community has a right to force another to be civilized. So long as the sufferers by the bad law do not invoke assistance from other communities, I cannot admit that persons entirely unconnected with them ought to step in and require that a condition of things with which all who are directly interested appear to be satisfied, should be put an end to because it is a scandal to persons some thousands of miles distant, who have no part or concern in it. Let them send missionaries, if they please, to preach against it; and let them, by any fair means, (of which silencing the teachers is not one,) oppose the progress of similar doctrines among their own people. If civilization has got the better of barbarism when barbarism had the world to itself, it is too much to profess to be afraid lest barbarism, after having been fairly got under, should revive and conquer civilization. A civilization that can thus succumb to its vanquished enemy must first have become so degenerate, that neither its appointed priests and teachers, nor anybody else, has the capacity, or will take the trouble, to stand up for it. If this be so, the sooner such a civilization receives notice to quit, the better. It can only go on from bad to worse, until destroyed and regenerated (like the Western Empire) by energetic barbarians.

CHAPTER V

APPLICATIONS

THE principles asserted in these pages must be more generally admitted as the basis for discussion of details, before a consistent application of them to all the various departments of government and morals can be attempted with any prospect of advantage. The few observations I propose to make on questions of detail, are designed to illustrate the principles, rather than to follow them out to their consequences. I offer, not so much applications, as specimens of application; which may serve to bring into greater clearness the meaning and limits of the two maxims which together form the entire doctrine of this Essay and to assist the judgment in holding the balance between them, in the cases where it appears doubtful which of them is applicable to the case.

The maxims are, first, that the individual is not accountable to society for his actions, in so far as these concern the interests of no person but himself. Advice, instruction, persuasion, and avoidance by other people, if thought necessary by them for their own good, are the only measures by which society can justifiably express its dislike or disapprobation of his conduct. Secondly, that for such actions as are prejudicial to the interests of others, the individual is accountable, and may be subjected either to social or to legal punishments, if society is of opinion that the one or the other is requisite for its protection.

In the first place, it must by no means be supposed, because damage, or probability of damage, to the interests of others, can alone justify the interference of society, that therefore it always does justify such interference. In many cases, an individual, in pursuing a legitimate object, necessarily and therefore legitimately causes pain or loss to others, or intercepts a good which they had a reasonable hope of obtaining. Such oppositions of interest between individuals often arise from bad social institutions, but are unavoidable while those institutions last; and some would be unavoidable under any institutions. Whoever succeeds in an overcrowded profession, or in a competitive examination; whoever is preferred to another in any contest for an object which both desire, reaps benefit from the loss of others, from their wasted exertion and their disappointment. But it is, by common admission, better for the general interest of mankind, that persons should pursue their objects undeterred by this sort of consequences. In other words, society admits no right, either legal or moral, in the disappointed competitors, to immunity from this kind of suffering; and feels called on to interfere, only when means of success have been employed which it is contrary to the general interest to permit—namely, fraud or treachery, and force.

Again, trade is a social act. Whoever undertakes to sell any description of goods to the public, does what affects the interest of other persons, and of society in general; and thus his conduct, in principle, comes within the jurisdiction of society: accordingly, it was once held to be the duty of governments, in all cases which were considered of importance, to fix prices, and regulate the processes of manufacture. But it is now recognized, though not till after a long struggle, that both the cheapness and the good quality of commodities are most effectually provided for by leaving the producers and sellers perfectly free, under the sole check of equal freedom to the buyers for supplying themselves elsewhere. This is the so-called doctrine of Free Trade, which rests on grounds different from, though equally solid with, the principle of individual liberty asserted in this Essay. Restrictions on trade, or on production for purposes of trade, are indeed restraints; and all restraint, quâ restraint, is an evil: but the restraints in question affect only that part of conduct which society is competent to restrain, and are wrong solely because they do not really produce the results which it is desired to produce by them. As the principle of individual liberty is not involved in the doctrine of Free Trade so neither is it in most of the questions which arise respecting the limits of that doctrine: as for example, what amount of public control is admissible for the prevention of fraud by adulteration; how far sanitary precautions, or arrangements to protect work-people employed in dangerous occupations, should be enforced on employers. Such questions involve considerations of liberty, only in so far as leaving people to themselves is always better, *cæteris paribus,* than controlling them: but that they may be legitimately controlled for these ends, is in principle undeniable. On the other hand, there are questions relating to interference with trade which are essentially questions of liberty; such as the Maine Law, already touched upon; the prohibition of the importation of opium into China; the restriction of the sale of poisons; all cases, in short, where the object of the interference is to make it impossible or difficult to obtain a particular commodity. These interferences are objectionable, not as infringements on the liberty of the producer or seller, but on that of the buyer.

One of these examples, that of the sale of poisons, opens a new question; the proper limits of what may be called the functions of police; how far liberty may legitimately be invaded for the prevention of crime, or of accident. It is one of the undisputed functions of government to take precautions against crime before it has been committed, as well as to detect and punish it afterwards. The preventive function of government, however, is far more liable to be abused, to the prejudice of liberty, than the punitory function; for there is hardly any part of the legitimate freedom of action of a human being which would not admit of being represented, and fairly too, as increasing the facilities for some form or other of delinquency. Nevertheless, if a public authority, or even a private person, sees any one evidently preparing to commit a crime, they are not bound to look on inactive until the crime is committed, but may interfere to prevent it. If poisons were never bought or used for any purpose except the commission of murder, it would be right to prohibit their manufacture and sale. They may, however, be wanted not only for innocent but for useful purposes, and restrictions cannot be imposed in the one case without operating in the other. Again, it is a proper office of public authority to guard against accidents. If either a public officer or any one else saw a person attempting to cross a bridge which had been ascertained to be unsafe, and there were no time to warn him of his danger, they might seize him and turn him back without any real infringement of his liberty; for liberty consists in doing what one desires, and he does not desire to fall into the river. Nevertheless, when there is not a certainty, but only a danger of mischief, no one but the person himself can judge of the sufficiency of the motive which may prompt him to incur the risk: in this case, therefore, (unless he is a child, or delirious, or in some state of excitement or absorption incompatible with the full use of the reflecting faculty,) he ought, I conceive, to be only warned of the danger; not forcibly prevented from exposing himself to it. Similar considerations, applied to such a question as the sale of poisons, may enable us to decide which among the possible modes of regulation are or are not contrary to principle. Such a precaution, for example, as that of labelling the drug with some word expressive of its dangerous character, may be enforced without violation of liberty: the buyer cannot wish not to know that the thing he possesses has poisonous qualities. But to require in all cases the certificate of a medical practitioner, would make it sometimes impossible, always expensive, to obtain the article for legitimate uses. The only mode apparent to me, in which difficulties may be thrown in the way of crime committed through this means, without any infringement, worth taking into account, upon the liberty of those who desire the poisonous substance for other purposes, consists in providing what, in the apt language of Bentham, is called "preappointed evidence." This provision is familiar to every one in the case of contracts. It is usual and right that the law, when a contract is entered into, should require as the condition of its enforcing performance, that certain formalities should be observed, such as signatures, attestation of witnesses, and the like, in order that in case of subsequent dispute, there may be evidence to prove that the contract was really entered into, and that there was nothing in the circumstances to render it legally invalid: the effect being, to throw great obstacles in the way of fictitious contracts, or contracts made in circumstances which, if known, would destroy their validity. Precautions of a similar nature might be enforced in the sale of articles adapted to be instruments of crime. The seller, for example, might be required to enter in a register the exact time of the transaction, the name and address of the buyer, the precise quality and quantity sold; to ask the purpose for which it was wanted, and record the answer he received. When there was no medical prescription, the presence of some third person might be required, to bring home the fact to the purchaser, in case there should afterwards be reason to believe that the article had been applied to criminal purposes. Such regulations would in general be no material impediment to obtaining the article, but a very considerable one to making an improper use of it without detection.

The right inherent in society, to ward off crimes against itself by antecedent precautions, suggests the obvious limitations to the maxim, that purely self-regarding misconduct cannot properly be meddled with in the way of prevention or punishment. Drunkennesses, for example, in ordinary cases, is not a fit subject for legislative interference; but I should deem it perfectly legitimate that a person, who had once been convicted of any act of violence to others under the influence of drink, should be placed under a special legal restriction, personal to himself; that if he were afterwards found drunk, he should be liable to a penalty, and that if when in that state he committed another offence, the punishment to which he would be liable for that other offence should be increased in severity. The making himself drunk, in a person whom drunkenness excites to do harm to others, is a crime against others. So, again, idleness, except in a person receiving support from the public, or except when it constitutes a breach of contract, cannot without tyranny be made a subject of legal punishment; but if either from idleness or from any other avoidable cause, a man fails to perform his legal duties to others, as for instance to support his children, it is no tyranny to force him to fulfil that obligation, by compulsory labor, if no other means are available.

Again, there are many acts which, being directly injurious only to the agents themselves, ougnt not to be legally inter-

dicted, but which, if done publicly, are a violation of good
manners, and coming thus within the category of offences
against others, may rightfully be prohibited. Of this kind
are offences against decency; on which it is unnecessary to
dwell, the rather as they are only connected indirectly with
our subject, the objection to publicity being equally strong
in the case of many actions not in themselves condemnable,
nor supposed to be so.

There is another question to which an answer must be
found, consistent with the principles which have been laid
down. In cases of personal conduct supposed to be blame-
able, but which respect for liberty precludes society from
preventing or punishing, because the evil directly resulting
falls wholly on the agent; what the agent is free to do,
ought other persons to be equally free to counsel or instigate? This question is not free from difficulty. The case
of a person who solicits another to do an act, is not strictly
a case of self-regarding conduct. To give advice or offer
inducements to any one, is a social act, and may therefore,
like actions in general which affect others, be supposed
amenable to social control. But a little reflection corrects
the first impression, by showing that if the case is not
strictly within the definition of individual liberty, yet the
reasons on which the principle of individual liberty is
grounded, are applicable to it. If people must be allowed, in
whatever concerns only themselves, to act as seems best to
themselves at their own peril, they must equally be free to
consult with one another about what is fit to be so done;
to exchange opinions, and give and receive suggestions.
Whatever it is permitted to do, it must be permitted to advise to do. The question is doubtful, only when the insti-
gator derives a personal benefit from his advice; when he
makes it his occupation, for subsistence, or pecuniary gain,
to promote what society and the State consider to be an evil.
Then, indeed, a new element of complication is introduced;
namely, the existence of classes of persons with an interest
opposed to what is considered as the public weal, and whose
mode of living is grounded on the counteraction of it. Ought
this to be interfered with, or not? Fornication, for example,
must be tolerated, and so must gambling; but should a per-

son be free to be a pimp, or to keep a gambling-house? The case is one of those which lie on the exact boundary line between two principles, and it is not at once apparent to which of the two it properly belongs. There are arguments on both sides. On the side of toleration it may be said, that the fact of following anything as an occupation, and living or profiting by the practice of it, cannot make that criminal which would otherwise be admissible; that the act should either be consistently permitted or consistently prohibited; that if the principles which we have hitherto defended are true, society has no business, *as* society, to decide anything to be wrong which concerns only the individual; that it cannot go beyond dissuasion, and that one person should be as free to persuade, as another to dissuade. In opposition to this it may be contended, that although the public, or the State, are not warranted in authoritatively deciding, for purposes of repression or punishment, that such or such conduct affecting only the interests of the individual is good or bad, they are fully justified in assuming, if they regard it as bad, that its being so or not is at least a disputable question: That, this being supposed, they cannot be acting wrongly in endeavoring to exclude the influence of solicitations which are not disinterested, of instigators who cannot possibly be impartial—who have a direct personal interest on one side, and that side the one which the State believes to be wrong, and who confessedly promote it for personal objects only. There can surely, it may be urged, be nothing lost, no sacrifice of good, by so ordering matters that persons shall make their election, either wisely or foolishly, on their own prompting, as free as possible from the arts of persons who stimulate their inclinations for interested purposes of their own. Thus (it may be said) though the statutes respecting unlawful games are utterly indefensible—though all persons should be free to gamble in their own or each other's houses, or in any place of meeting established by their own subscriptions, and open only to the members and their visitors—yet public gambling-houses should not be permitted. It is true that the prohibition is never effectual, and that whatever amount of tyrannical power is given to the police, gambling-houses can always be maintained under other pretences; but they may be compelled to conduct their operations with a certain degree of secrecy and mystery, so that nobody knows anything about them but those who seek them; and more than this, society ought not to aim at. There is considerable force in these arguments. I will not venture to decide whether they are sufficient to justify the moral anomaly of punishing the accessary, when the principal is (and must be) allowed to go free; of fining or imprisoning the procurer, but not the fornicator, the gambling-house keeper, but not the gambler. Still less ought the common operations of buying and selling to be interfered with on analogous grounds. Almost every article which is bought and sold may be used in excess, and the sellers have a pecuniary interest in encouraging that excess; but no argument can be founded on this, in favor, for instance, of the Maine Law; because the class of dealers in strong drinks, though interested in their abuse, are indispensably required for the sake of their legitimate use. The interest, however, of these dealers in promoting intemperance is a real evil, and justifies the State in imposing restrictions and requiring guarantees, which but for that justification would be infringements of legitimate liberty.

A further question is, whether the State while it permits, should nevertheless indirectly discourage conduct which it deems contrary to the best interests of the agent; whether, for example, it should take measures to render the means of drunkenness more costly, or add to the difficulty of procuring them, by limiting the number of the places of sale. On this as on most other practical questions, many distinctions require to be made. To tax stimulants for the sole purpose of making them more difficult to be obtained, is a measure differing only in degree from their entire prohibition; and would be justifiable only if that were justifiable. Every increase of cost is a prohibition, to those whose means do not come up to the augmented price; and to those who do, it is a penalty laid on them for gratifying a particular taste. Their choice of pleasures, and their mode of expending their income, after satisfying their legal and moral obligations to the State and to individuals, are their own concern, and must rest with their own judgment. These

considerations may seem at first sight to condemn the selection of stimulants as special subjects of taxation for purposes of revenue. But it must be remembered that taxation for fiscal purposes is absolutely inevitable; that in most countries it is necessary that a considerable part of that taxation should be indirect; that the State, therefore, cannot help imposing penalties, which to some persons may be prohibitory, on the use of some articles of consumption. It is hence the duty of the State to consider, in the imposition of taxes, what commodities the consumers can best spare; and *à fortiori,* to select in preference those of which it deems the use, beyond a very moderate quantity, to be positively injurious. Taxation, therefore, of stimulants, up to the point which produces the largest amount of revenue (supposing that the State needs all the revenue which it yields) is not only admissible, but to be approved of.

The question of making the sale of these commodities a more or less exclusive privilege, must be answered differently, according to the purposes to which the restriction is intended to be subservient. All places of public resort require the restraint of a police, and places of this kind peculiarly, because offences against society are especially apt to originate there. It is, therefore, fit to confine the power of selling these commodities (at least for consumption on the spot) to persons of known or vouched-for respectability of conduct; to make such regulations respecting hours of opening and closing as may be requisite for public surveillance, and to withdraw the license if breaches of the peace repeatedly take place through the connivance or incapacity of the keeper of the house, or if it becomes a rendezvous for concocting and preparing offences against the law. Any further restriction I do not conceive to be, in principle, justifiable. The limitation in number, for instance, of beer and spirit-houses, for the express purpose of rendering them more difficult of access, and diminishing the occasions of temptation, not only exposes all to an inconvenience because there are some by whom the facility would be abused, but is suited only to a state of society in which the laboring classes are avowedly treated as children or savages, and placed under an education of restraint, to fit them for future admission to the privileges of freedom. This is not the principle on which the laboring classes are professedly governed in any free country; and no person who sets due value on freedom will give his adhesion to their being so governed, unless after all efforts have been exhausted to educate them for freedom and govern them as freemen, and it has been definitively proved that they can only be governed as children. The bare statement of the alternative shows the absurdity of supposing that such efforts have been made in any case which needs be considered here. It is only because the institutions of this country are a mass of inconsistencies, that things find admittance into our practice which belong to the system of despotic, or what is called paternal, government, while the general freedom of our institutions precludes the exercise of the amount of control necessary to render the restraint of any real efficacy as a moral education.

It was pointed out in an early part of this Essay, that the liberty of the individual, in things wherein the individual is alone concerned, implies a corresponding liberty in any number of individuals to regulate by mutual agreement such things as regard them jointly, and regard no persons but themselves. This question presents no difficulty, so long as the will of all the persons implicated remains unaltered; but since that will may change, it is often necessary, even in things in which they alone are concerned, that they should enter into engagements with one another; and when they do, it is fit, as a general rule, that those engagements should be kept. Yet in the laws probably, of every country, this general rule has some exceptions. Not only persons are not held to engagements which violate the rights of third parties, but it is sometimes considered a sufficient reason for releasing them from an engagement, that it is injurious to themselves. In this and most other civilized countries, for example, an engagement by which a person should sell himself, or allow himself to be sold, as a slave, would be null and void; neither enforced by law nor by opinion. The ground for thus limiting his power of voluntarily disposing of his own lot in life, is apparent, and is very clearly seen in this extreme case. The reason for not interfering, unless for the sake of others, with a person's voluntary acts, is consideration for his liberty. His voluntary choice is evidence that what he so chooses is desirable, or at the least endurable, to him, and his good is on the whole best provided for by allowing him to take his own means of pursuing it. But by selling himself for a slave, he abdicates his liberty; he foregoes any future use of it, beyond that single act. He therefore defeats, in his own case, the very purpose which is the justification of allowing him to dispose of himself. He is no longer free; but is thenceforth in a position which has no longer the presumption in its favor, that would be afforded by his voluntarily remaining in it. The principle of freedom cannot require that he should be free not to be free. It is not freedom, to be allowed to alienate his freedom. These reasons, the force of which is so conspicuous in this peculiar case, are evidently of far wider application; yet a limit is everywhere set to them by the necessities of life, which continually require, not indeed that we should resign our freedom, but that we should consent to this and the other limitation of it. The principle, however, which demands uncontrolled freedom of action in all that concerns only the agents themselves, requires that those who have become bound to one another, in things which concern no third party, should be able to release one another from the engagement: and even without such voluntary release, there are perhaps no contracts or engagements, except those that relate to money or money's worth, of which one can venture to say that there ought to be no liberty whatever of retractation. Baron Wilhelm von Humboldt, in the excellent Essay from which I have already quoted, states it as his conviction, that engagements which involve personal relations or services, should never be legally binding beyond a limited duration of time; and that the most important of these engagements, marriage, having the peculiarity that its objects are frustrated unless the feelings of both the parties are in harmony with it, should require nothing more than the declared will of either party to dissolve it. This subject is too important, and too complicated, to be discussed in a parenthesis, and I touch on it only so far as is necessary for purposes of illustration. If the conciseness and generality of Baron Humboldt's dissertation had not obliged him in this instance to content himself with enunciating his conclusion without discussing the premises, he would doubtless have recognized that the question cannot be decided on grounds so simple as those to which he confines himself. When a person, either by express promise or by conduct, has encouraged another to rely upon his continuing to act in a certain way—to build expectations and calculations, and stake any part of his plan of life upon that supposition, a new series of moral obligations arises on his part towards that person, which may possibly be overruled, but can not be ignored. And again, if the relation between two contracting parties has been followed by consequences to others; if it has placed third parties in any peculiar position, or, as in the case of marriage, has even called third parties into existence, obligations arise on the part of both the contracting parties towards those third persons, the fulfilment of which, or at all events, the mode of fulfilment, must be greatly affected by the continuance or disruption of the relation between the original parties to the contract. It does not follow, nor can I admit, that these obligations extend to requiring the fulfilment of the contract at all costs to the happiness of the reluctant party; but they are a necessary element in the question; and even if, as Von Humboldt maintains, they ought to make no difference in the *legal* freedom of the parties to release themselves from the engagement (and I also hold that they ought not to make *much* difference), they necessarily make a great difference in the *moral* freedom. A person is bound to take all these circumstances into account, before resolving on a step which may affect such important interests of others; and if he does not allow proper weight to those interests, he is morally responsible for the wrong. I have made these obvious remarks for the better illustration of the general principle of liberty, and not because they are at all needed on the particular question, which, on the contrary, is usually discussed as if the interest of children was everything, and that of grown persons nothing.

I have already observed that, owing to the absence of any recognized general principles, liberty is often granted where it should be withheld, as well as withheld where it should be granted; and one of the cases in which, in the modern European world, the sentiment of liberty is the strongest, is a case where, in my view, it is altogether misplaced. A person should be free to do as he likes in his own concerns; but he ought not to be free to do as he likes in acting for another under the pretext that the affairs of another are his own affairs. The State, while it respects the liberty of each in what specially regards himself, is bound to maintain a vigilant control over his exercise of any power which it allows him to possess over others. This obligation is almost entirely disregarded in the case of the family relations, a case, in its direct influence on human happiness, more important than all the others taken together. The almost despotic power of husbands over wives needs not be enlarged upon here, because nothing more is needed for the complete removal of the evil, than that wives should have the same rights, and should receive the protection of law in the same manner, as all other persons; and because, on this subject, the defenders of established injustice do not avail themselves of the plea of liberty, but stand forth openly as the champions of power. It is in the case of children, that misapplied notions of liberty are a real obstacle to the fulfilment by the State of its duties. One would almost think that a man's children were supposed to be literally, and not metaphorically, a part of himself, so jealous is opinion of the smallest interference of law with his absolute and exclusive control over them; more jealous than of almost any interference with his own freedom of action: so much less do the generality of mankind value liberty than power. Consider, for example, the case of education. Is it not almost a self-evident axiom, that the State should require and compel the education, up to a certain standard, of every human being who is born its citizen? Yet who is there that is not afraid to recognize and assert this truth? Hardly any one indeed will deny that it is one of the most sacred duties of the parents (or, as law and usage now stand, the father), after summoning a human being into the world, to give to that being an education fitting him to perform his part well in life towards others and towards himself. But while this is unanimously declared to be the father's duty, scarcely anybody, in this country, will bear to hear of obliging him to perform it. Instead of his being required to make any exertion or sacrifice for securing education to the child, it is left to his choice to accept it or not when it is provided gratis! It still remains unrecognized, that to bring a child into existence without a fair prospect of being able, not only to provide food for its body, but instruction and training for its mind, is a moral crime, both against the unfortunate offspring and against society; and that if the parent does not fulfil this obligation, the State ought to see it fulfilled, at the charge, as far as possible, of the parent.

Were the duty of enforcing universal education once admitted, there would be an end to the difficulties about what the State should teach, and how it should teach, which now convert the subject into a mere battle-field for sects and parties, causing the time and labor which should have been spent in educating, to be wasted in quarrelling about education. If the government would make up its mind to *require* for every child a good education, it might save itself the trouble of *providing* one. It might leave to parents to obtain the education where and how they pleased, and content itself with helping to pay the school fees of the poorer classes of children, and defraying the entire school expenses of those who have no one else to pay for them. The objections which are urged with reason against State education, do not apply to the enforcement of education by the State, but to the State's taking upon itself to direct that education: which is a totally different thing. That the whole or any large part of the education of the people should be in State hands, I go as far as any one in deprecating. All that has been said of the importance of individuality of character, and diversity in opinions and modes of conduct, involves, as of the same unspeakable importance, diversity of education. A general State education is a mere contrivance for moulding people to be exactly like one another: and as the mould in which it casts them is that which pleases the predominant power in the government, whether this be a monarch, a priesthood, an aristocracy, or the majority of the existing generation, in proportion as it is efficient and successful, it establishes a despotism over the mind, leading by natural tendency to one over the body. An education established and controlled by the State, should only exist, if it exist at all, as one among many competing experiments, carried on for the purpose of example and stimulus, to keep the others up to a certain standard of excellence. Unless, indeed, when society in general is in so backward a state that it could not or would not provide for itself any proper institutions of education, unless the government undertook the task; then, indeed, the government may, as the less of two great evils, take upon itself the business of schools and universities, as it may that of joint-stock companies, when private enterprise, in a shape fitted for undertaking great works of industry does not exist in the country. But in general, if the country contains a sufficient number of persons qualified to provide education under government auspices, the same persons would be able and willing to give an equally good education on the voluntary principle, under the assurance of remuneration afforded by a law rendering education compulsory, combined with State aid to those unable to defray the expense.

The instrument for enforcing the law could be no other than public examinations, extending to all children, and beginning at an early age. An age might be fixed at which every child must be examined, to ascertain if he (or she) is able to read. If a child proves unable, the father, unless he has some sufficient ground of excuse, might be subjected to a moderate fine, to be worked out, if necessary, by his labor, and the child might be put to school at his expense. Once in every year the examination should be renewed, with a gradually extending range of subjects, so as to make the universal acquisition, and what is more, retention, of a certain minimum of general knowledge, virtually compulsory. Beyond that minimum, there should be voluntary examinations on all subjects, at which all who come up to a certain standard of proficiency might claim a certificate. To prevent the State from exercising through these arrangements, an improper influence over opinion, the knowledge required for passing an examination (beyond the merely instrumental parts of knowledge, such as languages and their use) should, even in the higher class of examinations, be confined to facts and positive science exclusively. The examinations on religion, politics, or other disputed topics, should not turn on the truth or falsehood of opinions, but on the matter of fact that such and such an opinion is held, on such grounds, by such authors, or schools, or churches. Under this system, the rising generation would be no worse off in regard to all disputed truths, than they are at present; they would be brought up either churchmen or dissenters as they now are, the State merely taking care that they should be instructed churchmen, or instructed dissenters. There would be nothing to hinder them from being taught religion, if their parents chose, at the same schools where they were taught other things. All attempts by the State to bias the conclusions of its citizens on disputed subjects, are evil; but it may very properly offer to ascertain and certify that a person possesses the knowledge requisite to make his conclusions, on any given subject, worth attending to. A student of philosophy would be the better for being able to stand an examination both in Locke and in Kant, whichever of the two he takes up with, or even if with neither: and there is no reasonable objection to examining an atheist in the evidences of Christianity, provided he is not required to profess a belief in them. The examinations, however, in the higher branches of knowledge should, I conceive, be entirely voluntary. It would be giving too dangerous a power to governments, were they allowed to exclude any one from professions, even from the profession of teacher, for alleged deficiency of qualifications: and I think, with Wilhelm von Humboldt, that degrees, or other public certificates of scientific or professional acquirements, should be given to all who present themselves for examination, and stand the test; but that such certificates should confer no advantage over competitors, other than the weight which may be attached to their testimony by public opinion.

It is not in the matter of education only that misplaced notions of liberty prevent moral obligations on the part of parents from being recognized, and legal obligations from being imposed, where there are the strongest grounds for the former always, and in many cases for the latter also. The fact itself, of causing the existence of a human being, is one of the most responsible actions in the range of human life. To undertake this responsibility—to bestow a life which may be either a curse or a blessing—unless the being on whom it is to be bestowed will have at least the ordinary chances of a desirable existence, is a crime against that being. And in a country either over-peopled or threatened with being so, to produce children, beyond a very small number, with the effect of reducing the reward of labor by their competition, is a serious offence against all who live by the remuneration of their labor. The laws which, in many countries on the Continent, forbid marriage unless the parties can show that they have the means of supporting a family, do not exceed the legitimate powers of the State: and whether such laws be expedient or not (a question mainly dependent on local circumstances and feelings), they are not objectionable as violations of liberty. Such laws are interferences of the State to prohibit a mischievous act—an act injurious to others, which ought to be a subject of reprobation, and social stigma, even when it is not deemed expedient to superadd legal punishment. Yet the current ideas of liberty, which bend so easily to real infringements of the freedom of the individual, in things which concern only himself, would repel the attempt to put any restraint upon his inclinations when the consequence of their indulgence is a life, or lives, of wretchedness and depravity to the offspring, with manifold evils to those sufficiently within reach to be in any way affected by their actions. When we compare the strange respect of mankind for liberty, with their strange want of respect for it, we might imagine that a man had an indispensable right to do harm to others, and no right at all to please himself without giving pain to any one.

I have reserved for the last place a large class of questions respecting the limits of government interference, which, though closely connected with the subject of this Essay, do not, in strictness, belong to it. These are cases in which the reasons against interference do not turn upon the principle of liberty: the question is not about restraining the actions of individuals, but about helping them: it is asked whether the government should do, or cause to be done, something for their benefit, instead of leaving it to be done by themselves, individually, or in voluntary combination.

The objections to government interference, when it is not

such as to involve infringement of liberty, may be of three kinds.

The first is, when the thing to be done is likely to be better done by individuals than by the government. Speaking generally, there is no one so fit to conduct any business, or to determine how or by whom it shall be conducted, as those who are personally interested in it. This principle condemns the interferences, once so common, of the legislature, or the officers of government, with the ordinary processes of industry. But this part of the subject has been sufficiently enlarged upon by political economists, and is not particularly related to the principles of this Essay.

The second objection is more nearly allied to our subject. In many cases, though individuals may not do the particular thing so well, on the average, as the officers of government, it is nevertheless desirable that it should be done by them, rather than by the government, as a means to their own mental education—a mode of strengthening their active faculties, exercising their judgment, and giving them a familiar knowledge of the subjects with which they are thus left to deal. This is a principal, though not the sole, recommendation of jury trial (in cases not political); of free and popular local and municipal institutions; of the conduct of industrial and philanthropic enterprises by voluntary associations. These are not questions of liberty, and are connected with that subject only by remote tendencies; but they are questions of development. It belongs to a different occasion from the present to dwell on these things as parts of national education; as being, in truth, the peculiar training of a citizen, the practical part of the political education of a free people, taking them out of the narrow circle of personal and family selfishness, and accustoming them to the comprehension of joint interests, the management of joint concerns—habituating them to act from public or semi-public motives, and guide their conduct by aims which unite instead of isolating them from one another. Without these habits and powers, a free constitution can neither be worked nor preserved, as is exemplified by the too-often transitory nature of political freedom in countries where it does not rest upon a sufficient basis of local liberties. The manage-

ment of purely local business by the localities, and of the
great enterprises of industry by the union of those who
voluntarily supply the pecuniary means, is further recommended by all the advantages which have been set forth in
this Essay as belonging to individuality of development, and
diversity of modes of action. Government operations tend
to be everywhere alike. With individuals and voluntary associations, on the contrary, there are varied experiments,
and endless diversity of experience. What the State can
usefully do, is to make itself a central depository, and active
circulator and diffuser, of the experience resulting from many
trials. Its business is to enable each experimentalist to benefit by the experiments of others, instead of tolerating no experiments but its own.

The third, and most cogent reason for restricting the
interference of government, is the great evil of adding un-
necessarily to its power. Every function superadded to those
already exercised by the government, causes its influence
over hopes and fears to be more widely diffused, and converts, more and more, the active and ambitious part of the
public into hangers-on of the government, or of some party
which aims at becoming the government. If the roads, the
railways, the banks, the insurance offices, the great joint-stock
companies, the universities, and the public charities, were all
of them branches of the government; if, in addition, the
municipal corporations and local boards, with all that now
devolves on them, became departments of the central administration; if the employes of all these different enterprises were appointed and paid by the government, and
looked to the government for every rise in life; not all the
freedom of the press and popular constitution of the legislature would make this or any other country free otherwise
than in name. And the evil would be greater, the more
efficiently and scientifically the administrative machinery
was constructed—the more skilful the arrangements for obtaining the best qualified hands and heads with which to
work it. In England it has of late been proposed that all
the members of the civil service of government should be
selected by competitive examination, to obtain for those employments the most intelligent and instructed persons pro-

curable; and much has been said and written for and against
this proposal. One of the arguments most insisted on by its
opponents is that the occupation of a permanent official ser-
vant of the State does not hold out sufficient prospects of
emolument and importance to attract the highest talents,
which will always be able to find a more inviting career in
the professions, or in the service of companies and other
public bodies. One would not have been surprised if this
argument had been used by the friends of the proposition, as
an answer to its principal difficulty. Coming from the opponents it is strange enough. What is urged as an objection
is the safety-valve of the proposed system. If indeed all the
high talent of the country *could* be drawn into the service of
the government, a proposal tending to bring about that result
might well inspire uneasiness. If every part of the business
of society which required organized concert, or large and
comprehensive views, were in the hands of the government,
and if government offices were universally filled by the ablest
men, all the enlarged culture and practised intelligence in the
country, except the purely speculative, would be concentrated in a numerous bureaucracy, to whom alone the rest
of the community would look for all things: the multitude
for direction and dictation in all they had to do; the able
and aspiring for personal advancement. To be admitted
into the ranks of this bureaucracy, and when admitted, to
rise therein, would be the sole objects of ambition. Under
this régime, not only is the outside public ill-qualified, for
want of practical experience, to criticize or check the mode
of operation of the bureaucracy, but even if the accidents
of despotic or the natural working of popular institutions occasionally raise to the summit a ruler or rulers of reforming
inclinations, no reform can be effected which is contrary to
the interest of the bureaucracy. Such is the melancholy
condition of the Russian empire, as is shown in the accounts
of those who have had sufficient opportunity of observation. The Czar himself is powerless against the bureaucratic
body: he can send any one of them to Siberia, but he cannot govern without them, or against their will. On every
decree of his they have a tacit veto, by merely refraining
from carrying it into effect. In countries of more advanced

civilization and of a more insurrectionary spirit the public, accustomed to expect everything to be done for them by the State, or at least to do nothing for themselves without asking from the State not only leave to do it, but even how it is to be done, naturally hold the State responsible for all evil which befalls them, and when the evil exceeds their amount of patience, they rise against the government and make what is called a revolution; whereupon somebody else, with or without legitimate authority from the nation, vaults into the seat, issues his orders to the bureaucracy, and everything goes on much as it did before; the bureaucracy being unchanged, and nobody else being capable of taking their place.

A very different spectacle is exhibited among a people accustomed to transact their own business. In France, a large part of the people having been engaged in military service, many of whom have held at least the rank of non-commissioned officers, there are in every popular insurrection several persons competent to take the lead, and improvise some tolerable plan of action. What the French are in military affairs, the Americans are in every kind of civil business; let them be left without a government, every body of Americans is able to improvise one, and to carry on that or any other public business with a sufficient amount of intelligence, order and decision. This is what every free people ought to be: and a people capable of this is certain to be free; it will never let itself be enslaved by any man or body of men because these are able to seize and pull the reins of the central administration. No bureaucracy can hope to make such a people as this do or undergo anything that they do not like. But where everything is done through the bureaucracy, nothing to which the bureaucracy is really adverse can be done at all. The constitution of such countries is an organization of the experience and practical ability of the nation, into a disciplined body for the purpose of governing the rest; and the more perfect that organization is in itself, the more successful in drawing to itself and educating for itself the persons of greatest capacity from all ranks of the community, the more complete is the bondage of all, the members of the bureaucracy included. For the governors are as much the slaves of their organization and discipline, as the governed are of the governors. A Chinese mandarin is as much the tool and creature of a despotism as the humblest cultivator. An individual Jesuit is to the utmost degree of abasement the slave of his order though the order itself exists for the collective power and importance of its members.

It is not, also, to be forgotten, that the absorption of all the principal ability of the country into the governing body is fatal, sooner or later, to the mental activity and progressiveness of the body itself. Banded together as they are—working a system which, like all systems, necessarily proceeds in a great measure by fixed rules—the official body are under the constant temptation of sinking into indolent routine, or, if they now and then desert that mill-horse round, of rushing into some half-examined crudity which has struck the fancy of some leading member of the corps: and the sole check to these closely allied, though seemingly opposite, tendencies, the only stimulus which can keep the ability of the body itself up to a high standard, is liability to the watchful criticism of equal ability outside the body. It is indispensable, therefore, that the means should exist, independently of the government, of forming such ability, and furnishing it with the opportunities and experience necessary for a correct judgment of great practical affairs. If we would possess permanently a skilful and efficient body of functionaries —above all, a body able to originate and willing to adopt improvements; if we would not have our bureaucracy degenerate into a pedantocracy, this body must not engross all the occupations which form and cultivate the faculties required for the government of mankind.

To determine the point at which evils, so formidable to human freedom and advancement begin, or rather at which they begin to predominate over the benefits attending the collective application of the force of society, under its recognized chiefs, for the removal of the obstacles which stand in the way of its well-being, to secure as much of the advantages of centralized power and intelligence, as can be had without turning into governmental channels too great a proportion of the general activity, is one of the most difficult and complicated questions in the art of government. It is, in a great measure, a question of detail, in which many and various considerations must be kept in view, and no absolute rule can be laid down. But I believe that the practical principle in which safety resides, the ideal to be kept in view, the standard by which to test all arrangements intended for overcoming the difficulty, may be conveyed in these words: the greatest dissemination of power consistent with efficiency; but the greatest possible centralization of information, and diffusion of it from the centre. Thus, in municipal administration, there would be, as in the New England States, a very minute division among separate officers, chosen by the localities, of all business which is not better left to the persons directly interested; but besides this, there would be, in each department of local affairs, a central superintendence, forming a branch of the general government. The organ of this superintendence would concentrate, as in a focus, the variety of information and experience derived from the conduct of that branch of public business in all the localities, from everything analogous which is done in foreign countries, and from the general principles of political science. This central organ should have a right to know all that is done, and its special duty should be that of making the knowledge acquired in one place available for others. Emancipated from the petty prejudices and narrow views of a locality by its elevated position and comprehensive sphere of observation, its advice would naturally carry much authority; but its actual power, as a permanent institution, should, I conceive, be limited to compelling the local officers to obey the laws laid down for their guidance. In all things not provided for by general rules, those officers should be left to their own judgment, under responsibility to their constituents. For the violation of rules, they should be responsible to law, and the rules themselves should be laid down by the legislature; the central administrative authority only watching over their execution, and if they were not properly carried into effect, appealing, according to the nature of the case, to the tribunal to enforce the law, or to the constituencies to dismiss the functionaries who had not executed it according to its spirit. Such, in its general conception, is the central superintendence which the Poor Law Board is intended to exercise over the administrators of the Poor Rate throughout the country. Whatever powers the Board exercises beyond this limit, were right and necessary in that peculiar case, for the cure of rooted habits of mal-administration in matters deeply affecting not the localities merely, but the whole community; since no locality has a moral right to make itself by mismanagement a nest of pauperism, necessarily overflowing into other localities, and impairing the moral and physical condition of the whole laboring community. The powers of administrative coercion and subordinate legislation possessed by the Poor Law Board (but which, owing to the state of opinion on the subject, are very scantily exercised by them), though perfectly justifiable in a case of a first-rate national interest, would be wholly out of place in the superintendence of interests purely local. But a central organ of information and instruction for all the localities, would be equally valuable in all departments of administration. A government cannot have too much of the kind of activity which does not impede, but aids and stimulates, individual exertion and development. The mischief begins when, instead of calling forth the activity and powers of individuals and bodies, it substitutes its own activity for theirs; when, instead of informing, advising, and upon occasion denouncing, it makes them work in fetters or bids them stand aside and does their work instead of them. The worth of a State, in the long run, is the worth of the individuals composing it; and a State which postpones the interests of *their* mental expansion and elevation, to a little more of administrative skill or that semblance of it which practice gives, in the details of business; a State, which dwarfs its men, in order that they may be more docile instruments in its hands even for beneficial purposes, will find that with small men no great thing can really be accomplished; and that the perfection of machinery to which it has sacrificed everything, will in the end avail it nothing, for want of the vital power which, in order that the machine might work more smoothly, it has preferred to banish.

CHARACTERISTICS
BY
THOMAS CARLYLE

INTRODUCTORY NOTE

THOMAS CARLYLE *was born at Ecclefechan in the south of Scotland, December 4, 1795. His father, a rigorous Calvinist belonging to the seceding "Burgher Kirk," was a stone-mason, a man of stern and upright character with a gift of fiery speech. Thomas began his education at home, went next to the village school, thence to the grammar school at Annan, and in 1809 walked to Edinburgh, a hundred miles away, and entered the University with a view to preparing for the ministry. On finishing his arts course, he was appointed mathematical usher at Annan and two years later at Kirkcaldy, where he formed an intimate friendship with Edward Irving. But he hated teaching, and, as he had abandoned his orthodox views and could no longer think of preaching, he returned to Edinburgh to study for the bar, supporting himself by private tutoring and writing for encyclopedias. These years, 1819-1822, he regarded as the most miserable of his life. Tormented with dyspepsia, torn with religious perplexity, with no prospects and no profession, he found comfort only in the affection of his family. It was about this time that the study of German led him to Goethe, who proved his chief aid in his struggles to gain spiritual peace.*

Through Irving Carlyle obtained a position as tutor to Charles and Arthur Buller at a salary that enabled him to help his family in substantial ways. This engagement lasted for two years, during which he translated Legendre's "Geometry" and Goethe's "Wilhelm Meister," and wrote a "Life of Schiller." His relation with the Bullers led him to London, and for a short time to Paris; and in his "Reminiscences" we have a graphic picture of the unfavorable impression made on him by fashionable and literary society.

He now retired to a farm near his father's house, and spent a peaceful year, chiefly in translating. In 1826 he married Jane Baillie Welsh, the brilliant and beautiful daughter of a doctor in Haddington, whom he had met through Irving. Miss Welsh was descended on one side from John Knox, on the other from the gipsies, and, it was claimed, William Wallace; and her temperament did not belie her ancestry. She had been much courted, and her wooing by Carlyle was as ominous as it was

329

extraordinary. Over their subsequent domestic relations there has been a vast amount of unseemly controversy, no one condemning Carlyle more severely than he did himself. Yet it may be argued that they found in their marriage as much satisfaction as either of them was capable of finding in wedded life. Carlyle's absorption in his work and his career undoubtedly led to much neglect and suffering on the part of his wife, but it is clear that the expressions of remorse in his writings after her death are not fairly to be taken as judicial evidence against him.

For the first eighteen months after marriage, the Carlyles lived in Edinburgh, where they shared in the most distinguished intellectual society of the city, and where Carlyle formed with Francis Jeffrey a pleasant and useful relation. Jeffrey accepted articles for the "Edinburgh Review," and their success there opened to Carlyle the pages of other periodicals. The first two reviews were on Richter and on German Literature, which, with his translations and later writings in the same field, gained him recognition as a pioneer of German literature in England, and brought him generous personal acknowledgments from Goethe.

In spite of these successes, the financial affairs of the Carlyles were still far from satisfactory, and to reduce expenses they retreated to the farm of Craigenputtock, which belonged to Mrs. Carlyle. Here they lived for more than six years, in an isolation broken only by occasional visits from guests, notable among whom were the Jeffreys and Emerson. It was here that the quasi-autobiographical "Sartor Resartus" was written, and more German articles, the market for which, however, grew duller and duller. A visit to London in 1831, for which he had to borrow money from Jeffrey, led to new relations with publishers and editors; and four months in Edinburgh broadened his range of subjects. But, finally, solitude and the need of money drove them to London, where they settled in 1834 in the house in Cheyne Row, Chelsea, where they lived for the rest of their lives.

The most important event of the earlier years of the London period was the ripening of Carlyle's friendship with J. S. Mill. To this intercourse was due his undertaking his "History of the French Revolution," published in 1837. Meanwhile, he succeeded in getting sorely needed funds by lecturing, giving four courses in successive springs, the last of which was his well-known "Heroes and Hero-worship." These relieved him from pressing necessities, and with the recognition of the brilliant qualities of his "French Revolution" came the turn in his fortunes. He gained many friends, among whom were such men as John Sterling, whose life he afterward was to write with sympathy and charm; F. D. Maurice, J. G. Lockhart, R. M. Milnes, afterwards Lord Houghton, and the Barings; and he was often sought out by young inquirers. Emerson had introduced his works to America, with the result of both fame and profit. He was already becoming a noted figure in intellectual circles in London.

His political ideas were put into definite shape in his "Chartism" (1839), and, if any one had ever doubted it, it now became clear that he was never to be classed with any of the established political parties. "Past and Present," a contrast between medieval monastic life and modern conditions, still further emphasized his separation from both Tories and Radicals. While these shorter works were being put forth, he was laboring on his next great book, the "Life and Letters of Oliver Cromwell"; and when this appeared in 1845 his position as one of the leading men of letters of the day was thoroughly established.

After a year or two mainly occupied with political writing, most of it at once powerful in style and ineffective in result, he settled down to another great task, a life of Frederick the Great, which occupied his main energies till 1865, and extended his reputation both on the Continent and at home. In this year he was elected Lord Rector of Edinburgh University. The Inaugural Address, which constitutes the sole duty of this honorary office, he delivered the next year; and on his journey south after a triumphal reception he was met at Dumfries by the news of his wife's death. She was buried in the Abbey Kirk at Haddington; and the epitaph which her husband placed upon her grave tells what the blow meant for him. It runs thus: "In her bright existence she had more sorrows than are common, but also a soft invincibility, a capacity of discernment, and a noble loyalty of heart which are rare. For forty years she was the true and loving helpmate of her husband, and by act and word unweariedly forwarded him as none else could in all of worthy that he did or attempted. She died at London, 21st April,

1866, suddenly snatched from him, and the light of his life as if gone out."

And, indeed, the light of his life had gone out. He was henceforth a broken man. He revised his collected works, wrote his "Reminiscences," but undertook no new tasks. He was now at the head of his profession, and surrounded by friends and admirers; honors were showered on him at home and abroad; but he lived in a gloom that deepened to the end. He died on February 4, 1881, and was buried in the old kirkyard at Ecclefechan.

Of the works by Carlyle here printed, "Characteristics" is a condensed and telling statement of some of his most fundamental ideas; the essay on "Sir Walter Scott" exhibits, both in its strength and in its shortcomings, the domination of ethical over esthetic considerations in his estimate of literature, and contains besides many characteristic generalizations on human life and conduct; the "Inaugural Address," the subject of which is nominally the "Reading of Books," summarizes rapidly his own intellectual history, and digresses in true Carlylean fashion into religion, ethics, history, and a variety of other topics. It is written in an exceptionally simple and straightforward style, admirably suited to the occasion; the two other papers represent more truly his habitual manner of expression—often abrupt, often exaggerated, sometimes grotesque, but, to use his own words of his "French Revolution," coming "direct and flamingly from the heart of a living man."

This style was, indeed, highly characteristic of its owner. The endless labor he put into his histories, the passion of his political convictions, the profound earnestness of his moral and religious preaching, were combined with a thirst for effective expression that led him to shatter any convention that stood in the way of truth, and gave a weight and edge to his utterance that make it a thing unique in English literature. Complex and inconsistent to the point of paradox, absolutely sincere yet exaggerated and over-emphatic, violent to brutality yet tender of heart, a Radical to the Tories and a Tory to the Radicals, Carlyle formed no school, yet was one of the most stimulating and potent influences of his century. Over his character and his message the voices of controversy have not yet died down, but whoever turns to his work finds coursing everywhere through it the red blood of a man.

CHARACTERISTICS[1]

[1831]

THE healthy know not of their health, but only the sick: this is the Physician's Aphorism; and applicable in a far wider sense than he gives it. We may say, it holds no less in moral, intellectual, political, poetical, than in merely corporeal therapeutics; that wherever, or in what shape soever, powers of the sort which can be named *vital* are at work, herein lies the test of their working right or working wrong.

In the Body, for example, as all doctors are agreed, the first condition of complete health is, that each organ perform its function, unconsciously, unheeded; let but any organ announce its separate existence, were it even boastfully, and for pleasure, not for pain, then already has one of those unfortunate 'false centres of sensibility' established itself, already is derangement there. The perfection of bodily well-being is that the collective bodily activities seem one; and be manifested, moreover, not in themselves, but in the action they accomplish. If a Dr. Kitchiner boast that his system is in high order, Dietetic Philosophy may indeed take credit; but the true Peptician was that Countryman who answered that, 'for his part, he had no system.' In fact, unity, agreement is always silent, or soft-voiced; it is only discord that loudly proclaims itself. So long as the several elements of Life, all fitly adjusted, can pour forth their movement like harmonious tuned strings, it is a melody and unison; Life,

[1] EDINBURGH REVIEW, No. 108.—1. *An Essay on the Origin and Prospects of Man.* By Thomas Hope. 3 vols. 8vo. London, 1831.
2. *Philosophische Vorlesungen, insbesondere über Philosophie der Sprache und des Wortes. Geschrieben und vorgetragen zu Dresden im December,* 1828, *und in den ersten Tagen des Januars,* 1829 (Philosophical Lectures, especially on the Philosophy of Langauge and the Gift of Speech. Written and delivered at Dresden in December, 1828, and the early days of January, 1829). By Friedrich von Schlegel. 8vo. Vienna, 1830.

from its mysterious fountains, flows out as in celestial music and diapason,—which also, like that other music of the spheres, even because it is perennial and complete, without interruption and without imperfection, might be fabled to escape the ear. Thus too, in some languages, is the state of health well denoted by a term expressing unity; when we feel ourselves as we wish to be, we say that we are *whole*.

Few mortals, it is to be feared, are permanently blessed with that felicity of 'having no system'; nevertheless, most of us, looking back on young years, may remember seasons of a light, aërial translucency and elasticity and perfect freedom; the body had not yet become the prison-house of the soul, but was its vehicle and implement, like a creature of the thought, and altogether pliant to its bidding. We knew not that we had limbs, we only lifted, hurled and leapt; through eye and ear, and all avenues of sense, came clear unimpeded tidings from without, and from within issued clear victorious force; we stood as in the centre of Nature, giving and receiving, in harmony with it all; unlike Virgil's Husbandmen, 'too happy *because* we did not know our blessedness.' In those days, health and sickness were foreign traditions that did not concern us; our whole being was as yet One, the whole man like an incorporated Will. Such, were Rest or ever-successful Labour the human lot, might our life continue to be: a pure, perpetual, unregarded music; a beam of perfect white light, rendering all things visible, but itself unseen, even because it was of that perfect whiteness, and no irregular obstruction had yet broken it into colours. The beginning of Inquiry is Disease: all Science, if we consider well, as it must have originated in the feeling of something being wrong, so it is and continues to be but Division, Dismemberment, and partial healing of the wrong. Thus, as was of old written, the Tree of Knowledge springs from a root of evil, and bears fruits of good and evil. Had Adam remained in Paradise, there had been no Anatomy and no Metaphysics.

But, alas, as the Philosopher declares, 'Life itself is a disease; a working incited by suffering'; action from passion! The memory of that first state of Freedom and paradisaic Unconsciousness has faded away into an ideal poetic dream. We stand here too conscious of many things: with Knowledge, the symptom of Derangement, we must even do our best to restore a little Order. Life is, in few instances, and at rare intervals, the diapason of a heavenly melody; oftenest the fierce jar of disruptions and convulsions, which, do what we will, there is no disregarding. Nevertheless, such is still the wish of Nature on our behalf; in all vital action, her manifest purpose and effort is, that we should be unconscious of it, and like the peptic Countryman, never know that we 'have a system.' For, indeed, vital action everywhere is emphatically a means, not an end; Life is not given us for the mere sake of Living, but always with an ulterior external Aim: neither is it on the process, on the means, but rather on the result, that Nature, in any of her doings, is wont to intrust us with insight and volition. Boundless as is the domain of man, it is but a small fractional proportion of it that he rules with Consciousness and by Forethought: what he can contrive, nay, what he can altogether know and comprehend, is essentially the mechanical, small; the great is ever, in one sense or other, the vital; it is essentially the mysterious, and only the surface of it can be understood. But Nature, it might seem, strives, like a kind mother, to hide from us even this, that she is a mystery: she will have us rest on her beautiful and awful bosom as if it were our secure home; on the bottomless boundless Deep, whereon all human things fearfully and wonderfully swim, she will have us walk and build, as if the film which supported us there (which any scratch of a bare bodkin will rend asunder, any sputter of a pistol-shot instantaneously burn up) were no film, but a solid rock-foundation. Forever in the neighbourhood of an inevitable Death, man can forget that he is born to die; of his Life, which, strictly meditated, contains in it an Immensity and an Eternity, he can conceive lightly, as of a simple implement wherewith to do day-labour and earn wages. So cunningly does Nature, the mother of all highest Art, which only apes her from afar, 'body forth the Finite from the Infinite'; and guide man safe on his wondrous path, not more by endowing him with vision, than, at the right place, with blindness! Under all her works, chiefly under her noblest work, Life, lies a basis of Darkness, which she benignantly conceals; in Life too, the roots and inward circulations which stretch down fearfully to the regions of Death and Night, shall not hint of their existence, and only the fair stem with its leaves and flowers, shone on by the fair sun, shall disclose itself, and joyfully grow.

However, without venturing into the abstruse, or too eagerly asking Why and How, in things where our answer must needs prove, in great part, an echo of the question, let us be content to remark farther, in the merely historical way, how that Aphorism of the bodily Physician holds good in quite other departments. Of the Soul, with her activities, we shall find it no less true than of the Body: nay, cry the Spiritualists, is not that very division of the unity, Man, into a dualism of Soul and Body, itself the symptom of disease; as, perhaps, your frightful theory of Materialism, of his being but a Body, and therefore, at least, once more a unity, may be the paroxysm which was critical, and the beginning of cure! But omitting this, we observe, with confidence enough, that the truly strong mind, view it as Intellect, as Morality, or under any other aspect, is nowise the mind acquainted with its strength; that here as before the sign of health is Unconsciousness. In our inward, as in our outward world, what is mechanical lies open to us: not what is dynamical and has vitality. Of our Thinking, we might say, it is but the mere upper surface that we shape into articulate Thoughts;—underneath the region of argument and conscious discourse, lies the region of meditation; here, in its quiet mysterious depths, dwells what vital force is in us; here, if aught is to be created, and not merely manufactured and communicated, must the work go on. Manufacture is intelligible, but trivial: Creation is great, and cannot be understood. Thus if the Debater and Demonstrator, whom we may rank as the lowest of true thinkers, knows what he has done, and how he did it, the Artist, whom we rank as the highest, knows not; must speak of Inspiration, and in one or the other dialect, call his work the gift of a divinity.

But on the whole, 'genius is ever a secret to itself'; of this old truth we have, on all sides, daily evidence. The Shakspeare takes no airs for writing *Hamlet* and the *Tempest*, understands not that it is anything surprising: Milton, again, is more conscious of his faculty, which accordingly is an inferior one. On the other hand, what cackling and strutting must we not often hear and see, when, in some shape of academical prolusion, maiden speech, review article, this or the other well-fledged goose has produced its goose-egg, of quite measurable value, were it the pink of its whole kind; and wonders why all mortals do not wonder!

Foolish enough, too, was the College Tutor's surprise at Walter Shandy: how, though unread in Aristotle, he could nevertheless argue; and not knowing the name of any dialectic tool, handled them all to perfection. Is it the skilfulest anatomist that cuts the best figure at Sadler's Wells? or does the boxer hit better for knowing that he has a *flexor longus* and a *flexor brevis?* But indeed, as in the higher case of the Poet, so here in that of the Speaker and Inquirer, the true force is an unconscious one. The healthy Understanding, we should say, is not the Logical, argumentative, but the Intuitive; for the end of Understanding is not to prove and find reasons, but to know and believe. Of logic, and its limits, and uses and abuses, there were much to be said and examined; one fact, however, which chiefly concerns us here, has long been familiar: that the man of logic and the man of insight; the Reasoner and the Discoverer, or even Knower, are quite separable,—indeed, for most part, quite separate characters. In practical matters, for example, has it not become almost proverbial that the man of logic cannot prosper? This is he whom business-people call Systematic and Theoriser and Word-monger; his *vital* intellectual force lies dormant or extinct, his whole force is mechanical, conscious: of such a one it is foreseen that, when once confronted with the infinite complexities of the real world, his little compact theorem of the world will be found wanting; that unless he can throw it overboard and become a new creature, he will necessarily founder. Nay, in mere Speculation itself, the most ineffectual of all characters, generally speaking, is your dialectic man-at-arms; were he armed cap-a-pie in syllogistic mail of proof, and perfect master of logic-fence, how little does it avail him! Consider the old Schoolmen, and their pilgrimage towards Truth: the faithfulest endeavour, incessant unwearied motion, often great natural vigour; only no progress: nothing but antic feats of one limb poised against the other; there they balanced, somersetted, and made postures; at best gyrated swiftly with some pleasure, like Spinning Dervishes, and ended where they began. So is it, so will it always be, with all System-makers and builders of logical card-castles; of which class a certain remnant must, in every age, as they do in our own, survive and build. Logic is good, but it is not the best. The Irrefragable Doctor, with his chains of induction, his corollaries, dilemmas and other cunning logical diagrams and apparatus, will cast you a beautiful horoscope, and speak reasonable things; nevertheless your stolen jewel, which you wanted him to find you, is not forthcoming. Often by some winged word, winged as the thunderbolt is, of a Luther, a Napoleon, a Goethe, shall we see the difficulty split asunder, and its secret laid bare; while the Irrefragable, with all his logical tools, hews at it, and hovers round it, and finds it on all hands too hard for him.

Again, in the difference between Oratory and Rhetoric, as indeed everywhere in that superiority of what is called the Natural over the Artificial, we find a similar illustration. The Orator persuades and carries all with him, he knows not how; the Rhetorician can prove that he ought to have persuaded and carried all with him: the one is in a state of healthy unconsciousness, as if he 'had no system'; the other, in virtue of regimen and dietetic punctuality, feels at best that 'his system is in high order.' So stands it, in short, with all the forms of Intellect, whether as directed to the finding of truth, or to the fit imparting thereof; to Poetry, to Eloquence, to depth of Insight, which is the basis of both these; always the characteristic of right performance is a certain spontaneity, an unconsciousness; 'the healthy know not of their health, but only the sick.' So that the old precept of the critic, as crabbed as it looked to his ambitious disciple, might contain in it a most fundamental truth, applicable to us all, and in much else than Literature: "Whenever you have written any sentence that looks particularly excellent, be sure to blot it out." In like manner, under milder phraseology, and with a meaning purposely much wider, a living Thinker has taught us: 'Of the Wrong we are always conscious, of the Right never.'

But if such is the law with regard to Speculation and the Intellectual power of man, much more is it with regard to Conduct, and the power, manifested chiefly therein, which we name Moral. 'Let not thy left hand know what thy right hand doeth': whisper not to thy own heart, How worthy is this action!—for then it is already becoming worthless. The good man is he who *works* continually in welldoing; to whom welldoing is as his natural existence, awakening no astonishment, requiring no commentary; but there, like a thing of course, and as if it could not but be so. Self-contemplation, on the other hand, is infallibly the symptom of disease, be it or be it not the sign of cure. An unhealthy Virtue is one that consumes itself to leanness in repenting and anxiety; or, still worse, that inflates itself into dropsical boastfulness and vain-glory: either way, there is a self-seeking; an unprofitable looking behind us to measure the way we have made: whereas the sole concern is to walk continually forward, and make more way. If in any sphere of man's life, then in the Moral sphere, as the inmost and most vital of all, it is good that there be wholeness; that there be unconsciousness, which is the evidence of this. Let the free, reasonable Will, which dwells in us, as in our Holy of Holies, be indeed free, and obeyed like a Divinity, as is its right and its effort: the perfect obedience will be the silent one. Such perhaps were the sense of that maxim, enunciating, as is usual, but the half of a truth: To say that we have a clear conscience, is to utter a solecism; had we never sinned, we should have had no conscience. Were defeat unknown, neither would victory be celebrated by songs of triumph.

This, true enough, is an ideal, impossible state of being; yet ever the goal towards which our actual state of being strives; which it is the more perfect the nearer it can approach. Nor, in our actual world, where Labour must often prove ineffectual, and thus in all senses Light alternate with Darkness, and the nature of an ideal Morality be much modified, is the case, thus far, materially different. It is a fact which escapes no one, that, generally speaking, whoso is acquainted with his worth has but a little stock to cultivate acquaintance with. Above all, the public acknowledgment of such acquaintance, indicating that it has reached quite an intimate footing, bodes ill. Already, to the popular judgment, he who talks much about Virtue in the abstract, begins to be suspect; it is shrewdly guessed that where there is great preaching, there will be little almsgiving. Or again, on a wider scale, we can remark that ages of Heroism are not ages of Moral Philosophy; Virtue, when it can be philosophised of, has become aware of itself, is sickly and beginning to decline. A spontaneous habitual all-pervading spirit of Chivalrous Valour shrinks together, and perks itself up into shrivelled Points of Honour; humane Courtesy and Nobleness of mind dwindle into punctilious Politeness, 'avoiding meats'; 'paying tithe of mint and anise, neglecting the weightier matters of the law.' Goodness, which was a rule to itself, must now appeal to Precept, and seek strength from Sanctions; the Freewill no longer reigns unquestioned and by divine right, but like a mere earthly sovereign, by expediency, by Rewards and Punishments: or rather, let us say, the Freewill, so far as may be, has abdicated and withdrawn into the dark, and a spectral nightmare of a Necessity usurps its throne; for now that mysterious Self-impulse of the whole man, heaven-inspired, and in all senses partaking of the Infinite, being captiously questioned in a finite dialect, and answering, as it needs must, by silence,—is conceived as non-extant, and only the outward Mechanism of it remains acknowledged: of Volition, except as the synonym of Desire, we hear nothing; of 'Motives,' without any Mover, more than enough.

So too, when the generous Affections have become wellnigh paralytic, we have the reign of Sentimentality. The greatness, the profitableness, at any rate the extremely ornamental nature of high feeling, and the luxury of doing good; charity, love, self-forgetfulness, devotedness and all manner of godlike magnanimity,—are everywhere insisted on, and pressingly inculcated in speech and writing, in prose and verse; Socinian Preachers proclaim 'Benevolence' to all the four winds, and have TRUTH engraved on their watch-seals: unhappily with little or no effect. Were the limbs in right walking order, why so much demonstrating of motion? The barrenest of all mortals is the Sentimentalist. Granting even that he were sincere, and did not wilfully deceive us, or without first deceiving himself, what good is in him? Does he not lie there as a perpetual lesson of despair, and type of bedrid valetudinarian impotence? His is emphatically a Virtue that has become, through every fibre, conscious of itself; it is all sick, and feels as if it were made of glass, and durst not touch or be touched; in the shape of work, it can do nothing; at the utmost, by incessant nursing and caudling, keep itself alive. As the last stage of all, when Virtue, properly so called, has ceased to be practised, and become extinct, and a mere remembrance, we have the era of Sophists, descanting of its existence, proving it, denying it, mechanically 'accounting' for it;— as dissectors and demonstrators cannot operate till once the body be dead.

Thus is true Moral genius, like true Intellectual, which indeed is but a lower phasis thereof, 'ever a secret to itself.' The healthy moral nature loves Goodness, and without wonder wholly lives in it: the unhealthy makes love to it, and would fain get to live in it; or, finding such courtship fruitless, turns round, and not without contempt abandons it. These curious relations of the Voluntary and Conscious to the Involuntary and Unconscious, and the small proportion which, in all departments of our life, the former bears to the latter,—might lead us into deep questions of Psychology and Physiology: such, however, belong not to our present object. Enough, if the fact itself become apparent, that Nature so meant it with us; that in this wise we are made. We may now say, that view man's individual Existence under what aspect we will, under the highest spiritual, as under the merely animal aspect, everywhere the grand vital energy, while in its sound state, is an unseen unconscious one; or, in the words of our old Aphorism, 'the healthy know not of their health, but only the sick.'

To understand man, however, we must look beyond the individual man and his actions or interests, and view him in combination with his fellows. It is in Society that man first feels what he is; first becomes what he can be. In Society an altogether new set of spiritual activities are evolved in him, and the old immeasurably quickened and strengthened. Society is the genial element wherein his nature first lives and grows; the solitary man were but a small portion of himself, and must continue forever folded in, stunted and only half alive. 'Already,' says a deep Thinker, with more meaning than will disclose itself at once, 'my opinion, my conviction, gains *infinitely* in strength and sureness, the moment a second mind has adopted it.' Such, even in its simplest form, is association; so wondrous the communion of soul with soul as directed to the mere act of Knowing! In other higher acts, the wonder is still more manifest; as in that portion of our being which we name the Moral: for properly, indeed, all communion is of a moral sort, whereof such intellectual communion (in the act of knowing) is itself an example. But with regard to Morals strictly so called, it is in Society, we might almost say, that Morality begins; here at least it takes an altogether new form, and on every side, as in living growth, expands itself. The Duties of Man to himself, to what is Highest in himself, make but the First Table of the Law: to the First Table is now superadded a Second, with the Duties of Man to his Neighbour; whereby also the significance of the First now assumes its true importance. Man has joined himself with man; soul acts and reacts on soul; a mystic miraculous unfathomable Union establishes itself; Life, in all its elements, has become intensated, consecrated. The lightning-spark of Thought, generated, or say rather heaven-kindled, in the solitary mind, awakens its express likeness in another mind, in a thousand other minds, and all blaze-up together in combined fire; reverberated from mind to mind, fed also with fresh fuel in each, it acquires incalculable new light as Thought, incalculable new heat as converted into Action. By and by, a common store of Thought can accumulate, and be transmitted as an everlasting possession: Literature, whether as preserved in the memory of Bards, in Runes and Hieroglyphs engraved on stone, **or** in Books of written or printed paper, comes into existence, and begins to play its wondrous part. Polities are formed; the weak

submitting to the strong; with a willing loyalty giving
obedience that he may receive guidance: or say rather, in
honour of our nature, the ignorant submitting to the wise;
for so it is in all even the rudest communities, man never
yields himself wholly to brute Force, but always to moral
Greatness; thus the universal title of respect, from the
Original *Sheik,* from the *Sachem* of the Red Indians, down
to our English *Sir,* implies only that he whom we mean to
honour is our *senior.* *Last,* as the crown and all-supporting
keystone of the fabric, Religion arises. The devout meditation of the isolated man, which flitted through his soul, like
a transient tone of Love and Awe from unknown lands,
acquires certainty, continuance, when it is shared-in by his
brother men. ' Where two or three are gathered together '
in the name of the Highest, then first does the Highest, as
it is written, ' appear among them to bless them'; then first
does an Altar and act of united Worship open a way from
Earth to Heaven; whereon, were it but a simple Jacob's-
ladder, the heavenly Messengers will travel, with glad tidings
and unspeakable gifts for men. Such is SOCIETY, the vital
articulation of many individuals into a new collective individual: greatly the most important of man's attainments
on this earth; that in which, and by virtue of which, all
his other attainments and attempts find their arena, and
have their value. Considered well, Society is the standing
wonder of our existence; a true region of the Supernatural;
as it were, a second all-embracing Life, wherein our first
individual Life becomes doubly and trebly alive, and whatever of Infinitude was in us bodies itself forth, and becomes
visible and active.

To figure Society as endowed with life is scarcely a meta-
phor; but rather the statement of a fact by such imperfect
methods as language affords. Look at it closely, that mystic
Union, Nature's highest work with man, wherein man's volition plays an indispensable yet so subordinate a part, and the
small Mechanical grows so mysteriously and indissolubly out
of the infinite Dynamical, like Body out of Spirit,—is truly
enough vital, what we can call vital, and bears the distinguishing character of life. In the same style also, we can
say that Society has its periods of sickness and vigour, of

youth, manhood, decrepitude, dissolution and new birth; in one or other of which stages we may, in all times, and all places where men inhabit, discern it; and do ourselves, in this time and place, whether as coöperating or as contending, as healthy members or as diseased ones, to our joy and sorrow, form part of it. The question, What is the actual condition of Society? has in these days unhappily become important enough. No one of us is unconcerned in that question; but for the majority of thinking men a true answer to it, such is the state of matters, appears almost as the one thing needful. Meanwhile, as the true answer, that is to say, the complete and fundamental answer and settlement, often as it has been demanded, is nowhere forthcoming, and indeed by its nature is impossible, any honest approximation towards such is not without value. The feeblest light, or even so much as a more precise recognition of the darkness, which is the first step to attainment of light, will be welcome.

This once understood, let it not seem idle if we remark that here too our old Aphorism holds; that again in the Body Politic, as in the animal body, the sign of right performances is Unconsciousness. Such indeed is virtually the meaning of that phrase, 'artificial state of society,' as contrasted with the natural state, and indicating something so inferior to it. For, in all vital things, men distinguish an Artificial and a Natural; founding on some dim perception or sentiment of the very truth we here insist on: the artificial is the conscious, mechanical; the natural is the unconscious, dynamical. Thus, as we have an artificial Poetry, and prize only the natural; so likewise we have an artificial Morality, an artificial Wisdom, an artificial Society. The artificial Society is precisely one that knows its own structure, its own internal functions; not in watching, not in knowing which, but in working outwardly to the fulfilment of its aim, does the wellbeing of a Society consist. Every Society, every Polity, has a spiritual principle; is the embodiment, tentative and more or less complete, of an Idea: all its tendencies of endeavour, specialties of custom, its laws, politics and whole procedure (as the glance of some Montesquieu, across innumerable superficial entanglements, can partly decipher), are prescribed by an Idea, and flow naturally from it, as movements from the living source of motion. This Idea, be it of devotion to a man or class of men, to a creed, to an institution, or even, as in more ancient times, to a piece of land, is ever a true Loyalty; has in it something of a religious, paramount, quite infinite character; it is properly the Soul of the State, its Life; mysterious as other forms of Life, and like these working secretly, and in a depth beyond that of consciousness.

Accordingly, it is not in the vigorous ages of a Roman Republic that Treatises of the Commonwealth are written: while the Decii are rushing with devoted bodies on the enemies of Rome, what need of preaching Patriotism? The virtue of Patriotism has already sunk from its pristine all-transcendent condition, before it has received a name. So long as the Commonwealth continues rightly athletic, it cares not to dabble in anatomy. Why teach obedience to the Sovereign; why so much as admire it, or separately recognise it, while a divine idea of Obedience perennially inspires all men? Loyalty, like Patriotism, of which it is a form, was not praised till it had begun to decline; the *Preux Chevaliers* first became rightly admirable, when 'dying for their king' had ceased to be a habit with chevaliers. For if the mystic significance of the State, let this be what it may, dwells vitally in every heart, encircles every life as with a second higher life, how should it stand self-questioning? It must rush outward, and express itself by works. Besides, if perfect, it is there as by necessity, and does not excite inquiry: it is also by nature infinite, has no limits; therefore can be circumscribed by no conditions and definitions; cannot be reasoned of; except *musically,* or in the language of Poetry, cannot yet so much as be spoken of.

In those days, Society was what we name healthy, sound at heart. Not indeed without suffering enough; not without perplexities, difficulty on every side: for such is the appointment of man; his highest and sole blessedness is, that he toil, and know what to toil at: not in ease, but in united victorious labour, which is at once evil and the victory over evil, does his Freedom lie. Nay, often, looking no deeper than such superficial perplexities of the early Time, historians have taught us that it was all one mass of contradiction and disease; and in the antique Republic or feudal Monarchy have seen only the confused chaotic quarry, not the robust labourer, or the stately edifice he was building of it.

If Society, in such ages, had its difficulty, it had also its strength; if sorrowful masses of rubbish so encumbered it, the tough sinews to hurl them aside, with indomitable heart, were not wanting. Society went along without complaint; did not stop to scrutinize itself, to say, How well I perform! or, Alas, how ill! Men did not yet feel themselves to be 'the envy of surrounding nations'; and were enviable on that very account. Society was what we can call *whole,* in both senses of the word. The individual man was in himself a whole, or complete union; and could combine with his fellows as the living member of a greater whole. For all men, through their life, were animated by one great Idea; thus all efforts pointed one way, everywhere there was *wholeness.* Opinion and Action had not yet become disunited; but the former could still produce the latter, or attempt to produce it; as the stamp does its impression while the wax is not hardened. Thought and the voice of thought were also a unison; thus, instead of Speculation, we had Poetry; Literature, in its rude utterance, was as yet a heroic Song, perhaps too a devotional Anthem.

Religion was everywhere; Philosophy lay hid under it, peaceably included in it. Herein, as in the life-centre of all, lay the true health and oneness. Only at a later era must Religion split itself into Philosophies; and thereby, the vital union of Thought being lost, disunion and mutual collision in all provinces of Speech and Action more and more prevail. For if the Poet, or Priest, or by whatever title the inspired thinker may be named, is the sign of vigour and well-being; so likewise is the Logician, or uninspired thinker, the sign of disease, probably of decrepitude and decay. Thus, not to mention other instances, one of them much nearer hand,—so soon as Prophecy among the Hebrews had ceased, then did the reign of Argumentation begin; and the ancient Theocracy, in its Sadduceeisms and Phariseeisms, and vain jangling of sects and doctors, give token that the *soul* of it had fled, and that the *body* itself, by natural dissolution, 'with the old forces still at work, but working in reverse order,' was on the road to final disappearance.

We might pursue this question into innumerable other ramifications; and everywhere, under new shapes, find the same truth, which we here so imperfectly enunciate, disclosed; that throughout the whole world of man, in all manifestations and performances of his nature, outward and inward, personal and social, the Perfect, the Great is a mystery to itself, knows not itself; whatsoever does know itself is already little, and more or less imperfect. Or otherwise, we may say, Unconsciousness belongs to pure unmixed life; Consciousness to a diseased mixture and conflict of life and death: Unconsciousness is the sign of creation; Consciousness, at best, that of manufacture. So deep, in this existence of ours, is the significance of Mystery. Well might the Ancients make Silence a god; for it is the element of all godhood, infinitude, or transcendental greatness; at once the source and the ocean wherein all such begins and ends. In the same sense, too, have Poets sung 'Hymns to the Night'; as if Night were nobler than Day; as if Day were but a small motley-coloured veil spread transiently over the infinite bosom of Night, and did but deform and hide from us its purely transparent eternal deeps. So likewise have they spoken and sung as if Silence were the grand epitome and complete sum-total of all Harmony; and Death, what mortals call Death, properly the beginning of Life. Under such figures, since except in figures there is no speaking of the Invisible, have men endeavoured to express a great Truth;—a Truth, in our Times, as nearly as is perhaps possible, forgotten by the most; which nevertheless continues forever true, forever all-important, and will one day, under new figures, be again brought home to the bosoms of all.

But indeed, in a far lower sense, the rudest mind has still some intimation of the greatness there is in Mystery. If Silence was made a god of by the Ancients, he still continues a government-clerk among us Moderns. To all quacks, moreover, of what sort soever, the effect of Mystery is well known: here and there some Cagliostro, even in latter days, turns it to notable account: the blockhead also, who is ambitious, and has no talent, finds sometimes in 'the talent of silence,' a kind of succedaneum. Or again, looking on the opposite side of the matter, do we not see, in the common understanding of mankind, a certain distrust, a certain contempt of what is altogether self-conscious and mechanical? As nothing that is wholly seen through has other than a trivial character; so anything professing to be great, and yet wholly to see through itself, is already known to be false, and a failure. The evil repute your 'theoretical men' stand in, the acknowledged inefficiency of 'paper constitutions,' and all that class of objects, are instances of this. Experience often repeated, and perhaps a certain instinct of something far deeper that lies under such experiences, has taught men so much. They know beforehand, that the loud is generally the insignificant, the empty. Whatsoever can proclaim itself from the house-tops may be fit for the hawker, and for those multitudes that must needs buy of him; but for any deeper use, might as well continue unproclaimed. Observe too, how the converse of the proposition holds; how the insignificant, the empty, is usually the loud; and, after the manner of a drum, is loud even because of its emptiness. The uses of some Patent Dinner Calefactor can be bruited abroad over the whole world in the course of the first winter; those of the Printing Press are not so well seen into for the first three centuries: the passing of the Select-Vestries Bill raises more noise and hopeful expectancy among mankind than did the promulgation of the Christian Religion. Again, and again, we say, the great, the creative and enduring is ever a secret to itself; only the small, the barren and transient is otherwise.

If we now, with a practical medical view, examine, by this same test of Unconsciousness, the Condition of our own Era, and of man's Life therein, the diagnosis we arrive at is nowise of a flattering sort. The state of Society in our days is, of all possible states, the least an unconscious one: this is specially the Era when all manner of Inquiries into what was once the unfelt, involuntary sphere of man's existence, find their place, and, as it were, occupy the whole domain of thought. What, for example, is all this that we hear, for the last generation or two, about the Improvement of the Age, the Spirit of the Age, Destruction of Prejudice, Progress of the Species, and the March of Intellect, but an unhealthy state of self-sentience, self-survey; the precursor and prognostic of still worse health? That Intellect do march, if possible at double-quick time, is very desirable; nevertheless, why should she turn round at every stride, and cry: See you what a stride I have taken! Such a marching of Intellect is distinctly of the spavined kind; what the Jockeys call 'all action and no go.' Or at best, if we examine well, it is the marching of that gouty Patient, whom his Doctors had clapt on a metal floor artificially heated to the searing point, so that he was obliged to march, and did march with a vengeance—nowhither. Intellect did not awaken for the first time yesterday; but has been under way from Noah's Flood downwards: greatly her best progress, moreover, was in the old times, when she said nothing about it. In those same 'dark ages,' Intellect (metaphorically as well as literally) could invent *glass,* which now she has enough ado to grind into *spectacles.* Intellect built not only Churches, but a Church, *the* Church, based on this firm Earth, yet reaching up, and leading up, as high as Heaven; and now it is all she can do to keep its doors bolted, that there be no tearing of the Surplices, no robbery of the Alms-box. She built a Senate-house likewise, glorious in its kind; and now it costs her a well-nigh mortal effort to sweep it clear of vermin, and get the roof made rain-tight.

But the truth is, with Intellect, as with most other things, we are now passing from that first or boastful stage of Self-sentience into the second or painful one: out of these often-asseverated declarations that 'our system is in high order,' we come now, by natural sequence, to the melancholy conviction that it is altogether the reverse. Thus, for instance, in the matter of Government, the period of the 'Invaluable Constitution' has to be followed by a Reform Bill; to laudatory De Lolmes succeed objurgatory Benthams. At any rate, what Treatises on the Social Contract, on the Elective Franchise, the Rights of Man, the Rights of Property, Codifications, Institutions, Constitutions, have we not, for long years, groaned under! Or again, with a wider survey, consider those Essays on Man, Thoughts on Man, Inquiries concerning Man; not to mention Evidences of the Christian Faith, Theories of Poetry, Considerations on the Origin of Evil, which during the last century have accumulated on us to a frightful extent. Never since the beginning of Time was there, that we hear or read of, so intensely self-conscious a Society. Our whole relations to the Universe and to our fellow-man have become an Inquiry, a Doubt; nothing will go on of its own accord, and do its function quietly; but all things must be probed into, the whole working of man's world be anatomically studied. Alas, anatomically studied, that it may be medically aided! Till at length indeed, we have come to such a pass, that except in this same *medicine,* with its artifices and appliances, few can so much as imagine any strength or hope to remain for us. The whole Life of Society must now be carried on by drugs: doctor after doctor appears with his nostrum, of Coöperative Societies, Universal Suffrage, Cottage-and-Cow systems, Repression of Population, Vote by ballot. To such height has the dyspepsia of Society reached: as indeed the constant grinding internal pain, or from time to time the mad spasmodic throes, of all Society do otherwise too mournfully indicate.

Far be it from us to attribute, as some unwise persons do, the disease itself to this unhappy sensation that there is a disease! The Encyclopedists did not produce the troubles of France; but the troubles of France produced the Encyclopedists, and much else. The Self-consciousness is the symptom merely; nay, it is also the attempt towards cure. We record the fact, without special censure; not wondering that Society should feel itself, and in all ways complain of aches and twinges, for it has suffered enough. Napoleon was but a Job's-comforter, when he told his wounded staff-officer, twice unhorsed by cannon-balls, and with half his limbs blown to pieces: *" Vous vous écoutez trop ! "*

On the outward, as it were Physical diseases of Society, it were beside our purpose to insist here. These are diseases which he who runs may read; and sorrow over, with or without hope. Wealth has accumulated itself into masses; and Poverty, also in accumulation enough, lies impassably separated from it; opposed, uncommunicating, like forces in positive and negative poles. The gods of this lower world sit aloft on glittering thrones, less happy than Epicurus's gods, but as indolent, as impotent; while the boundless living chaos of Ignorance and Hunger welters terrific, in its dark fury, under their feet. How much among us might be likened to a whited sepulchre; outwardly all pomp and strength; but inwardly full of horror and despair and dead-men's bones! Iron highways, with their wains fire-winged, are uniting all ends of the firm Land; quays and moles, with their innumerable stately fleets, tame the Ocean into our pliant bearer of burdens; Labour's thousand arms of sinew and of metal, all-conquering everywhere, from the tops of the mountain down to the depths of the mine and the caverns of the sea, ply unweariedly for the service of man: yet man remains unserved. He has subdued this Planet, his habitation and inheritance; yet reaps no profit from the victory.

Sad to look upon: in the highest stage of civilisation, nine-tenths of mankind have to struggle in the lowest battle of savage or even animal man, the battle against Famine. Countries are rich, prosperous in all manner of increase, beyond example: but the Men of those countries are poor, needier than ever of all sustenance outward and inward; of Belief, of Knowledge, of Money, of Food. The rule, *Sic vos non vobis,* never altogether to be got rid of in men's Industry, now presses with such incubus weight, that Industry must shake it off, or utterly be strangled under it; and, alas, can as yet but gasp and rave, and aimlessly struggle, like one in the final deliration. Thus Change, or the inevitable approach of Change, is manifest everywhere. In one Country we have seen lava-torrents of fever-frenzy envelop all things; Government succeed Government, like the phantasms of a dying brain. In another Country, we can even now see, in maddest alternation, the Peasant governed by such guidance as this: To labour earnestly one month in raising wheat, and the next month labour earnestly in burning it. So that Society, were it not by nature immortal, and its death ever a new-birth, might appear, as it does in the eyes of some, to be sick to dissolution, and even now writhing in its last agony. Sick enough we must admit it to be, with disease enough, a whole nosology of diseases; wherein he perhaps is happiest that is

not called to prescribe as physician;—wherein, however, one
small piece of policy, that of summoning the Wisest in the
Commonwealth, by the sole method yet known or thought
of, to come together and with their whole soul consult for it,
might, but for late tedious experiences, have seemed unquestionable enough.

But leaving this, let us rather look within, into the
Spiritual condition of Society, and see what aspects and
prospects offer themselves there. For after all, it is there
properly that the secret and origin of the whole is to be
sought: the Physical derangements of Society are but the
image and impress of its Spiritual; while the heart continues
sound, all other sickness is superficial, and temporary. False
Action is the fruit of false Speculation; let the spirit of
Society be free and strong, that is to say, let true Principles
inspire the members of Society, then neither can disorders
accumulate in its Practice; each disorder will be promptly,
faithfully inquired into, and remedied as it arises. But alas,
with us the Spiritual condition of Society is no less sickly
than the Physical. Examine man's internal world, in any of
its social relations and performances, here too all seems diseased self-consciousness, collision and mutually-destructive
struggle. Nothing acts from within outwards in undivided
healthy force; everything lies impotent, lamed, its force
turned inwards, and painfully ' listens to itself.'

To begin with our highest Spiritual function, with Religion, we might ask, Whither has Religion now fled? Of
Churches and their establishments we here say nothing; nor
of the unhappy domains of Unbelief, and how innumerable
men, blinded in their minds, have grown to 'live without
God in the world'; but, taking the fairest side of the matter,
we ask, What is the nature of that same Religion, which
still lingers in the hearts of the few who are called, and call
themselves, specially the Religious? Is it a healthy religion,
vital, unconscious of itself; that shines forth spontaneously
in doing of the Work, or even in preaching of the Word?
Unhappily, no. Instead of heroic martyr Conduct, and inspired and soul-inspiring Eloquence, whereby Religion itself
were brought home to our living bosoms, to live and reign
there, we have ' Discourses on the Evidences,' endeavouring,

with smallest result, to make it probable that such a thing as Religion exists. The most enthusiastic Evangelicals do not preach a Gospel, but keep describing how it should and might be preached: to awaken the sacred fire of faith, as by a sacred contagion, is not their endeavour; but, at most, to describe how Faith shows and acts, and scientifically distinguish true Faith from false. Religion, like all else, is conscious of itself, listens to itself; it becomes less and less creative, vital; more and more mechanical. Considered as a whole, the Christian Religion of late ages has been continally dissipating itself into Metaphysics; and threatens now to disappear, as some rivers do, in deserts of barren sand.

Of Literature, and its deep-seated, wide-spread maladies, why speak? Literature is but a branch of Religion, and always participates in its character: however, in our time, it is the only branch that still shows any greenness; and, as some think, must one day become the main stem. Now, apart from the subterranean and tartarean regions of Literature; —leaving out of view the frightful, scandalous statistics of Puffing, the mystery of Slander, Falsehood, Hatred and other convulsion-work of rabid Imbecility, and all that has rendered Literature on that side a perfect ' Babylon the mother of Abominations,' in very deed making the world ' drunk' with the wine of her iniquity;—forgetting all this, let us look only to the regions of the upper air; to such Literature as can be said to have some attempt towards truth in it, some tone of music, and if it be not poetical, to hold of the poetical. Among other characteristics, is not this manifest enough: that it knows itself? Spontaneous devotedness to the object, being wholly possessed by the object, what we can call Inspiration, has well-nigh ceased to appear in Literature. Which melodious Singer forgets that he is singing melodiously? We have not the love of greatness, but the love of the love of greatness. Hence infinite Affectations, Distractions; in every case inevitable Error. Consider, for one example, this peculiarity of Modern Literature, the sin that has been named View-hunting. In our elder writers, there are no paintings of scenery for its own sake; no euphuistic gallantries with Nature, but a constant heartlove for her, a constant dwelling in communion with her. View-hunting, with so much else that is of kin to it, first came decisively into action through the *Sorrows of Werter;* which wonderful Performance, indeed, may in many senses be regarded as the progenitor of all that has since become popular in Literature; whereof, in so far as concerns spirit and tendency, it still offers the most instructive image; for nowhere, except in its own country, above all in the mind of its illustrious Author, has it yet fallen wholly obsolete. Scarcely ever, till that late epoch, did any worshipper of Nature become entirely aware that he was worshipping, much to his own credit; and think of saying to himself: Come, let us make a description! Intolerable enough: when every puny whipster plucks out his pencil, and insists on painting you a scene; so that the instant you discern such a thing as ' wavy outline,' ' mirror of the lake,' ' stern headland,' or the like, in any Book, you tremulously hasten on; and scarcely the Author of Waverley himself can tempt you not to skip.

Nay, is not the diseased self-conscious state of Literature disclosed in this one fact, which lies so near us here, the prevalence of Reviewing! Sterne's wish for a reader ' that would give-up the reins of his imagination into his author's hands, and be pleased he knew not why, and cared not wherefore,' might lead him a long journey now. Indeed, for our best class of readers, the chief pleasure, a very stinted one, is this same knowing of the Why; which many a Kames and Bossu has been, ineffectually enough, endeavouring to teach us: till at last these also have laid down their trade; and now your Reviewer is a mere *taster;* who tastes, and says, by the evidence of such palate, such tongue, as he has got, It is good, It is bad. Was it thus that the French carried out certain inferior creatures on their Algerine Expedition, to taste the wells for them, and try whether they were poisoned? Far be it from us to disparage our own craft, whereby we have our living! Only we must note these things: that Reviewing spreads with strange vigour; that such a man as Byron reckons the Reviewer and the Poet equal; that at the last Leipzig Fair, there was advertised a Review of Reviews. By and by it will be found that all Literature has become one boundless self-devouring Review; and, as in London routs, we have to *do* nothing, but only **to** *see* others do nothing.—Thus does Literature also, like a sick thing, superabundantly 'listen to itself.'

No less is this unhealthy symptom manifest, if we cast a glance on our Philosophy, on the character of our speculative Thinking. Nay, already, as above hinted, the mere existence and necessity of a Philosophy is an evil. Man is sent hither not to question, but to work: 'the end of man,' it was long ago written, 'is an Action, not a Thought.' In the perfect state, all Thought were but the picture and inspiring symbol of Action; Philosophy, except as Poetry and Religion, would have no being. And yet how, in this imperfect state, can it be avoided, can it be dispensed with? Man stands as in the centre of Nature; his fraction of Time encircled by Eternity, his handbreadth of Space encircled by Infinitude: how shall he forbear asking himself, What am I; and Whence; and Whither? How too, except in slight partial hints, in kind asseverations and assurances, such as a mother quiets her fretfully inquisitive child with, shall he get answer to such inquiries?

The disease of Metaphysics, accordingly, is a perennial one. In all ages, those questions of Death and Immortality, Origin of Evil, Freedom and Necessity, must, under new forms, anew make their appearance; ever, from time to time, must the attempt to shape for ourselves some Theorem of the Universe be repeated. And ever unsuccessfully: for what Theorem of the Infinite can the Finite render complete? We, the whole species of Mankind, and our whole existence and history, are but a floating speck in the illimitable ocean of the All; yet *in* that ocean; indissoluble portion thereof; partaking of its infinite tendencies: borne this way and that by its deep-swelling tides, and grand ocean currents;—of which what faintest chance is there that we should ever exhaust the significance, ascertain the goings and comings? A region of Doubt, therefore, hovers forever in the background; in Action alone can we have certainty. Nay, properly Doubt is the indispensable, inexhaustible material whereon Action works, which Action has to fashion into Certainty and Reality; only on a canvas of Darkness, such is man's way of being, could the manycoloured picture of our Life paint itself and shine.

Thus if our eldest system of Metaphysics is as old as the *Book of Genesis,* our latest is that of Mr. Thomas Hope, published only within the current year. It is a chronic malady that of Metaphysics, as we said, and perpetually recurs on us. At the utmost, there is a better and a worse in it; a stage of convalescence, and a stage of relapse with new sickness: these forever succeed each other, as is the nature of all Life-movement here below. The first, or convalescent stage, we might also name that of Dogmatical or Constructive Metaphysics; when the mind constructively endeavours to scheme out and assert for itself an actual Theorem of the Universe, and therewith for a time rests satisfied. The second or sick stage might be called that of Sceptical or Inquisitory Metaphysics; when the mind having widened its sphere of vision, the existing Theorem of the Universe no longer answers the phenomena, no longer yields contentment; but must be torn in pieces, and certainty anew sought for in the endless realms of denial. All Theologies and sacred Cosmogonies belong, in some measure, to the first class; in all Pyrrhonism, from Pyrrho down to Hume and the innumerable disciples of Hume, we have instances enough of the second. In the former, so far as it affords satisfaction, a temporary anodyne to doubt, an arena for wholesome action, there may be much good; indeed in this case, it holds rather of Poetry than of Metaphysics, might be called Inspiration rather than Speculation. The latter is Metaphysics proper; a pure, unmixed, though from time to time a necessary evil.

For truly, if we look into it, there is no more fruitless endeavour than this same, which the Metaphysician proper toils in: to educe Conviction out of Negation. How, by merely testing and rejecting what is not, shall we ever attain knowledge of what is? Metaphysical Speculation, as it begins in No or Nothingness, so it must needs end in Nothingness; circulates and must circulate in endless vortices; creating, swallowing—itself. Our being is made up of Light and Darkness, the Light resting on the Darkness, and balancing it; everywhere there is Dualism, Equipoise; a perpetual Contradiction dwells in us: 'where shall I place myself to escape from my own shadow?' Consider it well,

Metaphysics is the attempt of the mind to rise above the mind; to environ and shut in, or as we say, *comprehend* the mind. Hopeless struggle, for the wisest, as for the foolishest! What strength of sinew, or athletic skill, will enable the stoutest athlete to fold his own body in his arms, and, by lifting, lift up *himself?* The Irish Saint swam the Channel, ' carrying his head in his teeth '; but the feat has never been imitated.

That this is the age of Metaphysics, in the proper, or sceptical Inquisitory sense; that there was a necessity for its being such an age, we regard as our indubitable misfortune. From many causes, the arena of free Activity has long been narrowing, that of sceptical Inquiry becoming more and more universal, more and more perplexing. The Thought conducts not to the Deed; but in boundless chaos, self-devouring, engenders monstrosities, phantasms, fire-breathing chimeras. Profitable Speculation were this: What is to be done; and How is it to be done? But with us not so much as the What can be got sight of. For some generations, all Philosophy has been a painful, captious, hostile question towards everything in the Heaven above, and in the Earth beneath: Why art thou there? Till at length it has come to pass that the worth and authenticity of all things seems dubitable or deniable: our best effort must be unproductively spent not in working, but in ascertaining our mere Whereabout, and so much as whether we are to work at all. Doubt, which, as was said, ever hangs in the background of our world, has now become our middleground and foreground; whereon, for the time, no fair Life-picture can be painted, but only the dark air-canvas itself flow round us, bewildering and benighting.

Nevertheless, doubt as we will, man is actually Here; not to ask questions, but to do work: in this time, as in all times, it must be the heaviest evil for him, if his faculty of Action lie dormant, and only that of sceptical Inquiry exert itself. Accordingly whoever looks abroad upon the world, comparing the Past with the Present, may find that the practical condition of man in these days is one of the saddest; burdened with miseries which are in a considerable degree peculiar. In no time was man's life what he calls a happy one; in no time can it be so. A perpetual dream there has been of Paradises, and some luxurious Lubberland, where the brooks should run wine, and the trees bend with ready-baked viands; but it was a dream merely; an impossible dream. Suffering, contradiction, error, have their quite perennial, and even indispensable abode in this Earth. Is not labour the inheritance of man? And what labour for the present is joyous, and not grievous? Labour, effort, is the very interruption of that ease, which man foolishly enough fancies to be his happiness; and yet without labour there were no ease, no rest, so much as conceivable. Thus Evil, what we call Evil, must ever exist while man exists: Evil, in the widest sense we can give it, is precisely the dark, disordered material out of which man's Freewill has to create an edifice of order and Good. Ever must Pain urge us to Labour; and only in free Effort can any blessedness be imagined for us.

But if man has, in all ages, had enough to encounter, there has, in most civilised ages, been an inward force vouchsafed him, whereby the pressure of things outward might be withstood. Obstruction abounded; but Faith also was not wanting. It is by Faith that man removes mountains: while he had Faith, his limbs might be wearied with toiling, his back galled with bearing; but the heart within him was peaceable and resolved. In the thickest gloom there burnt a lamp to guide him. If he struggled and suffered, he felt that it even should be so; knew for what he was suffering and struggling. Faith gave him an inward Willingness; a world of Strength wherewith to front a world of Difficulty. The true wretchedness lies here: that the Difficulty remain and the Strength be lost; that Pain cannot relieve itself in free Effort; that we have the Labour, and want the Willingness. Faith strengthens us, enlightens us, for all endeavours and endurances; with Faith we can do all, and dare all, and life itself has a thousand times been joyfully given away. But the sum of man's misery is even this, that he feel himself crushed under the Juggernaut wheels, and know that Juggernaut is no divinity, but a dead mechanical idol.

Now this is specially the misery which has fallen on man in our Era. Belief, Faith has well-nigh vanished from the

world. The youth on awakening in this wondrous Universe
no longer finds a competent theory of its wonders. Time
was, when if he asked himself, What is man, What are the
duties of man? the answer stood ready written for him. But
now the ancient ' ground-plan of the All ' belies itself when
brought into contact with reality; Mother Church has, to
the most, become a superannuated Step-mother, whose lessons go disregarded; or are spurned at, and scornfully gainsaid. For young Valour and thirst of Action no ideal
Chivalry invites to heroism, prescribes what is heroic: the
old ideal of Manhood has grown obsolete, and the new is
still invisible to us, and we grope after it in darkness, one
clutching this phantom, another that; Werterism, Byronism,
even Brummelism, each has its day. For Contemplation and
love of Wisdom, no Cloister now opens its religious shades;
the Thinker must, in all senses, wander homeless, too often
aimless, looking up to a Heaven which is dead for him, round
to an Earth which is deaf. Action, in those old days, was
easy, was voluntary, for the divine worth of human things
lay acknowledged; Speculation was wholesome, for it ranged
itself as the handmaid of Action; what could not so range
itself died out by its natural death, by neglect. Loyalty still
hallowed obedience, and made rule noble; there was still
something to be loyal to: the Godlike stood embodied under
many a symbol in men's interests and business; the Finite
shadowed forth the Infinite; Eternity looked through Time.
The Life of man was encompassed and overcanopied by a
glory of Heaven, even as his dwelling-place by the azure
vault.

How changed in these new days! Truly may it be said,
the Divinity has withdrawn from the Earth; or veils himself
in that wide-wasting Whirlwind of a departing Era, wherein
the fewest can discern his goings. Not Godhead, but an
iron, ignoble circle of Necessity embraces all things; binds
the youth of these times into a sluggish thrall, or else exas-
perates him into a rebel. Heroic Action is paralysed; for
what worth now remains unquestionable with him? At the
fervid period when his whole nature cries aloud for Action,
there is nothing sacred under whose banner he can act; the
course and kind and conditions of free Action are all but

undiscoverable.   Doubt storms-in on him through every
avenue; inquiries of the deepest, painfulest sort must be engaged with; and the invincible energy of young years waste
itself in sceptical, suicidal cavillings; in passionate 'questionings of Destiny,' whereto no answer will be returned.

For men, in whom the old perennial principle of Hunger
(be it Hunger of the poor Day-drudge who stills it with
eighteenpence a-day, or of the ambitious Placehunter who
can nowise still it with so little) suffices to fill-up existence,
the case is bad; but not the worst.   These men have an aim,
such as it is; and can steer towards it, with chagrin enough
truly; yet, as their hands are kept full, without desperation.
Unhappier are they to whom a higher instinct has been
given; who struggle to be persons, not machines; to whom
the Universe is not a warehouse, or at best a fancy-bazaar,
but a mystic temple and hall of doom.   For such men there
lie properly two courses open.   The lower, yet still an estimable class, take up with worn-out Symbols of the Godlike;
keep trimming and trucking between these and Hypocrisy,
purblindly enough, miserably enough.   A numerous intermediate class end in Denial; and form a theory that there
is no theory; that nothing is certain in the world, except
this fact of Pleasure being pleasant; so they try to realise
what trifling modicum of Pleasure they can come at, and to
live contented therewith, winking hard.   Of those we speak
not here; but only of the second nobler class, who also have
dared to say No, and cannot yet say Yea; but feel that in
the No they dwell as in a Golgotha, where life enters not,
where peace is not appointed them.

Hard, for most part, is the fate of such men; the harder
the nobler they are.   In dim forecastings, wrestles within
them the 'Divine Idea of the World,' yet will nowhere visibly
reveal itself.   They have to realise a Worship for themselves,
or live unworshipping.   The Godlike has vanished from the
world; and they, by the strong cry of their soul's agony, like
true wonder-workers, must again evoke its presence.   This
miracle is their appointed task; which they must accomplish,
or die wretchedly: this miracle has been accomplished by
such; but not in our land; our land yet knows not of it.   Behold a Byron, in melodious tones, 'cursing his day': he

mistakes earthborn passionate Desire for heaven-inspired Freewill; without heavenly loadstar, rushes madly into the dance of meteoric lights that hover on the mad Mahlstrom; and goes down among its eddies. Hear a Shelley filling the earth with inarticulate wail; like the infinite, inarticulate grief and weeping of forsaken infants. A noble Friedrich Schlegel, stupefied in that fearful loneliness, as of a silenced battle-field, flies back to Catholicism; as a child might to its slain mother's bosom, and cling there. In lower regions, how many a poor Hazlitt must wander on God's verdant earth, like the Unblest on burning deserts; passionately dig wells, and draw up only the dry quicksand; believe that he is seeking Truth, yet only wrestle among endless Sophisms, doing desperate battle as with spectre-hosts; and die and make no sign!

To the better order of such minds any mad joy of Denial has long since ceased: the problem is not now to deny, but to ascertain and perform. Once in destroying the False, there was a certain inspiration; but now the genius of Destruction has done its work, there is now nothing more to destroy. The doom of the Old has long been pronounced, and irrevocable; the Old has passed away: but, alas, the New appears not in its stead; the Time is still in pangs of travail with the New. Man has walked by the light of conflagrations, and amid the sound of falling cities; and now there is darkness, and long watching till it be morning. The voice even of the faithful can but exclaim: 'As yet struggles the twelfth hour of the Night: birds of darkness are on the wing, spectres uproar, the dead walk, the living dream.— Thou, Eternal Providence, wilt cause the day to dawn!'[1]

Such being the condition, temporal and spiritual, of the world at our Epoch, can we wonder that the world 'listens to itself,' and struggles and writhes, everywhere externally and internally, like a thing in pain? Nay, is not even this unhealthy action of the world's Organisation, if the symptom of universal disease, yet also the symptom and sole means of restoration and cure? The effort of Nature, exerting her medicative force to cast-out foreign impediments, and once more become One, become whole? In Practice, still more in

[1] Jean Paul's *Hesperus* (Vorrede).

Opinion, which is the precursor and prototype of Practice, there must needs be collision, convulsion; much has to be ground away. Thought must needs be Doubt and Inquiry, before it can again be Affirmation and Sacred Precept. Innumerable 'Philosophies of Man,' contending in boundless hubbub, must annihilate each other, before an inspired Poesy and Faith for Man can fashion itself together.

From this stunning hubbub, a true Babel-like confusion of tongues, we have here selected two Voices; less as objects of praise or condemnation, than as signs how far the confusion has reached, what prospect there is of its abating. Friedrich Schlegel's *Lectures* delivered at Dresden, and Mr. Hope's *Essay* published in London, are the latest utterances of European Speculation: far asunder in external place, they stand at a still wider distance in inward purport; are, indeed, so opposite and yet so cognate that they may, in many senses, represent the two Extremes of our whole modern system of Thought; and be said to include between them all the Metaphysical Philosophies, so often alluded to here, which, of late times, from France, Germany, England, have agitated and almost overwhelmed us. Both in regard to matter and to form, the relation of these two Works is significant enough.

Speaking first of their cognate qualities, let us remark, not without emotion, one quite extraneous point of agreement; the fact that the Writers of both have departed from this world; they have now finished their search, and had all doubts resolved: while we listen to the voice, the tongue that uttered it has gone silent forever. But the fundamental, all-pervading similiarity lies in this circumstance, well worthy of being noted, that both these Philosophies are of the Dogmatic or Constructive sort: each in its way is a kind of Genesis; an endeavour to bring the Phenomena of man's Universe once more under some theoretic Scheme: in both there is a decided principle of unity; they strive after a result which shall be positive; their aim is not to question, but to establish. This, especially if we consider with what comprehensive concentrated force it is here exhibited, forms a new feature in such works.

Under all other aspects, there is the most irreconcilable

opposition; a staring contrariety, such as might provoke contrasts, were there far fewer points of comparison. If Schlegel's Work is the apotheosis of Spiritualism; Hope's again is the apotheosis of Materialism: in the one, all Matter is evaporated into a Phenomenon, and terrestrial Life itself, with its whole doings and showings, held out as a Disturbance (*Zerrüttung*) produced by the *Zeitgeist* (Spirit of Time); in the other, Matter is distilled and sublimated into some semblance of Divinity: the one regards Space and Time as mere forms of man's mind, and without external existence or reality; the other supposes Space and Time to be 'incessantly created,' and rayed-in upon us like a sort of gravitation.' Such is their difference in respect of purport: no less striking is it in respect of manner, talent, success and all outward characteristics. Thus, if in Schlegel we have to admire the power of Words, in Hope we stand astonished, it might almost be said, at the want of an articulate Language. To Schlegel his Philosophic Speech is obedient, dexterous, exact, like a promptly ministering genius; his names are so clear, so precise and vivid, that they almost (sometimes altogether) become things for him: with Hope there is no Philosophical Speech; but a painful, confused stammering, and struggling after such; or the tongue, as in doatish forgetfulness, maunders, low, long-winded, and speaks not the word intended, but another; so that here the scarcely intelligible, in these endless convolutions, becomes the wholly unreadable; and often we could ask, as that mad pupil did of his tutor in Philosophy, " But whether is Virtue a fluid, then, or a gas?" If the fact, that Schlegel, in the city of Dresden, could find audience for such high discourse, may excite our envy; this other fact, that a person of strong powers, skilled in English Thought and master of its Dialect, could write the *Origin and Prospects of Man,* may painfully remind us of the reproach, that England has now no language for Meditation; that England, the most calculative, is the least meditative, of all civilised countries.

It is not our purpose to offer any criticism of Schlegel's Book; in such limits as were possible here, we should despair of communicating even the faintest image of its significance. To the mass of readers, indeed, both among the Germans themselves, and still more elsewhere, it nowise addresses itself, and may lie forever sealed. We point it out as a remarkable document of the Time and of the Man; can recommend it, moreover, to all earnest Thinkers, as a work deserving their best regard; a work full of deep meditation, wherein the infinite mystery of Life, if not represented, is decisively recognised. Of Schlegel himself, and his character, and spiritual history, we can profess no thorough or final understanding; yet enough to make us view him with admiration and pity, nowise with harsh contemptuous censure; and must say, with clearest persuasion, that the outcry of his being ' a renegade,' and so forth, is but like other such outcries, a judgment where there was neither jury, nor evidence, nor judge. The candid reader, in this Book itself, to say nothing of all the rest, will find traces of a high, farseeing, earnest spirit, to whom ' Austrian Pensions,' and the Kaiser's crown, and Austria altogether, were but a light matter to the finding and vitally appropriating of Truth. Let us respect the sacred mystery of a Person; rush not irreverently into man's Holy of Holies! Were the lost little one, as we said already, found ' sucking its dead mother, on the field of carnage,' could it be other than a spectacle for tears? A solemn mournful feeling comes over us when we see this last Work of Friedrich Schlegel, the unwearied seeker, end abruptly in the middle; and, as if he *had not* yet found, as if emblematically of much, end with an *' Aber—,'* with a ' But—'! This was the last word that came from the Pen of Friedrich Schlegel: about eleven at night he wrote it down, and there paused sick; at one in the morning, Time for him had merged itself in Eternity; he was, as we say, no more.

Still less can we attempt any criticism of Mr. Hope's new Book of Genesis. Indeed, under any circumstances, criticism of it were now impossible. Such an utterance could only be responded to in peals of laughter; and laughter sounds hollow and hideous through the vaults of the dead. Of this monstrous Anomaly, where all sciences are heaped and huddled together, and the principles of all are, with a childlike innocence, plied hither and thither, or wholly abolished in case of need; where the First Cause is figured as a huge

Circle, with nothing to do but radiate ' gravitation ' towards its centre; and so construct a Universe, wherein all, from the lowest cucumber with its coolness, up to the highest seraph with his love, were but ' gravitation,' direct or reflex, ' in more or less central globes,'—what can we say, except, with sorrow and shame, that it could have originated nowhere save in England? It is a general agglomerate of all facts, notions, whims and observations, as they lie in the brain of an English gentleman; as an English gentleman, of unusual thinking power, is led to fashion them, in his schools and in his world: all these thrown into the crucible, and if not fused, yet soldered or conglutinated with boundless patience; and now tumbled out here, heterogeneous, amorphous, unspeakable, a world's wonder. Most melancholy must we name the whole business; full of long-continued thought, earnestness, loftiness of mind; not without glances into the Deepest, a constant fearless endeavour after truth; and with all this nothing accomplished, but the perhaps absurdest Book written in our century by a thinking man. A shameful Abortion; which, however, need not now be smothered or mangled, for it is already dead; only, in our love and sorrowing reverence for the writer of *Anastasius,* and the heroic seeker of Light, though not bringer thereof, let it be buried and forgotten.

For ourselves, the loud discord which jars in these two Works, in innumerable works of the like import, and generally in all the Thought and Action of this period, does not any longer utterly confuse us. Unhappy who, in such a time, felt not, at all conjunctures, ineradicably in his heart the knowledge that a God made this Universe, and a Demon not! And shall Evil always prosper then? Out of all Evil comes Good? and no Good that is possible but shall one day be real. Deep and sad as is our feeling that we stand yet in the bodeful Night; equally deep, indestructible is our assurance that the Morning also will not fail. Nay, already, as we look round, streaks of a dayspring are in the east; it is dawning; when the time shall be fulfilled, it will be day. The progress of man towards higher and nobler developments of whatever is highest and noblest in him, lies not only prophesied to Faith, but now written to the eye of Observation, so that he who runs may read.

One great step of progress, for example, we should say, in actual circumstances, was this same; the clear ascertainment that we are in progress. About the grand Course of Providence, and his final Purposes with us, we can know nothing, or almost nothing: man begins in darkness, ends in darkness: mystery is everywhere around us and in us, under our feet, among our hands. Nevertheless so much has become evident to every one, that this wondrous Mankind is advancing somewhither; that at least all human things are, have been and forever will be, in Movement and Change;—as, indeed, for beings that exist in Time, by virtue of Time, and are made of Time, might have been long since understood. In some provinces, it is true, as in Experimental Science, this discovery is an old one; but in most others it belongs wholly to these latter days. How often, in former ages, by eternal Creeds, eternal Forms of Government and the like, has it been attempted, fiercely enough, and with destructive violence, to chain the Future under the Past; and say to the Providence, whose ways with man are mysterious, and through the great deep: Hitherto shalt thou come, but no farther! A wholly insane attempt; and for man himself, could it prosper, the frightfulest of all enchantments, a very Life-in-Death. Man's task here below, the destiny of every individual man, is to be in turns Apprentice and Workman; or say rather, Scholar, Teacher, Discoverer: by nature he has a strength for learning, for imitating; but also a strength for acting, for knowing on his own account. Are we not in a world seen to be Infinite; the relations lying closest together modified by those latest discovered and lying farthest asunder? Could you ever spell-bind man into a Scholar merely, so that he had nothing to discover, to correct; could you ever establish a Theory of the Universe that were entire, unimprovable, and which needed only to be got by heart; man then were spiritually defunct, the Species we now name Man had ceased to exist. But the gods, kinder to us than we are to ourselves, have forbidden such suicidal acts. As Phlogiston is displaced by Oxygen, and the Epicycles of Ptolemy by the Ellipses of Kepler; so does Paganism give place to

Catholicism, Tyranny to Monarchy, and Feudalism to Representative Government,—where also the process does not stop. Perfection of Practice, like completeness of Opinion, is always approaching, never arrived; Truth, in the words of Schiller, *immer wird, nie ist;* never *is,* always *is a-being.*

Sad, truly, were our condition did we know but this, that Change is universal and inevitable. Launched into a dark shoreless sea of Pyrrhonism, what would remain for us but to sail aimless, hopeless; or make madly merry, while the devouring Death had not yet ingulfed us? As indeed, we have seen many, and still see many do. Nevertheless so stands it not. The venerator of the Past (and to what pure heart is the Past, in that 'moonlight of memory,' other than sad and holy?) sorrows not over its departure, as one utterly bereaved. The true Past departs not, nothing that was worthy in the Past departs; no Truth of Goodness realised by man ever dies, or can die; but is all still here, and, recognised or not, lives and works through endless changes. If all things, to speak in the German dialect, are discerned by us, and exist for us, in an element of Time, and therefore of Mortality and Mutability; yet Time itself reposes on Eternity: the truly Great and Transcendental has its basis and substance in Eternity; stands revealed to us as Eternity in a vesture of Time. Thus in all Poetry, Worship, Art, Society, as one form passes into another, nothing is lost; it is but the superficial, as it were the *body* only, that grows obsolete and dies; under the mortal body lies a *soul* which is immortal; which anew incarnates itself in fairer revelation; and the Present is the living sum-total of the whole Past.

In Change, therefore, there is nothing terrible, nothing supernatural: on the contrary, it lies in the very essence of our lot and life in this world. Today is not yesterday: we ourselves change; how can our Works and Thoughts, if they are always to be the fittest, continue always the same? Change, indeed, is painful; yet ever needful; and if Memory have its force and worth, so also has Hope. Nay, if we look well to it, what is all Derangement, and necessity of great Change, in itself such an evil, but the product simply of *increased resources* which the old *methods* can no longer administer; of new wealth which the old scoffers will no longer

contain? What is it, for example, that in our own day
bursts asunder the bonds of ancient Political Systems, and
perplexes all Europe with the fear of Change, but even this:
the increase of social resources, which the old social methods
will no longer sufficiently administer? The new omnipotence
of the Steam-engine is hewing asunder quite other mountains
than the physical. Have not our economical distresses, those
barnyard Conflagrations themselves, the frightfulest madness
of our mad epoch, their rise also in what is a real increase:
increase of Men; of human Force; properly, in such a Planet
as ours, the most precious of all increases? It is true again,
the ancient methods of administration will no longer suffice.
Must the indomitable millions, full of old Saxon energy
and fire, lie cooped-up in this Western Nook, choking one
another, as in a Blackhole of Calcutta, while a whole fertile
untenanted Earth, desolate for want of the ploughshare,
cries: Come and till me, come and reap me? If the ancient
Captains can no longer yield guidance, new must be sought
after: for the difficulty lies not in nature, but in artifice; the
European Calcutta-Blackhole has no walls but air ones and
paper ones.—So too, Scepticism itself, with its innumerable
mischiefs, what is it but the sour fruit of a most blessed
increase, that of Knowledge; a fruit too that will not always
continue *sour?*

In fact, much as we have said and mourned about the
unproductive prevalence of Metaphysics, it was not without
some insight into the use that lies in them. Metaphysical
Speculation, if a necessary evil, is the forerunner of much
good. The fever of Scepticism must needs burn itself out,
and burn out thereby the Impurities that caused it; then
again will there be clearness, health. The principle of life,
which now struggles painfully, in the outer, thin and barren
domain of the Conscious or Mechanical, may then withdraw
into its inner sanctuaries, its abysses of mystery and miracle;
withdraw deeper than ever into that domain of the Unconscious, by nature infinite and inexhaustible; and creatively
work there. From that mystic region, and from that alone,
all wonders, all Poesies, and Religions, and Social Systems
have proceeded: the like wonders, and greater and higher,
lie slumbering there; and, brooded on by the spirit of the

waters, will evolve themselves, and rise like exhalations from the Deep.

Of our Modern Metaphysics, accordingly, may not this already be said, that if they have produced no Affirmation, they have destroyed much Negation? It is a disease expelling a disease: the fire of Doubt, as above hinted, consuming away the Doubtful; that so the Certain come to light, and again lie visible on the surface. English or French Metaphysics, in reference to this last stage of the speculative process, are not what we allude to here; but only the Metaphysics of the Germans. In France or England, since the days of Diderot and Hume, though all thought has been of a sceptico-metaphysical texture, so far as there was any Thought, we have seen no Metaphysics; but only more or less ineffectual questionings whether such could be. In the Pyrrhonism of Hume and the Materialism of Diderot, Logic had, as it were, overshot itself, overset itself. Now, though the athlete, to use our old figure, cannot, by much lifting, lift up his own body, he may shift it out of a laming posture, and get to stand in a free one. Such a service have German Metaphysics done for man's mind. The second sickness of Speculation has abolished both itself and the first. Friedrich Schlegel complains much of the fruitlessness, the tumult and transiency of German as of all Metaphysics; and with reason. Yet in that wide-spreading, deep-whirling vortex of Kantism, so soon metamorphosed into Fichteism, Schellingism, and then as Hegelism, and Cousinism, perhaps finally evaporated, is not this issue visible enough, That Pyrrhonism and Materialism, themselves necessary phenomena in European culture, have disappeared; and a Faith in Religion has again become possible and inevitable for the scientific mind; and the word *Free*-thinker no longer means the Denier or Caviller, but the Believer, or the Ready to believe? Nay, in the higher Literature of Germany, there already lies, for him that can read it, the beginning of a new revelation of the Godlike; as yet unrecognised by the mass of the world; but waiting there for recognition, and sure to find it when the fit hour comes. This age also is not wholly without its Prophets.

Again, under another aspect, if Utilitarianism, or Radicalism, or the Mechanical Philosophy, or by whatever name it is called, has still its long task to do; nevertheless we can now see through it and beyond it: in the better heads, even among us English, it has become obsolete; as in other countries, it has been, in such heads, for some forty or even fifty years. What sound mind among the French, for example, now fancies that men can be governed by ' Constitutions'; by the never so cunning mechanising of Self-interests, and all conceivable adjustments of checking and balancing; in a word, by the best possible solution of this quite insoluble and impossible problem, *Given a world of Knaves, to produce an Honesty from their united action?* Were not experiments enough of this kind tried before all Europe, and found wanting, when, in that doomsday of France, the infinite gulf of human Passion shivered asunder the thin rinds of Habit; and burst forth all-devouring, as in seas of Nether Fire? Which cunningly-devised ' Constitution,' constitutional, republican, democratic, sansculottic, could bind that raging chasm together? Were they not all burnt up, like paper as they were, in its molten eddies; and still the fire-sea raged fiercer than before? It is not by Mechanism, but by Religion; not by Self-interest, but by Loyalty, that men are governed or governable.

Remarkable it is, truly, how everywhere the eternal fact begins again to be recognised, that there is a Godlike in human affairs; that God not only made us and beholds us, but is in us and around us; that the Age of Miracles, as it ever was, now is. Such recognition we discern on all hands and in all countries: in each country after its own fashion. In France, among the younger nobler minds, strangely enough; where, in their loud contention with the Actual and Conscious, the Ideal or Unconscious is, for the time, without exponent ; where Religion means not the parent of Polity, as of all that is highest, but Polity itself; and this and the other earnest man has not been wanting, who could audibly whisper to himself: ' Go to, I will make a religion.' In England still more strangely; as in all things, worthy England will have its way: by the shrieking of hysterical women, casting out of devils, and other ' gifts of the Holy Ghost.' Well might Jean Paul say, in this his twelfth hour of the Night, 'the living dream'; well might he say, 'the dead walk.' Meanwhile let us rejoice rather that so much has been seen into, were it through never so diffracting media, and never so madly distorted; that in all dialects, though but half-articulately, this high Gospel begins to be preached: Man is still Man. The genius of Mechanism, as was once before predicted, will not always sit like a choking incubus on our soul; but at length, when by a new magic Word the old spell is broken, become our slave, and as familiar-spirit do all our bidding. 'We are near awakening when we dream that we dream.'

He that has an eye and a heart can even now say: Why should I falter? Light has come into the world; to such as love Light, so as Light must be loved, with a boundless all-doing, all-enduring love. For the rest, let that vain struggle to read the mystery of the Infinite cease to harass us. It is a mystery which, through all ages, we shall only read here a line of, there another line of. Do we not already know that the name of the Infinite is GOOD, is GOD? Here on Earth we are Soldiers, fighting in a foreign land; that understand not the plan of the campaign, and have no need to understand it; seeing well what is at our hand to be done. Let us do it like Soldiers; with submission, with courage, with a heroic joy. 'Whatsoever thy hand findeth to do, do it with all thy might.' Behind us, behind each one of us, lie Six Thousand Years of human effort, human conquest: before us is the boundless Time, with its as yet uncreated and unconquered Continents and Eldorados, which we, even we, have to conquer, to create; and from the bosom of Eternity there shine for us celestial guiding stars.

'My inheritance how wide and fair!
Time is my fair seed-field, of Time I'm heir.'

INAUGURAL ADDRESS AT
EDINBURGH UNIVERSITY
BY
THOMAS CARLYLE

INAUGURAL ADDRESS AT EDINBURGH

2ND APRIL 1866

ON BEING INSTALLED AS RECTOR OF THE UNIVERSITY THERE

GENTLEMEN,—I have accepted the office you have elected me to, and it is now my duty to return thanks for the great honour done me. Your enthusiasm towards me, I must admit, is in itself very beautiful, however undeserved it may be in regard to the object of it. It is a feeling honourable to all men, and one well known to myself when I was of an age like yours, nor is it yet quite gone. I can only hope that, with you, too, it may endure to the end,—this noble desire to honour those whom you think worthy of honour; and that you will come to be more and more select and discriminate in the choice of the object of it:—for I can well understand that you will modify your opinions of me and of many things else, as you go on [*Laughter and cheers*]. It is now fifty-six years, gone last November, since I first entered your City, a boy of not quite fourteen; to 'attend the classes' here, and gain knowledge of all kinds, I could little guess what, my poor mind full of wonder and awe-struck expectation; and now, after a long course, this is what we have come to [*Cheers*]. There is something touching and tragic, and yet at the same time beautiful, to see, as it were, the third generation of my dear old native land rising up and saying, "Well, you are not altogether an unworthy labourer in the vineyard; you have toiled through a great variety of fortunes, and have had many judges: this is our judgment of you!" As the old proverb says, 'He that builds by the wayside has many masters.' We must expect a variety of judges: but the voice of young Scotland, through you, is really of some value to me; and I return you many thanks for it,—though I cannot go into describing my emotions to you, and perhaps they will be much more perfectly conceivable if expressed in silence [*Cheers*].

When this office was first proposed to me, some of you know I was not very ambitious to accept it, but had my doubts rather. I was taught to believe that there were certain more or less important duties which would lie in my power. This, I confess, was my chief motive in going into it, and overcoming the objections I felt to such things: if it could do anything to serve my dear old *Alma Mater* and you, why should not I? [*Loud cheers.*] Well, but on practically looking into the matter when the office actually came into my hands, I find it grows more and more uncertain and abstruse to me whether there is much real duty that I can do at all. I live four hundred miles away from you, in an entirely different scene of things; and my weak health, with the burden of the many years now accumulating on me, and my total unacquaintance with such subjects as concern your affairs here,—all this fills me with apprehension that there is really nothing worth the least consideration that I can do on that score. You may depend on it, however, that if any such duty does arise in any form, I will use my most faithful endeavour to do in it whatever is right and proper, according to the best of my judgment [*Cheers*].

Meanwhile, the duty I at present have,—which might be very pleasant, but which is not quite so, for reasons you may fancy,—is to address some words to you, if possible not quite useless, nor incongruous to the occasion, and on subjects more or less cognate to the pursuits you are engaged in. Accordingly, I mean to offer you some loose observations, loose in point of order, but the truest I have, in such form as they may present themselves; certain of the thoughts that are in me about the business you are here engaged in, what kind of race it is that you young gentlemen have started on, and what sort of arena you are likely to find in this world. I ought, I believe, according to custom, to have written all that down on paper, and had it read out. That would have been much handier for me at the present moment [*A laugh*];

—but on attempting the thing, I found I was not used to write speeches, and that I didn't get on very well. So I flung that aside; and could only resolve to trust, in all superficial respects, to the suggestion of the moment, as you now see. You will therefore have to accept what is readiest; what comes direct from the heart; and you must just take that in compensation for any good order or arrangement there might have been in it. I will endeavour to say nothing that is not true, so far as I can manage; and that is pretty much all I can engage for [*A laugh*].

Advices, I believe, to young men, as to all men, are very seldom much valued. There is a great deal of advising, and very little faithful performing; and talk that does not end in any kind of action is better suppressed altogether. I would not, therefore, go much into advising; but there is one advice I must give you. In fact, it is the summary of all advices, and doubtless you have heard it a thousand times; but I must nevertheless let you hear it the thousand-and-first time, for it is most intensely true, whether you will believe it at present or not:—namely, That above all things the interest of your whole life depends on your being *diligent*, now while it is called to-day, in this place where you have come to get education! Diligent: that includes in it all virtues that a student can have; I mean it to include all those qualities of conduct that lead on to the acquirement of real instruction and improvement in such a place. If you will believe me, you who are young, yours is the golden season of life. As you have heard it called, so it verily is, the seed-time of life; in which, if you do not sow, or if you sow tares instead of wheat, you cannot expect to reap well afterwards, and you will arrive at little. And in the course of years when you come to look back, if you have not done what you have heard from your advisers,—and among many counsellors there is wisdom,—you will bitterly repent when it is too late. The habits of study acquired at Universities are of the highest importance in after-life. At the season when you are young in years, the whole mind is, as it were, fluid, and is capable of forming itself into any shape that the owner of the mind pleases to allow it, or constrain it, to form itself into. The mind is then in a plastic or fluid state;

but it hardens gradually, to the consistency of rock or of
iron, and you cannot alter the habits of an old man: he, as
he has begun, so he will proceed and go on to the last.

By diligence I mean, among other things, and very chiefly
too,—honesty, in all your inquiries, and in all you are about.
Pursue your studies in the way your conscience can name
honest. More and more endeavour to do that. Keep, I
should say for one thing, an accurate separation between
what you have really come to know in your minds and what
is still unknown. Leave all that latter on the hypothetical
side of the barrier, as things afterwards to be acquired, if
acquired at all; and be careful not to admit a thing as
known when you do not yet know it. Count a thing known
only when it is imprinted clearly on your mind, and has
become transparent to you, so that you may survey it on
all sides with intelligence. There is such a thing as a man
endeavouring to persuade himself, and endeavouring to
persuade others, that he knows things, when he does not
know more than the outside skin of them; and yet he goes
flourishing about with them [*Hear, hear, and a laugh*].
There is also a process called cramming, in some Universities
[*A laugh*],—that is, getting-up such points of things as the
examiner is likely to put questions about. Avoid all that,
as entirely unworthy of an honourable mind. Be modest,
and humble, and assiduous in your attention to what your
teachers tell you, who are profoundly interested in trying to
bring you forward in the right way, so far as they have been
able to understand it. Try all things they set before you,
in order, if possible, to understand them, and to follow and
adopt them in proportion to their fitness for you. Gradually
see what kind of work you individually can do; it is the
first of all problems for a man to find out what kind of
work he is to do in this universe. In short, morality as
regards study is, as in all other things, the primary consideration, and overrules all others. A dishonest man cannot
do anything real; he never will study with real fruit; and
perhaps it would be greatly better if he were tied up from
trying it. He does nothing but darken counsel by the words
he utters. That is a very old doctrine, but a very true one;
and you will find it confirmed by all the thinking men that

have ever lived in this long series of generations of which we are the latest.

I dare say you know, very many of you, that it is now some seven hundred years since Universities were first set-up in this world of ours. Abelard and other thinkers had arisen with doctrines in them which people wished to hear of, and students flocked towards them from all parts of the world. There was no getting the thing recorded in books, as you now may. You had to hear the man speaking to you, vocally, or else you could not learn at all what it was that he wanted to say. And so they gathered together, these speaking ones, —the various people who had anything to teach;—and formed themselves gradually, under the patronage of kings and other potentates who were anxious about the culture of their populations, and nobly studious of their best benefit; and became a body-corporate, with high privileges, high dignities, and really high aims, under the title of a University.

Possibly too you may have heard it said that the course of centuries has changed all this; and that ' the true University of our days is a Collection of Books.' And beyond doubt, all this is greatly altered by the invention of Printing, which took place about midway between us and the origin of Universities. Men have not now to go in person to where a Professor is actually speaking; because in most cases you can get his doctrine out of him through a book; and can then read it, and read it again and again, and study it. That is an immense change, that one fact of Printed Books. And I am not sure that I know of any University in which the whole of that fact has yet been completely taken in, and the studies moulded in complete conformity with it. Nevertheless, Universities have, and will continue to have, an indispensable value in society;—I think, a very high, and it might be, almost the highest value. They began, as is well known, with their grand aim directed on Theology,—their eye turned earnestly on Heaven. And perhaps, in a sense, it may be still said, the very highest interests of man are virtually intrusted to them. In regard to theology, as you are aware, it has been, and especially was then, the study of the deepest heads that have come into the world.—what is the nature of this stupendous Universe, and what are our relations to it, and to all things knowable by man, or known only to the great Author of man and it. Theology was once the name for all this; all this is still alive for man, however dead the name may grow! In fact, the members of the Church keeping theology in a lively condition [*Laughter*] for the benefit of the whole population, theology was the great object of the Universities. I consider it is the same intrinsically now, though very much forgotten, from many causes, and not so successful [*A laugh*] as might be wished, by any manner of means!

It remains, however, practically a most important truth, what I alluded to above, that the main use of Universities in the present age is that, after you have done with all your classes, the next thing is a collection of books, a great library of good books, which you proceed to study and to read. What the Universities can mainly do for you,—what I have found the University did for me, is, That it taught me to read, in various languages, in various sciences; so that I could go into the books which treated of these things, and gradually penetrate into any department I wanted to make myself master of, as I found it suit me.

Well, Gentlemen, whatever you may think of these historical points, the clearest and most imperative duty lies on every one of you to be assiduous in your reading. Learn to be good readers,—which is perhaps a more difficult thing than you imagine. Learn to be discriminative in your reading; to read faithfully, and with your best attention, all kinds of things which you have a real interest in, a real not an imaginary, and which you find to be really fit for what you are engaged in. Of course, at the present time, in a great deal of the reading incumbent on you, you must be guided by the books recommended by your Professors for assistance towards the effect of their prelections. And then, when you leave the University, and go into studies of your own, you will find it very important that you have chosen a field, some province specially suited to you, in which you can study and work. The most unhappy of all men is the man who cannot tell what he is going to do, who has got no work cut-out for him in the world, and does not go into it. For work is the grand cure of all the maladies and miseries that ever beset mankind,—honest work, which you intend getting done.

If, in any vacant vague time, you are in a strait as to choice of reading,—a very good indication for you, perhaps the best you could get, is toward some book you have a great curiosity about. You are then in the readiest and best of all possible conditions to improve by that book. It is analogous to what doctors tell us about the physical health and appetites of the patient. You must learn, however, to distinguish between false appetite and true. There is such a thing as a false appetite, which will lead a man into vagaries with regard to diet; will tempt him to eat spicy things, which he should not eat at all, nor would, but that the things are toothsome, and that he is under a momentary baseness of mind. A man ought to examine and find out what he really and truly has an appetite for, what suits his constitution and condition; and that, doctors tell him, is in general the very thing he ought to have. And so with books.

As applicable to all of you, I will say that it is highly expedient to go into History; to inquire into what has passed before you on this Earth, and in the Family of Man.

The history of the Romans and Greeks will first of all concern you; and you will find that the classical knowledge you have got will be extremely applicable to elucidate that. There you have two of the most remarkable races of men in the world set before you, calculated to open innumerable reflections and considerations; a mighty advantage, if you can achieve it;—to say nothing of what their two languages will yield you, which your Professors can better explain; model languages, which are universally admitted to be the most perfect forms of speech we have yet found to exist among men. And you will find, if you read well, a pair of extremely remarkable nations, shining in the records left by themselves, as a kind of beacon, or solitary mass of illumination, to light-up some noble forms of human life for us, in the otherwise utter darkness of the past ages; and it will be well worth your while if you can get into the understanding of what these people were, and what they did. You will find a great deal of hearsay, of empty rumour and tradition, which does not touch on the matter; but perhaps some of you will get to see the old Roman and the old Greek face to face; you will know in some measure how they contrived to exist, and to perform their feats in the world.

I believe, also, you will find one important thing not much noted, That there was a very great deal of deep religion in both nations. This is pointed out by the wiser kind of historians, and particularly by Ferguson, who is very well worth reading on Roman History,—and who, I believe, was an alumnus of our own University. His book is a very creditable work. He points out the profoundly religious nature of the Roman people, notwithstanding their ruggedly positive, defiant and fierce ways. They believed that Jupiter Optimus Maximus was lord of the universe, and that he had appointed the Romans to become the chief of nations, provided they followed his commands,—to brave all danger, all difficulty, and stand up with an invincible front, and be ready to do and die; and also to have the same sacred regard to truth of promise, to thorough veracity, thorough integrity, and all the virtues that accompany that noblest quality of man, valour,—to which latter the Romans gave the name of 'virtue' proper (*virtus,* manhood), as the crown and summary of all that is ennobling for a man. In the literary ages of Rome this religious feeling had very much decayed away; but it still retained its place among the lower classes of the Roman people. Of the deeply religious nature of the Greeks, along with their beautiful and sunny effulgences of art, you have striking proof, if you look for it. In the tragedies of Sophocles there is a most deep-toned recognition of the eternal justice of Heaven, and the unfailing punishment of crime against the laws of God. I believe you will find in all histories of nations, that this has been at the origin and foundation of them all; and that no nation which did not contemplate this wonderful universe with an awe-stricken and reverential belief that there was a great unknown, omnipotent, and all-wise and all-just Being, superintending all men in it, and all interest in it,—no nation ever came to very much, nor did any man either, who forgot that. If a man did forget that, he forgot the most important part of his mission in this world.

Our own history of England, which you will naturally take

a great deal of pains to make yourselves acquainted with, you will find beyond all others worthy of your study. For indeed I believe that the British nation,—including in that the Scottish nation,—produced a finer set of men than any you will find it possible to get anywhere else in the world [*Applause*]. I don't know, in any history of Greece or Rome, where you will get so fine a man as Oliver Cromwell, for example [*Applause*]. And we too have had men worthy of memory, in our little corner of the Island here, as well as others; and our history has had its heroic features all along; and did become great at last in being connected with world-history:—for if you examine well, you will find that John Knox was the author, as it were, of Oliver Cromwell; that the Puritan revolution never would have taken place in England at all, had it not been for that Scotchman [*Applause*]. That is an authentic fact, and is not prompted by national vanity on my part, but will stand examining [*Laughter and applause*].

In fact, if you look at the struggle that was then going on in England, as I have had to do in my time, you will see that people were overawed by the immense impediments lying in the way. A small minority of God-fearing men in that country were flying away, with any ship they could get, to New England, rather than take the lion by the beard. They durst not confront the powers with their most just complaints, and demands to be delivered from idolatry. They wanted to make the nation altogether conformable to the Hebrew Bible, which they, and all men, understood to be the exact transcript of the Will of God;—and could there be, for man, a more legitimate aim? Nevertheless, it would have been impossible in their circumstances, and not to be attempted at all, had not Knox succeeded in it here, some fifty years before, by the firmness and nobleness of his mind. For he also is of the select of the earth to me,—John Knox [*Applause*]. What he has suffered from the ungrateful generations that have followed him should really make us humble ourselves to the dust, to think that the most excellent man our country has produced, to whom we owe everything that distinguishes us among the nations, should have been so sneered at, misknown, and abused [*Applause*]. Knox was heard by Scotland; the people heard him, believed him to the marrow of their bones: they took up his doctrine, and they defied principalities and powers to move them from it. "We must have it," they said; "we will and must!" It was in this state of things that the Puritan struggle arose in England; and you know well how the Scottish earls and nobility, with their tenantry, marched away to Dunse Hill in 1639, and sat down there: just at the crisis of that struggle, when it was either to be suppressed or brought into greater vitality, they encamped on Dunse Hill,—thirty-thousand armed men, drawn out for that occasion, each regiment round its landlord, its earl, or whatever he might be called, and zealous all of them 'For Christ's Crown and Covenant.' That was the signal for all England's rising up into unappeasable determination to have the Gospel there also; and you know it went on, and came to be a contest whether the Parliament or the King should rule; whether it should be old formalities and use-and-wont, or something that had been of new conceived in the souls of men, namely, a divine determination to walk according to the laws of God here, as the sum of all prosperity; which of these should have the mastery: and after a long, long agony of struggle, it was decided—the way we know.

I should say also of that Protectorate of Oliver Cromwell's, notwithstanding the censures it has encountered, and the denial of everybody that it could continue in the world, and so on, it appears to me to have been, on the whole, the most salutary thing in the modern history of England. If Oliver Cromwell had continued it out, I don't know what it would have come to. It would have got corrupted probably in other hands, and could not have gone on; but it was pure and true, to the last fibre, in his mind; there was perfect truth in it while he ruled over it.

Macchiavelli has remarked, in speaking of the Romans, that Democracy cannot long exist anywhere in the world; that as a mode of government, of national management or administration, it involves an impossibility, and after a little while must end in wreck. And he goes on proving that, in his own way. I do not ask you all to follow him in that conviction [*Hear*],—but it is to him a clear truth; he considers it a solecism and impossibility that the universal mass of men should ever govern themselves. He has to admit of the Romans, that they continued a long time; but believes it was purely in virtue of this item in their constitution, namely, of their all having the conviction in their minds that it was solemnly necessary, at times, to appoint a Dictator; a man who had the power of life and death over everything, who degraded men out of their places, ordered them to execution, and did whatever seemed to him good in the name of God above him. He was commanded to take care that the republic suffer no detriment. And Macchiavelli calculates that this was the thing which purified the social system from time to time, and enabled it to continue as it did. Probable enough, if you consider it. And an extremely proper function surely, this of a Dictator, if the republic was composed of little other than bad and tumultuous men, triumphing in general over the better, and all going the bad road, in fact. Well, Oliver Cromwell's Protectorate, or Dictatorate if you will let me name it so, lasted for about ten years, and you will find that nothing which was contrary to the laws of Heaven was allowed to live by Oliver [*Applause*].

For example, it was found by his Parliament of Notables, what they call the ' Barebones Parliament,'—the most zealous of all Parliaments probably [*Laughter*],—that the Court of Chancery in England was in a state which was really capable of no apology; no man could get up and say that that was a right court. There were, I think, fifteen-thousand, or fifteen-hundred [*Laughter*],—I really don't remember which, but we will call it by the latter number, to be safe [*Renewed laughter*];—there were fifteen-hundred cases lying in it undecided; and one of them, I remember, for a large amount of money, was eighty-three years old, and it was going on still; wigs were wagging over it, and lawyers were taking their fees, and there was no end of it. Upon view of all which, the Barebones people, after deliberation about it, thought it was expedient, and commanded by the Author of Man and Fountain of Justice, and in the name of what was true and right, to abolish said court. Really, I don't know who could have dissented from that opinion. At the same time, it was thought by those who were wiser in their generation, and had more experience of the world, that this was a very dangerous thing, and wouldn't suit at all. The lawyers began to make an immense noise about it [*Laughter*]. All the public, the great mass of solid and well-disposed people who had got no deep insight into such matters, were very adverse to it: and the Speaker of the Parliament, old Sir Francis Rous,—who translated the Psalms for us, those that we sing here every Sunday in the Church yet; a very good man, and a wise and learned, Provost of Eton College afterwards,—he got a great number of the Parliament to go to Oliver the Dictator, and lay down their functions altogether, and declare officially, with their signature, on Monday morning, that the Parliament was dissolved. The act of abolition had been passed on Saturday night; and on Monday morning Rous came and said, " We cannot carry-on the affair any longer, and we remit it into the hands of your Highness." Oliver in that way became Protector, virtually in some sort a Dictator, for the first time.

And I give you this as an instance that Oliver did faithfully set to doing a Dictator's function, and of his prudence in it as well. Oliver felt that the Parliament, now dismissed, had been perfectly right with regard to Chancery, and that there was no doubt of the propriety of abolishing Chancery, or else reforming it in some kind of way. He considered the matter, and this is what he did. He assembled fifty or sixty of the wisest lawyers to be found in England. Happily, there were men great in the law; men who valued the laws of England as much as anybody ever did; and who knew withal that there was something still more sacred than any of these [*A laugh*]. Oliver said to them, " Go and examine this thing, and in the name of God inform me what is necessary to be done with it. You will see how we may clean-out the foul things in that Chancery Court, which render it poison to everybody." Well, they sat down accordingly, and in the course of six weeks,—(there was no public speaking then, no reporting of speeches, and no babble of any kind, there was just the business in hand)—they got some sixty propositions fixed in their minds as the sum-

mary of the things that required to be done. And upon
these sixty propositions, Chancery was reconstituted and
remodelled; and so it got a new lease of life, and has lasted
to our time. It had become a nuisance, and could not have
continued much longer. That is an instance of the manner
of things that were done when a Dictatorship prevailed in
the country, and that was how the Dictator did them. I
reckon, all England, Parliamentary England, got a new
lease of life from that Dictatorship of Oliver's; and, on
the whole, that the good fruits of it will never die while
England exists as a nation.

In general, I hardly think that out of common history-
books you will ever get into the real history of this country,
or ascertain anything which can specially illuminate it for
you, and which it would most of all behoove you to know.
You may read very ingenious and very clever books, by men
whom it would be the height of insolence in me to do other
than express my respect for. But their position is essentially
sceptical. God and the Godlike, as our fathers would have
said, has fallen asleep for them; and plays no part in their
histories. A most sad and fatal condition of matters; who
shall say how fatal to us all! A man unhappily in that condition will make but a temporary explanation of anything:—in
short, you will not be able, I believe, by aid of these men,
to understand how this Island came to be what it is. You
will not find it recorded in books. You will find recorded
in books a jumble of tumults, disastrous ineptitudes, and all
that kind of thing. But to get what you want, you will
have to look into side sources, and inquire in all directions.

I remember getting Collins's *Peerage* to read,—a very poor
performance as a work of genius, but an excellent book for
diligence and fidelity. I was writing on Oliver Cromwell
at the time [*Applause*]. I could get no biographical diction-
ary available; and I thought the Peerage Book, since most
of my men were peers or sons of peers, would help me,
at least would tell me whether people were old or young,
where they lived, and the like particulars, better than absolute nescience and darkness. And accordingly I found amply
all I had expected in poor Collins, and got a great deal

of help out of him. He was a diligent dull London book-
seller, of about a hundred years ago, who compiled out of
all kinds of parchments, charter-chests, archives, books that
were authentic, and gathered far and wide, wherever he
could get it, the information wanted. He was a very
meritorious man.

I not only found the solution of everything I had expected
there, but I began gradually to perceive this immense fact,
which I really advise every one of you who read history to
look out for, if you have not already found it. It was that
the Kings of England, all the way from the Norman Conquest down to the times of Charles I., had actually, in a good
degree, so far as they knew, been in the habit of appointing
as Peers those who *deserved* to be appointed. In general, I
perceived, those Peers of theirs were all royal men of a sort,
with minds full of justice, valour and humanity, and all
kinds of qualities that men ought to have who rule over
others. And then their genealogy, the kind of sons and
descendants they had, this also was remarkable:—for there
is a great deal more in genealogy than is generally believed at present. I never heard tell of any clever man
that came of entirely stupid people [*Laughter*]. If you look
around, among the families of your acquaintance, you will
see such cases in all directions;—I know that my own experience is steadily that way; I can trace the father, and the
son, and the grandson, and the family stamp is quite distinctly legible upon each of them. So that it goes for a
great deal, the hereditary principle,—in Government as in
other things; and it must be again recognised as soon as
there is any fixity in things. You will remark, too, in your
Collins, that, if at any time the genealogy of a peerage goes
awry, if the man that actually holds the peerage is a fool,—
in those earnest practical times, the man soon gets into mischief, gets into treason probably,—soon gets himself and
his peerage extinguished altogether, in short. [*Laughter*].

From those old documents of Collins, you learn and ascertain that a peer conducts himself in a pious, high-minded,
grave, dignified and manly kind of way, in his course through
life, and when he takes leave of life:—his last will is often
a remarkable piece, which one lingers over. And then you

perceive that there was kindness in him as well as rigour,
pity for the poor; that he has fine hospitalities, generosities,
—in fine, that he is throughout much of a noble, good and
valiant man. And that in general the King, with a beautiful approximation to accuracy, had nominated this kind of
man; saying, " Come you to me, sir. Come out of the
common level of the people, where you are liable to be
trampled upon, jostled about, and can do in a manner nothing with your fine gift; come here and take a district of
country, and make it into your own image more or less;
be a king under me, and understand that that is your function." I say this is the most divine thing that a human being can do to other human beings, and no kind of thing
whatever has so much of the character of God Almighty's
Divine Government as that thing, which, we see, went on all
over England for about six hundred years. That is the grand
soul of England's history [*Cheers*]. It is historically true
that, down to the time of James, or even Charles I., it was
not understood that any man was made a Peer without having merit in him to constitute him a proper subject for a
peerage. In Charles I.'s time it grew to be known or said
that, if a man was born a gentleman, and cared to lay out
10,000 *l.* judiciously up and down among courtiers, he could
be made a Peer. Under Charles II. it went on still faster,
and has been going-on with ever-increasing velocity, until
we see the perfectly breakneck pace at which they are going
now [*A laugh*], so that now a peerage is a paltry kind of
thing to what it was in those old times. I could go into
a great many more details about things of that sort, but
I must turn to another branch of the subject.

First, however, one remark more about your reading. I
do not know whether it has been sufficiently brought home to
you that there are two kinds of books. When a man is
reading on any kind of subject, in most departments of
books,—in all books, if you take it in a wide sense,—he will
find that there is a division into good books and bad books.
Everywhere a good kind of book and a bad kind of book
I am not to assume that you are unacquainted, or ill acquainted, with this plain fact; but I may remind you that it
is becoming a very important consideration in our day. And

we have to cast aside altogether the idea people have, that if they are reading any book, that if an ignorant man is reading any book, he is doing rather better than nothing at all. I must entirely call that in question; I even venture to deny that [*Laughter and cheers*]. It would be much safer and better for many a reader, that he had no concern with books at all. There is a number, a frightfully increasing number, of books that are decidedly, to the readers of them, not useful [*Hear*]. But an ingenuous reader will learn, also, that a certain number of books were written by a supremely noble kind of people,—not a very great number of books, but still a number fit to occupy all your reading industry, do adhere more or less to that side of things. In short, as I have written it down somewhere else, I conceive that books are like men's souls; divided into sheep and goats [*Laughter and cheers*]. Some few are going up, and carrying us up, heavenward; calculated, I mean, to be of priceless advantage in teaching,—in forwarding the teaching of all generations. Others, a frightful multitude, are going down, down; doing ever the more and the wider and the wilder mischief. Keep a strict eye on that latter class of books, my young friends!—

And for the rest, in regard to all your studies and readings here, and to whatever you may learn, you are to remember that the object is not particular knowledges,—not that of getting higher, and higher in technical perfections, and all that sort of thing. There is a higher aim lying at the rear of all that, especially among those who are intended for literary or speaking pursuits, or the sacred profession. You are ever to bear in mind that there lies behind that the acquisition of what may be called wisdom;—namely, sound appreciation and just decision as to all the objects that come round you, and the habit of behaving with justice, candour, clear insight, and loyal adherence to fact. Great is wisdom; infinite is the value of wisdom. It cannot be exaggerated; it is the highest achievement of man: ' Blessed is he that getteth understanding.' And that, I believe, on occasion, may be missed very easily; never more easily than now, I sometimes think. If that is a failure, all is failure!—However, I will not touch further upon that matter.

But I should have said, in regard to book-reading, if it be so very important, how very useful would an excellent library be in every University! I hope that will not be neglected by the gentlemen who have charge of you; and, indeed, I am happy to hear that your library is very much improved since the time I knew it, and I hope it will go on improving more and more. Nay, I have sometimes thought, why should not there be a library in every county town, for benefit of those that could read well and might if permitted? True, you require money to accomplish that;—and withal, what perhaps is still less attainable at present, you require judgment in the selectors of books; real insight into what is for the advantage of human souls, the exclusion of all kinds of clap-trap books which merely excite the astonishment of foolish people [*Laughter*], and the choice of wise books, as much as possible of good books. Let us hope the future will be kind to us in this respect.

In this University, as I learn from many sides, there is considerable stir about endowments; an assiduous and praise-worthy industry for getting new funds collected to encourage the ingenuous youth of Universities, especially of this our chief University [*Hear, hear*]. Well, I entirely participate in everybody's approval of the movement. It is very desirable. It should be responded to, and one surely expects it will. At least, if it is not, it will be shameful to the country of Scotland, which never was so rich in money as at the present moment, and never stood so much in need of getting noble Universities, and institutions to counteract many influences that are springing up alongside of money. It should not be slack in coming forward in the way of endowments [*A laugh*]; at any rate, to the extent of rivalling our rude old barbarous ancestors, as we have been pleased to call them. Such munificence as theirs is beyond all praise; and to them, I am sorry to say, we are not yet by any manner of means equal, or approaching equality [*Laughter*]. There is an abundance and over-abundance of money. Sometimes I cannot help thinking that probably never has there been, at any other time, in Scotland, the hundredth part of the money that now is, or even the thousandth part. For wherever I

go, there is that same gold-nuggeting [*A laugh*],—that ' unexampled prosperity,' and men counting their balances by
the million sterling. Money was never so abundant, and
nothing that is good to be done with it [*Hear, hear, and a
laugh*]. No man knows,—or very few men know,—what
benefit to get out of his money. In fact, it too often is
secretly a curse to him. Much better for him never to have
had any. But I do not expect that generally to be believed
[*Laughter*]. Nevertheless, I should think it would be a
beneficent relief to many a rich man who has an honest purpose struggling in him, to bequeath some house of refuge,
so to speak, for the gifted poor man who may hereafter be
born into the world, to enable him to get on his way a little.
To do, in fact, as those old Norman kings whom I have
been describing; to raise some noble poor man out of the dirt
and mud, where he is getting trampled on unworthily by the
unworthy, into some kind of position where he might acquire the power to do a little good in his generation! I hope
that as much as possible will be achieved in this direction;
and that efforts will not be relaxed till the thing is in a
satisfactory state. In regard to the classical department,
above all, it surely is to be desired by us that it were properly
supported,—that we could allow the fit people to have their
scholarships and subventions, and devote more leisure to
the cultivation of particular departments. We might have
more of this from Scotch Universities than we have; and I
hope we shall.

I am bound, however, to say that it does not appear as if,
of late times, endowment were the real soul of the matter.
The English, for example, are the richest people in the world
for endowments in their Universities; and it is an evident
fact that, since the time of Bentley, you cannot name anybody that has gained a European name in scholarship, or
constituted a point of revolution in the pursuits of men in
that way. The man who does so is a man worthy of being
remembered; and he is poor, and not an Englishman. One
man that actually did constitute a revolution was the son
of a poor weaver in Saxony; who edited his Tibullus, in
Dresden, in a poor comrade's garret, with the floor for his
bed, and two folios for pillow; and who, while editing his

Tibullus, had to gather peasecods on the streets and boil them for his dinner. That was his endowment [*Laughter*]. But he was recognised soon to have done a great thing. His name was Heyne [*Cheers*]. I can remember, it was quite a revolution in my mind when I got hold of that man's edition of Virgil. I found that, for the first time, I understood Virgil; that Heyne had introduced me, for the first time, into an insight of Roman life and ways of thought; had pointed out the circumstances in which these works were written, and given me their interpretation. And the process has gone on in all manner of developments, and has spread out into other countries.

On the whole, there is one reason why endowments are not given now as they were in old days, when men founded abbeys, colleges, and all kinds of things of that description, with such success as we know. All that has now changed; a vast decay of zeal in that direction. And truly the reason may in part be, that people have become doubtful whether colleges are now the real sources of what I called wisdom; whether they are anything more, anything much more, than a cultivating of man in the specific arts. In fact, there has been in the world a suspicion of that kind for a long time [*A laugh*]. There goes a proverb of old date, 'An ounce of mother-wit is worth a pound of clergy' [*Laughter*]. There is a suspicion that a man is perhaps not nearly so wise as he looks, or because he has poured out speech so copiously [*Laughter*]. When 'the seven free arts,' which the old Universities were based on, came to be modified a little, in order to be convenient for the wants of modern society,—though perhaps some of them are obsolete enough even yet for some of us,—there arose a feeling that mere vocality, mere culture of speech, if that is what comes out of a man, is not the synonym of wisdom by any means! That a man may be a 'great speaker,' as eloquent as you like, and but little real substance in him,—especially if that is what was required and aimed at by the man himself, and by the community that set him upon becoming a learned man. Maidservants, I hear people complaining, are getting instructed in the 'ologies,' and are apparently becoming more and more ignorant of brewing, boiling, and baking [*Laughter*]; and above all, are not taught what is necessary to be known, from the highest of us to the lowest,—faithful obedience, modesty, humility, and correct moral conduct.

Oh, it is a dismal chapter all that, if one went into it,— what has been done by rushing after fine speech! I have written down some very fierce things about that, perhaps considerably more emphatic than I could now wish them to be; but they were and are deeply my conviction [*Hear, hear*]. There is very great necessity indeed of getting a little more silent than we are. It seems to me as if the finest nations of the world,—the English and the American, in chief,—were going all off into wind and tongue [*Applause and laughter*]. But it will appear sufficiently tragical by and by, long after I am away out of it. There is a time to speak, and a time to be silent. Silence withal is the eternal duty of a man. He won't get to any real understanding of what is complex, and what is more than aught else pertinent to his interests, without keeping silence too. ' Watch the tongue,' is a very old precept, and a most true one.

I don't want to discourage any of you from your Demosthenes, and your studies of the niceties of language, and all that. Believe me, I value that as much as any one of you. I consider it a very graceful thing, and a most proper, for every human creature to know what the implement which he uses in communicating his thoughts is, and how to make the very utmost of it. I want you to study Demosthenes, and to know all his excellencies. At the same time, I must say that speech, in the case even of Demosthenes, does not seem, on the whole, to have turned to almost any good account. He advised next to nothing that proved practicable; much of the reverse. Why tell me that a man is a fine speaker, if it is not the truth that he is speaking? Phocion, who mostly did not speak at all, was a great deal nearer hitting the mark than Demosthenes [*Laughter*]. He used to tell the Athenians, " You can't fight Philip. Better if you don't provoke him, as Demosthenes is always urging you to do. You have not the slightest chance with Philip. He is a man who holds his tongue; he has great disciplined armies; a full treasury; can bribe anybody you like in your cities here; he is going on steadily with an unvarying aim towards his object; while you, with your idle clamourings, with your Cleon the Tanner spouting to you what you take for wisdom—! Philip will infallibly beat any set of men such as you, going on raging from shore to shore with all that rampant nonsense." Demosthenes said to him once, "Phocion, you will drive the Athenians mad some day, and they will kill you." "Yes," Phocion answered, "me, when they go mad; and as soon as they get sane again, you!" [*Laughter and applause.*]

It is also told of him how he went once to Messene, on some deputation which the Athenians wanted him to head, on some kind of matter of an intricate and contentious nature: Phocion went accordingly; and had, as usual, a clear story to have told for himself and his case. He was a man of few words, but all of them true and to the point. And so he had gone on telling his story for a while, when there arose some interruption. One man, interrupting with something, he tried to answer; then another, the like; till finally, too many went in, and all began arguing and bawling in endless debate. Whereupon Phocion struck-down his staff; drew back altogether, and would speak no other word to any man. It appears to me there is a kind of eloquence in that rap of Phocion's staff which is equal to anything Demosthenes ever said: "Take your own way, then; I go out of it altogether" [*Applause*].

Such considerations, and manifold more connected with them,—innumerable considerations, resulting from observation of the world at this epoch,—have led various people to doubt of the salutary effect of vocal education altogether. I do not mean to say it should be entirely excluded; but I look to something that will take hold of the matter much more closely, and not allow it to slip out of our fingers, and remain worse than it was. For, if a 'good speaker,' never so eloquent, does not see into the fact, and is not speaking the truth of that, but the untruth and the mistake of that,—is there a more horrid kind of object in creation? [*Loud Cheers.*] Of such speech I hear all manner of people say "How excellent!" Well, really it is not the speech, but the thing spoken, that I am anxious about! I really care very little how the man said it, provided I understand him, and it be true. Excellent speaker? But what if he is telling me things that are contrary to the fact; what if he has formed a wrong judgment about the fact,—if he has in his mind (like Phocion's friend, Cleon the Tanner) no power to form a right judgment in regard to the matter? An excellent speaker of that kind is, as it were, saying, " Ho, every one that wants to be persuaded of the thing that is not true; here is the man for you! " [*Great laughter and applause.*] I recommend you to be very chary of that kind of excellent speech [*Renewed laughter*].

Well, all that sad stuff being the too well-known product of our method of vocal education,—the teacher merely operating on the tongue of the pupil, and teaching him to wag it in a particular way [*Laughter*],—it has made various thinking men entertain a distrust of this not very salutary way of procedure; and they have longed for some less theoretic, and more practical and concrete way of working out the problem of education;—in effect, for an education not vocal at all, but mute except where speaking was strictly needful. There would be room for a great deal of description about this, if I went into it; but I must content myself with saying that the most remarkable piece of writing on it is in a book of Goethe's,—the whole of which you may be recommended to take up, and try if you can study it with understanding. It is one of his last books; written when he was an old man above seventy years of age: I think, one of the most beautiful he ever wrote; full of meek wisdom, of intellect and piety; which is found to be strangely illuminative, and very touching, by those who have eyes to discern and hearts to feel it. This about education is one of the pieces in *Wilhelm Meister's Travels;* or rather, in a fitful way, it forms the whole gist of the book. I first read it many years ago; and, of course, I had to read into the very heart of it while I was translating it [*Applause*] ; and it has ever since dwelt in my mind as perhaps the most remarkable bit of writing which I have known to be executed in these late centuries. I have often said that there are some ten pages of that, which, if ambition had been my only rule, I would rather have written, been able to write, than have written all the books that have appeared since I came into the world [*Cheers*]. Deep, deep is the meaning of what is said there. Those pages turn on the Christian religion, and the religious phenomena of the modern and the ancient world: altogether sketched out in the most aërial, graceful, delicately wise kind of way, so as to keep himself out of the common controversies of the street and of the forum, yet to indicate what was the result of things he had been long meditating upon.

Among others, he introduces in an airy, sketchy kind of way, with here and there a touch,—the sum-total of which grows into a beautiful picture,—a scheme of entirely mute education, at least with no more speech than is absolutely necessary for what the pupils have to do. Three of the wisest men discoverable in the world have been got together, to consider, to manage and supervise, the function which transcends all others in importance,—that of building up the young generation so as to keep it free from that perilous stuff that has been weighing us down, and clogging every step;—which function, indeed, is the only thing we can hope to go on with, if we would leave the world a little better, and not the worse, of our having been in it, for those who are to follow. The Chief, who is the Eldest of the three, says to Wilhelm: " Healthy well-formed children bring into the world with them many precious gifts; and very frequently these are best of all developed by Nature herself, with but slight assistance, where assistance is seen to be wise and profitable, and with forbearance very often on the part of the overseer of the process. But there is one thing which no child brings into the world with him, and without which all other things are of no use." Wilhelm, who is there beside him, asks, " And what is that ? " " All want it," says the Eldest; " perhaps you yourself." Wilhelm says, " Well, but tell me what it is ? " " It is," answers the other, " Reverence *(Ehrfurcht);* Reverence ! " Honour done to those who are greater and better than ourselves; honour distinct from fear. *Ehrfurcht;* the soul of all religion that has ever been among men, or ever will be.

And then he goes into details about the religions of the modern and the ancient world. He practically distinguishes the kinds of religion that are, or have been, in the world; and says that for men there are three reverences. The boys are all trained to go through certain gesticulations; to lay their hands on their breasts and look up to heaven, in sign of the first reverence; other forms for the other two: so they give their three reverences. The first and simplest is that of reverence for what is above us. It is the soul of all the Pagan religion; there is nothing better in the antique man than that. Then there is reverence for what is around us,— reverence for our equals, to which he attributes an immense power in the culture of man. The third is reverence for what is beneath us; to learn to recognise in pain, in sorrow and contradiction, even in those things, odious to flesh and blood, what divine meanings are in them; to learn that there lies in these also, and more than in any of the preceding, a priceless blessing. And he defines that as being the soul of the Christian religion,—the highest of all religions; 'a height,' as Goethe says (and that is very true, even to the letter, as I consider), 'a height to which mankind was fated and enabled to attain; and from which, having once attained it, they can never retrograde.' Man cannot quite lose that (Goethe thinks), or permanently descend below it again; but always, even in the most degraded, sunken and unbelieving times, he calculates there will be found some few souls who will recognise what this highest of the religions meant; and that, the world having once received it, there is no fear of its ever wholly disappearing.

The eldest then goes on to explain by what methods they seek to educate and train their boys; in the trades, in the arts, in the sciences, in whatever pursuit the boy is found best fitted for. Beyond all, they are anxious to discover the boy's aptitudes; and they try him and watch him continually, in many wise ways, till by degrees they can discover this. Wilhelm had left his own boy there, perhaps expecting they would make him a Master of Arts, or something of the kind; and on coming back for him, he sees a thunder-cloud of dust rushing over the plain, of which he can make nothing. It turns out to be a tempest of wild horses, managed by young lads who had a turn for horsemanship, for hunting, and being grooms. His own son is among them; and he finds that the breaking of colts has been the thing *he* was most suited for [*Laughter*].

The highest outcome, and most precious of all the fruits that are to spring from this ideal mode of educating, is what Goethe calls Art:—of which I could at present give no definition that would make it clear to you, unless it were clearer already than is likely [*A laugh*]. Goethe calls it music, painting, poetry: but it is in quite a higher sense than the common one; and a sense in which, I am afraid, most of our painters, poets and music-men would not pass muster [*A laugh*]. He considers this as the highest pitch to which human culture can go; infinitely valuable and ennobling; and he watches with great industry how it is to be brought about in the men who have a turn for it. Very wise and beautiful his notion of the matter is. It gives one an idea that something far better and higher, something as high as ever, and indubitably true too, is still possible for man in this world.— And that is all I can say to you of Goethe's fine theorem of mute education.

I confess it seems to me there is in it a shadow of what will one day be; will and must, unless the world is to come to a conclusion that is altogether frightful: some kind of scheme of education analogous to that; presided over by the wisest and most sacred men that can be got in the world, and watching from a distance: a training in practicality at every turn; no speech in it except speech that is to be followed by action, for that ought to be the rule as nearly as possible among men. Not very often or much, rarely rather, should a man speak at all, unless it is for the sake of something that is to be done; this spoken, let him go and do his part in it, and say no more about it.

I will only add, that it is possible, all this fine theorem of Goethe's, or something similar! Consider what we have already; and what 'difficulties' we have overcome. I should say there is nothing in the world you can conceive so difficult, *prima facie,* as that of getting a set of men gathered together as soldiers. Rough, rude, ignorant, disobedient people; you gather them together, promise them a shilling a day; rank them up, give them very severe and sharp drill; and by bullying and drilling and compelling (the word *drilling,* if you go to the original, means 'beating,' 'steadily *tormenting*' to the due pitch), they do learn what it is necessary to learn; and there is your man in red coat, a trained soldier; piece of an animated machine incomparably the most potent in this world; a wonder of wonders to look at. He will go where bidden; obeys one man, will walk into the cannon's mouth for him; does punctually whatever is commanded by his general officer. And, I believe, all manner of things of this kind could be accomplished, if there were the same attention bestowed. Very many things could be regimented, organised into this mute system;—and perhaps in some of the mechanical, commercial and manufacturing departments some faint incipiences may be attempted before very long. For the saving of human labour, and the avoidance of human misery, the effects would be incalculable, were it set about and begun even in part.

Alas, it is painful to think how very far away it all is, any real fulfilment of such things! For I need not hide from you, young Gentlemen,—and it is one of the last things I am going to tell you,—that you have got into a very troublous epoch of the world; and I don't think you will find your path in it to be smoother than ours has been, though you have many advantages which we had not. You have careers open to you, by public examinations and so on, which is a thing much to be approved of, and which we hope to see perfected more and more. All that was entirely unknown in my time, and you have many things to recognise as advantages. But you will find the ways of the world, I think, more anarchical than ever. Look where one will, revolution has come upon us. We have got into the age of revolutions. All kinds of things are coming to be subjected to fire, as it were: hotter and hotter blows the element round everything. Curious to see how, in Oxford and other places that used to seem as lying at anchor in the stream of time, regardless of all changes, they are getting into the highest humour of mutation, and all sorts of new ideas are afloat. It is evident that whatever is not inconsumable, made of *asbestos,* will have to be burnt, in this world. Nothing other will stand the heat it is getting exposed to.

And in saying that, I am but saying in other words that

we are in an epoch of anarchy. Anarchy *plus* a constable! [*Laughter.*] There is nobody that picks one's pocket without some policeman being ready to take him up [*Renewed laughter*]. But in every other point, man is becoming more and more the son, not of Cosmos, but of Chaos. He is a disobedient, discontented, reckless and altogether waste kind of object (the commonplace man is, in these epochs); and the wiser kind of man,—the select few, of whom I hope you will be part,—has more and more to see to this, to look vigilantly forward; and will require to move with double wisdom. Will find, in short, that the crooked things he has got to pull straight in his own life all round him, wherever he may go, are manifold, and will task all his strength, however great it be.

But why should I complain of that either? For that is the thing a man is born to, in all epochs. He is born to expend every particle of strength that God Almighty has given him, in doing the work he finds he is fit for; to stand up to it to the last breath of life, and do his best. We are called upon to do that; and the reward we all get,—which we are perfectly sure of, if we have merited it,—is that we have got the work done, or at least that we have tried to do the work. For that is a great blessing in itself; and I should say, there is not very much more reward than that going in this world. If the man gets meat and clothes, what matters it whether he buy those necessaries with seven thousand a year, or with seven million, could that be, or with seventy pounds a year? He can get meat and clothes for that; and he will find intrinsically, if he is a wise man, wonderfully little real difference [*Laughter*].

On the whole, avoid what is called ambition; that is not a fine principle to go upon,—and it has in it all degrees of *vulgarity,* if that is a consideration. 'Seekest thou great things, seek them not:' I warmly second that advice of the wisest of men. Don't be ambitious; don't too much need success; be loyal and modest. Cut down the proud towering thoughts that get into you, or see that they be pure as well as high. There is a nobler ambition than the gaining of all California would be, or the getting of all the suffrages that are on the Planet just now [*Loud and prolonged cheers*].

Finally, Gentlemen, I have one advice to give you, which is practically of very great importance, though a very humble one. In the midst of your zeal and ardour,—for such, I foresee, will rise high enough, in spite of all the counsels to moderate it that I can give you,—remember the care of health. I have no doubt you have among you young souls ardently bent to consider life cheap, for the purpose of getting forward in what they are aiming at of high; but you are to consider throughout, much more than is done at present, and what it would have been a very great thing for me if I had been able to consider, that health is a thing to be attended to continually; that you are to regard that as the very highest of all temporal things for you [*Applause*]. There is no kind of achievement you could make in the world that is equal to perfect health. What to it are nuggets and millions? The French financier said, " Why, is there no sleep to be sold! " Sleep was not in the market at any quotation [*Laughter and applause*].

It is a curious thing, which I remarked long ago, and have often turned in my head, that the old word for ' holy ' in the Teutonic languages, *heilig,* also means ' healthy.' Thus *Heilbronn* means indifferently ' holy-well ' or ' health-well.' We have in the Scotch, too, ' hale,' and its derivatives; and, I suppose, our English word ' whole ' (with a ' w '), all of one piece, without any *hole* in it, is the same word. I find that you could not get any better definition of what ' holy ' really is than ' healthy.' Completely healthy; *mens sana in corpore sano* [*Applause*]. A man all lucid, and in equilibrium. His intellect a clear mirror geometrically plane, brilliantly sensitive to all objects and impressions made on it, and imagining all things in their correct proportions; not twisted up into convex or concave, and distorting everything, so that he cannot see the truth of the matter without endless groping and manipulation: healthy, clear and free, and discerning truly all round him. We never can attain that at all. In fact, the operations we have got into are destructive of it. You cannot, if you are going to do any decisive intellectual operation that will last a long while; if, for instance, you are going to write a book,—you cannot manage it (at least, I never could) without getting decidedly made ill by it: and really one nevertheless must; if it is your business, you are obliged to follow out what you are at, and to do it, if even at the expense of health. Only remember, at all times, to get back as fast as possible out of it into health; and regard that as the real equilibrium and centre of things You should always look at the *heilig,* which means ' holy ' as well as ' healthy.'

And that old etymology,—what a lesson it is against certain gloomy, austere, ascetic people, who have gone about as if this world were all a dismal prison-house! It has indeed got all the ugly things in it which I have been alluding to; but there is an eternal sky over it; and the blessed sunshine, the green of prophetic spring, and rich *harvests* coming,—all this is in it too. Piety does not mean that a man should make a sour face about things, and refuse to enjoy wisely what his Maker has given. Neither do you find it to have been so with the best sort,—with old Knox, in particular. No; if you look into Knox, you will find a beautiful Scotch humour in him, as well as the grimmest and sternest truth when necessary, and a great deal of laughter. We find really some of the sunniest glimpses of things come out of Knox that I have seen in any man; for instance, in his *History of the Reformation,*—which is a book I hope every one of you will read [*Applause*], a glorious old book.

On the whole, I would bid you stand up to your work, whatever it may be, and not be afraid of it; not in sorrows or contradictions to yield, but to push on towards the goal. And don't suppose that people are hostile to you or have you at ill-will, in the world. In general, you will rarely find anybody designedly doing you ill. You may feel often as if the whole world were obstructing you, setting itself against you: but you will find that to mean only, that the world is travelling in a different way from you, and, rushing on in its own path, heedlessly treads on you. That is mostly all: to you no specific ill-will;—only each has an extremely goodwill to himself, which he has a right to have, and is rushing on towards his object. Keep out of literature, I should say also, as a general rule [*Laughter*],—though that is by the bye. If you find many people who are hard and indifferent to you, in a world which you consider to be inhospitable and

cruel, as often indeed happens to a tender-hearted, striving
young creature, you will also find there are noble hearts
who will look kindly on you; and their help will be precious
to you beyond price. You will get good and evil as you go
on, and have the success that has been appointed you.

I will wind-up with a small bit of verse, which is from
Goethe also, and has often gone through my mind. To me
it has something of a modern psalm in it, in some measure.
It is deep as the foundations, deep and high, and it is true
and clear:—no clearer man, or nobler and grander intellect
has lived in the world, I believe, since Shakespeare left it.
This is what the poet sings;—a kind of road-melody or
marching-music of mankind:

> ' The future hides in it
> Gladness and sorrow;
> We press still thorow,
> Nought that abides in it
> Daunting us,—onward.
>
> And solemn before us,
> Veiled, the dark Portal;
> Goal of all mortal:—
> Stars silent rest o'er us,
> Graves under us silent!
>
> While earnest thou gazest,
> Comes boding of terror,
> Comes phantasm and error;
> Perplexes the bravest
> With doubt and misgiving.
>
> But heard are the Voices,
> Heard are the Sages,
> The Worlds and the Ages:
> " Choose well; your choice is
> Brief, and yet endless.
>
> Here eyes do regard you,
> In Eternity's stillness;
> Here is all fulness,
> Ye brave, to reward you;
> Work, and despair not." '

Work, and despair not: *Wir heissen euch hoffen,* ' We bid
you be of hope!'—let that be my last word. Gentlemen, I

thank you for your great patience in hearing me; and, with many most kind wishes, say Adieu for this time.

FINIS OF RECTORSHIP.—'*Edinburgh University*. Mr. Carlyle ex-Lord Rector of the University of Edinburgh, has been asked to deliver a valedictory address to the students, but has declined. The following is a copy of the correspondence.

'2 S.-W. Circus Place, Edinburgh, 3d December 1868.

'SIR,—On the strength of being Vice-President of the Committee for your election as Lord Rector of the University of Edinburgh, I have been induced to write to you, in order to know if you will be able to deliver a Valedictory Address to the Students. Mr. Gladstone gave us one, and we fondly hope you will find it convenient to do so as well. Your Inaugural Address is still treasured up in our memories, and I am sure nothing could give us greater pleasure than once more to listen to your words. I trust you will pardon me for this intrusion; and hoping to receive a favourable answer, I am, etc., A. ROBERTSON, M. A.

'T. CARLYLE, ESQ.'

'Chelsea, 9th December 1868.

'DEAR SIR,—I much regret that a Valedictory Speech from me, in present circumstances, is a thing I must not think of. Be pleased to assure the young Gentlemen who were so friendly towards me, that I have already sent them, in silence, but with emotions deep enough, perhaps too deep, my loving Farewell, and that ingratitude, or want of regard, is by no means among the causes that keep me absent. With a fine youthful enthusiasm, beautiful to look upon, they bestowed on me that bit of honour, loyally all they had; and it has now, for reasons one and another, become touchingly memorable to me,—touchingly, and even grandly and tragically,—never to be forgotten for the remainder of my life.

'Bid them, in my name, if they still love me, fight the good fight, and quit themselves like men in the warfare, to which *they* are as if conscript and consecrated, and which lies ahead. Tell them to consult the eternal oracles (not yet inaudible, nor ever to become so, when worthily inquired of):

and to disregard, nearly altogether, in comparison, the temporary noises, menacings and deliriums. May they love Wisdom as Wisdom, if she is to yield *her* treasures, must be loved,—piously, valiantly, humbly, beyond life itself or the prizes of life, with all one's heart, and all one's soul:— in that case (I will say again), and not in any other case, it shall be well with them. Adieu, my young Friends, a long adieu.—Yours with great sincerity, T. CARLYLE.

'A. ROBERTSON, ESQ.'[1]

[1] Edinburgh Newspapers of December 12-13, 1868.

SIR WALTER SCOTT

BY

THOMAS CARLYLE

SIR WALTER SCOTT[1]

[1838]

AMERICAN Cooper asserts, in one of his books, that there
is ' an instinctive tendency in men to look at any man
who has become distinguished.' True, surely: as all
observation and survey of mankind, from China to Peru,
from Nebuchadnezzar to Old Hickory, will testify! Why
do men crowd towards the improved-drop at Newgate, eager
to catch a sight? The man about to be hanged is in a distinguished situation. Men crowd to such extent, that Green-
acre's is not the only life choked-out there. Again, ask of
these leathern vehicles, cabriolets, neat-flies, with blue men
and women in them, that scour all thoroughfares, Whither
so fast? To see dear Mrs. Rigmarole, the distinguished
female; great Mr. Rigmarole, the distinguished male! Or,
consider that crowning phenomenon, and summary of modern civilisation, a *soirée* of lions. Glittering are the rooms,
well-lighted, thronged; bright flows their undulatory flood of
blonde-gowns and dress-coats, a soft smile dwelling on all
faces; for behold there also flow the lions, hovering distinguished: oracles of the age, of one sort or another. Oracles
really pleasant to see; whom it is worth while to go and see:
look at them, but inquire not of them, depart rather and be
thankful. For your lion-*soirée* admits not of speech; there
lies the specialty of it. A meeting together of human creatures; and yet (so high has civilisation gone) the primary
aim of human meeting, that soul might in some articulate
utterance unfold itself to soul, can be dispensed with in it.
Utterance there is not; nay, there is a certain grinning play
of tongue-fence, and make-believe of utterance, considerably

[1] LONDON AND WESTMINSTER REVIEW, No. 12.—*Memoirs of the Life of
Sir Walter Scott, Baronet.* Vols. i.-vi. Edinburgh, 1837.

worse than none. For which reason it has been suggested, with an eye to sincerity and silence in such lion-*soirées*, Might not each lion be, for example, ticketed, as wine-decanters are? Let him carry, slung round him, in such ornamental manner as seemed good, his silver label with name engraved; you lift his label, and read it, with what farther ocular survey you find useful, and speech is not needed at all. O Fenimore Cooper, it is most true there is ' an instinctive tendency in men to look at any man that has become distinguished'; and, moreover, an instinctive desire in men to become distinguished and be looked at!

For the rest, we will call it a most valuable tendency this; indispensable to mankind. Without it, where were star-and-garter, and significance of rank; where were all ambition, money-getting, respectability of gig or no gig; and, in a word, the main impetus by which society moves, the main force by which it hangs together? A tendency, we say, of manifold results; of manifold origin, not ridiculous only, but sublime;—which some incline to deduce from the mere gregarious purblind nature of man, prompting him to run, ' as dim-eyed animals do, towards any glittering object, were it but a scoured tankard, and mistake it for a solar luminary,' or even ' sheeplike, to run and crowd because many *have* already run'! It is indeed curious to consider how men do make the gods that themselves worship. For the most famed man, round whom all the world rapturously huzzahs and venerates, as if his like were not, is the same man whom all the world was wont to jostle into the kennels; not a changed man, but in every fibre of him the same man. Foolish world, what went ye out to see? A tankard scoured bright: and do there not lie, of the self-same pewter, whole barrowfuls of tankards, though by worse fortune all still in the dim state?

And yet, at bottom, it is not merely our gregarious sheeplike quality, but something better, and indeed best: which has been called ' the perpetual fact of hero-worship'; our inborn sincere love of great men! Not the gilt farthing, for its own sake, do even fools covet; but the gold guinea which they mistake it for. Veneration of great men is perennial in the nature of man; this, in all times, especially in these, is one of the blessedest facts predicable of him. In all times, even in these seemingly so disobedient times, ' it remains a blessed fact, so cunningly has Nature ordered it, *that whatsoever man ought to obey, he cannot but obey.* Show the dullest clodpole, show the haughtiest featherhead, that a soul higher than himself is actually here; were his knees stiffened into brass, he must down and worship.' So it has been written; and may be cited and repeated till known to all. Understand it well, this of ' hero-worship' was the primary creed, and has intrinsically been the secondary and ternary, and will be the ultimate and final creed of mankind; indestructible, changing in shape, but in essence unchangeable; whereon polities, religions, loyalties, and all highest human interests have been and can be built, as on a rock that will endure while man endures. Such is hero-worship; so much lies in that our inborn sincere love of great men!— In favour of which unspeakable benefits of the reality, what can we do but cheerfully pardon the multiplex ineptitudes of the semblance; cheerfully wish even lion-*soirées,* with labels for their lions or without that improvement, all manner of prosperity? Let hero-worship flourish, say we; and the more and more assiduous chase after gilt farthings while guineas are not yet forthcoming. Herein, at lowest, is proof that guineas exist, that they are believed to exist, and valued. Find great men, if you can; if you cannot, still quit not the search; in defect of great men, let there be noted men, in such number, to such degree of intensity as the public appetite can tolerate.

Whether Sir Walter Scott was a great man, is still a question with some; but there can be no question with any one that he was a most noted and even notable man. In this generation there was no literary man with such a popularity in any country; there have only been a few with such, taking-in all generations and all countries. Nay, it is farther to be admitted that Sir Walter Scott's popularity was of a select sort rather; not a popularity of the populace. His admirers were at one time almost all the intelligent of civilised countries; and to the last included, and do still include, a great portion of that sort. Such fortune he had, and has continued to maintain for a space of some twenty or thirty years. So long the observed of all observers; a great man or only a considerable man; here surely, if ever, is a singular circumstanced, is a 'distinguished' man! In regard to whom, therefore, the 'instinctive tendency' on other men's part cannot be wanting. Let men look, where the world has already so long looked. And now, while the new, earnestly expected *Life* 'by his son-in-law and literary executor' again summons the whole world's attention round him, probably for the last time it will ever be so summoned; and men are in some sort taking leave of a notability, and about to go their way, and commit him to his fortune on the flood of things,—why should not this Periodical Publication likewise publish its thought about him? Readers of miscellaneous aspect, of unknown quantity and quality, are waiting to hear it done. With small inward vocation, but cheerfully obedient to destiny and necessity, the present reviewer will follow a multitude: to do evil or to do no evil, will depend not on the multitude but on himself. One thing he did decidedly wish; at least to wait till the Work were finished: for the six promised Volumes, as the world knows, have flowed over into a Seventh, which will not for some weeks yet see the light. But the editorial powers, wearied with waiting, have become peremptory; and declare that, finished or not finished, they will have their hands washed of it at this opening of the year. Perhaps it is best. The physiognomy of Scott will not be much altered for us by that Seventh Volume; the prior Six have altered it but little;—as, indeed, a man who has written some two-hundred volumes of his own, and lived for thirty years amid the universal speech of friends, must have already left some likeness of himself. Be it as the peremptory editorial powers require.

First, therefore, a word on the *Life* itself. Mr. Lockhart's known powers justify strict requisition in his case. Our verdict in general would be, that he has accomplished the work he schemed for himself in a creditable workmanlike manner. It is true, his notion of what the work was, does not seem to have been very elevated. To picture-forth the life of Scott according to any rules of art or composition, so that a reader, on adequately examining it, might say to himself, "There is Scott, there is the physiognomy and meaning of Scott's appearance and transit on this earth; such was he by nature, so did the world act on him, so he on the world, with such result and significance for himself and us ": this was by no manner of means Mr. Lockhart's plan. A plan which, it is rashly said, should preside over every biography! It might have been fulfilled with all degrees of perfection, from that of the *Odyssey* down to *Thomas Ellwood* or lower. For there is no heroic poem in the world but is at bottom a biography, the life of a man: also, it may be said, there is no life of a man, faithfully recorded, but is a heroic poem of its sort, rhymed or unrhymed. It is a plan one would prefer, did it otherwise suit; which it does not, in these days. Seven volumes sell so much dearer than one; are so much easier to write than one. The *Odyssey*, for instance, what were the value of the *Odyssey* sold per sheet? One paper of *Pickwick;* or say, the inconsiderable fraction of one. This, in commercial algebra, were the equation: *Odyssey* equal to *Pickwick* divided by an unknown integer.

There is a great discovery still to be made in Literature, that of paying literary men by the quantity they *do not* write. Nay, in sober truth, is not this actually the rule in all writing; and, moreover, in all conduct and acting? Not what stands above ground, but what lies unseen *under* it, as the root and subterrene element it sprang from and emblemed forth, determines the value. Under all speech that is good for anything there lies a silence that is better. Silence is deep as Eternity: speech is shallow as Time. Paradoxical does it seem? Woe for the age, woe for the man, quack-ridden, bespeeched, bespouted, blown about like barren Sahara, to whom this world-old truth were altogether strange!—Such we say is the rule, acted on or not, recognised or not; and he who departs from it, what can he do but spread himself into breadth and length, into superficiality and saleability; and, except as filigree, become comparatively useless? One thinks, Had but the hogshead of thin wash, which sours in a week ready for the kennels, been *distilled,* been concentrated! Our dear Fenimore Cooper, whom we started with, might, in that way, have given us one *Natty Leatherstocking,* one melodious synopsis of Man and Nature in the West (for it lay in him to do it), almost as a Saint-Pierre did for the Islands of the East; and the hundred Incoherences, cobbled hastily together by order of Colburn and Company, had slumbered in Chaos, as all incoherences ought if possible to do. Verily this same genius of diffuse-writing, of diffuse-acting, is a Moloch; and souls pass through the fire to him, more than enough. Surely, if ever discovery was valuable and needful, it were that above indicated, of paying by the work *not* visibly done!—Which needful discovery we will give the whole projecting, railwaying, knowledge-diffusing, march-of-intellect and otherwise promotive and locomotive societies in the Old and New World, any required length of centuries to make. Once made, such discovery once made, we too will fling cap into the air, and shout, *"Io Pæan!* the Devil *is* conquered";—and, in the *mean* while, study to think it nothing miraculous that seven biographical volumes are given where one had been better; and that several other things happen, very much as they from of old were known to do, and are like to continue doing.

Mr. Lockhart's aim, we take it, was not that of producing any such highflown work of art as we hint at: or indeed to do much other than to print, intelligently bound together by order of time, and by some requisite intercalary exposition, all such letters, documents and notices about Scott as he found lying suitable, and as it seemed likely the world would undertake to read. His Work, accordingly, is not so much a composition, as what we may call a compilation well done. Neither is this a task of no difficulty; this too is a task that may be performed with extremely various degrees of talent: from the *Life and Correspondence of Hannah More,* for instance, up to this *Life of Scott,* there is a wide range indeed! Let us take the Seven Volumes, and be thankful that they are genuine in their kind. Nay, as to that of their being seven and not one, it is right to say that the public so required it. To have done other, would have shown little policy in an author. Had Mr. Lockhart laboriously compressed himself, and instead of well-done compilation, brought out the well-done composition, in one volume instead of seven, which not many men in England are better qualified to do, there can be no doubt but his readers for the time had been immeasurably fewer. If the praise of magnanimity be denied him, that of prudence must be conceded, which perhaps he values more.

The truth is, the work, done in this manner too, was good to have: Scott's Biography, if uncomposed, lies printed and indestructible here, in the elementary state, and can at any time be composed, if necessary, by whosoever has a call to that. As it is, as it was meant to be, we repeat, the work is vigorously done. Sagacity, decision, candour, diligence, good manners, good sense: these qualities are throughout observable. The dates, calculations, statements, we suppose to be all accurate; much laborious inquiry, some of it impossible for another man, has been gone into, the results of which are imparted with due brevity. Scott's letters, not interesting generally, yet never absolutely without interest, are copiously given; copiously, but with selection; the answers to them still more select. Narrative, delineation, and at length personal reminiscences, occasionally of much merit, of a certain rough force, sincerity and picturesqueness, duly intervene. The scattered members of Scott's Life do lie here, and could be disentangled. In a word, this compilation is the work of a manful, clear-seeing, conclusive man, and has been executed with the faculty and combination of faculties the public had a right to expect from the name attached to it.

One thing we hear greatly blamed in Mr. Lockhart: that he has been too communicative, indiscreet, and has recorded much that ought to have lain suppressed. Persons are mentioned, and circumstances, not always of an ornamental sort. It would appear there is far less reticence than was looked for! Various persons, name and surname, have 'received pain': nay, the very Hero of the Biography is rendered unheroic; unornamental facts of him, and of those he had to do with, being set forth in plain English: hence 'personality,' 'indiscretion,' or worse, 'sanctities of private life,' etc., etc. How delicate, decent is English Biography, bless its mealy mouth! A Damocles' sword of *Respectability* hangs forever over the poor English Life-writer (as it does over poor English Life in general), and reduces him to the verge of paralysis. Thus it has been said 'there are no English lives worth reading except those of Players, who by the nature of the case have bidden Respectability good-day.' The English biographer has long felt that if in writing his Man's Biography, he wrote down anything that could by possibility offend any man, he had written wrong. The plain consequence was, that, properly speaking, no biography whatever could be produced. The poor biographer, having the fear *not* of God before his eyes, was obliged to retire as it were into vacuum; and write in the most melancholy, straitened manner, with only vacuum for a result. Vain that he wrote, and that we kept reading volume on volume: there was no biography, but some vague ghost of a biography, white, stainless; without feature or substance; *vacuum,* as we say, and wind and shadow,—which indeed the material of it was.

No man lives without jostling and being jostled; in all ways he has to *elbow* himself through the world, giving and receiving offence. His life is a battle, in so far as it is an entity at all. The very oyster, we suppose, comes in collision with oysters: undoubtedly enough it does come in collision with Necessity and Difficulty; and helps itself through, not as a perfect ideal oyster, but as an imperfect real one. Some kind of remorse must be known to the oyster; certain hatreds, certain pusillanimities. But as for man, his conflict is continual with the spirit of contradiction, that is without and within; with the evil spirit (or call it, with the weak, most necessitous, pitiable spirit), that is in others and in himself. His walk, like all walking (say the mechanicians), is a series of *falls*. To paint man's life is to represent these things. Let them be represented, fitly, with dignity and measure; but above all, let them be represented. No tragedy of *Hamlet* with the part of Hamlet omitted by particular desire! No ghost of a biography, let the Damocles' sword of Respectability (which, after all, is but a pasteboard one) threaten as it will. One hopes that the public taste is much mended in this matter; that vacuum-biographies, with a good many other vacuities related to them, are withdrawn or withdrawing into vacuum. Probably it was Mr. Lockhart's feeling of what the great public would approve, that led him, open-eyed, into this offence against the small criticising public: we joyfully accept the omen.

Perhaps then, of all the praises copiously bestowed on his Work, there is none in reality so creditable to him as this same censure, which has also been pretty copious. It is a censure better than a good many praises. He is found guilty of having said this and that, calculated not to be entirely pleasant to this man and that; in other words, calculated to give him and the thing he worked in a living set of features, not leave him vague, in the white beatified-ghost condition. Several men, as we hear, cry out, " See, there is something written not entirely pleasant to me! " Good friend, it is pity; but who can help it? They that will crowd about bonfires may, sometimes very fairly, get their beards singed; it is the price they pay for such illumination; natural twilight is safe and free to all. For our part, we hope all manner of biographies that are written in England will henceforth be written so. If it is fit that they be written otherwise, then it is still fitter that they be not written at all: to produce not things but ghosts of things can never be the duty of man.

The biographer has this problem set before him: to delineate a likeness of the earthly pilgrimage of a man. He will compute well what profit is in it, and what disprofit; under which latter head this of offending any of his fellow-creatures will surely not be forgotten. Nay, this may so swell the disprofit side of his account, that many an enterprise of biography, otherwise promising, shall require to be renounced. But once taken up, the rule before all rules is to do *it,* not to do the ghost of it. In speaking of the man and men he has to deal with, he will of course keep all his charities about him; but all his eyes open. Far be it from him to set down aught *untrue;* nay, not to abstain from, and leave in oblivion much that is true. But having found a thing or things essential for his subject, and well computed the for and against, he will in very deed set down such thing or things, nothing doubting,—*having,* we may say, the fear of God before his eyes, and no other fear whatever. Censure the biographer's prudence; dissent from the computation he made, or agree with it; be all malice of his, be all falsehood, nay, be all offensive avoidable inaccuracy, condemned and consumed; but know that by this plan only, executed as was possible, could the biographer hope to make a biography; and blame him not that he did what it had been the worst fault not to do.

As to the accuracy or error of these statements about the Ballantynes and other persons aggrieved, which are questions much mooted at present in some places, we know nothing at all. If they are inaccurate, let them be corrected; if the inaccuracy was avoidable, let the author bear rebuke and punishment for it. We can only say, these things carry no look of inaccuracy on the face of them; neither is anywhere the smallest trace of ill-will or unjust feeling discernible. Decidedly the probabilities are, and till better evidence arise, the fair conclusion is, that this matter stands very much as it ought to do. Let the clatter of censure, therefore, propagate itself as far as it can. For Mr. Lockhart it virtually amounts to this very considerable praise, that, standing full in the face of the public, he has set at naught, and been among the first to do it, a public piece of cant; one of the commonest we have, and closely allied to many others of the fellest sort, as smooth as it looks.

The other censure, of Scott being made unheroic, springs from the same stem; and is, perhaps, a still more wonderful flower of it. Your true hero must have no features, but be white, stainless, an impersonal ghost-hero! But connected with this, there is a hypothesis now current, due probably to some man of name, for its own force would not carry it far: That Mr. Lockhart at heart has a dislike to Scott, and has done his best in an underhand treacherous manner to dis-hero him! Such hypothesis is actually current: he that has ears may hear it now and then. On which astonishing hypothesis, if a word must be said, it can only be an apology for silence,—" That there are things at which one stands struck silent, as at first sight of the Infinite." For if Mr. Lockhart is fairly chargeable with any radical defect, if on any side his insight entirely fails him, it seems even to be in this: that Scott is altogether lovely to him; that Scott's greatness spreads out for him on all hands beyond reach of eye; that his very faults become beautiful, his vulgar worldli-nesses are solid prudences, proprieties; and of his worth there is no measure. Does not the patient Biographer dwell on his *Abbots, Pirates,* and hasty theatrical scene-paintings; affec-tionately analysing them, as if they were Raphael-pictures, time-defying *Hamlets, Othellos?* The Novel-manufactory,

with its 15,000*l.* a-year, is sacred to him as creation of a
genius, which carries the noble victor up to Heaven. Scott
is to Lockhart the unparalleled of the time; an object
spreading-out before him like a sea without shore. Of *that*
astonishing hypothesis, let expressive silence be the only
answer.

And so in sum, with regard to *Lockhart's Life of Scott,*
readers that believe in us shall read it with the feeling that a
man of talent, decision and insight wrote it; wrote it in seven
volumes, not in one, because the public would pay for it better in that state; but wrote it with courage, with frankness,
sincerity; on the whole, in a very readable, recommendable
manner, as things go. Whosoever needs it can purchase it,
or purchase the loan of it, with assurance more than usual
that he has ware for his money. And now enough of the
written *Life;* we will glance a little at the man and his
acted life.

Into the question whether Scott was a great man or not,
we do not propose to enter deeply. It is, as too usual, a
question about words. There can be no doubt but many men
have been named and printed *great* who were vastly smaller
than he: as little doubt moreover that of the specially *good,*
a very large portion, according to any genuine standard of
man's worth, were worthless in comparison to him. He for
whom Scott is great may most innocently name him so; may
with advantage admire his great qualities, and ought with
sincere heart to emulate them. At the same time, it is good
that there be a certain degree of precision in our epithets.
It is good to understand, for one thing, that no popularity,
and open-mouthed wonder of all the world, continued even
for a long series of years, can make a man great. Such popularity is a remarkable fortune; indicates a great adaptation
of the man to his element of circumstances; but may or may
not indicate anything great in the man. To our imagination,
as above hinted, there is a certain apotheosis in it; but in the
reality no apotheosis at all. Popularity is as a blaze of
illumination, or alas, of conflagration, kindled round a man;
showing what is in him; not putting the smallest item more
into him; often abstracting much from him; conflagrating

the poor man himself into ashes and *caput mortuum!* And then, by the nature of it, such popularity is transient; your 'series of years,' quite unexpectedly, sometimes almost all on a sudden, terminates! For the stupidity of men, especially of men congregated in masses round any object, is extreme. What illuminations and conflagrations have kindled themselves, as if new heavenly suns had risen, which proved only to be tar-barrels and terrestrial locks of straw! Profane Princesses cried out, "One God, one Farinelli!"—and whither now have they and Farinelli danced?

In Literature too there have been seen popularities greater even than Scott's, and nothing perennial in the interior of them. Lope de Vega, whom all the world swore by, and made a proverb of; who could make an acceptable five-act tragedy in almost as many hours; the greatest of all popularities past or present, and perhaps one of the greatest men that ever ranked among popularities. Lope himself, so radiant, far-shining, has not proved to be a sun or star of the firmament; but is as good as lost and gone out; or plays at best in the eyes of some few as a vague aurora-borealis, and brilliant ineffectuality. The great man of Spain sat obscure at the time, all dark and poor, a maimed soldier; writing his *Don Quixote* in prison. And Lope's fate withal was sad, his popularity perhaps a curse to him; for in this man there was something ethereal too, a divine particle traceable in few other popular men; and such far-shining diffusion of himself, though all the world swore by it, would do nothing for the true life of him even while he lived: he had to creep into a convent, into a monk's cowl, and learn, with infinite sorrow, that his blessedness had lain elsewhere; that when a man's life feels itself to be sick and an error, no voting of bystanders can make it well and a truth again.

Or coming down to our own times, was not August Kotzebue popular? Kotzebue, not so many years since, saw himself, if rumour and hand-clapping could be credited, the greatest man going; saw visibly his Thoughts, dressed-out in plush and pasteboard, permeating and perambulating civilised Europe; the most iron visages weeping with him, in all theatres from Cadiz to Kamtchatka; his own 'astonishing genius' meanwhile producing two tragedies or so per month:

he, on the whole, blazed high enough: he too has gone out into Night and *Orcus,* and already is not. We will omit this of popularity altogether; and account it as making simply nothing towards Scott's greatness or non-greatness, as an accident, not a quality.

Shorn of this falsifying *nimbus,* and reduced to his own natural dimensions, there remains the reality, Walter Scott, and what we can find in him: to be accounted great, or not great, according to the dialects of men. Friends to precision of epithet will probably deny his title to the name 'great.' It seems to us there goes other stuff to the making of great men than can be detected here. One knows not what idea worthy of the name of great, what purpose, instinct or tendency, that could be called great, Scott ever was inspired with. His life was worldly; his ambitions were worldly. There is nothing spiritual in him; all is economical, material, of the earth earthy. A love of picturesque, of beautiful, vigorous and graceful things; a genuine love, yet not more genuine than has dwelt in hundreds of men named minor poets: this is the highest quality to be discerned in him.

His power of representing these things, too, his poetic power, like his moral power, was a genius *in extenso,* as we may say, not *in intenso.* In action, in speculation, *broad* as he was, he rose nowhere high; productive without measure as to quantity, in quality he for the most part transcended but a little way the region of commonplace. It has been said, 'no man has written as many volumes with so few sentences that can be quoted.' Winged words were not his vocation; nothing urged him that way: the great Mystery of Existence was not great to him; did not drive him into rocky solitudes to wrestle with it for an answer, to be answered or to perish. He had nothing of the martyr; into no 'dark region to slay monsters for us,' did he, either led or driven, venture down: his conquests were for his own behoof mainly, conquests over common market-labour, and reckonable in good metallic coin of the realm. The thing he had faith in, except power, power of what sort soever, and even of the rudest sort, would be difficult to point out. One sees not that he believed in anything; nay, he did not even disbelieve; but quietly acquiesced, and made himself at home in a world of conventionalities; the false, the semi-false and the true were alike true in this, that they were there, and had power in their hands more or less. It was well to feel so; and yet not well! We find it written, 'Woe to them that are at ease in Zion'; but surely it is a double woe to them that are at ease in Babel, in Domdaniel. On the other hand, he wrote many volumes, amusing many thousands of men. Shall we call this great? It seems to us there dwells and struggles another sort of spirit in the inward parts of great men!

Brother Ringletub, the missionary, inquired of Ram-Dass, a Hindoo man-god, who had set up for godhood lately, What he meant to do, then, with the sins of mankind? To which Ram-Dass at once answered, He had *fire enough in his belly* to burn-up all the sins in the world. Ram-Dass was right so far, and had a spice of sense in him; for surely it is the test of every divine man this same, and without it he is not divine or great,—that he *have* fire in him to burn-up somewhat of the sins of the world, of the miseries and errors of the world: why else is he there? Far be it from us to say that a great man must needs, with benevolence prepense, become a 'friend of humanity'; nay, that such professional self-conscious friends of humanity are not the fatalest kind of persons to be met with in our day. All greatness is unconscious, or it is little and nought. And yet a great man without *such* fire in him, burning dim or developed, as a divine behest in his heart of hearts, never resting till it be fulfilled, were a solecism in Nature. A great man is ever, as the Transcendentalists speak, possessed with an *idea*.

Napoleon himself, not the superfinest of great men, and ballasted sufficiently with prudences and egoisms, had nevertheless, as is clear enough, an idea to start with: the idea that Democracy was the Cause of Man, the right and infinite Cause. Accordingly he made himself 'the armed Soldier of Democracy'; and did vindicate it in a rather great manner. Nay, to the very last, he had a kind of idea; that, namely, of *La carrière ouverte aux talens,* The tools to him that can handle them'; really one of the best ideas yet promulgated on that matter, or rather the one true central idea, towards which all the others, if they tend anywhither, must tend.

Unhappily it was in the military province only that Napoleon could realise this idea of his, being forced to fight for himself the while: before he got it tried to any extent in the civil province of things, his head by much victory grew light (no head can stand more than its quantity); and he lost head, as they say, and became a selfish ambitionist and quack, and was hurled out; leaving his idea to be realised, in the civil province of things, by others! Thus was Napoleon; thus are all great men: children of the idea; or, in Ram-Dass's phraseology, furnished with fire to burn-up the miseries of men. Conscious or unconscious, latent or unfolded, there is small vestige of any such fire being extant in the inner-man of Scott.

Yet on the other hand, the surliest critic must allow that Scott was a genuine man, which itself is a great matter. No affectation, fantasticality or distortion dwelt in him; no shadow of cant. Nay, withal, was he not a right brave and strong man, according to his kind? What a load of toil, what a measure of felicity, he quietly bore along with him; with what quiet strength he both worked on this earth, and enjoyed in it; invincible to evil fortune and to good! A most composed, invincible man; in difficulty and distress knowing no discouragement, Samson-like carrying off on his strong Samson-shoulders the gates that would imprison him: in danger and menace laughing at the whisper of fear. And then, with such a sunny current of true humour and humanity, a free joyful sympathy with so many things; what of fire he had all lying so beautifully *latent,* as radical latent heat, as fruitful internal warmth of life; a most robust, healthy man! The truth is, our best definition of Scott were perhaps even this, that he was, if no great man, then something much pleasanter to be, a robust, thoroughly healthy and withal very prosperous and victorious man. An eminently well-conditioned man, healthy in body, healthy in soul; we will call him one of the *healthiest* of men.

Neither is this a small matter: health is a great matter, both to the possessor of it and to others. On the whole, that humorist in the Moral Essay was not so far out, who determined on honouring health only; and so instead of humbling himself to the high-born, to the rich and well-dressed, insisted on doffing hat to the healthy: coroneted carriages with pale faces in them passed by as failures, miserable and lamentable; trucks with ruddy-cheeked strength dragging at them were greeted as successful and venerable. For does not health mean harmony, the synonym of all that is true, justly-ordered, good; is it not, in some sense, the net-total, as shown by experiment, of whatever worth is in us? The healthy man is the most meritorious product of Nature so far as he goes. A healthy body is good; but a soul in right health,—it is the thing beyond all others to be prayed for; the blessedest thing this earth receives of Heaven. Without artificial medicament of philosophy, or tight-lacing of creeds (always very questionable), the healthy soul discerns what is good, and adheres to it, and retains it; discerns what is bad, and spontaneously casts it off. An instinct from Nature herself, like that which guides the wild animals of the forest to their food, shows him what he shall do, what he shall abstain from. The false and foreign will not adhere to him; cant and all fantastic diseased incrustations are impossible;—as Walker the *Original,* in such eminence of health was *he* for his part, *could* not, by much abstinence from soap-and-water, attain to a dirty face! This thing thou canst work with and profit by, this thing is substantial and worthy; that other thing thou canst not work with, it is trivial and inapt: so speaks unerringly the inward monition of the man's whole nature. No need of logic to prove the most argumentative absurdity absurd; as Goethe says of himself, ' all this ran down from me like water from a man in wax-cloth dress.' Blessed is the healthy nature; it is the coherent, sweetly coöperative, not incoherent, self-distracting, self-destructive one! In the harmonious adjustment and play of all the faculties, the just balance of oneself gives a just feeling towards all men and all things. Glad light from within radiates outwards, and enlightens and embellishes.

Now all this can be predicated of Walter Scott, and of no British literary man that we remember in these days, to any such extent,—if it be not perhaps of one, the most opposite imaginable to Scott, but his equal in this quality and what holds of it: William Cobbett! Nay, there are other similarities, widely different as they two look; nor be the comparison disparaging to Scott: for Cobbett also, as the pattern John Bull of his century, strong as the rhinoceros, and with singular humanities and genialities shining through his thick skin, is a most brave phenomenon. So bounteous was Nature to us; in the sickliest of recorded ages, when British Literature lay all puking and sprawling in Werterism, Byronism, and other Sentimentalism tearful or spasmodic (fruit of internal *wind*). Nature was kind enough to send us two healthy Men, of whom she might still say, not without pride, "These also were made in England; such limbs do I still make there!" It is one of the cheerfulest sights, let the question of its greatness be settled as you will. A healthy nature may or may not be great; but there is no great nature that is not healthy.

Or, on the whole, might we not say, Scott, in the new vesture of the nineteenth century, was intrinsically very much the old fighting Borderer of prior centuries; the kind of man Nature did of old make in that birthland of his? In the saddle, with the foray-spear, he would have acquitted himself as he did at the desk with his pen. One fancies how, in stout *Beardie* of Harden's time, he could have played Beardie's part; and *been* the stalwart buff-belted *terræ filius* he in this late time could only delight to draw. The same stout self-help was in him; the same oak and triple brass round his heart. He too could have fought at Redswire, cracking crowns with the fiercest, if that had been the task; could have harried cattle in Tynedale, repaying injury with compound interest; a right sufficient captain of men. A man without qualms or fantasticalities; a hard-headed, sound-hearted man, of joyous robust temper, looking to the main chance, and fighting direct thitherward; *valde stalwartus homo!*—How much in that case had slumbered in him, and passed away without sign! But indeed who knows how much slumbers in many men? Perhaps our greatest poets are the *mute* Miltons; the vocals are those whom by happy accident we lay hold of, one here, one there, as it chances, and *make* vocal. It is even a question, whether, had not want, discomfort and distress-warrants been busy at Stratford-on-Avon, Shakspeare himself had not lived killing calves or combing wool! Had the Edial Boarding-school turned out well, we had never heard of Samuel Johnson; Samuel Johnson had been a fat schoolmaster and dogmatic gerundgrinder, and never known that he was more. Nature is rich: those two eggs thou art eating carelessly to breakfast, could they not have been hatched into a pair of fowls, and have covered the whole world with poultry?

But it was not harrying of cattle in Tynedale, or cracking of crowns at Redswire, that this stout Border-chief was appointed to perform. Far other work. To be the song-singer and pleasant tale-teller to Britain and Europe, in the beginning of the artificial nineteenth century; here, and not there, lay his business. Beardie of Harden would have found it very amazing. How he shapes himself to this new element; how he helps himself along in it, makes it to do for him, lives sound and victorious in it, and leads over the marches such a spoil as all the cattle-droves the Hardens ever took were poor in comparison to; this is the history of the life and achievements of *our* Sir Walter Scott, Baronet; —whereat we are now to glance for a little! It is a thing remarkable; a thing substantial; of joyful, victorious sort; not unworthy to be glanced at. Withal, however, a glance here and there will suffice. Our limits are narrow; the thing, were it never so victorious, is not of the sublime sort, nor extremely edifying; there is nothing in it to censure vehemently, nor love vehemently; there is more to wonder at than admire; and the whole secret is not an abstruse one.

Till towards the age of thirty, Scott's life has nothing in it decisively pointing towards Literature, or indeed towards distinction of any kind; he is wedded, settled, and has gone through all his preliminary steps, without symptom of renown as yet. It is the life of every other Edinburgh youth of his station and time. Fortunate we must name it, in many ways. Parents in easy or wealthy circumstances, yet unencumbered with the cares and perversions of aristocracy; nothing eminent in place, in faculty or culture, yet nothing deficient; all around is methodic regulation, prudence, prosperity, kindheartedness; an element of warmth and light, of affection, industry, and burgherly comfort, heightened into

elegance; in which the young heart can wholesomely grow.
A vigorous health seems to have been given by Nature; yet,
as if Nature had said withal, " Let it be a health to express
itself by mind, not by body," a lameness is added in childhood; the brave little boy, instead of romping and bickering,
must learn to think; or at lowest, what is a great matter, to
sit still. No rackets and trundling-hoops for this young
Walter; but ballads, history-books and a world of legendary
stuff, which his mother and those near him are copiously
able to furnish. Disease, which is but superficial, and issues
in outward lameness, does not cloud the young existence;
rather forwards it towards the expansion it is fitted for. The
miserable disease had been one of the internal nobler parts,
marring the general organisation; under which no Walter
Scott could have been forwarded, or with all his other endowments could have been producible or possible. ' Nature
gives healthy children much; how much! Wise education
is a wise unfolding of this; often it unfolds itself better of
its own accord.'

Add one other circumstance: the place where; namely,
Presbyterian Scotland. The influences of this are felt incessantly, they stream-in at every pore. ' There is a country
accent,' says La Rochefoucauld, ' not in speech only, but in
thought, conduct, character and manner of existing, which
never forsakes a man.' Scott, we believe, was all his days
an Episcopalian Dissenter in Scotland; but that makes little
to the matter. Nobody who knows Scotland and Scott can
doubt but Presbyterianism too had a vast share in the forming of him. A country where the entire people is, or even
once has been, laid hold of, filled to the heart with an infinite
religious idea, has ' made a step from which it cannot retrograde.' Thought, conscience, the sense that man is denizen
of a Universe, creature of an Eternity, has penetrated to
the remotest cottage, to the simplest heart. Beautiful and
awful, the feeling of a Heavenly Behest, of Duty god-com-
manded, over-canopies all life. There is an inspiration in
such a people: one may say in a more special sense, ' the
inspiration of the Almighty giveth them understanding.'
Honour to all the brave and true; everlasting honour to
brave old Knox, one of the truest of the true! That, in the

moment while he and his cause, amid civil broils, in convulsion and confusion, were still but struggling for life, he sent the schoolmaster forth to all corners, and said, " Let the people be taught "; this is but one, and indeed an inevitable and comparatively inconsiderable item in his great message to men. His message, in its true compass, was, " Let men know that they are men; created by God, responsible to God; who work in any meanest moment of time what will last throughout eternity." It is verily a great message. Not ploughing and hammering machines, not patent-digesters (never so ornamental) to digest the produce of these: no, in no wise; born slaves neither of their fellow-men, nor of their own appetites; but men! This great message Knox did deliver, with a man's voice and strength; and found a people to believe him.

Of such an achievement, we say, were it to be made once only, the results are immense. Thought, in such a country, may change its form, but cannot go out; the country has attained *majority;* thought, and a certain spiritual manhood, ready for all work that man can do, endures there. It may take many forms: the form of hard-fisted money-getting industry, as in the vulgar Scotchman, in the vulgar New Englander; but as compact developed force and alertness of faculty, it is still there; it may utter itself one day as the colossal Scepticism of a Hume (beneficent this too though painful, wrestling Titan-like through doubt and inquiry towards new belief) ; and again, some better day, it may utter itself as the inspired Melody of a Burns: in a word, it is there, and continues to manifest itself, in the Voice and the Work of a Nation of hardy endeavouring considering men, with whatever that may bear in it, or unfold from it. The Scotch national character originates in many circumstances; first of all, in the Saxon stuff there was to work on; but next, and beyond all else except that, in the Presbyterian Gospel of John Knox. It seems a good national character; and on some sides not so good. Let Scott thank John Knox, for he owed him much, little as he dreamed of debt in that quarter! No Scotchman of his time was more entirely Scotch than Walter Scott: the good and the not so good, which all Scotchmen inherit, ran through every fibre of him.

Scott's childhood, school-days, college-days, are pleasant
to read of, though they differ not from those of others in his
place and time. The memory of him may probably enough
last till this record of them become far more curious than it
now is. " So lived an Edinburgh Writer to the Signet's son
in the end of the eighteenth century," may some future
Scotch novelist say to himself in the end of the twenty-first!
The following little fragment of infancy is all we can extract. It is from an Autobiography which he had begun,
which one cannot but regret he did not finish. Scott's best
qualities never shone out more freely than when he went
upon anecdote and reminiscence. Such a master of narrative and of himself could have done personal narrative well.
Here, if anywhere, his knowledge was complete, and all his
humour and good-humour had free scope:

'An odd incident is worth recording. It seems, my mother had
sent a maid to take charge of me, at this farm of Sandy-Knowe, that
I might be no inconvenience to the family. But the damsel sent on
that important mission had left her heart behind her, in the keeping
of some wild fellow, it is likely, who had done and said more to her
than he was like to make good. She became extremely desirous to
return to Edinburgh; and, as my mother made a point of her remaining where she was, she contracted a sort of hatred at poor me, as
the cause of her being detained at Sandy-Knowe. This rose, I suppose, to a sort of delirious affection; for she confessed to old Alison
Wilson, the housekeeper, that she had carried me up to the craigs
under a strong temptation of the Devil to cut my throat with her
scissors, and bury me in the moss. Alison instantly took possession
of my person, and took care that her confidant should not be subject to any farther temptation, at least so far as I was concerned.
She was dismissed of course, and I have heard afterwards became a
lunatic.

'It is here, at Sandy-Knowe, in the residence of my paternal
grandfather, already mentioned, that I have the first consciousness
of existence; and I recollect distinctly that my situation and appearance were a little whimsical. Among the odd remedies recurred
to, to aid my lameness, some one had recommended that so often as a
sheep was killed for the use of the family, I should be stripped, and
swathed-up in the skin warm as it was flayed from the carcass of
the animal. In this Tartar-like habiliment I well remember lying
upon the floor of the little parlour in the farmhouse, while my grandfather, a venerable old man with white hair, used every excitement
to make me try to crawl. I also distinctly remember the late Sir
George M'Dougal of Mackerstown, father of the present Sir Henry
Hay M'Dougal, joining in the attempt. He was, God knows how, a
relation of ours; and I still recollect him, in his old-fashioned mili-

tary habit (he had been Colonel of the Greys), with a small cocked-hat deeply laced, an embroidered scarlet waistcoat, and a light-coloured coat, with milk-white locks tied in a military fashion, kneeling on the ground before me, and dragging his watch along the carpet to induce me to follow it. The benevolent old soldier, and the infant wrapped in his sheepskin, would have afforded an odd group to uninterested spectators. This must have happened about my third year (1774), for Sir George M'Dougal and my grandfather both died shortly after that period.'[2]

We will glance next into the '*Liddesdale Raids.*' Scott has grown-up to be a brisk-hearted jovial young man and Advocate: in vacation-time he makes excursions to the Highlands, to the Border Cheviots and Northumberland; rides free and far, on his stout galloway, through bog and brake, over the dim moory Debatable Land,—over Flodden and other fields and places, where, though he yet knew it not, his work lay. No land, however dim and moory, but either has had or will have its poet, and so become not unknown in song. Liddesdale, which was once as prosaic as most dales, having now attained illustration, let us glance thitherward: Liddesdale too is on this ancient Earth of ours, under this eternal Sky; and gives and takes, in the most incalculable manner, with the Universe at large! Scott's experiences there are rather of the rustic Arcadian sort; the element of whisky not wanting. We should premise that here and there a feature has, perhaps, been aggravated for effect's sake:

'During seven successive years,' writes Mr. Lockhart (for the Autobiography has long since left us), 'Scott made a *raid,* as he called it, into Liddesdale with Mr. Shortreed, sheriff-substitute of Roxburgh, for his guide; exploring every rivulet to its source, and every ruined *peel* from foundation to battlement. At this time no wheeled carriage had ever been seen in the district;—the first, indeed, was a gig, driven by Scott himself for a part of his way, when on the last of these seven excursions. There was no inn nor publichouse of any kind in the whole valley; the travellers passed from the shepherd's hut to the minister's manse, and again from the cheerful hospitality of the manse to the rough and jolly welcome of the homestead; gathering, wherever they went, songs and tunes, and occasionally more tangible relics of antiquity, even such a "rowth of auld knicknackets" as Burns ascribes to Captain Grose. To these rambles Scott owed much of the materials of his *Minstrelsy of the Scottish Border;* and not less of that intimate acquaintance with

the living manners of these unsophisticated regions, which constitutes the chief charm of one of the most charming of his prose
works. But how soon he had any definite object before him in his
researches seems very doubtful. "He was *makin' himsell* a' the
time," said Mr. Shortreed; "but he didna ken maybe what he was
about till years had passed: at first he thought o' little, I daresay, but
the queerness and the fun."

'"In those days," says the Memorandum before me, "advocates
were not so plenty—at least about Liddesdale;" and the worthy
Sheriff-substitute goes on to describe the sort of bustle, not unmixed
with alarm, produced at the first farmhouse they visited (Willie
Elliot's at Millburnholm), when the honest man was informed of
the quality of one of his guests. When they dismounted, accordingly, he received Mr. Scott with great ceremony, and insisted upon
himself leading his horse to the stable. Shortreed accompanied
Willie, however; and the latter, after taking a deliberate peep at
Scott, "out-by the edge of the door-cheek," whispered, "Weel,
Robin, I say, de'il hae me if I's be a bit feared for him now; he's
just a chield like ourselves, I think." Half-a-dozen dogs of all
degrees had already gathered round "the advocate," and his way
of returning their compliments had set Willie Elliott at once at
his ease.

' According to Mr. Shortreed, this good man of Millburnholm was
the great original of Dandie Dinmont.' * * * ' They dined at Millburnholm; and, after having lingered over Willie Elliot's punch-
bowl, until, in Mr. Shortreed's phrase, they were "half-glowrin',"
mounted their steeds again, and proceeded to Dr. Elliot's at Cleugh-
head, where ("for," says my Memorandum, "folk werena very
nice in those days") the two travellers slept in one and the same
bed,—as, indeed, seems to have been the case with them throughout
most of their excursions in this primitive district. Dr. Elliot (a
clergyman) had already a large MS. collection of the ballads Scott
was in quest of.' * * * ' Next morning they seem to have ridden a
long way for the express purpose of visiting one "auld Thomas
o' Tuzzilehope," another Elliot, I suppose, who was celebrated for
his skill on the Border pipe, and in particular for being in possession of the real *lilt*[3] of *Dick o' the Cowe*. Before starting, that
is, at six o'clock, the ballad-hunters had, "just to lay the stomach,
a devilled duck or twae and some *London* porter." Auld Thomas
found them, nevertheless, well disposed for "breakfast" on their
arrival at Tuzzilehope; and this being over, he delighted them with
one of the most hideous and unearthly of all specimens of "riding
music," and, moreover, with considerable libations of whisky-punch,
manufactured in a certain wooden vessel, resembling a very small
milkpail, which he called "Wisdom," because it "made" only a few
spoonfuls of spirits,—though he had the art of replenishing it so
adroitly, that it had been celebrated for fifty years as more fatal to
sobriety than any bowl in the parish. Having done due honour to
"Wisdom," they again mounted, and proceeded over moss and moor

[3] Loud tune: German, *lallen*.

to some other equally hospitable master of the pipe. " Ah me," says Shortreed, " sic an endless fund o' humour and drollery as he then had wi' him ! Never ten yards but we were either laughing or roaring and singing. Wherever we stopped, how brawlie he suited himsell to everybody ! He aye did as the lave did ; never made himsell the great man, or took ony airs in the company. I've seen him in a' moods in these jaunts, grave and gay, daft and serious, sober and drunk—(this, however, even in our wildest rambles, was rare)—but, drunk or sober, he was aye the gentleman. He lookit excessively heavy and stupid when he was *fou*, but he was never out o' gude humour." '

These are questionable doings, questionably narrated ; but what shall we say of the following, wherein the element of whisky plays an extremely prominent part ? We will say that it *is* questionable, and not exemplary, whisky mounting clearly beyond its level ; that indeed charity hopes and conjectures here may be some aggravating of features for effect's sake !

' On reaching, one evening, some *Charlieshope* or other (I forget the name) among those wildernesses, they found a kindly reception, as usual ; but, to their agreeable surprise after some days of hard living, a measured and orderly hospitality as respected liquor. Soon after supper, at which a bottle of elderberry-wine alone had been produced, a young student of divinity, who happened to be in the house, was called upon to take the " big ha' Bible," in the good old fashion of Burns's " Saturday Night " ; and some progress had been already made in the service, when the good-man of the farm, whose " tendency," as Mr. Mitchell says, " was soporific," scandalised his wife and the dominie by starting suddenly from his knees, and, rubbing his eyes, with a stentorian exclamation of " By ——, here's the keg at last ! " and in tumbled, as he spoke the word, a couple of sturdy herdsmen, whom, on hearing a day before of the advocate's approaching visit, he had despatched to a certain smuggler's haunt, at some considerable distance, in quest of a supply of *run* brandy from the Solway Frith. The pious " exercise " of the household was hopelessly interrupted. With a thousand apologies for his hitherto shabby entertainment, this jolly Elliot, or Armstrong, had the welcome *keg* mounted on the table without a moment's delay ; and gentle and simple, not forgetting the dominie, continued carousing about it until daylight streamed-in upon the party. Sir Walter Scott seldom failed, when I saw him in company with his Liddesdale companion, to mimic with infinite humour the sudden outburst of his old host on hearing the clatter of horses' feet, which he knew to indicate the arrival of the keg—the consternation of the dame—and the rueful despair with which the young clergyman closed the book.' [4]

[4] Vol. i. pp. 195-199.

From which Liddesdale *raids,* which we here, like the young clergyman, close not without a certain rueful despair, let the reader draw what nourishment he can. They evince satisfactorily, though in a rude manner, that in those days young advocates, and Scott like the rest of them, were *alive* and alert,—whisky sometimes preponderating. But let us now fancy that the jovial young Advocate has pleaded his first cause; has served in yeomanry drills; been wedded, been promoted Sheriff, without romance in either case; dabbling a little the while, under guidance of Monk Lewis, in translations from the German, in translation of Goethe's *Götz with the Iron Hand;*—and we have arrived at the threshold of the *Minstrelsy of the Scottish Border,* and the opening of a new century.

Hitherto, therefore, there has been made out, by Nature and Circumstance working together, nothing unusually remarkable, yet still something very valuable; a stout effectual man of thirty, full of broad sagacity and good humour, with faculties in him fit for any burden of business, hospitality and duty, legal or civic:—with what other faculties in him no one could yet say. As indeed, who, after lifelong inspection, can say what is in any man? The uttered part of a man's life, let us always repeat, bears to the unuttered unconscious part a small unknown proportion; he himself never knows it, much less do others. Give him room, give him *impulse;* he reaches down to the Infinite with that so straitly-imprisoned soul of his; and *can* do miracles if need be! It is one of the comfortablest truths that great men abound, though in the unknown state. Nay, as above hinted, our greatest, being also by nature our *quietest,* are perhaps those that remain unknown! Philosopher Fichte took comfort in this belief, when from all pulpits and editorial desks, and publications periodical and stationary, he could hear nothing but the infinite chattering and twittering of commonplace become ambitious; and in the infinite stir of motion nowhither, and of din which should have been silence, all seemed churned into one tempestuous yeasty froth, and the stern Fichte almost desired 'taxes on knowledge' to allay it a little;—he comforted himself, we say, by the unshaken belief that Thought did still exist in Germany; that thinking

men, each in his own corner, were verily doing their work,
though in a silent latent manner.[5]

Walter Scott, as a latent Walter, had never amused all
men for a score of years in the course of centuries and eter-
nities, or gained and lost several hundred thousand pounds
sterling by Literature; but he might have been a happy and
by no means a useless,—nay, who knows at bottom whether
not a still usefuler Walter! However, that was not his
fortune. The Genius of rather a singular age,—an age at
once destitute of faith and terrified at scepticism, with little
knowledge of its whereabout, with many sorrows to bear or
front, and on the whole with a life to lead in these new circumstances,—had said to himself: What man shall be the
temporary comforter, or were it but the spiritual comfit-
maker, of this my poor singular age, to solace its dead tedium
and manifold sorrows a little? So had the Genius said,
looking over all the world, What man? and found him walking the dusty Outer Parliament-house of Edinburgh, with
his advocate-gown on his back; and exclaimed, That is he!

The *Minstrelsy of the Scottish Border* proved to be a well
from which flowed one of the broadest rivers. Metrical
Romances (which in due time pass into Prose Romances);
the old life of men resuscitated for us: it is a mighty word!
Not as dead tradition, but as a palpable presence, the past
stood before us. There they were, the rugged old fighting
men; in their doughty simplicity and strength, with their
heartiness, their healthiness, their stout self-help, in their
iron basnets, leather jerkins, jack-boots, in their quaintness
of manner and costume; there as they looked and lived: it
was like a new-discovered continent in Literature; for the
new century, a bright El Dorado,—or else some fat beatific
land of Cockaigne, and Paradise of Donothings. To the
opening nineteenth century, in its languor and paralysis,
nothing could have been welcomer. Most unexpected, most
refreshing and exhilarating; behold our new El Dorado; our
fat beatific Lubberland, where one can enjoy and do nothing!
It was the time for such a new Literature; and this Walter
Scott was the man for it. The *Lays,* the *Marmions,* the
Ladys and *Lords* of Lake and Isles, followed in quick suc-

[5] Fichte, *Über das Wesen des Gelehrten.*

cession, with ever-widening profit and praise. How many thousands of guineas were paid-down for each new Lay; how many thousands of copies (fifty and more sometimes) were printed off, then and subsequently; what complimenting, reviewing, renown and apotheosis there was: all is recorded in these Seven Volumes, which will be valuable in literary statistics. It is a history, brilliant, remarkable; the outlines of which are known to all. The reader shall recall it, or conceive it. No blaze in his fancy is likely to mount higher than the reality did.

At this middle period of his life, therefore, Scott, enriched with copyrights, with new official incomes and promotions, rich in money, rich in repute, presents himself as a man in the full career of success. ' Health, wealth, and wit to guide them' (as his vernacular Proverb says), all these three are his. The field is open for him, and victory there; his own faculty, his own self, unshackled, victoriously unfolds itself, —the highest blessedness that can befall a man. Wide circle of friends, personal loving admirers; warmth of domestic joys, vouchsafed to all that can true-heartedly nestle down among them; light of radiance and renown given only to a few: who would not call Scott happy? But the happiest circumstance of all is, as we said above, that Scott had in himself a right healthy soul, rendering him little dependent on outward circumstances. Things showed themselves to him not in distortion or borrowed light or gloom, but as they were. Endeavour lay in him and endurance, in due measure; and clear vision of what was to be endeavoured after. Were one to preach a Sermon on Health, as really were worth doing, Scott ought to be the text. Theories are demonstrably true in the way of logic; and then in the way of practice they prove true or else not true: but here is the grand experiment, Do they turn-out well? What boots it that a man's creed is the wisest, that his system of principles is the superfinest, if, when set to work, the life of him does nothing but jar, and fret itself into *holes?* They are untrue in that, were it in nothing else, these principles of his; openly convicted of untruth;—fit only, shall we say, to be rejected as counterfeits, and flung to the dogs? We say not that; but we do say, that ill-health, of body or of mind, is *defeat,* is battle (in a good or in a bad cause) with bad success; that health alone is victory. Let all men, if they can manage it, contrive to be healthy! He who in what cause soever sinks into pain and disease, let him take thought of it; let him know well that it is not good *he* has arrived at yet, but surely evil,—may, or may not be, on the way towards good.

Scott's healthiness showed itself decisively in all things, and nowhere more decisively than in this: the way in which he took his fame; the estimate he from the first formed of fame. Money will buy money's worth; but the thing men call fame, what is it? A gaudy emblazonry, not good for much,—except, indeed, as it too may turn to money. To Scott it was a profitable pleasing superfluity, no necessary of life. Not necessary, now or ever! Seemingly without much effort, but taught by Nature, and the instinct which instructs the sound heart what is good for it and what is not, he felt that he could always do without this same emblazonry of reputation; that he ought to put no trust in it; but be ready at any time to see it pass away from him, and to hold on his way as before. It is incalculable, as we conjecture, what evil he escaped in this manner; what perversions, irritations, mean agonies without a name, he lived wholly apart from, knew nothing of. Happily before fame arrived, he had reached the mature age at which all this was easier to him. What a strange Nemesis lurks in the felicities of men! In thy mouth it shall be sweet as honey, in thy belly it shall be bitter as gall! Some weakly-organised individual, we will say at the age of five-and-twenty, whose main or whole talent rests on some prurient susceptivity, and nothing under it but shallowness and vacuum, is clutched hold of by the general imagination, is whirled aloft to the giddy height; and taught to believe the divine-seeming message that he is a great man: such individual seems the luckiest of men: and, alas, is he not the unluckiest? Swallow not the Circe-draught, O weakly-organised individual; it is fell poison; it will dry up the fountains of thy whole existence, and all will grow withered and parched; thou shalt be wretched under the sun!

Is there, for example, a sadder book than that *Life of Byron* by Moore? To omit mere prurient susceptivities that

rest on vacuum, look at poor Byron, who really had much
substance in him. Sitting there in his self-exile, with a
proud heart striving to persuade itself that it despises the
entire created Universe; and far off, in foggy Babylon, let
any pitifulest whipster draw pen on him, your proud Byron
writhes in torture,—as if the pitiful whipster were a magician, or his pen a galvanic wire struck into the Byron's
spinal marrow! Lamentable, despicable,—one had rather be
a kitten and cry mew! O son of Adam, great or little,
according as thou art lovable, those thou livest with will
love thee. Those thou livest *not* with, is it of moment that
they have the alphabetic letters of thy name engraved on
their memory, with some signpost likeness of thee (as like
as I to Hercules) appended to them? It is not of moment;
in sober truth, not of any moment at all! And yet, behold,
there is no soul now whom thou canst love freely,—from
one soul only art thou always sure of reverence enough; in
presence of no soul is it rightly well with thee! How is
thy world become desert; and thou, for the sake of a little
babblement of tongues, art poor, bankrupt, insolvent not in
purse, but in heart and mind! 'The Golden Calf of self-
love,' says Jean Paul, 'has grown into a burning Phalaris'
Bull, to consume its owner and worshipper.' Ambition, the
desire of shining and outshining, was the beginning of Sin
in this world. The man of letters who founds upon his
fame, does he not thereby alone declare himself a follower
of Lucifer (named *Satan,* the Enemy), and member of the
Satanic school?——

It was in this poetic period that Scott formed his connexion with the Ballantynes; and embarked, though under
cover, largely in trade. To those who regard him in the
heroic light, and will have *Vates* to signify Prophet as well
as Poet, this portion of his biography seems somewhat incongruous. Viewed as it stood in the reality, as he was and as
it was, the enterprise, since it proved so unfortunate, may be
called lamentable, but cannot be called unnatural. The
practical Scott, looking towards practical issues in all things,
could not but find hard cash one of the most practical. If
by any means cash could be honestly produced, were it by

writing poems, were it by printing them, why not? Great
things might be done ultimately; great difficulties were at
once got rid of,—manifold higglings of booksellers, and contradictions of sinners hereby fell away. A printing and
bookselling speculation was not so alien for a maker of
books. Voltaire, who indeed got no copyrights, made much
money by the war-commissariat, in his time; we believe, by
the victualling branch of it. St. George himself, they say,
was a dealer in bacon in Cappadocia. A thrifty man will
help himself towards his object by such steps as lead to
it. Station in society, solid power over the good things
of this world, was Scott's avowed object; towards which
the precept of precepts is that of Iago, *Put money in
thy purse.*

Here, indeed, it is to be remarked, that perhaps no literary
man of any generation has less value than Scott for the
immaterial part of his mission in any sense: not only for
the fantasy called fame, with the fantastic miseries attendant
thereon; but also for the spiritual purport of his work,
whether it tended hitherward or thitherward, or had any
tendency whatever; and indeed for all purports and results
of his working, except such, we may say, as offered themselves to the eye, and could, in one sense or the other, be
handled, looked at and buttoned into the breeches-pocket.
Somewhat too little of a fantast, this *Vates* of ours! But so
it was: in this nineteenth century, our highest literary man,
who immeasurably beyond all others commanded the world's
ear, had, as it were, no message whatever to deliver to the
world; wished not the world to elevate itself, to amend itself,
to do this or to do that, except simply pay him for the books
he kept writing. Very remarkable; fittest, perhaps, for an
age fallen languid, destitute of faith and terrified at scepticism? Or, perhaps, for quite another sort of age, an age all
in peaceable triumphant motion? Be this as it may, surely
since Shakspeare's time there has been no great speaker so
unconscious of an aim in speaking as Walter Scott. Equally
unconscious these two utterances: equally the sincere complete products of the minds they came from: and now if
they were equally *deep?* Or, if the one was living fire, and
the other was futile phosphorescence and mere resinous fire-

work? It will depend on the relative worth of the minds; for both were equally spontaneous, both equally expressed themselves unencumbered by an ulterior aim. Beyond drawing audiences to the Globe Theatre, Shakspeare contemplated no result in those plays of his. Yet they have had results! Utter with free heart what thy own *dæmon* gives thee: if fire from heaven, it shall be well; if resinous firework, it shall be—as well as it could be, or better than otherwise!

The candid judge will, in general, require that a speaker, in so extremely serious a Universe as this of ours, have something to speak about. In the heart of the speaker there ought to be some kind of gospel-tidings, burning till it be uttered; otherwise it were better for him that he altogether held his peace. A gospel somewhat more decisive than this of Scott's,—except to an age altogether languid, without either scepticism or faith! These things the candid judge will demand of literary men; yet withal will recognise the great worth there is in Scott's honesty if in nothing more, in his being the thing he was with such entire good faith. Here is a something, not a nothing. If no skyborn messenger, heaven looking through his eyes; then neither is it a chimera with his systems, crotchets, cants, fanaticisms, and 'last infirmity of noble minds,'—full of misery, unrest and ill-will; but a substantial, peaceable, terrestrial man. Far as the Earth is under the Heaven does Scott stand below the former sort of character; but high as the cheerful flowery Earth is above waste Tartarus does he stand above the latter. Let him live in his own fashion, and do honour to him in that.

It were late in the day to write criticisms on those Metrical Romances: at the same time, we may remark, the great popularity they had seems natural enough. In the first place, there was the indisputable impress of worth, of genuine human force, in them. This, which lies in some degree, or is thought to lie, at the bottom of all popularity, did to an unusual degree disclose itself in these rhymed romances of Scott's. Pictures were actually painted and presented; human emotions conceived and sympathised with. Considering what wretched Della-Cruscan and other vamp-

ing-up of old worn-out tatters was the staple article then, it
may be granted that Scott's excellence was superior and
supreme. When a Hayley was the main singer, a Scott
might well be hailed with warm welcome. Consider whether
the *Loves of the Plants,* and even the *Loves of the Triangles,*
could be worth the loves and hates of men and women!
Scott was as preferable to what he displaced, as the substance
is to wearisomely repeated shadow of a substance.

But, in the second place, we may say that the *kind* of
worth which Scott manifested was fitted especially for the
then temper of men. We have called it an age fallen into
spiritual languor, destitute of belief, yet terrified at Scepticism; reduced to live a stinted half-life, under strange new
circumstances. Now vigorous whole-life, this was what of
all things these delineations offered. The reader was carried
back to rough strong times, wherein those maladies of ours
had not yet arisen. Brawny fighters, all cased in buff and
iron, their hearts too sheathed in oak and triple brass,
caprioled their huge war-horses, shook their death-doing
spears; and went forth in the most determined manner,
nothing doubting. The reader sighed, yet not without a
reflex solacement: "O, that I too had lived in those times,
had never known these logic-cobwebs, this doubt, this sickli-
ness; and been and felt myself alive among men alive!"
Add lastly, that in this new-found poetic world there was no
call for effort on the reader's part; what excellence they had,
exhibited itself at a glance. It was for the reader, not the
El Dorado only, but a beatific land of Cockaigne and
Paradise of Donothings! The reader, what the vast majority
of readers so long to do, was allowed to lie down at his ease,
and be ministered to. What the Turkish bathkeeper is said
to aim at with his frictions, and shampooings, and foment-
ings, more or less effectually, that the patient in total idleness may have the delights of activity,—was here to a
considerable extent realised. The languid imagination fell
back into its rest; an artist was there who could supply it
with high-painted scenes, with sequences of stirring action,
and whisper to it, Be at ease, and let thy tepid element be
comfortable to thee. 'The rude man,' says a critic, 'requires
only to see something going on. The man of more refine-

ment must be made to feel. The man of complete refinement must be made to reflect.'

We named the *Minstrelsy of the Scottish Border* the fountain from which flowed this great river of Metrical Romances; but according to some they can be traced to a still higher, obscurer spring; to Goethe's *Götz von Berlichingen with the Iron Hand;* of which, as we have seen, Scott in his earlier days executed a translation. Dated a good many years ago, the following words in a criticism on Goethe are found written; which probably are still new to most readers of this Review:

' The works just mentioned, *Götz* and *Werter,* though noble specimens of youthful talent, are still not so much distinguished by their intrinsic merits as by their splendid fortune. It would be difficult to name two books which have exercised a deeper influence on the subsequent literature of Europe than these two performances of a young author; his first-fruits, the produce of his twenty-fourth year. *Werter* appeared to seize the hearts of men in all quarters of the world, and to utter for them the word which they had long been waiting to hear. As usually happens too, this same word, once uttered, was soon abundantly repeated; spoken in all dialects, and chanted through all notes of the gamut, till the sound of it had grown a weariness rather than a pleasure   Sceptical sentimentality, view-hunting, love, friendship, suicide and desperation, became the staple of literary ware; and though the epidemic, after a long course of years, subsided in Germany, it reappeared with various modifications in other countries, and everywhere abundant traces of its good and bad effects are still to be discerned. The fortune of *Berlichingen with the Iron Hand,* though less sudden, was by no means less exalted. In his own country, *Götz,* though he now stands solitary and childless, became the parent of an innumerable progeny of chivalry plays, feudal delineations, and poetico-antiquarian performances; which, though long ago deceased, made noise enough in their day and generation: and with ourselves his influence has been perhaps still more remarkable. Sir Walter Scott's first literary enterprise was a translation of *Götz von Berlichingen:* and, if genius could be communicated like instruction, we might call this work of Goethe's the prime cause of *Marmion* and the *Lady of the Lake,* with all that has followed from the same creative hand. Truly, a grain of seed that has lighted in the right soil! For if not firmer and fairer, it has grown to be taller and broader than any other tree; and all the nations of the earth are still yearly gathering of its fruit.'

How far *Götz von Berlichingen* actually affected Scott's literary destination, and whether without it the rhymed romances, and then the prose romances of the Author of

Waverley, would not have followed as they did, must remain a very obscure question; obscure and not important. Of the fact, however, there is no doubt, that these two tendencies, which may be named *Götzism* and *Werterism,* of the former of which Scott was representative with us, have made, and are still in some quarters making the tour of all Europe. In Germany too there was this affectionate half-regretful looking-back into the Past; Germany had its buff-belted watch-tower period in literature, and had even got done with it before Scott began. Then as to *Werterism,* had not we English our Byron and his genus? No form of Werterism in any other country had half the potency; as our Scott carried Chivalry Literature to the ends of the world, so did our Byron Werterism. France, busy with its Revolution and Napoleon, had little leisure at the moment for Götzism or Werterism; but it has had them both since, in a shape of its own: witness the whole 'Literature of Desperation' in our own days; the beggarliest form of Werterism yet seen, probably its expiring final form: witness also, at the other extremity of the scale, a noble-gifted Chateaubriand, Götz and Werter both in one.—Curious: how all Europe is but like a set of parishes of the same county; participant of the self-same influences, ever since the Crusades, and earlier;—and these glorious wars of ours are but like parish-brawls, which begin in mutual ignorance, intoxication and boastful speech; which end in broken windows, damage, waste and bloody noses; and which one hopes the general good sense is now in the way towards putting down, in some measure!

But leaving this to be as it can, what it concerned us here to remark, was that British Werterism, in the shape of those Byron Poems, so potent and poignant, produced on the languid appetite of men a mighty effect. This too was a 'class of feelings deeply important to modern minds; feelings which arise from *passion incapable of being converted into action,* which belong to an age as indolent, cultivated and unbelieving as our own'! The 'languid age without either faith or scepticism' turned towards Byronism with an interest altogether peculiar: here, if no cure for its miserable paralysis and languor, was at least an indignant statement of

the misery; an indignant Ernulphus' curse read over it,—
which all men felt to be something. Half-regretful look-
ings in the Past gave place, in many quarters, to Ernulphus'
cursings of the Present. Scott was among the first to perceive that the day of Metrical Chivalry Romances was declining. He had held the sovereignty for some half-score of
years, a comparatively long lease of it; and now the time
seemed come for dethronement, for abdication: an unpleasant business; which however he held himself ready, as a
brave man will, to transact with composure and in silence.
After all, Poetry was not his staff of life; Poetry had
already yielded him much money; *this* at least it would not
take back from him. Busy always with editing, with com-
piling, with multiplex official commercial business, and solid
interests, he beheld the coming change with unmoved eye.

Resignation he was prepared to exhibit in this matter;—
and now behold there proved to be no need of resignation.
Let the Metrical Romance become a Prose one; shake off
its rhyme-fetters, and try a wider sweep! In the spring of
1814 appeared *Waverley;* an event memorable in the annals
of British Literature; in the annals of British Bookselling
thrice and four times memorable. Byron sang, but Scott
narrated; and when the song had sung itself out through all
variations onwards to the *Don Juan* one, Scott was still
found narrating, and carrying the whole world along with
him. All bygone popularity of chivalry-lays was swallowed
up in a far greater. What 'series' followed out of *Waverley*, and how and with what result, is known to all men;
was witnessed and watched with a kind of rapt astonishment
by all. Hardly any literary reputation ever rose so high in
our Island; no reputation at all ever spread so wide. Walter
Scott became Sir Walter Scott, Baronet, of Abbotsford; on
whom Fortune seemed to pour her whole cornucopia of
wealth, honour and worldly goods; the favourite of Princes
and of Peasants, and all intermediate men. His 'Waverley
series,' swift-following one on the other apparently without
end, was the universal reading; looked for like an annual
harvest, by all ranks, in all European countries.

A curious circumstance superadded itself, that the author
though known was unknown. From the first most people

suspected, and soon after the first, few intelligent persons much doubted, that the Author of *Waverley* was Walter Scott. Yet 'a certain mystery was still kept up; rather piquant to the public; doubtless very pleasant to the author, who saw it all; who probably had not to listen, as other hapless individuals often had, to this or the other long-drawn 'clear proof at last,' that the author was not Walter Scott, but a certain astonishing Mr. So-and-so;—one of the standing miseries of human life in that time. But for the privileged Author it was like a king travelling incognito. All men know that he is a high king, chivalrous Gustaf or Kaiser Joseph; but he mingles in their meetings without cumber of etiquette or lonesome ceremony, as Chevalier du Nord, or Count of Lorraine: he has none of the weariness of royalty, and yet all the praise, and the satisfaction of hearing it with his own ears. In a word, the Waverley Novels circulated and reigned triumphant; to the general imagination the 'Author of *Waverley*' was like some living mythological personage, and ranked among the chief wonders of the world.

How a man lived and demeaned himself in such unwonted circumstances, is worth seeing. We would gladly quote from Scott's correspondence of this period; but that does not much illustrate the matter. His letters, as above stated, are never without interest, yet also seldom or never very interesting. They are full of cheerfulness, of wit and ingenuity; but they do not treat of aught intimate; without impeaching their sincerity, what is called sincerity, one may say they do not, in any case whatever, proceed from the innermost parts of the mind. Conventional forms, due consideration of your own and your correspondent's pretensions and vanities, are at no moment left out of view. The epistolary stream runs on, lucid, free, gladflowing; but always, as it were, *parallel* to the real substance of the matter, never coincident with it. One feels it hollowish under foot. Letters they are of a most humane man of the world, even exemplary in that kind; but with the man of the world always visible in them;—as indeed it was little in Scott's way to speak, perhaps even with himself, in any other fashion.

We select rather some glimpses of him from Mr. Lockhart's record. The first is of dining with Royalty or Prince-Regentship itself; an almost official matter:

' On hearing from Mr. Croker (then Secretary to the Admiralty) that Scott was to be in town by the middle of March (1815), the Prince said, " Let me know when he comes, and I'll get-up a snug little dinner that will suit him;" and after he had been presented and graciously received at the *levée,* he was invited to dinner accordingly, through his excellent friend Mr. Adam (now Lord Chief Commissioner of the Jury Court in Scotland), who at that time held a confidential office in the royal household. The Regent had consulted with Mr. Adam, also, as to the composition of the party. " Let us have," said he, " just a few friends of his own, and the more Scotch the better;" and both the Commissioner and Mr. Croker assure me that the party was the most interesting and agreeable one in their recollection. It comprised, I believe, the Duke of York—the Duke of Gordon (then Marquess of Huntly)—the Marquess of Hertford (then Lord Yarmouth)—the Earl of Fife—and Scott's early friend, Lord Melville. " The Prince and Scott," says Mr. Croker, " were the two most brilliant story-tellers, in their several ways, that I have ever happened to meet; they were both aware of their *forte,* and both exerted themselves that evening with delightful effect. On going home, I really could not decide which of them had shone the most. The Regent was enchanted with Scott, as Scott with him; and on all his subsequent visits to London, he was a frequent guest at the royal table." The Lord Chief Commissioner remembers that the Prince was particularly delighted with the poet's anecdotes of the old Scotch judges and lawyers, which his Royal Highness sometimes *capped* by ludicrous traits of certain ermine sages of his own acquaintance. Scott told, among others, a story, which he was fond of telling, of his old friend the Lord Justice-Clerk Braxfield; and the commentary of his Royal Highness on hearing it amused Scott, who often mentioned it afterwards. The anecdote is this: Braxfield, whenever he went on a particular circuit was in the habit of visiting a gentleman of good fortune in the neighbourhood of one of the assize towns, and staying at least one night, which, being both of them ardent chess-players, they usually concluded with their favourite game. One Spring circuit the battle was not decided at daybreak; so the Justice-Clerk said, " Weel, Donald, I must e'en come back this gate, and let the game lie ower for the present:" and back he came in October, but not to his old friend's hospitable house; for that gentleman had in the interim been apprehended on a capital charge (of forgery), and his name stood on the *Porteous Roll,* or list of those who were about to be tried under his former guest's auspices. The laird was indicted and tried accordingly, and the jury returned a verdict of *guilty.* Braxfield forthwith put on his cocked hat (which answers to the black cap in England), and pronounced the sentence of the law in the usual terms—" To be hanged by the neck until you be dead; and may the Lord have mercy upon your unhappy soul ! "

Having concluded this awful formula in his most sonorous cadence, Braxfield, dismounting his formidable beaver, gave a familiar nod to his unfortunate acquaintance, and said to him in a sort of chuckling whisper, "And now, Donald my man, I think I've checkmated you for ance." The Regent laughed heartily at this specimen of Macqueen's brutal humour; and "I' faith, Walter," said he, "this old big-wig seems to have taken things as coolly as my tyrannical self. Don't you remember Tom Moore's description of me at breakfast—

> "The table spread with tea and toast,
> Death-warrants and the *Morning Post?*"

'Towards midnight the Prince called for "a bumper, with all the honours, to the Author of *Waverley*"; and looked significantly, as he was charging his own glass, to Scott. Scott seemed somewhat puzzled for a moment, but instantly recovering himself, and filling his glass to the brim, said, "Your Royal Highness looks as if you thought I had some claim to the honours of this toast. I have no such pretensions; but shall take good care that the real Simon Pure hears of the high compliment that has now been paid him." He then drank-off his claret; and joined with a stentorian voice in the cheering, which the Prince himself timed. But before the company could resume their seats, his Royal Highness, "Another of the same, if you please, to the Author of *Marmion*,—and now, Walter my man, I have checkmated you for *ance*." The second bumper was followed by cheers still more prolonged: and Scott then rose, and returned thanks in a short address, which struck the Lord Chief Commissioner as "alike grave and graceful." This story has been circulated in a very perverted shape.' * * * 'Before he left town he again dined at Carlton House, when the party was a still smaller one than before, and the merriment if possible still more free. That nothing might be wanting, the Prince sang several capital songs.'[6]

Or take, at a very great interval in many senses, this glimpse of another dinner, altogether *un*officially and much better described. It is James Ballantyne the printer and publisher's dinner, in St. John Street, Canongate, Edinburgh, on the birth-eve of a Waverley Novel:

'The feast was, to use one of James's own favourite epithets, *gorgeous;* an aldermanic display of turtle and venison, with the suitable accompaniments of iced punch, potent ale, and generous Madeira. When the cloth was drawn, the burly *præses* arose, with all he could master of the port of John Kemble, and spouted with a sonorous voice the formula of Macbeth,

> "Fill full!
> I drink to the general joy of the whole table!"

[6] Vol. iii. pp. 340-343.

This was followed by "the King, God bless him!" and second came —"Gentlemen, there is another toast which never has been nor shall be omitted in this house of mine: I give you the health of Mr. Walter Scott, with three times three!" All honour having been done to this health, and Scott having briefly thanked the company, with some expressions of warm affection to their host, Mrs. Ballantyne retired;—the bottles passed round twice or thrice in the usual way; and then James rose once more, every vein on his brow distended; his eyes solemnly fixed on vacancy, to propose, not as before in his stentorian key, but with "'bated breath," in the sort of whisper by which a stage-conspirator thrills the gallery,—" *Gentlemen, a bumper to the immortal Author of Waverley!* "—The uproar of cheering, in which Scott made a fashion of joining, was succeeded by deep silence; and then Ballantyne proceeded—

"In his Lord-Burleigh look, serene and serious,
A something of imposing and mysterious "—

to lament the obscurity, in which his illustrious but too modest correspondent still chose to conceal himself from the plaudits of the world; to thank the company for the manner in which the *nominis umbra* had been received; and to assure them that the Author of *Waverley* would, when informed of the circumstance, feel highly delighted—"the proudest hour of his life," etc., etc. The cool, demure fun of Scott's features during all this mummery was perfect; and Erskine's attempt at a gay *nonchalance* was still more ludicrously meritorious. Aldiborontiphoscophornio, however, bursting as he was, knew too well to allow the new Novel to be made the subject of discussion. Its name was announced, and success to it crowned another cup; but after that, no more of Jedediah. To cut the thread, he rolled out unbidden some one of his many theatrical songs, in a style that would have done no dishonour to almost any orchestra— *The Maid of Lodi*, or perhaps *The Bay of Biscay, O!*—or *The sweet little cherub that sits up aloft*. Other toasts followed, interspersed with ditties from other performers; old George Thomson, the friend of Burns, was ready, for one, with *The Moorland Wedding*, or *Willie brew'd a peck o' maut;*—and so it went on, until Scott and Erskine, with any clerical or very staid personage that had chanced to be admitted, saw fit to withdraw. Then the scene was changed. The claret and olives made way for broiled bones and a mighty bowl of punch; and when a few glasses of the hot beverage had restored his powers, James opened *ore rotundo* on the merits of the forthcoming Romance. "One chapter—one chapter only!" was the cry. After *"Nay by'r Lady, nay!"* and a few more coy shifts, the proofsheets were at length produced, and James, with many a prefatory "hem," read aloud what he considered as the most striking dialogue they contained.

'The first I heard so read was the interview between Jeanie Deans, the Duke of Argyle and Queen Caroline, in Richmond Park; and, notwithstanding some spice of the pompous tricks to which he was addicted, I must say he did the inimitable scene great justice. At all events, the effect it produced was deep and memorable; and no wonder that the exulting typographer's *one bumper more to Jedediah Cleishbotham* preceded his parting-stave, which was uniformly *The Last Words of Marmion,* executed certainly with no contemptible rivalry of Braham.' [7]

Over at Abbotsford things wear a still more prosperous aspect. Scott is building there, by the pleasant banks of the Tweed; he has bought and is buying land there; fast as the new gold comes in for a new Waverley Novel, or even faster, it changes itself into moory acres, into stone, and hewn or planted wood.

'About the middle of February' (1820), says Mr. Lockhart, 'it having been ere that time arranged that I should marry his eldest daughter in the course of the spring,—I accompanied him and part of his family on one of those flying visits to Abbotsford, with which he often indulged himself on a Saturday during term. Upon such occasions, Scott appeared at the usual hour in court, but wearing, instead of the official suit of black, his country morning-dress, green jacket and so forth, under the clerk's gown '—' At noon, when the Court broke up, Peter Mathieson was sure to be in attendance in the Parliament Close; and, five minutes after, the gown had been tossed off; and Scott, rubbing his hands for glee, was under weigh for Tweedside. As we proceeded,' etc.

'Next morning there appeared at breakfast John Ballantyne, who had at this time a shooting or hunting-box a few miles off, in the vale of the Leader, and with him Mr. Constable, his guest; and it being a fine clear day, as soon as Scott had read the church-service and one of Jeremy Taylor's sermons, we all sallied out before noon on a perambulation of his upland territories; Maida (the hound) and the rest of the favourites accompanying our march. At starting we were joined by the constant henchman, Tom Purdie,—and I may save myself the trouble of any attempt to describe his appearance, for his master has given us an inimitably true one in introducing a certain personage of his Red-gauntlet:—" He was, perhaps, sixty years old; yet his brow was not much furrowed, and his jet-black hair was only grizzled, not whitened, by the advance of age. All his motions spoke strength unabated; and, though rather undersized, he had very broad shoulders, was square-made, thin-flanked, and apparently combined in his frame muscular strength and activity; the last somewhat impaired, perhaps, by years, but the first remaining in full vigor. A hard and harsh countenance; eyes far sunk under projecting eyebrows, which were grizzled like his hair; a wide mouth, furnished from ear to ear with a range of unimpaired teeth of uncommon whiteness, and a size and breadth which might have become the jaws of an ogre, completed this delightful portrait."

[7] Vol. iv. pp. 166-168.

Equip this figure in Scott's cast-off green jacket, white hat and drab trousers; and imagine that years of kind treatment, comfort and the honest consequence of a confidential *grieve*[8] had softened away much of the hardness and harshness originally impressed on the visage by anxious penury, and the sinister habits of a *black-fisher;*—and the Tom Purdie of 1820 stands before us.

'We were all delighted to see how completely Scott had recovered his bodily vigour, and none more so than Constable, who, as he puffed and panted after him, up one ravine and down another, often stopped to wipe his forehead, and remarked, that "it was not every author who should lead him such a dance." But Purdie's face shone with rapture as he observed how severely the swag-bellied book-seller's activity was tasked. Scott exclaimed exultingly, though, per-haps, for the tenth time, "This will be a glorious spring for our trees, Tom!"—"You may say that, Sheriff," quoth Tom,—and then lingering a moment for Constable—"My certy," he added, scratching his head, "and I think it will be a grand season for *our buiks* too." But indeed Tom always talked of *our buiks,* as if they had been as regular products of the soil as *our aits* and *our birks.* Having threaded first the Hexilcleugh and then the Rhymer's Glen, we arrived at Huntly Burn, where the hospitality of the kind *Weird Sisters,* as Scott called the Miss Fergusons, reanimated our exhausted bibliopoles, and gave them courage to extend their walk a little farther down the same famous brook. Here there was a small cottage in a very sequestered situation' (named Chiefswood), 'by making some little additions to which Scott thought it might be converted into a suitable summer residence for his daughter and future son-in-law.' * * * 'As we walked homeward, Scott being a little fatigued, laid his left hand on Tom's shoulder, and leaned heavily for sup-port, chatting to his "Sunday pony," as he called the affectionate fellow, just as freely as with the rest of the party; and Tom put-in his word shrewdly and manfully, and grinned and grunted whenever the joke chanced to be within his apprehension. It was easy to see that his heart swelled within him from the moment the Sheriff got his collar in his gripe.'[9]

That Abbotsford became infested to a great degree with tourists, wonder-hunters, and all that fatal species of people, may be supposed. Solitary Ettrick saw itself populous: all paths were beaten with the feet and hoofs of an endless miscellany of pilgrims. As many as 'sixteen parties' have arrived at Abbotsford in one day; male and female; peers, Socinian preachers, whatsoever was distinguished, whatso-ever had love of distinction in it! Mr. Lockhart thinks there was no literary shrine ever so bepilgrimed, except Ferney in Voltaire's time, who, however, was not half so

[8] Overseer; German, *graf.*   [9] Vol. iv. pp. 349-353.

accessible. A fatal species! These are what Schiller calls
the 'flesh-flies'; buzzing swarms of bluebottles, who never
fail where any taint of human glory or other corruptibility
is in the wind. So has Nature decreed. Scott's *healthiness,*
bodily and mental, his massive solidity of character, nowhere
showed itself more decisively than in his manner of en-
countering this part of his fate. That his bluebottles were
blue, and of the usual tone and quality, may be judged. Hear
Captain Basil Hall (in a very compressed state):

'We arrived in good time, and found several other guests at dinner. The public rooms are lighted with oil-gas, in a style of extraordinary splendour. The' etc.—'Had I a hundred pens, each of
which at the same time should separately write down an anecdote, I
could not hope to record one half of those which our host, to use
Spenser's expression, "welled out alway." '—'Entertained us all the
way with an endless string of anecdotes;'—'came like a stream of
poetry from his lips;'—'path muddy and scarcely passable, yet I do
not remember ever to have seen any place so interesting as the skill
of this mighty magician had rendered this narrow ravine.'—'Im-
posible to touch on any theme, but straightway he has an anecdote
to fit it.'—'Thus we strolled along, borne, as it were, on the stream
of song and story.'—'In the evening we had a great feast indeed.
Sir Walter asked us if we had ever read Christabel.'—'Interspersed
with these various readings were some hundreds of stories, some
quaint, some pathetical.'—'At breakfast today we had, as usual, some
150 stories—God knows how they came in.'—'In any man so gifted
—so qualified to take the loftiest, proudest line at the head of the
literature, the taste, the imagination of the whole world!'—'For
instance, he never sits at any particular place at table, but takes'
etc. etc.[10]

Among such worshippers, arriving in 'sixteen parties a-
day,' an ordinary man might have grown buoyant; have felt
the god, begun to nod, and seemed to shake the spheres. A
slightly splenetic man, possessed of Scott's sense, would have
swept his premises clear of them: Let no blue bottle approach here, to disturb a man in his work,—under pain of
sugared *squash* (called quassia) and king's yellow! The
good Sir Walter, like a quiet brave man, did neither. He let
the matter take its course; enjoyed what was enjoyable in
it; endured what could not well be helped; persisted meanwhile in writing his daily portion of romance-*copy,* in preserving his composure of heart;—in a word, accommodated

[10] Vol. v. pp. 375-402.

himself to this loud-buzzing environment, and made it serve him, as he would have done (perhaps with more ease) to a silent, poor and solitary one. No doubt it affected him too, and in the lamentable way fevered his internal life, though he kept it well down; but it affected him *less* than it would have done almost any other man. For his guests were not all of the bluebottle sort; far from that. Mr. Lockhart shall furnish us with the brightest aspect a British Ferney ever yielded, or is like to yield: and therewith we will quit Abbotsford and the dominant and culminant period of Scott's life:

'It was a clear, bright September morning, with a sharpness in the air that doubled the animating influence of the sunshine, and all was in readiness for a grand coursing-match on Newark Hill. The only guest who had chalked-out other sport for himself was the stanchest of anglers, Mr. Rose; but he too was there on his *shelty,* armed with his salmon-rod and landing-net, and attended by his Hinves, and Charlie Purdie, a brother of Tom, in those days the most celebrated fisherman of the district. This little group of Waltonians, bound for Lord Somerville's preserve, remained loung-ing about, to witness the start of the main cavalcade. Sir Walter, mounted on Sibyl, was marshalling the order of procession with a huge hunting-whip; and among a dozen frolicsome youths and maid-ens, who seemed disposed to laugh at all discipline, appeared, each on horseback, each as eager as the youngest sportsman in the troop, Sir Humphry Davy, Dr. Wollaston, and the patriarch of Scottish belles-lettres, Henry Mackenzie. The Man of Feeling, however, was persuaded with some difficulty to resign his steed for the present to his faithful negro follower, and to join Lady Scott in the sociable, until we should reach the ground of our *battue.* Laidlaw, on a strong-tailed wiry Highlander, yclept *Hoddin Grey,* which carried him nimbly and stoutly, although his feet almost touched the ground as he sat, was the adjutant. But the most picturesque figure was the illustrious inventor of the safety-lamp. He had come for his favourite sport of angling, and had been practising it successfully with Rose, his travelling companion, for two or three days pre-ceding this; but he had not prepared for coursing fields, or had left Charlie Purdie's troop for Sir Walter's on a sudden thought, and his fisherman's costume—a brown hat with flexible brim, sur-rounded with line upon line of catgut, and innumerable fly-hooks—jack-boots worthy of a Dutch smuggler, and a fustian surtout dabbled with the blood of salmon, made a fine contrast with the smart jackets, white-cord breeches, and well-polished jockey-boots of the less distinguished cavaliers about him. Dr. Wollaston was in black; and with his noble serene dignity of countenance might have passed for a sporting archbishop. Mr. Mackenzie, at this time in the 76th year of his age, with a white hat turned up with green, green spec-

tacles, green jacket, and long brown leathern gaiters, buttoned upon
his nether anatomy, wore a dog-whistle round his neck, and had, all
over, the air of as resolute a devotee as the gay captain of Huntly
Burn. Tom Purdie and his subalterns had preceded us by a few
hours with all the greyhounds that could be collected at Abbotsford,
Darnick, and Melrose; but the giant Maida had remained as his
master's orderly, and now gambolled about Sibyl Grey, barking for
mere joy like a spaniel puppy.

'The order of march had been all settled, and the sociable was
just getting under weigh, when *the Lady Anne* broke from the line,
screaming with laughter, and exclaimed, "Papa, papa, I knew you
could never think of going without your pet!" Scott looked round,
and I rather think there was a blush as well as a smile upon his
face, when he perceived a little black pig frisking about his pony,
and evidently a self-elected addition to the party of the day. He
tried to look stern, and cracked his whip at the creature, but was in
a moment obliged to join in the general cheers. Poor piggy soon
found a strap round its neck, and was dragged into the background;—Scott, watching the retreat, repeated with mock pathos the
first verse of an old pastoral song—

> "What will I do gin my hoggie die?
>   My joy, my pride, my hoggie!
> My only beast, I had na mae,
>   And wow! but I was vogie!"

—the cheers were redoubled—and the squadron moved on.

'This pig had taken, nobody could tell how, a most sentimental
attachment to Scott, and was constantly urging its pretensions to be
admitted a regular member of his *tail* along with the greyhounds and
terriers: but, indeed, I remember him suffering another summer
under the same sort of pertinacity on the part of an affectionate
hen. I leave the explanation for philosophers;—but such were the
facts. I have too much respect for the vulgarly calumniated
donkey, to name him in the same category of pets with the pig and
the hen; but a year or two after this time, my wife used to drive
a couple of these animals in a little garden-chair, and whenever her
father appeared at the door of our cottage, we were sure to see
Hannah More and Lady Morgan (as Anne Scott had wickedly
christened them) trotting from their pasture, to lay their noses over
the paling, and, as Washington Irving says of the old white-haired
hedger with the Parisian snuff-box, "to have a pleasant crack wi'
the laird." [11]

[11] Vol. v. pp. 7-10.
On this subject let us report an anecdote furnished by a correspondent of
our own, whose accuracy we can depend on: 'I myself was acquainted with
a little Blenheim cocker, one of the smallest, beautifulest and wisest of lap-
dogs or dogs, which, though Sir Walter knew it not, was very singular in
its behaviour towards him. *Shandy*, so hight this remarkable cocker, was
extremely shy of strangers: promenading on Princes Street, which in fine
weather used to be crowded in those days, he seemed to live in perpetual
fear of being stolen; if any one but looked at him admiringly, he would

'There' at Chiefswood 'my wife and I spent this summer and autumn of 1821; the first of several seasons which will ever dwell on my memory as the happiest of my life. We were near enough Abbotsford to partake as often as we liked of its brilliant and constantly varying society; yet could do so without being exposed to the worry and exhaustion of spirit which the daily reception of newcomers entailed upon all the family, except Sir Walter himself. But, in truth, even he was not always proof against the annoyances connected with such a style of open housekeeping. Even his temper sank sometimes under the solemn applauses of learned dulness, the vapid raptures of painted and periwigged dowagers, the horse-leech avidity with which underbred foreigners urged their questions, and the pompous simpers of condescending magnates. When sore beset at home in this way, he would every now and then discover that he had some very particular business to attend to on an outlying part of his estate; and, craving the indulgence of his guests over-night, appear at the cabin in the glen before its inhabitants were astir in the morning. The clatter of Sibyl Grey's hoofs, the yelping of Mustard and Spice, and his own joyous shout of *réveillée* under our windows, were the signal that he had burst his toils, and meant for that day to "take his ease in his inn." On descending, he was to be found seated with all his dogs and ours about him, under a spreading ash that overshadowed half the bank between the cottage and the brook, pointing the edge of his woodman's axe,

draw-back with angry timidity, and crouch towards his own lady-mistress. One day, a tall, irregular, busy-looking man came halting by; the little dog ran towards him, began fawning, frisking, licking at his feet: it was Sir Walter Scott! Had Shandy been the most extensive reader of Reviews, he could not have done better. Every time he saw Sir Walter afterwards, which was some three or four times in the course of visiting Edinburgh, he repeated his demonstrations, ran leaping, frisking, licking the author of *Waverley's* feet. The good Sir Walter endured it with good humour; looked down at the little wise face, at the silky shag-coat of snow-white and chestnut-brown; smiled, and avoided hitting him as they went on,—till a new division of streets or some other obstacle put an end to the interview. In fact, he was a strange little fellow, this Shandy. He has been known to sit for hours looking out at the summer moon, with the saddest, wistfulest expression of countenance; altogether like a Werterean Poet. He would have been a poet, I daresay, if he could have found a *publisher*. But his moral tact was the most amazing. Without reason shown, without word spoken, or act done, he took his likings and dislikings; unalterable; really almost unerring. His chief aversion, I should say, was to the genus *quack*, above all, to the genus *acrid-quack*, these, though never so clear-starched, bland-smiling and beneficent, he absolutely would have no trade with. Their very sugar-cake was unavailing. He said with emphasis, as clearly as barking could say it: "Acrid-quack, avaunt!" Would to Heaven many a prime-minister and high-person in authority had such an invaluable talent! On the whole, there is more in this universe than our philosophy has dreamt of. A dog's instinct is a voice of Nature too; and farther, *it* has never babbled itself away in idle jargon and hypothesis, but always adhered to the practical, and grown in silence by continual communion with fact. We do the animals injustice. Their body resembles our body, Buffon says; with its four limbs, with its spinal marrow, main organs in the head, and so forth: but have they not a kind of soul, equally the rude draught and imperfect imitation of ours? It is a strange, an almost solemn and pathetic thing to see an intelligence imprisoned in that dumb rude form; struggling to express itself out of that;—even as we do out of our imprisonment; and succeed very imperfectly!'

and listening to Tom Purdie's lecture touching the plantation that most needed thinning. After breakfast he would take possession of a dressing-room upstairs, and write a chapter of *The Pirate;* and then, having made-up and despatched his packet for Mr. Ballantyne, away to join Purdie wherever the foresters were at work—and sometimes to labour among them as strenuously as John Swanston—until it was time either to rejoin his own party at Abbotsford, or the quiet circle of the cottage. When his guests were few and friendly, he often made them come over and meet him at Chiefswood in a body towards evening; and surely he never appeared to more amiable advantage than when helping his young people with their little arrangements upon such occasions. He was ready with all sorts of devices to supply the wants of a narrow establishment; he used to delight particularly in sinking the wine in a well under the *brae* ere he went out, and hauling up the basket just before dinner was announced,—this primitive device being, he said, what he had always practised when a young housekeeper, and in his opinion far superior in its results to any application of ice: and in the same spirit, whenever the weather was sufficiently genial, he voted for dining out of doors altogether, which at once got rid of the inconvenience of very small rooms, and made it natural and easy for the gentlemen to help the ladies, so that the paucity of servants went for nothing.' [12]

Surely all this is very beautiful; like a picture of Boccaccio's; the ideal of a country life in our time. Why could it not last? Income was not wanting: Scott's official permanent income was amply adequate to meet the expense of all that was valuable in it; nay, of all that was not harassing, senseless and despicable. Scott had some 2,000*l.* a-year without writing books at all. Why should he manufacture and not create, to make more money; and rear mass on mass for a dwelling to himself, till the pile toppled, sank crashing, and buried him in its ruins, when he had a safe pleasant dwelling ready of its own accord? Alas, Scott, with all his health, was *infected;* sick of the fearfulest malady, that of Ambition! To such a length had the King's baronetcy, the world's favour and 'sixteen parties a day,' brought it with him. So the inane racket must be kept up, and rise ever higher. So masons labour, ditchers delve; and there is endless altogether deplorable correspondence about marble-slabs for tables, wainscoting of rooms, curtains and the trimmings of curtains, orange-coloured or fawn-coloured: Walter Scott, one of the gifted of the world, whom his admirers call the

[12] Vol. v. pp. 123, 124.

most gifted, must kill himself that he may be a country
gentleman, the founder of a race of Scottish lairds.

It is one of the strangest, most tragical histories ever enacted under this sun. So poor a passion can lead so strong
a man into such mad extremes. Surely, were not man a fool
always, one might say there was something eminently dis-
tracted in this, *end* as it would, of a Walter Scott writing
daily with the ardour of a steam-engine, that he might make
15,000*l*. a-year, and buy upholstery with it. To cover the
walls of a stone house in Selkirkshire with nicknacks, ancient armour and genealogical shields, what can we name it
but a being bit with delirium of a kind? That tract after
tract of moorland in the shire of Selkirk should be joined
together on parchment and by ring-fence, and named after
one's name,—why, it is a shabby small type edition of your
vulgar Napoleons, Alexanders, and conquering heroes, not
counted venerable by any teacher of men!—

> ' The whole world was not half so wide
> To Alexander when he cried
> Because he had but one to subdue,
> As was a narrow paltry tub to
> Diogenes; who ne'er was said,
> For aught that ever I could read,
> To whine, put finger i' the eye and sob,
> Because he had ne'er another tub.'

Not he! And if, ' looked at from the Moon, which itself is
far from Infinitude,' Napoleon's dominions were as small as
mine, *what,* by any chance of possibility, could Abbotsford
landed-property ever have become? As the Arabs say, there
is a black speck, were it no bigger than a bean's eye, in
every soul; which once set it a-working, will overcloud the
whole man into darkness and quasi-madness, and hurry him
balefully into Night!

With respect to the literary character of these Waverley
Novels, so extraordinary in their commercial character, there
remains, after so much reviewing, good and bad, little that
it were profitable at present to say. The great fact about
them is, that they were faster written and better paid for
than any other books in the world. It must be granted,
moreover, that they have a worth far surpassing what is

usual in such cases; nay, that if Literature had no task but
that of harmlessly amusing indolent languid men, here was
the very perfection of Literature; that a man, here more emphatically than ever elsewhere, might fling himself back, ex-
claiming, "Be mine to lie on this sofa, and read everlasting
Novels of Walter Scott!" The composition, slight as it
often is, usually hangs together in some measure, and *is* a
composition. There is a free flow of narrative, of incident
and sentiment; an easy masterlike coherence throughout, as
if it were the free dash of a master's hand, 'round as the O
of Giotto.' [13] It is the perfection of extemporaneous writing.
Farthermore, surely he were a blind critic who did not
recognise here a certain genial sunshiny freshness and picturesqueness; paintings both of scenery and figures, very
graceful, brilliant, occasionally full of grace and glowing
brightness blended in the softest composure; in fact, a deep
sincere love of the beautiful in Nature and Man, and the
readiest faculty of expressing this by imagination and by
word. No fresher paintings of Nature can be found than
Scott's; hardly anywhere a wider sympathy with man. From
Davie Deans up to Richard Cœur-de-Lion; from Meg Mer-
rilies to Die Vernon and Queen Elizabeth! It is the utterance
of a man of open soul; of a brave, large, free-seeing man,
who has a true brotherhood with all men. In joyous picturesqueness and fellow-feeling, freedom of eye and heart;
or to say it in a word, in general *healthiness* of mind, these
Novels prove Scott to have been amongst the foremost
writers.

Neither in the higher and highest excellence, of drawing
character, is he at any time altogether deficient; though at
no time can we call him, in the best sense, successful. His
Bailie Jarvies, Dinmonts, Dalgettys (for their name is
legion), do look and talk like what they give themselves out

[13] 'Venne a Firenze' (il cortigiano del Papa), 'e andato una mattina in
bottega di Giotto, che lavorava, gli chiese un poco di disegno per mandarlo a sua
Santità. Giotto, che garbatissimo era, prese un foglio, ed in quello con un
pennello tinto di rosso, fermato il braccio al fianco per farne compasso, e
girato la mano fece un tondo sì pari di sesto e di profilo, che fu a vederlo
una maraviglia. Ciò fatto ghignando disse al cortigiano, Eccovi il disegno.'
. . . 'Onde il Papa, e molti cortigiani intendenti conobbero perciò, quanto
Giotto avanzasse d' eccellenza tutti gli altri pittori del suo tempo. Divolga-
tasi poi questa cosa, ne nacque il proverbio, che ancora è in uso dirsi a gli
uomini di grossa pasta: *Tu sei più tondo che l' O di Giotto.*'—Vasari, *Vite*
(Roma, 1759), i. 46.

for; they are, if not *created* and made poetically alive, yet
deceptively *enacted* as a good player might do them. What
more is wanted, then? For the reader lying on a sofa,
nothing more; yet for another sort of reader, much. It were
a long chapter to unfold the difference in drawing a character between a Scott, and a Shakspeare, a Goethe. Yet it is a
difference literally immense; they are of different species;
the value of the one is not to be counted in the coin of the
other. We might say in a short word, which means a long
matter, that your Shakspeare fashions his characters from
the heart outwards; your Scott fashions them from the skin
inwards, never getting near the heart of them! The one set
become living men and women; the other amount to little
more than mechanical cases, deceptively painted automatons.
Compare Fenella with Goethe's Mignon, which, it was once
said, Scott had 'done Goethe the honour' to borrow. He has
borrowed what he could of Mignon. The small stature, the
climbing talent, the trickiness, the *mechanical case,* as we
say, he has borrowed; but the soul of Mignon is left behind.
Fenellà is an unfavorable specimen for Scott; but it illustrates in the aggravated state, what is traceable in all the
characters he drew.

To the same purport indeed we are to say that these famed
books are altogether addressed to the every-day mind; that
for any other mind there is next to no nourishment in them.
Opinions, emotions, principles, doubts, beliefs, beyond what
the intelligent country gentleman can carry along with him,
are not to be found. It is orderly, customary, it is prudent,
decent; nothing more. One would say, it lay not in Scott
to give much more; getting out of the ordinary range, and
attempting the heroic, which is but seldom the case, he falls
almost at once into the rose-pink sentimental,—descries the
Minerva Press from afar, and hastily quits that course; for
none better than he knew it to lead nowhither. On the whole,
contrasting *Waverley,* which was carefully written, with
most of its followers, which were written extempore, one
may regret the extempore method. Something very perfect
in its kind might have come from Scott; nor was it a low
kind: nay, who knows how high, with studious self-concen-
tration, he might have gone; what wealth Nature had im-

planted in him, with his circumstances, most unkind while seeming to be kindest, had never impelled him to unfold?

But after all, in the loudest blaring and trumpeting of popularity, it is ever to be held in mind, as a truth remaining true forever, that Literature *has* other aims than that of harmlessly amusing indolent languid men: or if Literature have them not, then Literature is a very poor affair; and something else must have them, and must accomplish them, with thanks or without thanks; the thankful or thankless world were not long a world otherwise! Under this head there is little to be sought or found in the Waverley Novels. Not profitable for doctrine, for reproof, for edification, for building up or elevating, in any shape! The sick heart will find no healing here, the darkly-struggling heart no guidance: the Heroic that is in all men no divine awakening voice. We say, therefore, that they do not found themselves on deep interests, but on comparatively trivial ones; not on the perennial, perhaps not even on the lasting. In fact, much of the interest of these Novels results from what may be called contrasts of costume. The phraseology, fashion of arms, of dress and life, belonging to one age, is brought suddenly with singular vividness before the eyes of another. A great effect this; yet by the very nature of it, an altogether temporary one. Consider, brethren, shall not we too one day be antiques, and grow to have as quaint a costume as the rest? The stuffed Dandy, only give him *time,* will become one of the wonderfulest mummies. In antiquarian museums, only two centuries hence, the steeple-hat will hang on the next peg to Franks and Company's patent, antiquarians deciding which is uglier: and the Stulz swallow-tail, one may hope, will seem as incredible as any garment that ever made ridiculous the respectable back of man. Not by slashed breeches, steeple-hats, buff-belts, or antiquated speech, can romance-heroes continue to interest us; but simply and solely, in the long-run, by being men. Buff-belts and all manner of jerkins and costumes are transitory; man alone is perennial. He that has gone deeper into this than other men, will be remembered longer than they; he that has not, not. Tried under this category, Scott, with his clear practical insight, joyous temper, and other sound faculties, is not to be accounted little,—among the ordinary circulating-library heroes he might well pass for a demi-god. Not little, yet neither is he great; there were greater, more than one or two, in his own age: among the great of all ages, one sees no likelihood of a place for him.

What, then, is the result of these Waverley Romances? Are they to amuse one generation only? One or more! As many generations as they can; but not all generations: ah no, when our swallow-tail has become fantastic as trunk-hose, they will cease to amuse!—Meanwhile, as we can discern, their results have been several-fold. First of all, and certainly not least of all, have they not perhaps had this result: that a considerable portion of mankind has hereby been sated with mere amusement, and set on seeking something better? Amusement in the way of reading can go no farther, can do nothing better, by the power of man; and men ask, Is this what it can do? Scott, we reckon, carried several things to their ultimatum and crisis, so that change became inevitable; a great service, though an indirect one.

Secondly, however, we may say, these Historical Novels have taught all men this truth, which looks like a truism, and yet was as good as unknown to writers of history and others, till so taught: that the bygone ages of the world were actually filled by living men, not by protocols, state-papers, controversies and abstractions of men. Not abstractions were they, not diagrams and theorems; but men, in buff or other coats and breeches, with colour in their cheeks, with passions in their stomach, and the idioms, features and vitalities of very men. It is a little word this; inclusive of great meaning! History will henceforth have to take thought of it. Her faint hearsays of 'philosophy teaching by experience' will have to exchange themselves everywhere for direct inspection and embodiment: this, and this only, will be counted experience; and till once experience have got in, philosophy will reconcile herself to wait at the door. It is a great service, fertile in consequences, this that Scott has done; a great truth laid open by him;—correspondent indeed to the substantial nature of the man; to his solidity and veracity even of imagination, which, with all his lively discursiveness, was the characteristic of him.

A word here as to the extempore style of writing, which is getting much celebrated in these days. Scott seems to have been a high proficient in it. His rapidity was extreme; and the matter produced was excellent, considering that: the circumstances under which some of his Novels, when he could not himself write, were dictated, are justly considered wonderful. It is a valuable faculty this of ready-writing; nay, farther, for Scott's purpose it was clearly the only good mode. By much labour he could not have added one guinea to his copyright; nor could the reader on the sofa have lain a whit more at ease. It was in all ways necessary that these works should be produced rapidly; and, round or not, be thrown off like Giotto's O. But indeed, in all things, writing or other, which a man engages in, there is the indispensablest beauty in knowing *how to get done.* A man frets himself to no purpose; he has not the sleight of the trade; he is not a craftsman, but an unfortunate borer and bungler, if he know not when to have done. Perfection is unattainable: no carpenter ever made a mathematically accurate right-angle in the world; yet all carpenters know when it is right enough, and do not botch it, and lose their wages, by making it too right. Too much painstaking speaks disease in one's mind, as well as too little. The adroit sound-minded man will endeavour to spend on each business approximately what of pains it deserves; and with a conscience void of remorse will dismiss it then. All this in favour of easy-writing shall be granted, and, if need were, enforced and inculcated.

And yet, on the other hand, it shall not less but more strenuously be inculcated, that in the way of writing, no great thing was ever, or will ever be done with ease, but with difficulty! Let ready-writers with any faculty in them lay this to heart. Is it with ease, or not with ease, that a man shall *do his best,* in any shape; above all, in this shape justly named of 'soul's travail,' working in the deep places of thought, embodying the True out of the Obscure and Possible, environed on all sides with the uncreated False? Not so, now or at any time. The experience of all men belies it; the nature of things contradicts it. Virgil and Tacitus, were they ready-writers? The whole *Prophecies of Isaiah* are not equal in extent to this cobweb of a Review Article. Shakspeare, we may fancy, wrote with rapidity; but not till he had thought with intensity: long and sore had this man thought, as the seeing eye may discern well, and had dwelt and wrestled amid dark pains and throes,—though his great soul is silent about all that. It was for him to write rapidly at fit intervals, being ready to do it. And herein truly lies the secret of the matter: such swiftness of mere writing, after due energy of preparation, is doubtless the right method; the hot furnace having long worked and simmered, let the pure gold flow out at one gush. It was Shakspeare's plan; no easy-writer he, or he had never been a Shakspeare. Neither was Milton one of the mob of gentlemen that write with ease; he did not attain Shakspeare's faculty, one perceives, of even writing fast *after* long preparation, but struggled while he wrote. Goethe also tells us he 'had nothing sent him in his sleep'; no page of his but he knew well how it came there. It is reckoned to be the best prose, accordingly, that has been written by any modern. Schiller, as an unfortunate and unhealthy man, '*könnte nie fertig werden*, never could get done'; the noble genius of him struggled not wisely but too well, and wore his life itself heroically out. Or did Petrarch write easily? Dante sees himself 'growing lean' over his *Divine Comedy;* in stern solitary death-wrestle with it, to prevail over it, and do it, if his uttermost faculty may: hence, too, it is done and prevailed over, and the fiery life of it endures forevermore among men.

No: creation, one would think, cannot be easy; your Jove has severe pains, and fire-flames, in the head out of which an armed Pallas is struggling! As for manufacture, that is a different matter, and may become easy or not easy, according as it is taken up. Yet of manufacture too, the general truth is that, given the manufacturer, it will be worthy in direct proportion to the pains bestowed upon it; and worthless always, or nearly so, with no pains. Cease, therefore, O ready-writer, to brag openly of thy rapidity and facility; to thee (if thou be in the manufacturing line) it is a benefit, an increase of wages; but to me it is sheer loss, worsening of my pennyworth: why wilt thou brag of it to me? Write easily, by steam if thou canst contrive it, and canst sell it;

but hide it like virtue! "Easy writing," said Sheridan, "is sometimes d—d hard reading." Sometimes; and always it is sure to be rather useless reading, which indeed (to a creature of few years and much work) may be reckoned the hardest of all.

Scott's productive facility amazed everybody; and set Captain Hall, for one, upon a very strange method of accounting for it without miracle;—for which see his Journal, above quoted from. The Captain, on counting line for line, found that he himself had written in that Journal of his almost as much as Scott, at odd hours in a given number of days; 'and as for the invention,' says he, 'it is known that this costs Scott nothing, but comes to him of its own accord.' Convenient indeed!—But for us too Scott's rapidity is great, is a proof and consequence of the solid health of the man, bodily and spiritual; great, but unmiraculous; not greater than that of many others besides Captain Hall. Admire it, yet with measure. For observe always, there are two conditions in work: let me fix the quality, and *you* shall fix the quantity! Any man may get through work rapidly who easily satisfies himself about it. Print the *talk* of any man, there will be a thick octavo volume daily; make his writing three times as good as his talk, there will be the third part of a volume daily, which still is good work. To write with never such rapidity in a passable manner, is indicative not of a man's genius, but of his habits; it will prove his soundness of nervous system, his practicality of mind, and in fine, that he has the knack of his trade. In the most flattering view, rapidity will betoken health of mind: much also, perhaps most of all, will depend on health of body. Doubt it not, a faculty of easy-writing is attainable by man! The human genius, once fairly set in this direction, will carry it far. William Cobbett, one of the healthiest of men, was a greater improviser even than Walter Scott: his writing, considered as to quality and quantity, of Rural Rides, Registers, Grammars, Sermons, Peter Porcupines, Histories of Reformation, everfresh denouncements of Potatoes and Paper-money, seems to us still more wonderful. Pierre Bayle wrote enormous folios, one sees not on what motive principle: he flowed-on forever, a mighty tide of ditch-water; and even died flowing, with the pen in his hand. But indeed the most unaccountable ready-writer of all is, probably, the common Editor of a Daily Newspaper. Consider his leading articles; what they treat of, how passably they are done. Straw that has been thrashed a hundred times without wheat; ephemeral sound of a sound; such portent of the hour as all men have seen a hundred times turn out inane: how a man with merely human faculty, buckles himself nightly with new vigour and interest to this thrashed straw, nightly thrashes it anew, nightly gets-up new thunder about it; and so goes on thrashing and thundering for a considerable series of years; this is a fact remaining still to be accounted for, in human physiology. The vitality of man is great.

Or shall we say, Scott, among the many things he carried towards their ultimatum and crisis, carried this of ready-writing too, that so all men might better see what was in it? It is a valuable consummation. Not without results;—results, at some of which Scott as a Tory politician would have greatly shuddered. For if once Printing have grown to be as Talk, then DEMOCRACY (if we look into the roots of things) is not a bugbear and probability, but a certainty, and event as good as come! ' Inevitable seems it me.' But leaving this, sure enough the triumph of ready-writing appears to be even now; everywhere the ready-writer is found bragging strangely of his readiness. In a late translated *Don Carlos,* one of the most indifferent translations ever done with any sign of ability, a hitherto unknown individual is found assuring his reader, ' The reader will possibly think it an excuse, when I assure him that the whole piece was completed within the space of ten weeks, that is to say, between the sixth of January and the eighteenth of March of this year (inclusive of a fortnight's interruption from over-exertion) ; that I often translated twenty pages a-day, and that the fifth act was the work of five days.'[14] O hitherto unknown individual, what is it to me what time it was the work of, whether five days or five decades of years? The only question is, How well hast thou done it?

So, however, it stands: the genius of Extempore irresistibly

[14] *Don Carlos,* a Dramatic Poem, from the German of Schiller. Mannheim and London, 1837.

lording it, advancing on us like ocean-tides, like Noah's
deluges—of ditch-water! The prospect seems one of the
lamentablest. To have all Literature swum away from us
in watery Extempore, and a spiritual time of Noah super-
vene? That surely is an awful reflection; worthy of dyspep-
tic Matthew Bramble in a London fog! Be of comfort, O
splenetic Matthew; it is not Literature they are swimming
away; it is only Book-publishing and Book-selling. Was
there not a Literature *before* Printing or Faust of Mentz, and
yet men wrote extempore? Nay, before Writing or Cadmus
of Thebes, and yet men spoke extempore? Literature is the
Thought of thinking Souls; this, by the blessing of God, can
in no generation be swum away, but remains with us to the
end.

Scott's career, of writing impromptu novels to buy farms
with, was not of a kind to terminate voluntarily, but to ac-
celerate itself more and more; and one sees not to what wise
goal it could, in any case, have led him. Bookseller Constable's bankruptcy was not the ruin of Scott; his ruin was,
that ambition, and even false ambition, had laid hold of him;
that his way of life was not wise. Whither could it lead?
Where could it stop? New farms there remained ever to
be bought, while new novels could pay for them. More
and more success but gave more and more appetite, more
and more audacity. The impromptu writing must have
waxed ever thinner; declined faster and faster into the questionable category, into the condemnable, into the generally
condemned. Already there existed, in secret, everywhere a
considerable opposition party; witnesses of the Waverley
miracles, but unable to believe in them, forced silently to
protest against them. Such opposition party was in the sure
case to grow; and even, with the impromptu process ever
going on, ever waxing thinner, to draw the world over to it.
Silent protest must at length have come to words; harsh
truths, backed by harsher facts of a world-popularity over-
wrought and worn-out, behoved to have been spoken;—such
as can be spoken now without reluctance, when they can pain
the brave man's heart no more. Who knows? Perhaps it
was better ordered to be all *otherwise*. Otherwise, at any

rate, it was. One day the Constable mountain, which seemed to stand strong like the other rock mountains, gave suddenly, as the icebergs do, a loud-sounding crack; suddenly, with huge clangor, shivered itself into ice-dust; and sank, carrying much along with it. In one day Scott's high-heaped money-wages became fairy-money and nonentity; in one day the rich man and lord of land saw himself penniless, landless, a bankrupt among creditors.

It was a hard trial. He met it proudly, bravely,—like a brave proud man of the world. Perhaps there had been a prouder way still: to have owned honestly that he *was* unsuccessful, then, all bankrupt, broken, in the world's goods and repute; and to have turned elsewhither for some refuge. Refuge did lie elsewhere; but it was not Scott's course, or fashion of mind, to seek it there. To say, Hitherto I have been all in the wrong, and this my fame and pride, now broken, was an empty delusion and spell of accursed witchcraft! It was difficult for flesh and blood! He said, I will retrieve myself, and make my point good yet, or die for it. Silently, like a proud strong man, he girt himself to the Hercules' task of removing rubbish-mountains, since that was it; of paying large ransoms by what he could still write and sell. In his declining years, too; misfortune is doubly and trebly unfortunate that befalls us then. Scott fell to his Hercules' task like a very man, and went on with it unweariedly; with a noble cheerfulness, while his life-strings were cracking, he grappled with it, and wrestled with it, years long, in death-grips, strength to strength;—and *it* proved the stronger; and his life and heart did crack and break: the cordage of a most strong heart! Over these last writings of Scott, his *Napoleons, Demonologies, Scotch Histories,* and the rest, criticism, finding still much to wonder at, much to commend, will utter no word of blame; this one word only, Woe is me! The noble war-horse that once laughed at the shaking of the spear, how is he doomed to toil himself dead, dragging ignoble wheels! Scott's descent was like that of a spent projectile; rapid, straight down;—perhaps mercifully so. It is a tragedy, as all life is; one proof more that Fortune stands on a restless *globe;* that Ambition, literary, warlike, politic, pecuniary, never yet profited any man.

Our last extract shall be from Volume Sixth; a very tragical one. Tragical, yet still beautiful; waste Ruin's havoc borrowing a kind of sacredness from a yet sterner visitation, that of Death! Scott has withdrawn into a solitary lodging-house in Edinburgh, to do daily the day's work there; and had to leave his wife at Abbotsford in the last stage of disease. He went away silently; looked silently at the sleeping face he scarcely hoped ever to see again. We quote from a Diary he had begun to keep in those months, on hint from Byron's *Ravenna Journal:* copious sections of it render this Sixth Volume more interesting than any of the former ones:

'*Abbotsford, May* 11 (1826).— * * It withers my heart to think of it, and to recollect that I can hardly hope again to seek confidence and counsel from that ear, to which all might be safely confided. But in her present lethargic state, what would my attendance have availed?—and Anne has promised close and constant intelligence. I must dine with James Ballantyne today *en famille.* I cannot help it; but would rather be at home and alone. However, I can go out too. I will not yield to the barren sense of hopelessness which struggles to invade me.'

'*Edinburgh,—Mrs. Brown's lodgings, North St. David Street—May* 12.—I passed a pleasant day with kind J. B., which was a great relief from the black dog, which would have worried me at home. He was quite alone.'

'Well, here I am in Arden. And I may say with Touchstone, "When I was at home I was in a better place"; I must, when there is occasion, draw to my own Bailie Nicol Jarvie's consolation—"One cannot carry the comforts of the Saut-Market about with one." Were I at ease in mind, I think the body is very well cared for. Only one other lodger in the house, a Mr. Shandy,—a clergyman, and, despite his name, said to be a quiet one.'

'*May* 14.—A fair good-morrow to you, Mr. Sun, who are shining so brightly on these dull walls. Methinks you look as if you were looking as bright on the banks of the Tweed; but look where you will, Sir Sun, you look upon sorrow and suffering.—Hogg was here yesterday, in danger, from having obtained an accommodation of 100*l.* from James Ballantyne, which he is now obliged to repay. I am unable to help the poor fellow, being obliged to borrow myself.'

'*May* 15.—Received the melancholy intelligence that all is over at Abbotsford.'

'*Abbotsford, May* 16.—She died at nine in the morning, after being very ill for two days—easy at last. I arrived here late last night. Anne is worn out, and has had hysterics, which returned on my arrival. Her broken accents were like those of a child, the language as well as the tones broken, but in the most gentle voice of submission. "Poor mamma—never return again—gone forever —a better place." Then, when she came to herself, she spoke with sense, freedom and strength of mind, till her weakness returned. It would have been inexpressibly moving to me as a stranger—what was it then to the father and the husband? For myself, I scarce know how I feel; sometimes as firm as the Bass Rock, sometimes as weak as the water that breaks on it. I am as alert at thinking and deciding as I ever was in my life. Yet, when I contrast what this place now is, with what it has been not long since, I think my heart will break. Lonely, aged, deprived of my family—all but poor Anne; an impoverished, an embarrassed man, deprived of the sharer of my thoughts and counsels, who could always talk-down my sense of the calamitous apprehensions which break the heart that must bear them alone.—Even her foibles were of service to me, by giving me things to think of beyond my weary self-reflections.

'I have seen her. The figure I beheld is, and is not, my Charlotte—my thirty-years companion. There is the same symmetry of form, though those limbs are rigid which were once so gracefully elastic—but that yellow mask, with pinched features, which seems to mock life rather than emulate it, can it be the face that was once so full of lively expression? I will not look on it again. Anne thinks her little changed, because the latest idea she had formed of her mother is as she appeared under circumstances of extreme pain. Mine go back to a period of comparative ease. If I write long in this way, I shall write-down my resolution, which I should rather write-up, if I could.'

'May 18.— * * Cerements of lead and of wood already hold her; cold earth must have her soon. But it is not my Charlotte, it is not the bride of my youth, the mother of my children, that will be laid among the ruins of Dryburgh, which we have so often visited in gaiety and pastime. No, no.'

'May 22.— * * Well, I am not apt to shrink from that which is my duty, merely because it is painful; but I wish this funeral-day over. A kind of cloud of stupidity hangs about me, as if all were unreal that men seem to be doing and talking.'

'May 26.— * * Were an enemy coming upon my house, would I not do my best to fight, although oppressed in spirits; and shall a similar despondency prevent me from mental exertion? It shall not, by Heaven!'

'Edinburgh, May 30.—Returned to town last night with Charles. This morning resume ordinary habits of rising early, working in the morning, and attending the Court. * * * I finished correcting the proofs for the Quarterly; it is but a flimsy article, but then the circumstances were most untoward.—This has been a melancholy day—most melancholy. I am afraid poor Charles found me weeping. I do not know what other folks feel, but with me the hysterical passion that impels tears is a terrible violence—a sort of throttling sensation—then succeeded by a state of dreaming stupidity, in which I ask if my poor Charlotte can actually be dead.' [15]

[15] Vol. vi. pp. 297-307.

This is beautiful as well as tragical. Other scenes, in that Seventh Volume, must come, which will have no beauty, but be tragical only. It is better that we are to end here.

And so the curtain falls; and the strong Walter Scott is with us no more. A possession from him does remain; widely scattered; yet attainable; not inconsiderable. It can be said of him, When he departed, he took a Man's life along with him. No sounder piece of British manhood was put together in that eighteenth century of Time. Alas, his fine Scotch face, with its shaggy honesty, sagacity and goodness, when we saw it latterly on the Edinburgh streets, was all worn with care, the joy all fled from it;—ploughed deep with labour and sorrow. We shall never forget it; we shall never see it again. Adieu, Sir Walter, pride of all Scotchmen, take our proud and sad farewell.